BEFORE THE TRUMPET YOUNG FRANKLIN ROOSEVELT 1882-1905

BEFORE THE TRUMPET

Young Franklin Roosevelt 1882-1905

GEOFFREY C. WARD

1817

HARPER & ROW, PUBLISHERS, New York
Cambridge, Philadelphia, San Francisco, London
Mexico City, São Paulo, Singapore, Sydney

For my mother and father

Unless otherwise indicated, all photographs are courtesy of the Franklin D. Roosevelt Library at Hyde Park.

 For information address Harper & Row, Publishers, Inc., 10 East 53rd Street, New York, N.Y. 10022. Published simultaneously in Canada by Fitzhenry & Whiteside Limited, Toronto.

FIRST EDITION

Designer: Sidney Feinberg

Library of Congress Cataloging in Publication Data

Ward, Geoffrey C.
Before the trumpet.

Bibliography: p.
Includes index.
1. Roosevelt, Franklin D. (Franklin Delano), 1882–1945
—Childhood and youth. 2. Presidents—United States—
Biography. I. Title.
E807.W327 1985 973.917'092'4 [B] 84-48755
ISBN 0-06-015451-9

---

85 86 87 88 89 HC 10 9 8 7 6 5 4 3 2 1

CONTENTS

PREFACE

Three years ago, it was part of my job as the editor of *American Heritage* magazine to help decipher secret recordings made by Franklin D. Roosevelt in the Oval Office of the White House in the autumn of 1940. As I eavesdropped, fascinated, on the private conversations of the most important President of this century, I was struck above all by the tireless ebullience with which FDR seemed to face the world. Despite the muffled, primitive recording, despite the crackling and static of forty years of disintegration, the vibrancy of his extraordinary personality comes through undimmed. There he sits—imprisoned in his chair, locked in political combat with Wendell Willkie, the most formidable opponent ever sent against him, facing the worst war in history—and he couldn't be having a better time. Nothing seems to faze him. He is amused and amusing, apparently unafraid of anything, and somehow serene in the conviction that whatever happens, everything will turn out fine, provided he's in charge.

That unshakable energy and optimism served him and his country well during the two most serious crises Americans have faced since the Civil War. But, I wondered as I listened, where did that self-assurance come from?

This book is an attempt at answering that question. It seeks the sources of Franklin Roosevelt's vivid personality—its boldness and caution, its deviousness and charm and underlying confidence—where common sense dictates they must be found, in his youth and young manhood. It is about the pre-eminent American politician of modern times, but it is not about politics. Nor is it a conventional full-scale biography. It begins long before its subject was born and ends in 1905 on the day of his marriage; in a second volume I hope to carry the story through his steely decision to return to political life despite his paralysis. It is the story of young Franklin Roosevelt, but it is also the story of the big uncommon family that helped shape him. It is based—so far as is possible more than a century after many of the events it describes—on primary sources; no historian is quoted anywhere in its pages, though the work of earlier biographers inevitably informs every page.

—Geoffrey C. Ward

New York City
November 25, 1984

Too often is the biographer tempted to confine himself to that comparatively brief period after the trumpet of fame has directed the eyes of the world upon him whose life story he writes. But to understand properly the greatness or littleness of any man we must know something of his whole life—what went before and what went after.

FRANKLIN D. ROOSEVELT

I have always been a great believer in heredity.

SARA DELANO ROOSEVELT

Franklin, Jr., and I had a very quiet afternoon and evening. He started me off on telling him stories about various members of the family whom he is too young to know anything about. After a while he remarked, "I think families are the most interesting things in the world," which of course is true, for in the story of every family is the stuff from which both novels and eventually history is written.

ELEANOR ROOSEVELT, *My Day,* 1938

PROLOGUE

THE RIVER ROAD

FDR was furious. "The old body snatcher," he muttered as his limousine moved along the wet street toward the White House. "The old body snatcher."

It was Sunday morning, March 4, 1934, cold and rainy in Washington, and the President was coming home from church. The Right Reverend James E. Freeman, the Episcopal Bishop of Washington, had invited Roosevelt and his Cabinet to attend a special service at the National Cathedral to celebrate the first anniversary of the President's inauguration. FDR, a lifelong churchman and senior warden of his own church, St. James, at Hyde Park, New York, had agreed to come.

Things had not gone well. Word got around that the President was to be there, and when he arrived many of the pews were already filled with tourists who stood and pointed and talked among themselves right through the service. Roosevelt resented being the focus of attention in church. "I can do almost anything in the goldfish bowl of the President's life," he once said, "but I'll be hanged if I can say my prayers in it. It bothers me to feel like something in the zoo."[1]

But it was what had happened after services ended that had angered

1. Roosevelt later became more relaxed about the inevitable attention his churchgoing received. Ultimately even the rector of St. James succumbed; during the war a small, discreetly lettered sign went up on the Albany Post Road proclaiming it "The Church of the President." On the way to services one Sunday, FDR noticed that someone had added, "(Formerly God's)." Roosevelt roared.

Source: Olin Dows, *Franklin Roosevelt at Hyde Park*, p. 66.

him. At sixty-seven, Bishop Freeman was more than twice as old as the great unfinished Gothic monument over which he presided. Its cornerstone had been laid in 1901, and the struggle to raise funds with which to complete it had grown more difficult as the Depression deepened. The bishop refused to be discouraged, however; the cathedral was the capstone of his life's work in the church. He was determined to make it a truly national institution, an American Westminster Abbey, where presidents came to worship and eminent citizens were laid to rest in its crypt of the Chapel of St. Joseph of Arimathea.

Roosevelt's attendance this Sunday understandably delighted him, and as the President made his slow, stiff-legged way up the aisle, smiling at the congregation while gripping the arm of his sturdy uniformed naval aide, Captain Walter Vernon, the bishop waited at the door to escort him to his car.

The men shook hands and Roosevelt complimented him on the aptness of his sermon and the beauty of his church. The bishop thanked the President for coming; his presence honored the cathedral, he said, and he hoped he would return often. Then, leaning closer, he reminded FDR that several distinguished Americans already rested in the cathedral crypt, Woodrow Wilson and Admiral George Dewey among them. When the time came, Bishop Freeman continued, he hoped President Roosevelt would consent to join them.

Roosevelt kept smiling. The bishop pushed on. He knew how busy the President must be in these difficult times. It was so easy to let things slip one's mind. Perhaps Mr. Roosevelt would be good enough to dictate a memorandum expressing his wish to be buried here—just so there would be no misunderstanding later on.

The President continued to smile as he was helped into his automobile, and he waved at the crowd standing in the rain on the cathedral steps until they could no longer see him. But he had been deeply offended. If he died in office, he told his staff back at the White House, he wanted no part of Bishop Freeman or his cathedral. There might be a simple ceremony in the East Room, just as there had been for several of his predecessors, but he would be buried at home, of course, at Hyde Park. In his mother's rose garden.

Several months later, taking his friend and Secretary of Labor Frances Perkins for a drive around Springwood, the family estate at Hyde Park, he stopped his open car outside the tall hemlock hedge that enclosed the garden. "That's where I'm going to be buried, Frances," he said. "Don't you ever let anyone try to bury me in any cathedral."[2]

On December 22, 1937, the newspapers announced that former Secretary of State Frank Kellogg had died the day before at his home in Minnesota. The funeral was to be held there, but the body was to be shipped to Washington for burial beneath the National Cathedral. Bishop Freeman, FDR noted, had done it again. The President did not plan to attend the interment services at the cathedral on the twenty-seventh, but they were evidently on his mind, for late in the evening on the twenty-sixth, seated in his study on the second floor of the White House, he had settled down with a pencil and a pad and had written out detailed instructions for his funeral and burial.

No member of his family or his staff saw this document before his sudden death from a cerebral hemorrhage at Warm Springs, Georgia, on April 12, 1945. Sealed in an envelope addressed to his eldest son, James, it had been placed in a safe in the President's bedroom and was not opened until several days after he was buried. Yet Franklin Roosevelt's feelings about his home at Hyde Park (and about the overeager Bishop of Washington) had become so well known to them that most of his wishes were carried out.

And so, at eight-fifty on the morning of Sunday, April 15, Franklin Roosevelt's train from Washington slid to a stop for the last time at the siding his father, James Roosevelt, had built long before, at the foot of his estate on the eastern shore of the Hudson River. There were seventeen Pullmans. The President's body had ridden alone in the last car, guarded through the night by just four servicemen—Army, Navy, Marine, and Coast Guard. Three of his own sons were away at war, but the rest of his immediate family was aboard the train; so were many of his friends and closest aides, members of his Cabinet, and the justices of the Supreme Court, as well as eighteen of the reporters who had covered him for so many years. The new President, Harry Truman,

2. Bishop Freeman was nothing if not persistent. According to the President's son James, the bishop asked to see Roosevelt alone at the White House not long after their encounter at the cathedral. FDR reluctantly agreed; he was too good a churchman to refuse to see his bishop. But just moments after the priest was ushered into the Oval Office, a buzzer sounded at the desk of the President's appointments secretary, Marvin McIntyre, the signal that Roosevelt wished the conversation interrupted. When the startled bishop had left, FDR ordered, "If that man ever asks to see me again, don't let him in!" The President's personal reaction to Freeman's death in 1943 is not recorded. The bishop was buried, of course, in the cathedral crypt.

Source: James Roosevelt and Sidney Shalett, *Affectionately, FDR*, p. 103.

with his wife and daughter, occupied the armor-plated presidential car, the *Ferdinand Magellan*, for the first time.

Few passengers had slept. A good deal of liquor had been poured during the long night. The great weight of the train had broken three couplings along the way and caused an hour's delay.

The slow trip north from Georgia through the warm southern spring had reminded some aboard of another train bearing another President home in another springtime, just eighty years before. FDR had been fond of trains since as a boy he had first eagerly watched the American countryside click past from the window of his father's private car; in fact, the southern tracks over which his funeral train had moved toward Washington had once been in his father's charge. Wherever he went as President, country people in twos and threes and tens had turned out to watch him pass, silent respectful knots of miners or fishermen or farmers. This time, they had come by the hundreds, even at night, standing at crossings and along the country roads to see the darkened train roll past, their eyes fixed on the brightly lit final car.

The crowds grew bigger in the towns and cities. At Charlotte, North Carolina, late on the night of the thirteenth, thousands of people, black and white, stood along the platform and stretched for several blocks on either side of the station. The train stopped, and a troop of Boy Scouts began to sing "Onward, Christian Soldiers." The rest of the crowd joined in. "It started ragged at first, but then it swelled," a reporter remembered. "Soon eight or ten thousand voices were singing like an organ. Those people were scared to death. They weren't singing for a single departed soul. They were singing for themselves, to hold themselves up." FDR had been President for so long, more than a dozen years, four years longer than any other man. The younger people in that crowd could not remember an America without him, and the radio had made him a familiar presence even in those living rooms where he had not always been welcome. Many could not even recall Harry Truman's name; still more had no idea what he looked like.

As the old hymn ended, the blacks in the crowd, most of whom had stood apart at one end of the platform, knelt together and began to sing a hymn of their own. Some whites sang with them as the train slowly began to move. "Most of the blacks never got to vote for FDR," another reporter noted, "but they came out late at night to pray for him."

FDR's distant cousin, the journalist Joseph Alsop, believed the

President's most lasting legacy had been his inclusion of the excluded. Until 1933, and despite their great and growing numbers, minority citizens—Catholics, blacks, Jews, and all the rest—were routinely excluded from government by the well-to-do white Anglo-Saxon Protestants who had jealously guarded their power since the Constitutional Convention. FDR, who was himself by birth and upbringing, education and expectation, a member of that ruling class, had been shrewd and self-confident enough to alter its ancient policy and welcome able men (and women) of every background to Washington, to make even the most rejected feel that they were somehow important to the American commonwealth.

In the process, he had made bitter enemies of the wealthy Protestants among whom he had lived most of his life. He had raised their taxes, regulated their business practices, threatened their dominance; he was, they said, a hypocrite, untrustworthy, demagogic, a "traitor to his class," and many of them, hating his name too much even to utter it, simply called him "That Man in the White House."[3]

To most Americans, though, he had seemed more savior than traitor. On March 4, 1933, the first of FDR's four inauguration days, the United States had been a haunted, frightened place, in the fourth year of a depression which had put one out of four wage earners out of work. Earlier that long cold winter, former President Calvin Coolidge, who had presided over the boom days of the 1920s that already seemed unimaginably distant, expressed something of the general despair. "In other periods of depression," he said, "it has always been possible to see some things which were solid and upon which you could base hope, but as I look about me I see nothing to give ground for hope—nothing of man."

Such talk was alien to Franklin Roosevelt's whole being. "This Nation asks for action, and action now," he said in his first inaugural address. "We must act quickly." He acted, and he continued to act. No President since Abraham Lincoln had come into office at a more critical moment. No President since Lincoln had been granted such powers to work his will. And no President, *including* Lincoln, did

3. Even FDR's death did not always diminish his enemies' hatred for him. Many years later, a man who had been a small boy in 1945, the son of an automobile executive living in the glossy Detroit suburb of Bloomfield Hills, recalled watching through the kitchen window one night that spring as his normally sedate mother and father and their nearest neighbors held hands and danced around a bonfire in the garden. His memory of that sight blurred over time, and he always assumed that his parents had been celebrating the end of the war in the Pacific that finally came late that summer. One day he asked his mother about it. "Oh, no, dear," she said. "We danced because Roosevelt was dead." *(Confidential source.)*

more to alter the old relationship between ordinary citizens and their government. Before FDR there was no unemployment compensation or Social Security; no regulation of the stock market; no federal guarantees of bank deposits or the right to bargain; no minimum wage or maximum hours; no price supports for farmers or federal funds for electric power with which to light their homes; no federal commitment to equal opportunity or high employment. Not all that had been done during his presidency had originated with him. Nor had all of it worked, but when it had not, he had often been willing to change his mind. "It is common sense to take a method and try it," he once said. "If it fails, admit it frankly and try another. But above all, try something." By the time of his death the government he had rebuilt had accepted responsibility for the welfare of those Americans who found themselves, through no fault of their own, in economic or social distress.

"The so-called New Deal," Eleanor Roosevelt once wrote, "was . . . nothing more than an effort to preserve our economic system." It had done that and more, but her husband's greatest achievement, she believed, was that he had been able to communicate his own assurance to others. He had restored the "people's sense of security and confidence in themselves," she said, without which no recovery would ever have been possible; and shortly after he died she told one of his closest aides that when the time came to place a headstone above his grave, she hoped it would be carved with the best-remembered words from his first inaugural address: ". . . the only thing we have to fear is fear itself."[4]

It was that will and spirit that the people remembered as they came out in the dark to see his funeral train pass by.

Now, at the end of the journey, the Roosevelts and Trumans waited on the train with the President's body while the rest of the party stepped down, bundled in coats and hats. It had been unseasonably hot in Washington the day before, and at the ceremony in the East Room the humid air was thick and sweet with the smell of the banked flowers behind the coffin. To keep from fainting, Margaret Truman had concentrated all her attention on the drop of perspiration that seemed to hang perpetually from the nose of the presiding clergyman.

Here on the Hudson it was barely spring. The morning sun was brilliant, but the branches of the trees were still bare, and a chill wind

4. This was not done. FDR had asked that only his and his wife's dates of birth and death appear on the simple stone.

blew in from the west, ruffling the surface of the water. A fleet of cars drove the mourners up through deep woods to the rose garden on the bluff above. Roosevelt had always called the winding gravel path they followed "the river road"; it, too, had been built by his father.

Earlier that morning, a second train of twelve cars carrying a large delegation from Congress had moved slowly past the first and continued north along the river to the Hyde Park village station. A small silent crowd of townspeople, Roosevelt's neighbors, waited in front of the little red brick depot whose eaves were hung with purple and black crape. Arms folded, they watched as the dignitaries from Washington talked together in clusters next to the steaming train, their breath coming in clouds, waiting for the Army staff sedans that were to ferry them to join the other guests assembling in the garden three miles away. Several of the men carried briefcases, the onlookers noticed; even this day, the business of government went on. At the back of the train, men unloaded armfuls of the flowers that had filled the East Room. The wind off the river tore at the blossoms and scattered petals along the track. The flowers filled two railroad cars, and they, too, were to be taken to the garden.

There, the evening before, men from the Roosevelt estate had dug the grave. William Plog, the bent gray-haired superintendent of the family acres who had been hired half a century earlier by Roosevelt's father, had supervised the work. A Poughkeepsie undertaker had offered to send in a crew to do the job. That wouldn't be necessary, Plog had told him. "I think the President would want his own men to do that, and we shall do it."

The grave stood empty now, black and shocking against the soft spring green of the grass, and as the mourners began streaming into the garden through openings in the south side of the hedge, Plog was still at work, directing state troopers as they heaped flowers behind the open grave. Three hundred uniformed servicemen lined the inside of the ten-foot hedge on three sides—the west was open to the river—and Robert Sherwood, the playwright and presidential speech writer, who was among the first to arrive, noticed that the medals and decorations they wore recalled the trials of the great war that Roosevelt had directed and whose end he had not lived to see—North Africa and Monte Cassino, Guadalcanal and Midway, Tarawa and Normandy.

It is given to few leaders adequately to meet one national crisis. Franklin Roosevelt mastered two. When FDR had come to office, America counted for little overseas; General Douglas MacArthur, then chief of staff, had ranked her army sixteenth in the world, behind those of Romania and Spain. When Roosevelt died, the United States and her allies were only weeks away from victory over the Axis powers, and America was the most powerful nation in history. Many factors contributed to that transformation, but none were more important than FDR's refusal to be intimidated by tyrants, his early sense that traditional American isolation would not work in the modern world, and his undiminished conviction that he and his country would prevail, whatever the odds. Because he was able to impart that confidence intact to his fellow citizens, Eleanor Roosevelt said, he "enabled us to produce as we did in the early days of the war and to go into the most terrible war in our history and win it."

Nor did illness or exhaustion ever dim his optimism. The final words of the speech he had intended to deliver on Jefferson Day restated the theme that suffused his whole presidency: "The only limit to our realization of tomorrow will be our doubts of today. Let us move forward with strong and active faith."

Doves could be heard in the trees and sparrows fluttered in and out of the hedge as the crowd of mourners grew; and as the guests waited for the final ceremony to begin, the men and women murmured to one another. Not everyone in the garden had admired Roosevelt; there had been an unseemly jostling to be here, even among congressmen who had opposed him. And there were others there who had been with him once and had fallen away. But most had remained his allies. They had fought alongside him, believed in him, worn themselves out in his service.

Still, no one waiting in that garden could claim really to have known Franklin Roosevelt. His big easy smile, his warmth, his obvious and unfeigned love of company and conversation and a good time, all had made him seem to outsiders the most accessible of men. He had called the people—*all* the people—"my friends." But the longer one knew him, and there were present men and women who had known him since he was born in the house that stood just yards away, the more evident it became that there were sides to him that he permitted no one to see.

Sherwood, who had studied him up close with a dramatist's shrewd eye for character, confessed that he had never been able to penetrate the President's "thickly forested interior." Roosevelt's personality was so mercurial, so filled with paradox, that he called it "multiplex." FDR was a conservative by training and instinct but utterly unafraid of experimentation; at once principled and pragmatic; unable to walk unaided and boundlessly optimistic.

Henry Morgenthau, Jr., Roosevelt's Secretary of the Treasury and Dutchess County neighbor since 1915, stood now near the grave trying to comfort his sobbing daughter Joan. He admitted that his old friend was "extraordinarily difficult to describe."

"Never let your left hand know what your right is doing," FDR had once said to him.

"Which hand am I, Mr. President?" Morgenthau asked.

"My right hand, but I keep my left hand under the table."

Frances Perkins, clutching her purse and wearing one of her familiar black hats, had known FDR even longer—since he first campaigned for a seat in the New York State Senate in 1910; she simply thought him "the most complicated human being I have ever known."

Even Eleanor Roosevelt, now preparing to leave the train and accompany her husband's body to the top of the hill, knew that she had never fully shared his inner life. No one had. "He had no real confidantes," she once said. "I don't think I was ever his confidante, either."

At a signal, eight uniformed pallbearers carried the casket from the train to a waiting hearse. High above them, artillery men began firing a twenty-one-gun salute, crash following crash every fifteen seconds, echoing and re-echoing across the Hudson.

A flight of twelve silver bombers drummed southward overhead.

As the hearse began moving up the road, several limousines fell in line behind. These bore the Trumans and the Roosevelts: the President's widow; his daughter, Anna, and her husband, Colonel John Boettiger; the second youngest Roosevelt son, Elliott (now a brigadier general), and his wife, the actress Faye Emerson; and the wives of his absent sons—James, Franklin, Jr., and John.

The limousines moved slowly up the road along which FDR had loved to speed, spinning around the bends in his open hand-controlled Ford, and leaving the Secret Service behind. Fallen logs, green with moss, lay across one another on the forest floor. Violets had begun to bloom among the logs and along the road, and here and there were the green and yellow spears of daffodils. Behind the cortege, the river was hidden now by the branches of giant poplars. Roosevelt had believed this stand of trees to be virgin forest, untouched since before Henry Hudson's day, and this largely fancied link with primeval America had been important to him; he had loved to show it to visitors.

Roosevelt was nearly home. The hearse glided past the ice pond where he had sometimes swum as a boy and where he had helped teach some of his children how to swim, and on up to the edge of the broad, sharply sloping meadow below his house, down which he had sledded every winter of his boyhood.

Here, where the path emerged from the woods, a gun carriage waited, drawn by six brown horses. Lines of servicemen—883 in all—stood along both sides of the road ahead. The casket, covered with a flag and somehow surprisingly small to contain a President—*the* President to a generation that had known no other—was lifted from the hearse and strapped tight to the carriage; the climb ahead was steep.

A seventh horse, riderless, walked behind, its head and body hooded, stirrups reversed; boots and a sword hung upside down from the left stirrup, traditional symbols of the fallen warrior. Ahead marched the U.S. Military Academy band. There was no music at first; the men needed their breath for climbing. But the cadence of its muffled drums could be heard now in the garden, growing closer, and so could the distant pealing of the bell of St. James.

At the head of the procession, in front of the bandsmen, came a battalion of honor, 600 West Point cadets, grave and wide-eyed in their gray uniforms, moving in perfect unison. A reporter noted that "not a crease of a bending knee [was] a quarter of an inch out of line." But at least one cadet had trouble controlling his emotions. "I felt a tear trickle down my cheek," he would confess to his parents; Roosevelt had been "my ideal in life, perhaps the greatest man the world has ever seen."

The procession halted just outside the hedge. The band played Chopin's funeral march while the cadets passed into the garden from the river side, one column after another swinging to a halt until the battalion formed a solid phalanx. Then it played "Nearer My God to Thee" as the two presidential families entered the garden and took their places near the grave. Mrs. Roosevelt was dry-eyed but haggard beneath her veil. On her black dress was a gold pin with the three feathers of the Roosevelt family crest worked out on it in diamonds. Her husband had given it to her on their wedding day forty years before.

To the east stood congressmen and Cabinet members; the military chiefs of staff and the members of the Supreme Court were to the west. Behind the wall of flowers to the north were friends and neighbors from Hyde Park.

Three elderly members of the President's family were too frail to stand while they waited. Uncle Fred Delano and Mrs. Price Collier, his late mother's surviving brother and sister, had come on the train from Washington; they had wanted to "ride home with Franklin," Mrs. Collier said. Betty Roosevelt, the second wife and widow of the President's half brother James Roosevelt Roosevelt, had been driven over from her home next door. Bundled in black, all three sat on massive chairs in the bright sunshine.

They struggled to their feet as a youthful crucifer passed through the leafy gateway, followed by the Reverend George Anthony, the aged rector of St. James, gaunt in his black velvet skullcap and cassock and white surplice. Behind him, pallbearers carried the coffin to the grave.

A lone bomber, unscheduled, flew over the garden, dipping its wings in salute.

Then there was only the sound of birds as the rector removed his cap, his white surplice blowing in the wind. His voice was strong and sure as he asked Christ's mercy on His departed servant, intoned the Lord's Prayer, and finally recited the first stanza of John Lodge Ellerton's elegy:

> *"Now the laborer's task is o'er;*
> *Now the battle day is past;*
> *Now upon the farther shore*
> *Lands the voyager at last.*
> *Father in thy gracious keeping*
> *Leave we now thy servant sleeping."*

The silence that followed was so complete that everyone in the garden could hear the squeaking of the leather straps that held the coffin as it was lowered into the earth.

West Point riflemen fired three volleys into the brilliant sky. The President's cousin Margaret Suckley held his Scottie on a leash; at the first volley, Fala began howling, rolling over and over in the grass.

A small child began to cry and was rushed away by its embarrassed father.

A West Point cornetist blew taps.

The family left the graveside; the other mourners followed them.

Franklin Roosevelt was left alone in his mother's garden at Hyde Park, just as he had wished.

The broad, slow-moving river and the big shabby comfortable house that overlooked it had been the great constants in his life. Always, no matter where he was or what he was doing, he had come back here to restore himself—as student, candidate, bureaucrat, businessman, invalid, governor, and perhaps two hundred times in his dozen years as President.

If there was an answer to the riddle of his personality, a way through that forested interior, surely it would be found in this place, among these people.

CHAPTER 1

MR. JAMES

Spring had come late to the Hudson Valley in 1867, too; and when James Roosevelt and his wife, Rebecca, drove up the long driveway to their new home on April 30 of that year, mist hid the hills beyond, and a cold, steady rain slanted down, driven by the wind off the river. The carriage splashed along the edge of a stubbled, muddy field beneath big trees, their bare limbs black and shiny with rain, and stopped in front of the house.

Dark and clapboarded, it was not large as Hudson River manors went—there were just seventeen rooms—and it was in poor repair. A three-storied tower stood at the southeast corner, and a deep veranda ran the full length of the front and around one side, its pillars thickly wound with ivy. The house's profile reminded James of a locomotive with a tall smokestack pulling a train of cars. Water dripped steadily from the overhanging eaves as the Roosevelts hurried inside.

They were a handsome couple. Rebecca, then thirty-six, was a merry woman, plump and attractive, and capable of putting almost anyone at ease. Her husband was more reserved; his servants, the townspeople, even some of his friends, found it most comfortable to call him "Mr. James." He was slender and erect, of medium height, with alert hazel eyes, a firm chin, and brown muttonchop whiskers just beginning to go gray at thirty-nine.

The Roosevelts had been happily married now for fourteen years and had one child, an amiable thirteen-year-old boy named James

Roosevelt Roosevelt, whom everyone including his parents called "Rosy." At the moment he was staying with his uncle, John Aspinwall Roosevelt, at his home just two miles down the Albany Post Road, but soon he would be coming to live in the new house as well.

Like many of their friends, the Roosevelts led a serene but peripatetic life, dividing the year between their country home on the Hudson, a house in New York City in which they spent the harshest winter months, and long vacations abroad.

They had been at Interlaken in the Swiss Alps in September of 1865, when word came that their old house in the country, Mount Hope, had been burned to the ground. James Roosevelt's grandfather had built Mount Hope; James himself had been born there, and he had inherited it at his grandfather's death. Its loss had seemed "a fearful dream," he wrote; he could not believe that his "dear old home is among the things of the past." Rather than rebuild, James had sold the land to the State of New York for $45,000—it became the site of the Hudson River State Hospital, a mental institution—and began looking for a place of his own to buy with the proceeds.

The house whose gloomy, vacant interior he and Rebecca were now exploring had not been their first choice. They had hoped to buy Ferncliffe, the far more opulent Hudson River estate of John Jacob Astor III at Rhinebeck. James Roosevelt was himself a wealthy man —general manager of the Cumberland and Pennsylvania Railroad, director of the Consolidated Coal Company of Maryland, responsible custodian of a considerable inheritance—but his fortune was inconsequential compared to that compiled by Astor's grandfather, and it had taken him three days to get up the nerve to call and make an offer for his house. He paced outside Astor's door for half an hour one morning, unable to bring himself to knock, and finally left, wandering the streets the rest of the day until a nervous headache drove him home. Rebecca spoke firmly to him, and two days later he managed to make it past the door. He offered $40,000. Astor turned him down; it was $50,000 or nothing.

The Roosevelts lowered their sights. They tried next to buy a more modest place on the river from Moses Beach, another New York businessman, only to find him unable to decide whether or not he really wanted to sell. (Rebecca was secretly relieved; she thought the Beach place "perfectly hopeless, on account of a villa he had built which would not do for a carriage house.")

The Hyde Park house the Roosevelts finally settled upon was built in 1826, and had been owned by a railroad executive named Josiah Wheeler. Not only was the house run-down, but Wheeler, whose heart had never been in farming, had neglected the fields and gardens, and all the outbuildings needed attention.

Still, Rebecca wrote, they were "quite satisfied with our purchase." There was a lot of work to do. But the house could fairly easily be put in good order. An enclosed garden filled with rosebushes and plum and pear trees stood just to the north, its tall hedges already almost half a century old. With the house and garden came 110 acres of land on which James could raise his trotting horses. (Later, he would buy up adjacent tracts until his estate encompassed almost 1,000 acres of fields and forests.) And even through the drizzle the view of the river from the veranda was majestic.

James threw himself into the work. Rebecca marveled at his energy. The first few weeks in their new home she hardly saw him between breakfast and supper as he strode from task to task, seeing that oilcloth and Brussels carpet were properly laid, checking to make sure the painters used the right shade of green on the piazza, supervising the installation of indoor plumbing in the house. Rebecca called him "Boss Plumber" for a time. He took charge of the land, too, riding over it daily with Rosy at his side, inspecting fences, seeing that his horses and his herd of Guernsey, Jersey, and Alderney cattle were well pastured, showing the gardener where Rebecca wanted her new plants set out. The gardener's name was Sebastian Bauman, but Mr. James addressed him and all the other men and women who worked on the place by their first names; so did Rebecca and Rosy.

One day James and Rosy called Rebecca out from the house to see a trembling newborn Alderney calf they had found in the woods. Sebastian had carried it home in his arms. Precisely one year later they found another one on the same spot.

Each morning, Rebecca wrote, she and James walked together in the enclosed garden, gathering "thousands of roses before breakfast." And when it grew too hot to do much during the day, James went on working at night. After supper one evening in June, Rebecca walked with him through the woods to the ice pond a quarter of the way down the bluff and sat beneath a tree while he raked leaves from its silver surface by the light of a young moon.

The fire that had razed Mount Hope had also taken with it all but a few of the family's possessions. "Our loss is total," Rebecca had confided to her journal in Switzerland. "Nothing left but three lamps and a little bedding." And when her mother-in-law sent her a charred book from the old library as a memento, she had wept.

Actually, it had not been quite that bad. A rosewood bed and bureau had been rescued, along with two small Duncan Phyfe chairs. So had a large silver tea service that had belonged to James's great-grandfather. And at either end of the table in their new dining room, James and Rebecca carefully placed a chair from the old house. Carved deeply into the back of each were the roses and plumes of the Roosevelt family crest.

Later, when he had his estate more or less the way he wanted it, James ordered his men to dig up the tall brownstone gateposts that had marked the entrance to his grandfather's house, haul them up the road by oxcart, and reinstall them on either side of the driveway to his own.

Continuity was important to him. He was very proud to be a Roosevelt.

The Roosevelts were an old New York family, but they came relatively late to the Hudson Valley. By the time Franklin Roosevelt's great-grandfather built Mount Hope in 1818, more wealthy and powerful clans such as the Livingstons, the Schuylers, the Verplancks, and the Van Rensselaers had already been living along the river for two centuries. In that anachronistic, almost feudal world, the Roosevelts were always parvenus.

They were descended from Claes Van Rosenvelt, a hardy Dutchman about whom little is known except that he was married to an Englishwoman named Thomas, came to New Amsterdam about 1650, and carved out for himself a comfortable farm on what is now the far eastern fringe of the garment district. Claes had a son named Nicholas, who in turn had three sons: one of these, Johannes, was the ancestor of Theodore Roosevelt; the line established by another son, Jacobus, would lead eventually to FDR.

The descendants of Jacobus—James in English—Roosevelt were able, energetic, and prosperous, noteworthy among the leaders of New York's Knickerbocker society only if unbroken solvency and good manners are thought exceptional. Their wealth came from Manhattan real estate, dry goods, and the West Indian sugar trade. And they had married well, linking their clan with the sons and daughters of other important families, both English and Dutch. In this way, Franklin Roosevelt would write, "the stock kept virile and abreast of the times."

One eighteenth-century Roosevelt stood out above the rest.

Remembered in the family as "the patriot," Isaac Roosevelt was a sugar merchant whose indignation at the way British trade laws cut into his profits, rather than any abstract concern with the rights of man, drove him to join the Revolutionary cause. (It was his elegant English tea service that had been salvaged from the ruins of Mount Hope.) He was a moderating influence among his fellow businessmen before the fighting began, determined to help win repeal of illicit taxes but hopeful always that there would be a reconciliation between king and colonies, and adamant against the violence to property encouraged by the Sons of Liberty. Still, when the crisis came in the summer of 1776, he voted for independence as a delegate to the Provincial Congress. It was not an easy decision. Many of his closest friends were Tories, and when English troops occupied New York he was forced to abandon his home and business and flee to Dutchess County for the duration.

Later, he helped fashion the new constitution that created New York State, doing all he could behind the scenes to limit the spread of democracy and safeguard the rights of men of property, and he helped win New York's ratification of the Federal Constitution as a member of the Constitutional Convention of 1788. During forty days and nights of sometimes angry debate at Poughkeepsie, he was a solid but silent member of the Federalist forces led by his friend Alexander Hamilton, never once taking the floor himself. His alliance with Hamilton carried over into his business life as well; he served as president of the Bank of New York, which he, Hamilton, and others had founded in 1784.

Isaac's son, James, inherited both his father's business and his politics, serving one uneventful year in the State Assembly. It was he who built Mount Hope on the Hudson, living there or on another farm in Harlem during the summer months and in a handsome town house at 18 South Street the rest of the year. During his long and largely tranquil life he had three wives and eleven children.[1]

1. The consistent conservatism of his ancestors evidently bothered FDR. Not long before his death he rather forlornly asked one of his secretaries, Jonathan Daniels, to see if the Library of Congress couldn't find some sort of link between his great-grandfather, Isaac the Patriot, and Thomas Jefferson, whom the President found much more congenial than Alexander Hamilton. The historian David C. Mearns, director of the reference department, did his best but neither he nor his staff could find any evidence that the two men had ever even met. A note of somewhat desperate cheer dominates Mearns's reply to Daniels:

> There is an interesting item in Jefferson's unpublished account book (for 1790), which reads "pd. Roosevelt 3 feather fans. 24/." Inasmuch as the New York directory for 1789 lists no fewer than five mercantile establishments under the name of Roosevelt, and Isaac and his son

Knickerbocker society, in which Isaac and James Roosevelt and their families were entirely at home, was closed and comfortable, still centered on Manhattan's tip, and surprisingly small. As late as 1830, a contemporary wrote, "a New Yorker of no very extended acquaintance could tell the names of all the principal merchants and where they lived."

Their homes were modest by later standards—narrow three- or four-story houses of brick on cobbled streets only a few steps from their places of business. Isaac Roosevelt lived on Pearl Street; his sugar refinery was just behind his house, his bank right across the street. There were few carriages—the city was small enough so that one could walk almost anywhere—and even the most prominent families rarely dined out in public. Guests were entertained in the parlor or strolled with their hosts along the Battery. The Sabbath was strictly observed, the whole family marching to church together three times during the day, their servants following along behind, one old New Yorker recalled, "as an evidence that the family was doing its whole duty."

If a strong sense of duty and of decorum united the society of old New York, so, too, did a century and a half of family alliances. Money alone provided no entree. "The applicant for admission" to New York society of that day, wrote a nostalgic member of it long after everything had changed, "must possess the requisite affinities and bear the unmistakable evidences which, the world over, proclaim the gentleman by sentiment and education. This idea of aristocracy pervaded Gotham . . . it underlay and formed the foundation of New York society. The good old fathers and their *Madames* were great sticklers for form and ceremony; their full ruffles and cuffs were starched, and unwittingly imparted to the wearer an air of dignified composure that would check the merest approach to familiarity from their juniors."

The dignified composure of the Roosevelts was especially memorable. Many years later, Philip Hone the diarist and former mayor of the city who as a boy had known Isaac Roosevelt, recalled that he and the members of his generation had been another "sort of people from those of the present day. Proud and aristocratical, they were the only nobility we had . . . men could not stand straight in their presence." Others agreed. The obituary notices of three successive Roosevelt patriarchs

were primarily dealers in sugar, it is impossible to link it to them. . . . Still, it is clear that when in New York, Thomas Jefferson obtained his feather fans from the Roosevelt family!

Source: Mearns to Daniels, April 9, 1945, Jonathan Daniels Papers, Franklin D. Roosevelt Library (hereafter designated FDRL).

use the identical phrase to describe the departed: Each had been "a gentleman of the old school."

And it is likely that they shared their friends' horror at the changes that were then disturbing the tranquillity of their little port city. Hundreds of immigrants disembarked at the Battery Park Wharf each day; their strange accents could be heard in every street. New York's outskirts edged steadily up the island of Manhattan to accommodate them, and the old families themselves eventually found themselves forced to follow suit. "The old down town burgomasters," wrote Philip Hone, "were marching reluctantly north to pitch their tents in places which in their time were orchards, cornfields or morasses, a pretty smart distance from town." James Roosevelt joined that genteel exodus in 1821, moving to a new house at 64 Bleecker Street in Greenwich Village, in the hope that his family would benefit from its more wholesome small-town atmosphere.

But more than the Knickerbocker neighborhoods was threatened. The political power the old New York families had once wielded so freely was also slipping away. Governing had been one thing; it was a gentleman's duty to help guide the destinies of persons less fortunate and less well informed than he, just as it was incumbent upon him to contribute to charity. Both Isaac and James Roosevelt were proud of having held public office. But electoral politics was quite another matter. Competing for votes was thought unseemly, unprincipled, vulgar. The Federalist Party having disintegrated, the Roosevelts of Jacobus' line became Whigs, but they no longer even considered an active part in political life.

In this they mirrored the attitudes of their friends and neighbors. The revulsion and fear the old families felt for the new and sweaty world of partisan politics was deep and long-lasting. Francis Grund, an Austrian nobleman who admired American democracy, was astonished by the enmity wealthy New Yorkers felt toward ordinary citizens during his visits to New York in the 1830s. It was as if the aristocrats thought "themselves beset by dogs," he wrote, "and are continually kicking for fear of being bitten."

Among the wealthy men and women with whom Grund spoke, politics was thought "wholly uninteresting except to tavern-keepers on election days . . . a subject unworthy of the pursuit of gentlemen, and a thing banished from people of fashion and good taste. . . . Thus a 'popular candidate for office' is equivalent to 'a vagabond who has no business of his own'; 'popularity' means 'the approbation of the mob.' " Grund added that "all these significations apply only to members of the *democratic* party . . . for it is easily understood why a man of property should be attached to his country; but the poor man has no right to be so, and is therefore justly suspected whenever he takes an interest in politics."

An elderly and oblivious woman of the sort who might well have visited the Roosevelt parlor confided to Grund that she had no objection to liberty in the abstract. "I think all men, with the exception of our negroes, ought to be free; but I cannot bear the ridiculous notion of equality which seems to have taken hold of our people." If not crushed soon, she continued, it would be "the ruin of our country."

The clamorous, noisome new city did not suit James Roosevelt's oldest son, Isaac, who was born in 1790. He was an unlikely member of his clan, lacking utterly the family's traditional self-assurance. While other Roosevelts delighted in the world, Isaac shrank from it. Educated at Princeton and then at the New York College of Physicians and Surgeons, from which he was graduated in 1812, he astonished his parents by announcing that he did not plan to practice medicine. The sight of blood was unbearable to him, he said; he could not tolerate the sounds of suffering. He lived with his parents in New York for a time, collecting books on the history of medicine and venturing out only to ride north into the countryside to conduct botanical experiments with his mentor, Dr. David Hosack, whose twenty-acre Elgin Botanical Garden then covered the land now occupied by Rockefeller Center.[2]

When Mount Hope was completed in 1820, he moved there, con-

2. Dr. Hosack eventually became Dr. Isaac Roosevelt's neighbor as well as his teacher. He was an extraordinary man—physician, botanist, educator, historian, biographer, public citizen. In 1828, he purchased a modest house and a large rolling riverfront tract just a few miles north of Mount Hope, at Hyde Park. Here he hoped to retire and indulge his many interests. He added two wings to the house, one in which his grandchildren could play chess and whist and offer musicales, the other for his collection of some 5,000 books. Six hundred English sheep kept the lawns clipped, and a herd of dairy cattle, also imported from the British Isles, was pastured on his land. The gardens, designed by a French landscape architect, were filled with exotic plants which envious townspeople sometimes spirited away. Dr. Hosack patrolled the village regularly in his carriage, spotting the stolen goods in other people's plots and politely asking for them back. His guests, who included Washington Irving and Frances Trollope, dined on the guavas, citron melons, and pineapples that flourished in his locked greenhouses. Mrs. Trollope, who found few things to admire in America, thought Hosack's estate "magnificent . . . it is hardly possible to imagine anything more beautiful."

Dr. Hosack died in 1835. His house burned to the ground ten years later. In 1898, Frederick H. Vanderbilt would build on the site a vast and showy Renaissance palace of fifty-five rooms, each furnished with truly awesome vulgarity.

Source: Christine Chapman Robbins, *David Hosack, Citizen of New York*, Philadelphia, 1964, pages 176–190.

tinuing his solitary studies and breeding cattle and horses. His brother-in-law once described Dr. Isaac as "of a delicate constitution and refined tastes." He was being charitable. In fact, Dr. Isaac was a hypochondriac, frightened of people, and paralyzed with dread. One's only duty in this life, he constantly reiterated, was to be prepared for the next: "We know not what a day may bring forth. 'Be ye also ready' is the warning voice." He seemed destined to remain an eccentric recluse to the end, a mild embarrassment to his prominent family, perhaps, but inoffensive if kept in the country.

Then, in 1827, another surprise: Dr. Isaac announced that he planned to marry his parents' neighbor on Bleecker Street, Mary Rebecca Aspinwall. She was eighteen; he was thirty-seven.

Once they had recovered from the shock, the elder Roosevelts must have been pleased. No one knows how the Aspinwalls took the news. The Roosevelts had been largely content to live on the fortunes their ancestors had built; the Aspinwalls, with their partners, the Howlands, were still aggressively amassing theirs. Transportation and shipping provided the means. They first made good in the whaling business; later the firm of Howland & Aspinwall became one of the most prosperous shipping companies in New York, its clippers familiar in the ports of every continent. Still later, they did well in railroads, and William Henry Aspinwall, Dr. Isaac's brother-in-law, built himself a fine mansion on University Place, and another even larger one at Barrytown, above Rhinebeck on the Hudson.

Little is known of Mary Rebecca Aspinwall other than that she was a patient and loving wife to her querulous husband, but her mother was a Howland, and it seems clear that she brought to the marriage a badly needed dash of the vigor with which her Yankee forebears on both sides had wrested their wealth from the sea.

For somehow their son, James, the President's father, inherited more than Dr. Isaac's fears. He grew to be a serious and upright man, but there lived in him, too, something of the gambler; he would prove willing, even eager, to take risks. The conservative and the gambler warred within James Roosevelt all his life, just as they would later war within his son. And when the time came for him to raise his own boys, he would work hard to recreate in minute detail the world in which he himself was raised.

James was born at Mount Hope on July 16, 1828, during the final year of the presidency of John Quincy Adams, and was baptized that winter in the old Dutch Reformed Church at Poughkeepsie. Soon thereafter, perhaps at the gentle urging of his wife, Dr. Isaac decided that he should at last have a home of his own. He purchased a large plot of land just across the Albany Post Road and built on it a big solid gabled dwelling with deep verandas on all four sides. He named it Rosedale, and around it he planted trees and shrubs so thickly that the river could only be glimpsed through the leaves and little light was allowed to enter the dark paneled rooms; Dr. Isaac discouraged even the sun from intruding upon his refuge.[3]

Here, James spent his first fourteen years. We know few details of his life at Rosedale—the fire that destroyed Mount Hope took with it most of the family papers—but it must have been at least outwardly tranquil and secure.

There can have been few steady playmates. Tutors taught him his first lessons. But his mother adored him and his father loved him with what Dr. Isaac himself called "a love inexpressible, pure and elevating." He had no rival for his parents' affection. Servants saw to his needs, and he was free to roam his family's lands with his black dog Billy; he hunted and fished, built a waterwheel on the ice pond, learned to ride and care for the fine horses his grandfather bred and trained on the other side of the road.

Still, the purity of his father's devotion was always alloyed by his fears, his constant warnings of the end that might come at any instant. These must have been especially frightening to a child because they had no apparent cause. If one needed to be fearful in the midst of Rosedale's placid and self-contained universe, no place was safe, nothing could be relied upon, the future was always filled with peril. Perhaps in response, James developed an air of sobriety beyond his years, at least in the presence of adults. He learned early that many things were better left unsaid, uncomfortable thoughts best swallowed. Even when he was a small boy few called him Jim or Jimmy; he was already James and would soon become Mr. James.

3. The biographer Kenneth S. Davis, visiting Rosedale in 1967, was shown a secret cellar, cement-walled. The family then living in the house told him that a plumber had uncovered it while doing some work in 1955, and that "historical research" led them to believe it had been a hideaway for runaway slaves, and that Dr. Isaac must therefore have been a stationmaster on the clandestine Underground Railroad that helped spirit fugitives north to Canada. Davis suggests quite rightly that Dr. Isaac's "peculiar psychology"—especially his near-obsession with privacy—would have made such a dangerous and secret activity perfectly plausible. It might also help explain the need for the shady screen that he grew around his house. On the other hand, it seems unlikely that even Dr. Isaac could have kept the presence of runaways secret from his sons, and impossible to believe that they would have kept their silence if they had learned of it, once the Civil War had ended. Nor did Dr. Isaac pass on any special sympathy for blacks to his children.

When he was nine years old, his parents enrolled him at the Poughkeepsie Collegiate School, established just the year before in a handsome pseudo-classical building on a summit east of town. From its white marble colonnade, young James could gaze across fields and farmhouses to the roofs and steeples of Poughkeepsie, then home to fewer than 7,000 persons, and to the river and the Catskills far beyond; if he turned his face northward he could just make out the roof of Rosedale above its screen of trees, three miles away. Unlike the other boys, James was a day student; the family carriage came to take him home each evening and brought him back the next morning.

The Collegiate School was intended for the sons of Hudson River gentlemen first, and then for boys of good family from as far away as Cuba, Mexico, and South America. James and his schoolmates, said the *Poughkeepsie Eagle,* were all "of the right sort" and enhanced the town by their attendance. They were led through a rigorous curriculum that included French and Spanish, Latin and Greek, rhetoric and logic, mathematics, natural philosophy, and history (especially "that of our country").

The school's founder, Mr. Charles Bartlett, A.M., was a pioneer in the gentling of education. His students were never beaten, as they routinely were at other private academies; rather, allowance was made for what Bartlett called "the nature of the juvenile mind," and discipline was achieved by "disapprobation of the instructors" and "private and public censure"; "rewards and punishments [were] of an intellectual and moral nature, addressed to the understanding of the heart."

James attended Mr. Bartlett's school for five years, but somehow its leniency did not seem to have the desired effect, or at least Dr. Isaac did not believe it had. He thought James "unruly." Whether the normal exuberance of boyhood was simply more than the nervous doctor could endure, or whether he felt his son was learning bad habits from his schoolmates, we cannot know. It is possible that James may really have been rebellious when away from home, for in 1840, when the boy was twelve (and his father was fifty), a brother, John Aspinwall Roosevelt, was born at Rosedale. James would not have been the first only child to feel threatened by a pink and shrieking intruder on what had been his own exclusive world.

In any case, in the fall of 1841, at the age of thirteen, James Roosevelt was sent away to Mr. Alexander Hyde's school at Lee, Massachusetts. If Dr. Isaac sought for his son a more pious and tranquil atmosphere far removed from worldly temptation, he chose well. For half a century, Lee had been the religious fiefdom of a singular Congregational minister, the Reverend Alvan Hyde, and of his schoolmaster son, Alexander.

It was a lovely little town at the foot of the Berkshires, peopled by independent-minded farmers. A good many men of Lee had marched with Daniel Shays during the farmers' rebellion of 1787, and when the young Reverend Hyde arrived from Connecticut to apply for the pastorate of the First Congregational Church in 1792 there had not been a permanent pastor for eight years. Several men had come to town "to preach with a view to settle," but the turbulent congregation had been unable to agree to hire any of them. One was rejected because he was thought guilty of "denying eternal punishment"; another because some churchmen did not like his "ideas of all mankind's being finally happy." A sympathetic parishioner warned Hyde that "we have been very Shaysy here, and you'll have to be wise as a serpent to keep peace among us."

Alvan Hyde, though only twenty-two, proved more lion than serpent. He overwhelmed the parish with his eloquence and zeal. His revivalist message was simple and terrifying, and there was no room in it for abstruse doctrinal differences. "His teachings were not overlaid and smothered by imported facts and notions," an admirer wrote. "Theory that did not lead to practice was a mere tinkling cymbal." Having heard him preach, the townspeople begged him to stay; they helped build him a house, offered him a larger salary than his predecessor had received, and when that did not suffice, supplemented it with produce. One member of the congregation brought him a year's supply of honey every autumn.

In return, the Reverend Hyde came very close to taking over their lives. He mediated town disputes, dominated town politics, supervised the schools, and so strengthened his congregation with the fierce urgency of his preaching—fired by rum in the years before the temperance enthusiasm caught up with him—that a new church had to be built to contain the newcomers.

A local historian recalled that Hyde had soon "trained up a townful of theologians. Men, women, and children discussed original sin and foreordination." Those who cursed or drank too much knew that he would learn of it and make awful examples of them on Sunday, when everyone would be at church and eager to hear the worst. A resident remembered that " 'I couldn't go a foot' was no excuse when Dr. Hyde —as he was sure to do—came during the week to find out the reasons for non-attendance." Village politics became uniform, too. "All good children were born whigs," wrote an old citizen of Lee, "and it took a good deal of other kinds of goodness to compensate for the sin of being a democrat . . . To indicate publicly any anxiety for an office always lessened one's chances; and to electioneer for one's self insured . . . defeat." That, too, must have comforted Dr. Isaac.

The Reverend Alvan Hyde died in 1833, but his memory and example gripped his town long after he had left the pulpit; and his son, Alexander, carried on his interest in education. Educated at Williams College, Alexander Hyde started a school for gentlemen's sons in rooms above the meeting house in 1835, and two years later opened a second school in his own home.

It was here that James Roosevelt came to live and learn. Alexander Hyde specialized in the pacification of troublesome boys. He put relentless emphasis on religion, with special attention to God's wrath toward the disobedient. Prayer services opened and closed each day. Sunday was entirely given over to worship: morning devotions, morning services at the church (where James and his fellow scholars were kept alert by an usher's horn-tipped rattan), Sunday school, afternoon prayers, and evening worship. The boys were sustained from dawn to supper on the Sabbath only by large spice cookies, gritty with caraway seeds and carried in their pockets.

Like Mr. Barrett of the Collegiate School, Alexander Hyde promised a homelike atmosphere—"a family school"—free of physical brutality. His patience had its limits, however, and recalcitrant scholars were likely to have their hair pulled. A middle-aged alumnus returning for a reunion in the 1870s joked to his old schoolmaster that he had been the cause of his baldness; Hyde said he had entirely forgotten the incident, but had no doubt it had been deserved.

Even at Hyde's school, James could not entirely escape the shadow of his father's fears. Dr. Isaac worried that his son might be reading the wrong sort of fiction, the kind that was not "well written and moral or religious," and he despaired even of his absent son's devotion: "I often wonder if the extent of your love is as great as mine."

And sometimes life seemed to confirm his worst fears. In 1842, he wrote to his son that all seven of his own brothers were now dead, the last just drowned in the Hudson and found floating several days later "so much changed" that he could be identified only by his watch. The body had been too bloated to fit into a coffin; and "owing to the condition of the corpse," Dr. Isaac explained, "no person attended the funeral but myself . . . the sexton & 2 assistants." He drew his customary conclusion: "How important, my dear son, that we should make it the great business of our lives to be prepared for another and a better world . . . Repent . . . Strive to correct your faults . . . be gentle and mild. Obtain the command of your temper."

Whether it was due to the boy's distance from his own anxieties or the discipline imposed by Dr. Hyde, James's father was at least momentarily pleased at his son's progress during the fall and winter of 1842. "Your improvement in learning and knowledge and good conduct," he told James, "will be such as will reflect credit to teachers and parents—and do honor to the name of Roosevelt." When James had been home for the holidays, Dr. Isaac told Dr. Hyde, the boy had been "amiable, disinterested and endeavored to please us in all things."

Not quite in all things, however. There was the matter of college. James was determined to attend the University of New York in Manhattan. His family, and especially his father, dreaded the corrupting influence of life in the city. If James was permitted to come to New York, his uncle Gardiner G. Howland warned, "he will become a Dandy & will walk Broadway with his cane." Dr. Isaac did not believe his son would fall so low as that. "You know you were created for better things," he wrote. "We live for God." But he much preferred that James avoid the risk and remain in some "quiet country village."

His son was adamant, however, and after consulting clergymen, relatives, and Dr. Hyde (who also distrusted the city), Dr. Isaac nervously acquiesced, requiring that James live at home with his grandparents on Bleecker Street, attending the university only during the day, and that he further promise to resist those temptations which "are mortifying to the feelings and put [boys'] tempers as well as their principles to a severe test."

James entered the University of New York as a freshman in the autumn of 1843, and did well enough at first, finding time to join a debating society and win a gold medal for his "Readiness in composition and facility in expressing his thoughts." But something did go wrong. In May, he and three friends were officially admonished for having caused "disorder" in the mathematics classroom, and in June he failed to appear for his final examinations in both mathematics and Latin.

Dr. Isaac sent him upstate the following fall, to Union College in the old Dutch city of Schenectady. The president of Union, the Reverend Dr. Eliphalet Nott, was another specialist in the education and improvement of difficult boys. His reputation for salvaging wayward students expelled from other schools was so widespread that Union was sometimes called "Botany Bay," after the Australian penal colony that gave English convicts their second chance. President Nott "rather gloried in this appellation," wrote one of James's fellow students, because "it indicated faith in his rare powers of reclamation."

He was a remarkable man, seventy-two years old when James arrived on campus, and beginning his fifth decade as Union's president. (He would serve sixty-two years in that post, the longest college presidency in American history.) He was famous for his oratory and his inventive genius as well as his educational reforms, holding patents on some thirty models of coal-burning stoves and an improved boiler that made steamboat travel less of a gamble. He had also devised the curious three-wheeled "chariot" in which he rode around the town greeting new students and their parents.

He had been a prodigy, had read the Bible through at four and earned his M.A. at Brown in a single year, and was raised by an admiring but unbending mother. When, at ten, he refused to eat his morning mush, the bowl was put before him again at lunch and supper; he gave in and ate it the next morning, he remembered, "ate the mush, and in addition, the red ants which had been attracted to it by the sugar in it." His older brother, the Reverend Samuel Nott, had been his teacher, a Calvinist so strict, Nott wrote, that "in addition to warnings and admonitions daily, if I was not whipped more than three times a week, I considered myself for a time peculiarly fortunate." While still a small boy, Nott had sworn that "If I lived to be a man, I would not be like other men in the treatment of their children."[4]

He was not. Boys were fundamentally good, he believed, in need only of self-discipline. An alumnus recalled that he "used to say that many a life that had germs of usefulness in it had been utterly ruined by unwise harshness and abandonment, when milder and more persuasive means would have restored and reformed it." Discipline at Union was "moral and parental," its catalogue promised. "Disgraceful punishments are not inflicted."

Dr. Nott wished to produce virtuous gentlemen, not mere scholars, men equipped to make their way in a new and increasingly democratic world. That world needed reforming, he believed, and it was the duty of a college to provide its graduates with as much practical knowledge

4. Samuel Nott had also been the mentor of the Reverend Alvan Hyde, the stern preacher of Lee; perhaps that fact had something to do with Dr. Isaac's decision to send James to Dr. Nott at Union.

as possible with which to meet that challenge. Academic traditionalists had been appalled when he introduced a separate scientific course of studies alongside the classics, and shocked again just a year before James Roosevelt arrived, when he engaged an instructor in the purely technical science of engineering.

To his critics, Dr. Nott's sense of the practical seemed somewhat overdeveloped. He had made his college the most solvent in the country through a series of statewide lotteries, and the lines between Union's proceeds and his own were sometimes blurred. "The financial mysteries of the college," wrote Silas Blunt of the class of 1849, "always suggesting the intimate blending of its funds with the private means of its president . . . occupied several legislative committees . . . but our cunning 'Old Prexy' invariably foiled them." (Nott would eventually bequeath some $600,000 to his college.)

Schenectady itself was then a "quaint, quiet town," Blunt remembered, "with the grass flourishing between the pavement stones in all the streets." Dr. Nott once confessed privately that he thought it "the town under the horse's tail." And the Union students, with their top hats and frock coats and tall white collars, were the targets of a good deal of hostility from the local boys. One upperclassman, a clergyman's son who stood more than six feet tall and favored a bottle-green jacket, was especially conspicuous. He was Chester A. Arthur, a future President of the United States, but then best known for the pranks he loved to lead.

The Union students had fistfights with the townboys (Dr. Nott himself rode out in his chariot on one occasion, to offer a battle plan). They stole pies and broke windows in the downtown stores, and they took part in smoke-outs, massing in a victim's dormitory room and puffing away on pipes and cigars until he was forced to flee. And they loved to harass the trainmen on the Utica and Schenectady Railroad as their trains inched through town on tracks already in such bad repair that engines were forbidden to move at more than ten miles an hour. The Union boys would jump onto the train from one side, jump off on the other, run around the front of the locomotive while the engineer and fireman pelted them with chunks of firewood, then leap on and start all over again.

Precisely what role James Roosevelt played in all this we do not know. Union students lived in two big brick dormitories, in sparsely furnished rooms with whitewashed walls and dark woodwork into which two generations of students had already carved their names.

(Chet Arthur did so at least twice.) And they were roused from bed each morning at six-thirty for roll call and prayers by a clanging bell that hung in the tower of West College Hall and dictated their comings and goings for the rest of the day. The boys grew to hate this bell, and Arthur once led a raiding party that threw it into the Erie Canal.

But James Roosevelt lived apart from his fellow students at Union, just as he had at the Collegiate School. He was one of only two students to reside off campus, in rooms rented from a Mr. Hearsey. His isolation was certainly not a matter of social standing. Among his fellow students were the sons of New York families every bit as old and distinguished as his own: Schuyler, Schermerhorn, and Van Wyck. Frederick W. Seward, the son of the Whig governor of New York, was a classmate. Perhaps it was James himself who insisted on the separation, a way of asserting at least a little of the independence he had hoped for during his short year in New York. More likely it was Dr. Isaac's doing, a means of reassuring himself that James would remain aloof from mischief.

If so, he was mistaken. "I was this morning both grieved and astonished by the reception of a letter from Dr. Nott, respecting your membership of a secret society contrary to the laws of the college," Dr. Isaac wrote to James in the fall of 1846. "I mean the society which holds its meetings at a tavern. I must request you to dissolve all connection *immediately* with this society. . . . Remember my dear son your *promise* that while at college you would not give your mother or me the *least anxiety* on your account."

It was not the secrecy of the society that was against the college rules. James had joined Delta Phi, the nation's first Greek letter fraternity, which had been born on the Union campus with Dr. Nott's blessing. Rather, it was the fact that it met in a tavern that had agitated the president. He was a celebrated temperance champion, known throughout the east for his *Ten Lectures on the Use of Intoxicating Liquors,* and in his zeal he was given to creative exaggeration. Those who drank, he warned his boys, risked the fate of a young inebriate who, he said, had been found "roasted from the crown of his head to the soles of his feet . . . standing erect in the midst of a widely extended silver-colored flame, bearing . . . exactly the appearance of the wick of a burning candle. . . . It was purely a case of spontaneous combustion."

Whether or not James ever believed such stories, he knew enough to say he did, and agreed to reform. Though intemperance was one of the very few causes for instant dismissal from Union, Dr. Nott evidently forgave him, for he was permitted to remain and to graduate with his class in July of 1847, and even to deliver the class oration.

Another conflict with his father followed. James was now determined to go abroad on his own, to make the Grand Tour of the Continent that was then considered the proper topping-off of every young gentleman's education. Dr. Isaac, of course, was against it. He could not bear to think of his son so far away. Wandering through Europe would be dangerous. Exotic diseases lurked everywhere. There were signs of political turmoil.

This time James's mother came to the rescue. Though she was at the bedside of her dying father in New York in the summer of 1847, she took the time to write her husband a chastening letter: "I do hope sincerely you will allow him to go . . . and leave him in the hands of our Heavenly Father. . . . Let us lay aside our own selfish feelings for the good of our dear child."

Dr. Isaac gave in. It was the greatest adventure of James Roosevelt's life. He was on his own at last, free to roam wherever he liked without the hobble of his father's fears. He spent eighteen months abroad, a time, his step-grandmother wrote, of "exciting scenes and hairs'-breadth escapes." He traveled through France, England, Germany, Spain, Italy, and the Holy Land. His father remained fearful throughout. He did not want James to visit the Middle East because of the malaria "that prevails on the coast of Syria, amid the ruins of dilapidated cities," and he was only briefly cheered when he learned that James had hired a guide to accompany him while traveling through "solitary plundering and thieving villages in Italy." Every letter from James brought tears of relief, and a new crop of worries.

His parents planned to join him in England in the spring of 1848, leaving eight-year-old Johnny with Dr. Hyde of Lee. Then, at the last possible moment, Dr. Isaac decided not to go. The first signs of the revolutions that would soon sweep through Europe could already be seen in France and Italy. The Continent was now "too excited and turbulent," he explained; travel would be "unpleasant and unsafe for a lady." The arbitrary suddenness of his decision tried the patience of the Aspinwalls. His grandmother wrote James that Dr. Isaac had consulted no one; his mother, her trunks already packed, was heartbroken.

Dr. Isaac continued to fret, and when he learned that James had left Italy and reached Munich safely, he was delighted. "Liberty in Europe," he warned his son, "is far different from the liberty we enjoy in our country, and I hope you will continue to take no active part in the revolutions which are agitating the Old World." (On the other hand, of course, there were worrisome things in Germany. "Abjure the pipes & beer & theology," he continued, "& adopt all that you find praiseworthy in [the German] character.")

The elder Roosevelts finally made it to Europe in the fall of 1848 and apparently spent the winter months with their son before returning to Mount Hope for the summer. As soon as they had left, if family legend is to be believed, James fulfilled his father's deepest fear: He went south, crossed the Swiss border into northern Italy, and joined the encamped army of Giuseppe Garibaldi at Rieti. There, he put on the red shirt and plumed hat of revolution and drilled alongside the liberator's peasant soldiers. It cannot have been easy duty for a wealthy young man. There were far more volunteers that spring than there were rations or arms, and the local blacksmiths had had to be persuaded to hammer out lances for those who had no guns. Still, James stuck it out for a month or so before moving on when he saw no immediate prospect of action.[5]

5. Mr. James's European adventures are scantily documented. None of his early letters written from the Continent survive, and we have only his father's and step-grandmother's letters to draw upon, plus family legends and Mr. James's passport, its fragile pages filled with blurred visas and consular stamps. Some scholars cannot bring themselves to believe that so conservative a man as Mr. James became could ever have been a revolutionary, however briefly. Their case is inadvertently strengthened by FDR's own version of the story. In October 1941, the President was presented with a desiccated cigar, alleged once to have belonged to Garibaldi. He was delighted with this trophy and sent it on to the new Franklin D. Roosevelt Library at Hyde Park, along with a memorandum in which he recorded what he remembered being told about his father's brief but romantic military career:

> He [James] became close friends with a mendicant priest—spoke only Latin with him—and the two of them proceeded on a walking tour in Italy. They came to Naples, and found the city besieged by Garibaldi's army. They both enlisted in this army, wore a red shirt for a month or so, and tiring of it, as there seemed to be little action, went to Garibaldi's tent and asked if they could receive their discharge. Garibaldi thanked the old priest and my father and the walking tour was resumed.

The trouble with this tale is that Garibaldi was nowhere near Naples during the time James Roosevelt was in Europe; his siege of that city did not begin until 1860.

Still, I believe something of the sort must have happened. James Roosevelt was many things, but he was not a liar, and there seems no reason for him to have invented such a tale about himself, especially one so utterly lacking in heroism.

The problem, I think, lies not with the basic facts of the story but with FDR's later embellishments of it. James did visit Naples (twice) during his Grand Tour, which may account for part of the confusion. And on his first sojourn in Italy he did have an Italian companion—not a priest, however, but a "courier," or professional guide, named Joseph Salerno. Dr. Isaac's relief that his son had taken no "*active* part in the revolution" (my italics) suggests that he was at least concerned about something of the kind. James may well once have conversed with a mendicant priest in Latin in Garibaldi's camp, whether or not the cleric had first swapped his cassock for a red shirt. Finally, Mr. James's passport shows that he did indeed go back into Italy in the spring of 1849, when Garibaldi was encamped at Rieti.

He sailed for home in May and entered Harvard Law School in the fall. There was family precedent for his decision. His grandfather and namesake had studied law and been admitted to the New York bar, though he had never practiced. James received his LL.B. on July 16, 1851, his twenty-third birthday, having so impressed the Harvard community with his congeniality and character that, two years after he left Cambridge, the Porcellian, Harvard's most prestigious club, made him an honorary member.

In the autumn of 1851, James entered the office of a prominent New York attorney, Benjamin Douglas Silliman. The busy Silliman firm practiced common, equity, and admiralty law, and included among its clients a good many of the new corporations then beginning to transform the character of American business. Family connections may have helped him obtain this prized position. Silliman's uncle, also named Benjamin, was a professor of chemistry at Yale, a prominent alumnus of Union College, and a friend of Samuel F. B. Morse, the artist and inventor of the telegraph, who was, in turn, a friend of Dr. Isaac. Morse and his wife lived just south of Poughkeepsie, and they and the elder Roosevelts visited one another's homes.

In any case, James remained with the firm for two years. He found the work tedious after his adventuring abroad, though Silliman himself was a major power among New York Whigs, and the office routine was sometimes relieved by intimate views of the inside of American politics. Once, James was sent to Washington to deliver some papers to Senator Sam Houston of Texas. He called at Houston's hotel to find the great man ill. A row of chairs ran from the door of the senator's room to the bed where he lay propped against pillows. An eager caller sat on each chair, and James took his seat at the end of the line nearest the door, moving up slowly as one by one the visitors approached the bedside, held a short murmured conversation, and hurried out with their marching orders. According to FDR, James always remembered "the Senator's splendid head . . . and his personality and force."

Among the most important clients of the Silliman firm was the newly organized Consolidated Coal Company of Maryland, and in 1852, less than a year out of law school, young James Roosevelt was elected to its board of directors. This was not entirely a tribute to his talents; his uncle William Henry Aspinwall had helped found the company. James took the work seriously, however, found that he much preferred it to what he called the "inactive" life of the law, and left Silliman the following year to devote himself to business. Shortly thereafter, he expanded his interests to include railroads. This, too, was a family tradition. Even timorous Dr. Isaac had invested heavily in the Hudson River line that had finally managed to stretch its tracks as far north as Poughkeepsie in 1847. Now his son became general manager of the Cumberland and Pennsylvania.[6]

James Roosevelt never became an economic royalist, but it was not for want of trying. At least three times during his long business career he tried to corner a major American industry and make himself truly rich, a rival of the Vanderbilts, Goulds, and Rockefellers. He never quite succeeded, and he may simply have lacked the requisite drive and ruthlessness to beat out his competitors. Nonetheless, the effort delighted him, providing the heady sense of risk and adventure that this genteel gambler seemed to need.

Having carved out a career more to his liking than the law had been, he now found himself a wife. On April 27, 1853, he married Rebecca Brien Howland. Their alliance further tangled the thicket of Roosevelt genealogy. His paternal grandfather's third wife, with whom he had lived while attending the University of New York, had been a Howland; so had his maternal grandmother; and his bride's father had been the late Gardiner G. Howland, the uncle who had worried that James might become a Broadway dandy.

After the wedding the couple went to Niagara Falls, already the mecca for American honeymooners. On their first morning together as husband and wife they found themselves eating breakfast in the hotel dining room with twenty-two other newlywed couples. They set up housekeeping at Mount Hope, and later in the year sailed for England and the Continent, setting the pattern they would follow regularly throughout their lives together.

In London they called upon the new American minister, James Buchanan, who was said to have taken an immediate liking to James. (Judge James Roosevelt, a distant cousin and prominent New York Democrat and a friend of Buchanan's, may have had something to do with the minister's hospitality toward the young visitor

6. The completeness of his initial break with the law seems open to question. As late as 1864 he was writing letters to his brother John on the stationery of the firm of [Albert] Mathews and [Otis] Swann, a Manhattan law firm with offices at 2 Hanover Street.

Source: Roosevelt Family Papers Donated by the Children, FDRL.

and his bride.) The embassy was temporarily shorthanded, and Buchanan asked James to serve as his secretary for a few weeks until a permanent replacement could arrive from America. James agreed.[7]

It was not an easy time for James Buchanan. A former Secretary of State and Democratic senator from Pennsylvania, he had hoped for a Cabinet post from President Franklin Pierce and had been bitterly disappointed at his posting to London. Only his sense of duty had made him take it. Ocean travel made him violently seasick. He detested everything about London; its weather, its high rents, its elaborate society. And his mood was not improved when even his clothes became an issue at court. Secretary of State William Marcy had ordered that American ambassadors were to wear nothing but "the simple costume of an American citizen" when calling upon foreign dignitaries. American ministers to the Court of St. James's had traditionally worn elaborate costumes, rich with braid and gold embroidery. Buchanan first thought he might solve the problem by dressing in the style of George Washington, but inspection of portraits of the first President made him abandon that idea. Appearing in a powdered wig and knee breeches would have made him a permanent laughingstock back home. Instead, he attended the queen's levee in early 1854 in a plain black suit, but wearing a dress sword at his side so as to avoid being confused with the palace servants. Queen Victoria was unruffled, but one London newspaper denounced Buchanan for his bold "puppyism."

What role the Roosevelts played in all this we do not know. Nor do we know how long they stayed abroad. But when they came home, Rebecca was pregnant, and on March 27, 1854, she gave birth to a son. By Roosevelt tradition, he should have been called Isaac, that name and James having been alternated for four generations. Instead, Mr. James named him after himself, and, not liking the diminutive "Junior" he had sometimes been forced to use to distinguish himself from his own grandfather, he added a redundant middle name, calling the infant

7. FDR told the story of his father's connection with James Buchanan in a letter to the historian Roy F. Nichols. In it, he seems to imply that his father served as Buchanan's London secretary while on his Grand Tour. But Buchanan was Secretary of State in Washington while young James was abroad for the first time; the historian George Bancroft was then minister to England, and both men's signatures appear on James Roosevelt's passport with their respective titles. Still, it is hard to see why Mr. James—or FDR—would have fabricated a link with so undistinguished a historical figure as Buchanan, and so I have assumed that the two men did at least meet in London, but in the 1850s. Buchanan served in London from 1853 to 1856.

Source: President's Personal File (hereafter PPF) 3012, FDRL.

James Roosevelt Roosevelt. Few who knew the boy ever bothered with his full name. He was just "Rosy."

He was a cheerful, open-faced child, the center of life at Mount Hope, precisely as his father had been at Rosedale a quarter of a century earlier. James Roosevelt—now known to nearly everyone outside the family as Mr. James—was at least as devoted a parent as Dr. Isaac had been. He spent whole days with his son, teaching him to shoot and fish, implanting in him his own love for horses that would become something of an obsession in the boy.

Rosy slept in his parents' bedroom every night until he was at least ten years old, and did not go to school at all. Mr. Abel, his tutor, came twice a week before breakfast to hear his lessons. His dancing master came regularly, too, and when a suitable partner could not be imported for him from a nearby estate, his nurse suggested that the scullery maid might stand in, a notion James and Rebecca found hilarious.

Rosy went everywhere with his parents, and in early 1861 they were in Paris, where he and his father posed together in a photographer's studio. Mr. James sits on a chair gripping a riding crop and the collar of a small terrier, standing on its hind legs for the camera; another bigger hunting dog sits at his feet. He wears boots, a hunter's coat, and a flat broad-brimmed hat. Beneath it, his gaze is direct, determined. Rosy, barely six, stands beside him wearing a cloak with a fur collar and trying very hard to match his father's expression.

Mr. James's determination did not extend to the battlefields of the Civil War. He was just thirty-two when the fighting began, but he made no effort to join the struggle, and the law then allowed wealthy men to hire substitutes to do their fighting for them.

Exactly what James Roosevelt did do during the war remains a mystery. Franklin Roosevelt alleged that his father had "rendered distinguished patriotic service" as a member of the Sanitary Commission, organized in 1861 to provide aid to sick and wounded soldiers and their families. He may well have done so—he was always conscious of his responsibilities as a wealthy citizen—but no one has ever found written evidence that he did. Nor did Mr. James himself mention such service in either of the two brief autobiographical sketches he wrote in his old age. Some have suggested that he might unofficially have brought his expert knowledge of railroad management to bear on the problems of Union transport and supply, and his postwar friendship with General Herman Haupt, the German-born engineer who served as chief of the U.S. military railroads, at least suggests that this may be the most likely story.[8]

In any case, when his younger brother threatened to enlist in 1864, James warned that if he did so it would break their mother's heart, but if John felt honor-bound to join up anyway, he should attach himself to the staff of General Marsena Patrick, the provost marshal of the Army of the Potomac, an old family friend. "The position would be a pleasant one," he promised, "and we would always have the consolation of knowing it would also be of comparative safety." (John Roosevelt evidently took his advice, for among his papers is a crumbling scrapbook in which there is a delicately colored map of Union supply lines, evidently drawn by him, on stationery headed "Headquarters, Army of the Potomac, Office of the Provost Marshal General.")

In 1915, Union College published a proud little volume summarizing the wartime service of all its alumni, north and south. Hundreds of Union men had served; sixty had given their lives, two of them from James Roosevelt's class. His name appears nowhere in its pages.[9]

Theodore Roosevelt, Sr., Mr. James's cousin, friend, and almost exact contemporary, also avoided the fighting. His reasons were perhaps more understandable. He had married a proud Georgian, Martha Bulloch, who could not bear to have him take up arms against her family's cause, and he had compensated for it by tireless labor on behalf of the Allotment Commission he had helped create to secure funds for the wives and children of the men at the front. Still, his decision not to enlist ate at his conscience all his life and embarrassment over the memory of it may have helped inspire his son's sometimes shrill bellicosity.

There is no evidence that Mr. James ever lost an hour's sleep over having stayed at home.

The death that Dr. Isaac had daily expected came for him in 1863

8. Mr. James became president of the Southern Railroads Security Company in 1872 and went south to survey his holdings early in the following year. General Haupt and his wife went along in the official party—Haupt was then general manager of the Richmond and Danville line, part of the S.R.S.C. network. He and Mr. James got along well; their wives did not, Rebecca finding Mrs. Haupt altogether too German for her tastes.

Source: Rebecca Roosevelt's journal, FDRL.

9. Certainly, Mr. James's loyalty to the Union was never seriously questioned; in fact it seems to have grown with the years. James Bulloch, the senior Theodore Roosevelt's brother-in-law, was a Confederate agent in England during the Civil War and was excluded from the amnesty that followed the fighting, continuing to live in Liverpool. Invited once to meet him by the family, Mr. James politely demurred; he did not dine with traitors.

at the age of seventy-three. James had already inherited Mount Hope from his grandfather, but he now received the lion's share of his father's fortune, enlarged over the years by the shrewd investment counsel of the Aspinwalls. A smaller legacy and Rosedale, where his mother still lived, went to John.

Two years later, James, Rebecca, and Rosy sailed for Europe, leaving Mount Hope in the hands of the William Griswolds of New York. With them went some twenty trunks and carpetbags; the false bottom of one trunk concealed $500 in gold as a hedge against emergency.

Some 30,000 Americans had traveled to Europe each year during the 1850s. The Civil War temporarily blocked the tourist stream, but its flow resumed almost the moment the fighting stopped. The morning the Roosevelts stepped onto the crowded deck of the *Scotia,* May 17, 1865, the trial of the conspirators in the assassination of Abraham Lincoln was just getting under way at Washington, and a ragged but defiant Confederate army was still at large in Louisiana.

Like most of their friends, the Roosevelts were at once cosmopolitan and provincial. They had lived abroad much of the time and knew Paris and London and the Alps as well as they knew the streets of lower Manhattan or their estates on the Hudson. They thought the English worth emulating. An unkind relative once said of Mr. James that with his side-whiskers and riding crop and Scottish tweeds, he sought to seem "like Lord Landsdowne [but] he succeeded only in mimicking Lord Landsdowne's coachman."

But the rest of the Old World was interesting to them only for its comforts and its culture. The ordinary people among whom they lived for months at a time—the French and Germans, Italians and Swiss and Spanish—were barely worthy of notice. Visitors like the Roosevelts learned European languages so that they might make sense of the opera and the theater—and give clear directions to the servants.

In fact, they had little need of European friends, for when they went abroad they took their own world with them. After the Civil War, a large segment of New York society simply reconstituted itself overseas each summer. There were always friends and acquaintances and sometimes kinsmen aboard the ships that took them across the Atlantic. And once ashore, the Roosevelts and their circle stayed at the same hotels (with reassuring names such as the Hotel du New York in Florence, and the Hotel de l'Oncle Tom at Paris). They dined at the same restaurants, wandered through the same palaces and picture galleries, attended one another's parties, worshipped together at the English or American chapels that offered Protestant services in nearly every city. On a single day at Geneva, Rebecca encountered—separately and entirely unexpectedly—four different close friends, two from New York and two from Poughkeepsie. "I wonder when we shall cease meeting people," she wrote that night. The next morning she met two more.

The *Scotia* was the finest and fastest ship in Cunard's fleet of sidewheel steamers, and she offered only first-class accommodations. Her passenger list was routinely published in the *New York Times*. Accompanying "James Roosevelt, Lady, and son" on this voyage was at least one couple who were close friends, Mr. and Mrs. William T. Blodgett of New York. He had made a fortune in the varnish business, collected art, and had paid $20,000 for Frederick Church's busy masterpiece, "Heart of the Andes." Seventeen years later, the Blodgetts' daughter, Nelly, would serve as Franklin Roosevelt's godmother.

The most celebrated of their fellow passengers were Mr. and Mrs. August Belmont, on their way to Europe for a brief vacation (accompanied by two servants). Belmont was an Austrian Jew, a banker who had come to America as the representative of the House of Rothschild and then struck out spectacularly on his own. His wealth, ambition, and ability had made him a power in the Democratic Party and bought him the American ministership to The Hague in 1853. He was also a well-known sportsman, president of the Jockey Club, and co-founder (with his friend Leonard Jerome) of the Jerome Park Racetrack, where he would often encounter Mr. James.

But the Belmonts were best known as leaders of New York society. Mrs. Belmont was Caroline Slidell Perry, the lovely if somewhat vague daughter of Commodore Matthew Perry, and they had been married by an Episcopal minister. With the awkward question of religion successfully muted, Belmont had set out to make his wife the city's leading hostess. The dining room in their mansion on lower Fifth Avenue seated 200 for dinner, served on gold plates by 200 servants wearing the full Belmont livery—maroon jackets with silver buttons and scarlet piping, black knee breeches, and a family coat of arms personally designed by the master of the house. There was also a cavernous ballroom in which precisely one party was given annually. The other 364 days of the year, noted Edith Wharton, it was kept in "shuttered darkness, with its gilt chairs stacked in a corner and its chandelier in a bag."

Belmont could be a charming companion when he wanted to be, and he tried at least to keep his wealth and power in perspective. "I prefer," he once wrote, "to leave my children instead of the gilded prospects of a New York merchant prince, the more enviable title of American citizen." The prospects of his children were not irreparably tarnished, however, and when Rebecca Roosevelt's younger brother, Samuel Howland III, married Frederika Belmont in 1876, she brought with her an enormous dowry; her wedding dress alone cost $30,000.

Captain Charles Marshall, seventy-three and white-bearded, was a familiar figure on the transatlantic run. He was an immensely wealthy shipping magnate, a friendly rival of the Howlands and Aspinwalls, and he had personally commanded ninety-nine crossings before settling permanently into office life. It was well that the Roosevelts had been acquainted with him before the *Scotia* left the dock, for he was not easy to get to know. When he died later that same year, even an admiring obituary writer admitted that the captain had "possessed an air of sternness about him that was somewhat repulsive to strangers."

Another bearded passenger was better company. He was thirty years old and, like Belmont, he had been an immigrant; unlike him, he had arrived in America dirt-poor and was happy at twelve to work as a bobbin boy in a cotton mill for $1.20 a week. The *Times* listed him as "A. Carnagie, Pittsburgh," and he was sailing to England on business. A cousin claimed to have perfected a process by which a steel coating could be permanently fused to iron rails. If it worked, and Carnegie could obtain the American patent on it, he would dominate the construction of railroads, bridges, and office buildings for decades to come. (It didn't work, in fact. Tested the next winter, the steel peeled away from the iron as soon as it got cold; Carnegie was only momentarily discouraged.) For all his canniness and drive, he did not like to talk business, much preferring to offer his voluble, good-humored opinions on everything from public education to the poetry of Robert Burns, which he loved to recite with special emphasis on the rolling Scottish "R's."

With these shipboard companions and others, the Roosevelts looked forward to a pleasant voyage. The only potentially discordant note, Rebecca wrote in the journal she began the evening the *Scotia* steamed out of New York harbor, was the presence of "the greatest number of Jews."

The passage began placidly enough. Two days out, thick fog surrounded the ship but she continued to make steady progress until noon, when her whistle shrieked just as the passengers sat down to luncheon. The *Scotia*'s wheels stopped churning. James rushed on deck, followed by Rebecca and Rosy. There was an eerie silence. Then, through the swirling fog off the port bow, James remembered, "not five feet from us, an iceberg was slowly drifting past, so near you could have easily jumped on it and so hard that there would have been instant destruction if we had struck it." Under way again that afternoon, the Roosevelts spotted a second cliff of floating ice less than a mile away. Rebecca slept in her clothes that night, terrified.

The rest of the trip was uneventful, however, and at Liverpool the Roosevelts were ferried directly to the steamer *Niagara* for the choppy trip across the English Channel to Le Havre. James was a veteran sailor and relentlessly cheerful. But this time even he took to his bed, and Rebecca wrote that she and Rosy were "much comforted" by having James continually moan, " 'Why did we come this way?' "

They stayed at Le Havre for nearly two months. Tutors in French and music came daily to Rosy's room, where a piano had been installed so that he and James might play duets in the evenings, just before the elder Roosevelts settled into their nightly game of bezique.

The little family spent hours on the stony beach, chasing the gray crabs that scuttled in and out of the waves, and whenever the timid North Atlantic sun permitted, they went into the water themselves. Rosy was frightened of the ocean at first, and his father made him pay for his own swimming lessons out of his allowance. The boy stuck with it to please Mr. James, and was rewarded with a handsome toy: "a beautiful screw boat," his father said, "a full-rigged steamer that winds up and goes ten minutes in the waves." Rebecca ventured out from a separate beach, holding on to ropes strung out through the surf for the safety of the ladies.

There were long strolls along the waterfront, interrupted often while James stopped to smoke his pipe and "talk horse" with idle coachmen. The Roosevelts' affection for animals of every kind seems to have been boundless. Rosy went to a pet shop every afternoon to feed apricots to an appreciative monkey. Rebecca had a pet snail which one day got loose and accompanied Mr. James on a promenade, clinging to his hat.

James himself longed "every day to have some kind of beast to handle. I always pat the horses in the street and speak to the dogs, sometimes to the disgust of their owners." Framed photographs of two dogs they had left behind at Mount Hope hung on the wall of their hotel room, and they finally broke down and bought a puppy that reminded them of their yellow terrier, "Jeff Davis." It proved troublesome at first, Rebecca noted, "pulling at one end of the string and James at the other, or else insisting upon walking with his head just under my petticoat." And it howled all night until James intimidated it into silence by "barking like a big dog."

Rosy made friends with three French children who were staying at the hotel with their parents, the Count and Countess Alexandre Walewski. The count was the president of the French Legislative Assembly and the natural child of Napoleon I and Marie Walewska of Poland. His resemblance to his father was so great that an old soldier, hearing him speak at a funeral, covered his face with his hands and wept. "I know this voice," he said. "I have loved it, and I never thought I would hear it again." One morning the Roosevelts and Walewskis rode out into the countryside to a wooded park where the children played beneath the great trees while their parents sat on blankets and ate their lunch of cherries and milk. They returned to the hotel just in time for dinner, Rebecca remembered, "loaded with wildflowers and roses, the children in a gale."

French nobles were worth cultivating. Commoners were not. James hiked to a likely-looking trout stream and was advised to ask the local miller for permission to fish. The miller turned out also to be the village mayor—"a consequential little Frenchman," James wrote—who declared the waters off limits: "*Défendu.*" James hired a small boy to point out the best holes and began casting anyway. He was arrested, taken before the mayor again, and released with a lecture. Unrepentant, he walked downstream two miles and "poached all day. I did not have much luck," he told John, "but enjoyed the forbidden fruit more than good sport easily obtained."

In early August, the Roosevelts started for Switzerland. They visited Rouen on the way, and showed Rosy the exact spot where Joan of Arc was burned. And they dined at an inn where "the Maitre D'Hôtel . . . portioned out food in such small quantities that it only made us wish for more. . . . Imagine the skill of a man who can so divide a small pair of boiled chickens among 35 people (counted) as to have half a chicken left."

At Geneva, they went to church one evening to hear the organ played. It was dark inside. A few dull lanterns dimly outlined the altar. Before it stood a coffin, covered by a black pall embroidered with skulls. "It certainly was spooky," Rebecca recalled, "and quite enough to unsettle Rosy, who commenced to tremble and cry, half with fear and half because he did not like to hear gay music when a dead man was in the church. We could not pacify him." Later, their hotelkeeper told James the coffin was a permanent fixture, carved from stone.

Rosy woke up shrieking a few nights later at Interlaken, and begged to sleep in his parents' bed. The first few days of their stay there, in lovely rooms overlooking the blinding wall of the Jungfrau, were otherwise marred only by the nationality of their fellow guests. "Oh, drat," Rebecca wrote. "Can we stand the clang of German women all winter? There are several in the house and besides eating with their knives, they are so noisy and greasy!"

Walking without James one afternoon, Rebecca and Rosy passed near an asylum on the slope. "Several awful-looking creatures came howling down the path," and again that night Rosy was too frightened to sleep alone. He was ill the next day, and the doctor came to dose him with castor oil.

That afternoon, September 17, the waiter brought their tea on a tray, and with it a letter from John Roosevelt. It told of the Mount Hope fire. "No word can express the shock of it," Rebecca said. James especially mourned the loss of 400 fine cigars, and urged his brother to search the ruins for a tin box that had held four gold watches, including "dear father's, with his chain and seal." (The box was evidently never found.) The fire's origins were mysterious. The Griswolds insisted it had been an accident, caused by a faulty flue in the library chimney. James was sure it had been deliberately set, and came to believe that the tenants' butler was the culprit, intending either to cover up his own looting of the place or simply because he had grown bored in the country and wanted to force his employer to move back to the city, where life was more exciting.

Rosy was not told of the disaster until he felt better the next morning. James and Rebecca agonized for several days, deciding whether or not to sail right home. They resolved finally to stay in Europe and to go on to Dresden for the winter, as planned.

There they rented a house at 4 Mosciasky Strasse and put an Irish servant, Marie Cork, in charge of the staff of three German women. Rosy was enrolled in a German school, the first school of any kind he had ever attended. It terrified him. He came home weeping the first day because the other boys had jeered when he had not known the songs they were singing, and he trembled going back the next morning because the master had announced to the class that he was about to buy a new cane. He had split his old one flogging last year's pupils. A few days later, Rosy came home with a bloody nose, James told John. "Of course, my first question was if he whipped his antagonist and felt quite satisfied with being informed that his foe retired with a loosened tooth."

Rosy's sleep continued to be troubled. When he was awakened suddenly one night, James noted, "he first talked German, then French, and wound up with English. Poor baby, how dreadful it must be to dream in three languages!"

It grew worse as tension at home was added to tension at school. The servant Marie proved difficult. Rebecca had to scold her for "having more clothes in the wash than I had. She has been sulking all day. We don't care." The German maids quit. Marie did, too, then promised to do better, continued to sulk. It got so bad, Rebecca wrote, that James was afraid to go downstairs, "as he is constantly seized and attacked." Finally they fired her, and James himself drove her to the railroad station. For the following twenty-four hours the Roosevelts survived a crisis whose seriousness perhaps only a couple of their time and class could fully appreciate: life without servants. James bought a German phrase book, conducting "experiments" in case conversation with tradesmen could not be avoided. Rebecca herself answered the doorbell. Actual cooking and washing were out of the question, of course; a hot supper was brought in from a nearby hotel, and a German girl came in afterwards to tidy up. Still, Rebecca wrote, since Marie left it had been "a most exciting day . . . and we marvel that we have no servant and everything more comfortable than if Marie was here. . . . If the house had been full of footmen in livery we could not have been more at our ease."

The next day they hired two new German women: "About Two our *'stube Mädchen'* came, a nice looking little thing. She . . . says *'Schön'* whenever we look at her. At five, the cook arrived with low curtseys and two yards of ear trumpet, a canary . . . and a dog."

The test of the new servants' skills came a few evenings later, when General and Mrs. George Brinton McClellan came to dinner. Everything went perfectly. The food was hot and good, and "our little frau" served it beautifully.

The McClellans were new and glamorous friends. Shortly after the Roosevelts settled in, they found that the general and his wife, Mary, were staying in a small house just around the corner at 2 Wiener Strasse. They had been in Europe for several months, having left America to ease the pain of the general's two great defeats: his removal as commander of the Army of the Potomac by the Illinois politician whom he had routinely dismissed as "Uncle Abraham," and the still greater humiliation of having been defeated for the presidency by the same tormentor.

The general liked Europe. Everywhere he went he was received as an important man. "I hear no slanders," he wrote home to his father-in-law, "all treat me as a gentleman. . . . If I were at home now there would probably be nothing for me to do but go into exile in Nevada or Utah . . . This side of the water is more pleasant, I assure you." He would stay in Europe for three years. Mary McClellan was pregnant with her first child. The baby was due momentarily, and the general had gone into what he called "winter quarters" at Dresden and sent for his mother to help with the delivery.

Mr. James called on him one morning, and the two men took an instant liking to one another. For the next eight months they managed to get away from the ladies long enough to take a stroll or have a smoke together nearly every day. In many ways they were natural companions. At thirty-nine, the general was just two years older than Mr. James, and like him was a member of two old and prosperous families, from Philadelphia rather than New York or New England, but at least as distinguished as the Roosevelts and Aspinwalls.

And they were both Democrats. James Roosevelt had stayed a Whig as long as he could. As the natural heirs of the Federalists, the Whigs had been the party of his father and grandfather, and James had been steeped in Whig traditions. He shared fully their belief in the Union and a genuinely national government, in the rights of property and the virtues of government by gentlemen—above all, in their abhorrence of the sort of executive power that had been so lustily enjoyed by the Whigs' Democratic nemesis, Andrew Jackson.

As late as 1848, Mr. James had been a loyal admirer of the perennial Whig presidential candidate, Henry Clay. No one knows precisely when he moved to the Democrats, but perhaps it was in 1856, the presidential year that forced most Whigs to find a new home. Their old party's inability to hammer out a coherent position on the great issue of slavery had rendered them largely impotent by then. The best candidate they could come up with was the colorless ex-President Millard Fillmore. Some Whigs, whose fear of immigrants neared paranoia, rallied to the short-lived American, or Know-Nothing, Party, which had also nominated Fillmore. Samuel F. B. Morse, the inventor and Poughkeepsie friend of the elder Roosevelts, had been a frenzied

Know-Nothing pamphleteer. Party members most strongly opposed to slavery enlisted in the bold new Republican Party, behind its dashing nominee, John Charles Fremont.

By contrast, the Democrats had managed to nominate a man who promised calm and moderation, a compromise candidate who belonged to neither the northern or southern factions of his party. He was James Buchanan of Pennsylvania, Mr. James's old friend from London.[10]

Many of James Roosevelt's friends and other members of the family made a different choice. Theodore Roosevelt, Sr., became a Republican during the Civil War, for example. So did Mr. James's former employer Benjamin Silliman and his uncle William Henry Aspinwall, who would serve as Lincoln's confidential agent in London.

Mr. James had joined the Democrats, and he now found special pleasure in discussing politics with his party's most recent presidential nominee. Despite the general's frequent boast that he was "utterly indifferent to contemporaneous praise or censure," he never forgot a slight. And as he and Mr. James took their evening walks, he railed against his enemies. He professed to have been appalled by Lincoln's murder: "All who know me must know that I regard it with unmingled horror and regret." But he was furious that the Secretary of War, Edwin M. Stanton—"that rascal," who he believed had poisoned Lincoln's mind against him—continued in office under the new President,

10. FDR seems to have believed that his father and grandfather were always Democrats, and most of his biographers have agreed. Many of the members of his Cousin Theodore's family were indeed members of that party long before the Civil War, and one of them, Judge James J. Roosevelt, was a Tammany sachem and member of Congress.

But the descendants of Jacobus Roosevelt were different. Franklin Roosevelt's grandfather was first a Federalist and then a Whig, and Mr. James remained a Whig about as long as there was any life left in the party of his fathers. A letter to James from Dr. Isaac, written on February 25, 1848, while his son was still touring Europe, makes this clear: "Uncle William [Henry Aspinwall] and John [Aspinwall] have become Taylorites [supporters of General Zachary Taylor for the upcoming Whig presidential nomination] & Zack I think will be our next President. We [the Whigs] had a large meeting in New York, William Vice President and John Sec'y. As soon as you get through your studies I suppose Zack, if you desert your old friend [Henry] Clay, will give you an office. I have not yet turned."

There is additional evidence that at least suggests James's Whiggery. The law itself was predominantly a Whig profession in the 1840s; most American lawyers were Whigs, Benjamin D. Silliman prominent among them. There must have been considerable clamor for jobs in Silliman's office among young lawyers with the proper Whig credentials, and it seems unlikely that he would have disappointed deserving members of his own party in favor of a Democrat, no matter how pleasant and well connected. The precise date of James Roosevelt's conversion to the Democrats is unknown; my account seems the most plausible to me, but further firsthand evidence may someday alter it.

Source: Isaac Roosevelt's letter to Mr. James, Roosevelt Family Papers (hereafter RFP), FDRL.

Andrew Johnson. And he took a dim view of the black troops who had helped win the war after he had left it: "I confess to a prejudice in favor of my own race, and I can't learn to like the odor of either Billy Goats or Niggers."

"I see a good deal of General McClellan," James told John, "and like him so much." The McClellans were again the Roosevelts' dinner guests on the evening of November 22, and a servant arrived the next morning with a note from the general. His wife, Mary, had given birth to a fine baby boy, and both the infant and his mother were doing well. "A few hours earlier," Rebecca wrote, "and it might have happened here."[11]

The months passed pleasantly at Dresden. It was a lovely place to spend the winter, a medieval city whose towers, bridges, artworks, and opera houses had earned it the title "Florence on the Elbe." Rosy did well in school despite his fears, winning one of five top prizes out of 240 boys. His father thought this a fine performance "for a Yankee boy. I only wish we could keep him for two or three years at the same school. He learns more in a month here than he would in a year at home. There is no shirking."

Still, Rosy was isolated at Dresden, not encouraged to bring German boys home after school, and lonely. The Roosevelts decided finally to have Rebecca's younger brother, Samuel Howland III, brought over to provide some company. In mid-April, James set out for England to pick up the boy. He was delayed by a storm while crossing the Channel—"I was turned nearly inside out," James wrote to John—and when he and Sam did not turn up in Dresden on the twenty-fifth as he had promised, Rebecca was inconsolable. She took to her bed, and even a visit from General McClellan did not help. She wept with fear the whole night. James and Sam arrived, tired but safe, on the twenty-sixth.

The next day was the thirteenth anniversary of their marriage, and James presented Rebecca with a piece of fine Dresden china. The Roosevelts were devoted to one another. She called him "my darling," or by a pet name, "Beamer," and worried extravagantly when he was ill, always crying when he was away too long. Once, in New York, she went to Grand Central to welcome him home from a business trip, and when he did not get off the train—he had missed his connection —was so distraught that she had to ask a policeman to take her home;

11. The baby boy was inevitably christened George Brinton McClellan, Jr.; he grew up to become twice the Democratic mayor of New York (1903–1910).

she repaid the young officer with a basket of grapes two days later. Her spontaneity and open affection pierced Mr. James's public reserve. "I walked up 6th Avenue with him . . . as far as 16th Street," she once confided to her journal, "and as he forgot to kiss me before he left home, I made him give me a kiss in the fish market, to the surprise of all the butchers."

James in turn called her "dear Becky." He rarely traveled far without her, showered her with presents, and made sure she was always surrounded by the flowers she loved. On her fortieth birthday in Naples in 1870, he and Rosy would get up before breakfast and arrange to have bouquets delivered to her all day long, "huge, thousands of roses and camelias," she marveled, "they measured together thirty-six feet in circumference."

But there was always another side to Mr. James, a free-wheeling, gusty side which he seems to have kept from Rebecca and reserved mostly for his brother, John. With him he joked freely about things that would have been thought unseemly by anyone else—the pretty girls in short skirts who skated at Dresden and whose "display of limbs is not modest," the dire effects of too much castor oil, the daring bathing costumes worn by Frenchmen: "Not much more than a figleaf . . . only a pair of worsted drawers with leg ends cut off near the thigh and does not even cover the 'ar.' " Their mother wrote that John was planning a trip to the south. "Why don't you bring back half a dozen buck niggers?" James asked his brother. "We would have such a shindy with the Paddys."

John got married while the Roosevelts were abroad, to Ellen Crosby, the daughter of a Poughkeepsie physician. "Well, my dear brother," James wrote, "you are in for it. There is no escape now except a divorce. How I pity you. No more nice jolly times. You are in the traces and if you attempt to kick over you will catch it. There is no use in trying to rebel—after an experience of thirteen years I find the best way is to submit and go along steady." He also offered a bit of advice: "Do not be nagged at any time, but especially in the early morning. It destroys the peace of the day and [is] trying to the nerves and constitution."

James shared the ups and downs of his business with his brother, too, and whenever he went abroad, John handled his investments, saw that his taxes were paid and watched over his estate. James had the *Times* mailed to him everywhere he traveled so that he could keep track of his stocks, and he worried constantly over the smallest details of life on his farm. Was the garden gate locked to keep out the pigs? Had the ice house been filled? Had the stables been properly cleaned, and had "Bessie" dropped a colt "all safe and sound?" If so, a check for $50 should go to the owner of its sire. An old express bill for the delivery of venison and game birds that had arrived at Hyde Park "rot-eaten" should not be paid without a fight.

Sam Howland was just a year older than Rosy, and the two boys became close if sometimes quarrelsome companions. "Here come the boys," James wrote one afternoon. "They make an awful racket and fight like cats. I have serious thoughts of having a pugilistic set-to with coats off and a fair stand-up fight which I think would end their everlasting skirmishings."

The Roosevelts left Dresden and began to make their meandering way home on May 17, 1866, a year to the day after they had departed from New York. They were now a party of five: Sam was still with them, and so was a governess, remembered now only as "Marie," of whom Rosy was very fond. Stopping for lunch on the road to Carlsbad, they were encircled by a crowd of ragged, jostling beggars clamoring for alms. It was frightening. "We had no money," Rebecca wrote, "and so gave them scraps of cold meat, which they took greedily and ate like dogs."

The Roosevelts hurried on to the Hotel King George, where they spent a placid month. The boys fetched fresh milk from a village cow every morning and sometimes walked out into the countryside to buy honey from the hive. James and Rebecca took the waters religiously, then they all lunched at a lake pavilion, where Rosy and Sam once each gave a large coin to "the little boy who opens the door, after which he made us the most profound bows." One afternoon, Rebecca and James came upon a merry-go-round set up in the square of the nearby town of Hammes. A crowd of village children looked on without the money for tickets. Mr. James offered the man in charge enough coins to keep the carousel spinning for half an hour. Some fifty shouting children clambered aboard "thick as berries in the boats," Rebecca wrote, "and two or three on each horse. The sound of the hand organ brought all the mothers to the doors with their knitting and . . . James was greeted with smiles all through the village."

In June, the Roosevelt party moved on to St. Moritz, where they went for donkey rides in the mountains. When Rosy's mount balked, Mr. James hired a small boy to run backwards ahead of him up the slope, holding out a fistful of thistles. They were driven up a glacier and got down from the carriage to scrape the snow away and peer into the clear green heart of the ice, and they climbed on foot up a mountainside to visit a frozen cave. It was a steep ascent. James had to pull Rebecca behind him, their guide pushing from below: "I could actually hear my heart beating," she remembered. On the way down, Rosy and Sam "snowballed" Mr. James. In the evenings, James and Rebecca enjoyed talking with an English guest, a Mr. Bullock, who had done what the young Mr. James had only dreamed of doing—he had fought alongside Garibaldi. He was very quiet, Mr. James wrote, "and rather Lord Dundrearish in his style, hair parted in the middle," but he had "led the assault [on Naples] and brought off under a heavy fire many wounded men. And all this for the mere *sport* of fighting."

In August they journeyed to Paris (after what Rosy described as a "sad parting" with Mademoiselle Marie), in time for a great city-wide fair. The fountains in the Place de la Concorde were "lighted with the electric light," Rosy wrote, "and the Obelisque was beautifully lighted by gas." The sky above the Tuileries exploded with fireworks; "the rockets were superb and burned in the air, letting fall thousands of little stars."

Then back to Le Havre—where, Rosy noted, "we had quite a pretty dish for dinner . . . eggshells blown out and filled with blancmange"—and on to London, Liverpool, and home.

On October 12, just four days from New York and shrouded again in fog, the *Scotia* churned past an immigrant ship, "so near," Rebecca wrote, "that we could see and hear the people on board distinctly."

The gulf between the America for which those immigrants were heading and that to which the Roosevelts now returned was nearly as broad as the Atlantic. The city had always been a necessary evil for Mr. James and Rebecca. He had to go there from time to time to tend to business; she went with him for the social season, to visit relatives, to attend the theater. A richly furnished brownstone at 15 Washington Square made all this possible; membership in the finest clubs—the Union, Metropolitan, Century, University—made it congenial. But the reeking, airless world of the tenement slum was as remote and mysterious to the Roosevelts as had been the world of the hungry beggars who had so alarmed them near Carlsbad.

Home was among the shady lawns and river breezes of Hyde Park.

"The Hudson at Hyde Park is a broad, tranquil and noble river," the editor and essayist Nathaniel Parker Willis had written in 1853, "of about the same character as the Bosphorus above Roumeli-bissar, or the Dardanelles at Abydos. The shores are cultivated by the water's edge, and lean up in graceful, rather than bold elevations; the eminences around are crested with the villas of the wealthy inhabitants of the metropolis at the river's mouth; summer-houses, belvideres and water-steps, give an air of refreshment to the banks."

Mr. James shared Willis' enthusiasm for his neighborhood, but he would not have been pleased with the writer's exotic analogy. It was England, not Turkey, that Hyde Park was meant to resemble; the life of the English country gentleman he and his neighbors labored to recreate. Their stationery was headed "Hyde Park on the Hudson." They gave their estates names that sounded as much as possible like those of country houses in England. Josiah Wheeler had called the Roosevelts' new home "Brierstone" when he had owned it. Mr. James renamed it "Springwood" soon after he and his family moved in. Neither name reflected anything about the land itself, but each had a nice English resonance.

The nineteenth-century American historian William Hickling Prescott visited England as a young man. He was not much impressed by London society; it seemed simply more opulent than that of his native Boston. But English country life was "quite another matter—altogether unique." The health and stability of English institutions, Prescott believed, rested on the "predominance of the country and the country interests" over those of the overcrowded turbulent city. In the American context, Thomas Jefferson would have agreed. So would Mr. James, and the habits and attitudes and hobbies of the English country gentleman as set forth by Prescott were precisely those he avidly adopted for himself.

The historian was not blind to the faults of the English aristocrat. The Englishman had an air of insufferable arrogance about him, Prescott admitted, especially when abroad. He was intolerant, "his bigotry surpassing everything in a quiet passive form that has been witnessed since the more active bigotry of the times of the Spanish Philips." And he was almost proud of the "exclusive, limited range of his knowledge." The Englishman traveled widely, Prescott said, but "the scope of his ideas" was not enlarged by it: "the body travels, not the mind."

But at home, in the country, he was different. "The Englishman is seen to most advantage in his country-house," he noted, "for he is constitutionally both domestic and rural in his habits. His fireside and his farm—these are the places in which one sees his simple and warm-hearted nature most freely unfolded. There is a shyness in an Englishman, a natural reserve which makes him cold to strangers, and difficult of approach. But corner him in his old house, a frank and full expression will be given to his feelings . . ."

Certainly that was true of Mr. James. He was fully himself only at Springwood, never happier than when involved in its everyday chores. "This afternoon we walked over the farm," Rebecca wrote one day in 1870, "saw the pigs which are to be killed on Tuesday, then went to the stable and fed Bill with carrots, then to the greenhouse with milk for Pussy and over to Sebastian's with corn for the white turkeys." Mr. James was proud that unlike the country seats of some of his neighbors, his place turned a profit; he liked to think of it as a working farm and objected when others called it an estate.

"I doubt," Prescott wrote of the English country gentleman, "if ever there was so high a standard of morality which has such means of self-indulgence at its command . . . and which occupies a position that secures so much deference. Their respect for religion, at least for the forms of it, is universal."

Mr. James inherited little of his father's pious desperation, but he was always a dedicated churchman. Shortly after his marriage he had left the Dutch Reform Church of his ancestors and joined the Episcopal Church in which Rebecca had been raised.

St. James Church at Hyde Park was a small but handsome pseudo-Gothic chapel, modeled after the country churches of England and built of red brick, blanketed with ivy and surrounded by evergreens. Mr. James served it all his life as a vestryman and sometimes as senior warden. The wealthiest parishioners sat nearest the altar; his pew, with its red silk cushions, was the third from the front on the left side of the aisle, its door marked with his brass nameplate: "J. Roosevelt."

Prescott was especially impressed by the English gentleman's commitment to his community. "There are few of the great proprietors . . ." he wrote, "who are not more or less occupied with improving their estates and providing for the comforts of their tenantry."

The village of Hyde Park was tiny—as late as 1925, fewer than 900 persons lived there—and almost all its residents depended for their livelihood on one or more of the great estates. Mr. James had a sober proprietary concern for their welfare. He took an interest in the public school and in conditions at the county jail, and served for many years as manager of the asylum that stood on the site of Mount Hope. And when news came of the great Chicago fire in 1870, he organized a subscription drive to help the city rebuild, canvassing his neighbors by carriage and raising $1,000 in a single day.

In 1871 he was elected to a two-year term as town supervisor on the Democratic ticket. In that post he may not have won friends among his less well-to-do colleagues on the board when he urged that no board member receive his three-dollar per diem allowance unless a meeting were actually held.

Three years later, local party officials tried to talk him into running for the State Senate. His attractions for them were obvious enough: He was by now a loyal Democrat, widely respected and admired, even by his predominantly Republican neighbors and, most important, he was wealthy enough to finance his own campaign. Politics clearly fascinated Mr. James, and Rebecca knew it. "James went to a political meeting," she wrote on October 18, 1874. "I was dreadfully afraid he would be nominated . . . but he got home safely." In an autobiographical fragment hastily written in his old age, Mr. James said, "[I] have always refused to accept any nomination for Public Office, repeatedly refused nomination for Congress, State Senate and Assembly." He was proud to have resisted temptation, as his father would have wanted him to do. But he was even prouder of having been asked.

The final near-universal characteristic among English country gentlemen noted by Prescott, was their love of the outdoors. "Every man hunts or shoots. No man is too old to be in the saddle some part of the day, and men of seventy years and more follow the hounds and take a five-barred gate at a leap." Mr. James hunted, fished, skated, and had his old boathouse poled downstream by canal boat from the riverfront at Rosedale and set up below Springwood so that he and Rosy could row in the evenings in their double wherry. He was a commodore in the local yacht club, and in the ice-boating club whose bladed vessels flashed across the river's frozen surface in winter.

But horses were his passion. He loved to ride and drive them. His barn held a bewildering assortment of vehicles—three sleighs, a high phaeton, a skeleton wagon, a rockaway, a landau, a spark, a station wagon (for carrying heavy trunks to and from the depot), and smaller versions of several of these, meant to be pulled by Rosy's ponies. There was also a fine carriage with brass fittings, made especially for Mr. James in London and so big that when it arrived in its crate at the Poughkeepsie landing, he had it unpacked at the riverside and proudly drove it home himself.

He was best known in sporting circles as a breeder of superb trotters. His prize was "Gloster," born at Springwood in 1870. A sleek brown gelding with a phenomenally long stride, it covered a mile in 2:17 ¼ seconds in October of 1873, setting a mark that stood for years.

Later that autumn, Franklin Roosevelt would write, "a gentleman who had driven up from the station in a frock coat and silk hat and introduced himself as Leland Stanford of California" offered Mr. James $15,000 for his champion. Stanford, who had built the Central Pacific Railroad and served as Republican governor of California, was a well-known sportsman, interested in the scientific breeding of horses. Mr. James accepted his offer. The horse was shipped west, but before it could race again it was killed in a train wreck.[12]

Shortly thereafter, perhaps guilty at having indirectly caused the death of his handsome horse, Mr. James withdrew entirely from the trotting world, saying that it was no longer a sport for gentlemen. He continued to keep horses, though, and like William Prescott's prototypical country gentleman, he managed a daily ride until just a few weeks before his death.

Despite the loss of Gloster, life at Springwood was almost uniformly tranquil. "A beautiful morning," Rebecca wrote. "Drove James to the station in the pony carriage and went for him in the evening. The day was a blank."

James got home from the city at three-thirty one morning. "One of my under-farmers met me at the station," he remembered, "and when I apologized for keeping him up so late, he said 'Oh! Mr. Roosevelt. I enjoyed it. I have never been up so late before in my life.' " The household staff was smoothly supervised by Elspeth McEachern, a brisk and cheerful Scotswoman, whom the Roosevelts called "Elespie."

Friends sometimes came out to play croquet on the sloping lawn or to ride or just to sit on the piazza and watch the steamboats glide by on the wide river below. One day a drunken coachman had to be dismissed; on another, there were "great scenes with Polly [the family parrot] who would not go back into her cage. Rosy finally got her in by fright and won five dollars from his Pops."

The outside world rarely intruded without invitation, though once all three Roosevelts hurried down to the front gate to watch the

12. The local stable boy who had gone west with Gloster managed to salvage the horse's flowing four-foot tail, and when FDR became governor of New York, he had it mounted on a wooden plaque for him as a gift. Roosevelt hung it in his bedroom, first in the governor's mansion at Albany, then in the White House. It is now displayed in a glass case in Mr. James's old stable at Hyde Park.

animals from Barnum's circus plod by, African lions roaring in painted cages and a herd of Indian elephants raising clouds of dust on the road to Poughkeepsie.

Mr. James did not discuss business at home. Rebecca kept a daily journal for nine years. There are in it only a handful of references to what her husband did on his trips to town, nearly all of them clustered in two years, 1873 and 1875. These years saw him disappointed—but not embittered—by the sudden and unexpected disintegration of two schemes through which he had hoped to become a man of great wealth and power.

Consolidated Coal was the first of these. It seemed a spectacular success, controlling five out of every six tons of bituminous coal shipped from the Cumberlands.

And so did the second scheme. In 1871, Thomas A. Scott, the able and aggressive senior vice president of the mighty Pennsylvania Railroad, sought to win control of all the railroad lines south of the Potomac—and to beat out the rival Baltimore & Ohio into the bargain. The instrument he chose was a holding company, the Southern Railway Security Company, which in conjunction with a number of prominent New York investors, flooded millions of dollars into southern rail stocks to build its network. James Roosevelt was a heavy investor, and in 1872 Scott made him its president. Under his leadership, Mr. James wrote, the S.R.S.C. came to control "all the southern lines . . . from Richmond to New Orleans and southwest to Memphis."

When Mr. James went south in early 1873 to inspect his railroads, Rebecca went with him. She found it a foreign country, far cruder than any of the European regions in which the Roosevelts had lived. At church in Richmond a "Vile little boy in the pew spitted a spittoon full." At Charlotte, the hotel was cold and filthy, and when Rebecca tried "to sit in the parlor while my room was cleaned . . . I found a lady? sitting there smoking a pipe over the fire." At Columbia, they were taken to see the state legislature in session: "What a sight! I hope I may never see it again. More than 2/3 members were negroes and some of them not a bit better than apes—writing or making believe to write. The senate was going through a fight. Two darkies calling each other awful names."

Their car was derailed in the middle of the night on the way to Atlanta. The Roosevelts crawled out a window and continued their journey in the mail car, Rebecca sitting on the sacks. And once they got to the Georgia capital, she wrote, "there was nothing to see except bad roads and jews shops, the Hotel and RR depot being the only two good buildings."

The Roosevelt train was held up again in Alabama so that the party could spend an hour or two "lingering over some very fine bridges which James walked over in his slippers." There were fleas on the train to Vicksburg, and heavy rains at Chattanooga, where "one evening we had a little supper of quail with toast, shivered in our damp bedroom, where the tides had been rising all day in one corner [and] could not sleep for ever so long, owing to the pigs and dogs outside the window and the rats in the walls."

They were glad to get back to Springwood for the summer. There, on September 19, Rebecca noted in her diary, "Terrible time in town. So many failures. James very much excited." Well he might have been. The great Philadelphia banking house of Jay Cooke & Company had collapsed without warning the day before, and the shock waves were spreading into every corner of the economy. They would continue to be felt for a decade and a half. Factories closed down, the laying of new railroad track halted, the demand for coal dwindled.

Just five days later, Mr. James was called to Philadelphia to confer with Scott and other officials of the Pennsylvania line. He returned the evening of the twenty-fourth, Rebecca noted, "and was *a little cross.*" On October 3, he was allowed to resign the presidency of the Southern Railway Security Company.

The stockholders of Consolidated Coal were more patient, but they too were dissatisfied by the plummeting value of their stock, and in the spring of 1875, Mr. James and his closest allies—including Uncle William Henry Aspinwall and his friend Warren Delano II of Newburgh—were swept from the board of directors.

Mr. James was momentarily depressed by these defeats. For several days after the Consolidated Coal vote Rebecca noted that he was "anxious" and "miserable." But he bounced back fast. He had never invested more money in any of his schemes than he could afford. He seems to have enjoyed business much as he had enjoyed trotting. It was a challenge and worth working at, but it never ran his life.

One afternoon at Springwood, he looked up from his writing table to see robins preparing to take possession of the corners of his piazza for their summer nests. "I often wonder," he wrote, "why men are satisfied to live all their lives between brick walls and thinking of nothing but money and the so-called recreations of so-called society when there is so much enjoyment in the country."

It was Rebecca's health, not business, that worried him most. It had begun to fail as early as 1869. She had grown heavy, suffered from chest pains, coughed constantly, tired easily. Nothing the doctor suggested seemed to help. "Dear Becky" spent three weeks in bed that spring, James noted, "very much blushed and prostrated." He had slowed down, too, suffering from ghostly back pains he believed only European waters could alleviate.

They went abroad again that summer. In England they inspected Rugby School (where James briefly thought he might send Rosy, now sixteen), and in London ordered fourteen silver-plated coats of arms, a new set of harness, and new coachmen's uniforms with silver buttons bearing the Roosevelt crest. In Paris, James and Rosy spun through the Bois de Boulogne on their velocipedes and spent one whole day shopping for "carriages and diamonds." The Roosevelts tried the grape cure at Merau, strolling slowly together beneath arbors heavy with blue clusters of fruit. "People stuff with them all day," Rebecca wrote, "and everyone carries a little open basket on their arm which is constantly replenished."

Nothing helped. Rebecca stayed in her hotel room during most of the trip, too weak to go out, while James and Rosy—"my two lovers"—saw the sights, then hurried back to her in the evenings with bouquets.

At Rome they met the energetic Theodore Roosevelt clan, then tumbling their way across Europe on their first family Grand Tour. Rosy was delighted. There were four other children with whom to see the sights: Anna (called "Bamie," and a great favorite of Mr. James), Theodore, Elliott, and Corinne. They all went together to St. Peter's to see Pope Pius IX carried past them in a sedan chair. The pontiff stopped in front of the massed Roosevelts and, as eleven-year-old Theodore boasted in his diary that night, "he extended his hand to me and I kissed it! Hem!! Hem!!"

The two families came home together, too, through very rough seas. Rebecca and Martha Roosevelt (whom everyone called "Mittie") spent days huddled together on the pitching deck, their steamer blankets soaked with spray, salt caked on their veils. Their deck chairs had to be lashed to the mast, but anything was better than trying to ride it out in the close air below deck.

Rebecca did not get better. The doctor ordered her to stop climbing stairs; a servant had to carry her gently up and down to bed in his arms. James had an elevator installed in the New York house, and another at Springwood. When he gave a supper for some 200 children at the Hyde Park schoolhouse he brought an easy chair for her so that she might watch the fun without growing too tired.

On a brilliant afternoon in early August 1876, James took her aboard his yacht for a cruise on Long Island Sound, hoping that the sun and sea air would ease her cough. Not long after they got under way she suffered a massive heart attack. James ordered the yacht back to the dock and helped carry her home to Washington Square.

She died there on the twenty-first.

Dr. Isaac had been buried in Greenwood Cemetery in Brooklyn, and he had wished that his sons and their families would be buried there, too. But for James and Rosy and for Rebecca, Hyde Park had been home, and her body was taken there, to the shady graveyard behind St. James. Mr. James hoped someday to be buried beside her, and drew up plans for a monument of Scotch granite large enough for both of them to be built above her grave upon his death.

"I don't care much where I go," James wrote to his mother from London that fall, "but . . . would rather keep on the move." Hyde Park held too many memories for him to spend the winter there, and for several months he visited old friends in England and wandered in France and Spain. Rosy had sailed with him in October, but had to return to Columbia College in January.

Mr. James came home alone in the spring, to Springwood, where he planned to live "very quietly." Elespie continued to run the household. He went into town on business, still dined at his clubs, and attended parties at the invitation of friends. But he was in his fifties now, his whiskers silvery, and he seemed sure to live out the remainder of his life a widower, comfortable and much admired, but lonely.

Then sometime in 1877 he fell in love again—with Anna Roosevelt, Bamie, Theodore Roosevelt's older sister. It was not surprising that he was drawn to a member of the family. It was a Roosevelt custom to marry cousins—he had already done it once himself—and the idea of linking the Hyde Park and Oyster Bay branches of the family must have appealed to him.

But Bamie was very young, just twenty-two in 1877, less than half his age, a full year younger than Rosy. Mr. James had always taken an avuncular interest in her, had liked to take her for long toboggan rides when she came up to Hyde Park to visit Rosy as a little girl. She was not beautiful; her heavy-lidded eyes made her look older than she was, and Pott's disease, a form of tuberculosis that assaults the bones, had left her with a distorted back and almost constant pain. But she was an extraordinary person: wise and capable well beyond her years—her niece Alice Roosevelt Longworth always insisted that had Bamie been born a man she would have become President, not her brother—and she was unusually sympathetic. People confided in her, and she was intensely interested in the lives of those who were doing things she could not do herself. All the members of her own family brought her their troubles. She was "kind of a feminine little Atlas," Theodore Roosevelt once said, "with a small world on her shoulders."

After Rebecca's death, Mr. James added to that burden, confiding his sadness to her as he did perhaps to no one else. He called frequently at the Roosevelt home on West Fifty-seventh Street, and he wrote to Bamie often. A few of his letters have survived. He had kept up a brave front during Christmas of 1877, for example—his second without Rebecca—but it had been "stupid," he told Bamie, "not gay."

In February of 1878, Theodore Roosevelt, Sr., died. Bamie had been his favorite child, and she had adored him in return. The loss was enormous. Mr. James offered sympathy. Perhaps in her grief she initially responded to his solicitude more strongly than she might have otherwise. Mr. James was in fact old enough to be her father. He even resembled him somewhat; they had sometimes been mistaken for one another on the street.

Mr. James felt encouraged. He continued to write to Bamie, pressing his suit more strongly now, but always couched in the most decorous and formal language.

"I am all alone in my country house this bright sunny Sunday afternoon," he wrote in March, "and seated before the fire, have been wondering if you would like to get a letter from me. I suppose I should have asked formal permission last Tuesday evening to write you, but I did not get a chance to, or perhaps to tell the truth, I still retain, old as I am, a certain shyness of my childhood days. . . . I hope however you will not think me too bold."

By May he was so eager for even a glimpse of her that any pretext would do. When he heard she would be traveling aboard a train that would halt briefly at Poughkeepsie, he promised that he would be waiting on the platform with his dog "*on* the arrival of the train in order that you may give dear little Budge the pleasure of a ten-minute interview. I am sure he will know you, as he never forgets people he liked."

He sent her little gifts, including a paper knife, hoping that "now and then, when you are using it, and deep in some book, it may serve to give you one little thought of me."

In the autumn of 1879, Mr. James was abroad again, and when he arrived at Pau in the French Pyrenees in October, he was delighted to find a letter from Bamie and hurried to answer it: "If you knew the pleasure it gave me to sit down in that bright sunlight to read all that you are doing . . . you would be fully repaid for your trouble and kindness," he wrote. "I must confess, however, that it made me fearfully homesick, as I have still such a longing to be with you all once more."

Because Bamie had never visited Pau, he continued, it would be "impossible for you to realize the contrast between this Sunday and the last. Last Sunday I was in London, yellow dank fog, so dark in the house that even lamps gave but little light; dismal gloomy streets deserted because one could not get about; you were so depressed that you felt even your best friends have deserted you. Today such a blue sky and warm sunlight as you only get in the South of France and Italy. I am writing with all my windows open looking out on the magnificent snow-clad chain of the Pyrenees. . . . The whole country is as green and fresh as May." The season had hardly begun, Mr. James continued, but every room was full. "I am happy so far to find only one American family. . . . I have never liked Pau because there are so many of my own country people here, and the set is not always the best. I do not expect I shall be so troubled by their society as a single man is not much sought after, unless he puts himself forward."

He was thinking constantly of Bamie now. She was working too hard on her charities; they would wear her down if she was not careful. He had gone riding one afternoon, along shady lanes that reminded him of the paths around her country home at Oyster Bay: "I so wish you could have been with me, it was such intense enjoyment."

And he worried that some of her letters seemed surprisingly remote: "Do you know I imagined your last letter was a *little* stiff? Sometimes I am afraid you think I write too freely to you, but you are the only person I ever go to with all my little trials, and I have always talked to you even more freely, and writing is only expressing one's thoughts on paper instead of orally, and I do not see the difference."

James returned to America early in 1880 and shortly thereafter asked Bamie to marry him. It was "rather terrifying for a young girl," a member of the family recalled. Mr. James was "an old man," remote and "rather stiff." Bamie liked him, but there had never been any question of love. She felt badly that he had so misunderstood her feelings and could not bring herself to hurt him directly.

Her mother, Mittie, stepped in, gently turning him away with the greatest possible tact. Mr. James seems to have taken it well. Perhaps it had simply been another gamble that had not quite paid off. He continued to call at West Fifty-seventh Street.

And there, one soft April evening in 1880, he attended a small dinner. Bamie and her sister Corinne were there. So was their mother. And so was an astonishingly beautiful young woman named Sara Delano, whom Bamie introduced as one of her closest friends.

"He talked to her the whole time," Mittie told Bamie after the guests had gone home. "Why, he never took his eyes off her."

CHAPTER 2

ALGONAC

Once during her son's presidency, Sara Delano Roosevelt was asked why the Oyster Bay Roosevelts had grown so antagonistic toward the Hyde Park branch of the family. "I can't imagine," she said, "unless it's because we're better-looking than they are."

Certainly Sara Delano was better-looking than almost anyone. A photograph of her, made about the time Mr. James first saw her, shows why he was transfixed. She was one of four daughters of Warren Delano II of Newburgh who were known to New York society as "the beautiful Delano sisters," and she is sometimes said to have resembled the ideal American beauty made popular a decade later by the artist Charles Dana Gibson. There is a superficial resemblance. She was tall and had the Gibson girl's long graceful neck, her large eyes and upswept hair, her fine regular features of the kind inevitably called "chiseled."

But she was not a girl in 1880. She was twenty-six, half Mr. James's age, and precisely Rosy's, but past the age when most women of her class married. Her chin was square and stubborn, and there was already something regal, reserved—substantive—about her.

She retained those qualities all her life. Even at eighty-six, in a newsreel made in Paris where she had gone to visit her sister Dora in the early spring of 1940, she has an extraordinary impact. Surrounded by photographers and by reporters shouting questions in two languages, she is unruffled, removed, yet somehow in charge. She stands straight, gazes directly into the camera, and answers the questions she wishes to answer slowly, with care, in a mellow, beautifully modulated voice. Her French is flawless; her accent when speaking English almost British in its crisp precision.

What are her impressions of France on this visit?

"*Pour moi, c'est toujours la belle France, sympathique et loyale.*"

Does she think France will be invaded?

She doesn't know, of course, but if so, the French army—which she has seen parading—"is ready for *anything.*"

Will FDR run again for the White House?

"I have never even heard him speak of a third term. He always considers the pleasure of returning to his home at Hyde Park."

What she says is banal. The way she says it—the fact that *she* has said it—makes it important.

She herself first experienced the pleasures of Hyde Park just a few weeks after she met Mr. James. She may have been invited to visit that very first evening, at Mittie Roosevelt's table. Mr. James knew her father fairly well; they had been allies on the board of Consolidated Coal. And he was at least slightly acquainted with her mother, Catherine Lyman Delano.

Now he wrote to Mrs. Delano directly, asking whether "Miss Sallie" might be allowed to visit Springwood with some friends in early May.

Mrs. Delano granted permission, and on April 7, Sara Delano came to Hyde Park for the first time, accompanied by a full complement of escorts: Bamie and Corinne Roosevelt, and their mother. They stayed a week, taking long carriage rides on the Albany Road beneath the branches of the big old trees that then formed an unbroken leafy vault that ran for miles. There were visits to St. James and to Rosedale, where Sara was introduced to Mr. James's brother and sister-in-law and to his mother, now an old lady in a lace cap. There were quiet strolls through the woods, boat rides on the river, tea on the piazza.

One morning, Mr. James asked Sara if she would be kind enough to arrange the flowers for the luncheon table. She agreed, gathering a bouquet from the enclosed garden and choosing a blue-green English bowl of Oriental design. It was shallow and wide-mouthed, not ideal for arranging flowers, but she fussed until she got them right, and Mr. James was delighted.

More than half a century later, in 1932, Sara wrote to her son how grateful she still was for that first invitation to Springwood. Had she not come, she said, "I should now be 'old Miss Delano' after a rather sad life." And as often as she could until the end—for some sixty years in all—she would continue to arrange fresh flowers daily in that bowl.

Before she returned to Algonac, her home, twenty miles downriver, she and Mr. James seem to have reached a secret understanding. He would ask her father for her hand. If her father agreed, she would gladly marry him.

Algonac's name was said to have been derived from the Algonquian words for "hill" and "river," and it was in every way a grander place than Springwood. It was more than twice as large, with forty rooms, and stood on the opposite side of the Hudson on a high hill that jutted far out into the river, so that the house was nearly surrounded on three sides by water. From its tall bracketed tower there were views of the sparkling Hudson and the far-off mountains, north and south. A wall of trees and flowering shrubs hid the compound from the road, and visitors passed through stone gates to approach the house along a graded gravel road that coiled through some sixty acres of lawns and orchards and formal beds of flowers.

Mr. James made that journey one bright morning in late May.

Warren Delano II, the absolute master and vigilant guardian of this tranquil walled-off world, was a formidable man, blind in one eye and able to walk only with a cane, but at seventy-one still big and fierce-looking. His gray side-whiskers were enhanced by a swooping mustache and a protruding tuft of beard below his lower lip.

He had decided views about everything, and they were rarely challenged, either by his eight children, his admiring wife, or his invited guests. His father had taught him that tuberculosis was the product of too little fat in the diet, and so a soft yellow brick of butter always sat in front of his plate from which he pared thick slices for his children—and made sure they ate them.

He had unshakable convictions about religion, too: "There is no standing room for any creed between our Unitarian faith and the Papal church." And about labor: "I cannot and will not pay any man more than $1.50 a day" for ten hours' work, he once told one of his sons; if workers complained, they could always be replaced by immigrants, "a new element that knows the value of shelter, food & clothing."

And he was an implacable Republican, fond of saying that while all Democrats were not horse thieves, it had been his experience that all horse thieves were Democrats.

He had subjected every suitor for his daughters' hands to an exacting interrogation. Some years earlier, Sara or one of her sisters had invited two young men to visit Algonac. One of them had been a Harvard classmate of Sara's brother Warren Delano III, and her father wrote to his son right away: "Mr. Coles is accredited with being your friend and seems . . . bright and intelligent and I dare say is better than he looks. . . . But what do you know of him and how did he stand at Cambridge and what is he doing now! Who and what are his parents and family, etc.?"

When another young man of whom Mr. Delano did not approve sent Sara flowers, he drafted a formal note—at once courteous and dismissive—which she dutifully copied out in her own hand and sent off.

Mr. Delano greeted Mr. James warmly, understandably thinking that he had simply come to make a social call on an old friend. The true purpose of the visit dawned slowly; and when things became clear, he was not pleased. There were plenty of objections to the match. Mr. James was an Episcopalian for one thing. Then, too, he and Sara had only known one another for a few weeks. Above all there was the question of Mr. James's age.

James Roosevelt was patient but persistent. He loved Sara, would always cherish her, could promise her a comfortable quiet life on the Hudson very much like that she had led at Algonac. Presumably he avoided discussing politics on this visit; some time would have to pass before Warren Delano grudgingly admitted that his son-in-law had demonstrated that one could simultaneously be a gentleman and a Democrat.

Certainly Mr. James's prosperity and good reputation were well established, and Mr. Delano liked him, though he had at least once confidentially questioned his sense of purpose. (During a short-lived internal squabble within Consolidated Coal he had worried to his son that Mr. Roosevelt's good manners and charm would make him "vibrate" between two factions when he should stand on principle—and side with Warren Delano.)

Sara was not present at these discussions about her future, of course, but she must have made her feelings known to her mother in private, and perhaps to her father as well. Perhaps, too, Mrs. Delano had delicately pointed out to her husband that she had been only slightly over half his age when they had been married thirty-seven years before.

In any case, Mr. Delano did not reject the suit outright, and a few days later, after Mr. James had returned to Springwood, Sara's older sister Dora and her husband, Will Forbes, went up for a five-day visit. Clearly they had been sent to inspect the Roosevelt holdings—and Mr. James himself.

They evidently pronounced themselves satisfied, for James Roosevelt continued to call at Algonac,[1] and in late July he and Sara announced their engagement.

Friends and family were astonished. Elliott Roosevelt thought Mr. James a "sly old chap" for having conducted his courtship in secret, but believed him devoted to Sara. Elliott's sister Bamie wrote to the couple expressing both her pleasure and her surprise. She was delighted that Sara and Mr. James had found one another—"it is hard to think of two people who will be more absolutely happy together than you both"—but she was a little concerned that everything had happened so fast. Their courtship had lasted just ten weeks.

Mr. James wrote back from his room at Algonac. "*I* do not think the affair has been in the least rapid or bewildering," he said. "As you know Miss Sallie rather well, you must know how very difficult it was to win her."

Mr. Delano wrote of the engagement to his son Warren III. The "suddenness or haste" with which everything had happened had so stunned him, he said, that "I can scarcely yet realize that it is a veritable fact." Still, he now professed to be pleased. "The great secret of our dear Sallie's life . . . is being divulged. . . . Of this choice of our dear one, I can say that it is very satisfactory to me, to Mama, to each and all of the family. Both Roosevelt and Sallie seem to be earnestly, seriously, entirely in love." (The use of "Roosevelt" rather than "James" in this letter at least suggests that Mr. Delano was still not entirely comfortable with the coming marriage; he called his other sons-in-law by their first names.) The engagement, he continued, "relieved my mind of many anxieties! It leaves my child within comparatively little distance from here . . . and so far as I can know or judge, it assures her of all the comforts and necessary luxuries of life."

The comforts and necessary luxuries with which Sara Delano had always been surrounded had been hard won by her father. The clandestine nature of the trade upon which he built much of his fortune,

1. Many years later the Roosevelt coachman was still grumbling to his family about the inconvenience of these visits: "I'd take him . . . there [to Algonac] and I never got back till five in the morning."

Source: Nancy Fogel interview with Albert and Mary Paul, FDRL.

his subsequent struggle to overcome financial disaster and rebuild, and his simultaneous effort to shield every member of his big family from the stern realities of life out from under Algonac's sheltering trees—all marked her character in ways that would in turn mark her son's.

The Delanos were an old family in America, older even than the Roosevelts, and at least as proud of their ancestry. Sara Delano was fond of saying that her son was "a Delano, not a Roosevelt at all."

The first American Delano was Philippe de la Noye, a Huguenot who arrived at Plymouth Colony in 1621. He came out of love, not religious zeal, hoping to marry Priscilla Mullens (the same Priscilla with whom Myles Standish and John Alden were later smitten). His dramatic arrival on her doorstep did him no good. She turned him down, and he did not marry for thirteen more years. When he did, he chose another Englishwoman, Hester Dewsbury, with whom he had several children. One of these, Jonathan Delano, married Mercy Warren, fought in King Philip's War, and was rewarded for his service with an 800-acre tract of land at New Bedford, Massachusetts, which then encompassed the coastal village of Fairhaven.[2]

There his sons and their sons prospered as mariners and whalers and shipbuilders, and there Warren Delano II was born in 1809. His grandfather Ephraim had been a sea captain. His father, the first Warren, had begun his career at sea at nineteen, ferrying cargoes of corn and salt, bathwood and potatoes to New Orleans and Liverpool and the Canary Islands. Later he purchased interests in a number of fine ships, came to own several more, and was captured at sea and endured two grim weeks aboard a British prison ship after the War of 1812 had officially ended. He returned to Fairhaven in 1815, alive but "sick enough," he said. After that he built himself a great rambling house and settled into a lucrative if less eventful life ashore as a whaling executive.

One of his eldest son's earliest memories was of being bundled up

2. An eager-to-please nineteenth-century genealogist once delighted his Delano patrons by tracing their forebears in Europe all the way back to a Roman patrician family, the Actii, who were said to have staked a claim to a corner of French Flanders in the final days of the Empire.

Whatever the truth of that story, the history of the American clan is rich enough in color and incident. Among its livelier members: Thomas Delano, Philippe's son, who was fined by the Massachusetts Bay Colony for having sexual relations with his wife before marriage, wed Mary Alden, the daughter of the girl his father had pursued to the New World; Captain Amasa Delano, who circled the globe three times and took down the first account of the *Bounty* mutineers' colony on Pitcairn Island; Captain Paul Delano, who commanded the Chilean fleet that helped end Spanish rule in Peru; and Dutch-born Adelaide Delannoy, seduced by the American actor Junius Brutus Booth, who became the mother of Edwin and John Wilkes Booth.

Sources: Daniel W. Delano, Jr., *Franklin Roosevelt and the Delano Influence*, and Nathan Miller, *The Roosevelt Chronicles*, pages 179–180.

by his mother and hurried aboard a boat and taken to Acushnet at the head of the Acushnet River during the war with England; a British frigate had sailed into Buzzards Bay and threatened to shell Fairhaven. So many women and children were sheltered in one house that night, Warren would later tell his grandson Franklin Roosevelt, that the smallest children were put to bed on the stairs.

It was probably inevitable that Warren II would first seek to make his fortune from the sea; it is unlikely that he ever seriously considered any other life. But his father knew from experience the risks of actual seafaring; the business side of the maritime trade was the place for a likely young man to make his mark. Young Warren was graduated from Fairhaven Academy at fifteen in 1824. Two years later, his father had him apprenticed as a junior clerk to Hathaway and Company, a Boston importer; later he worked for Goodhue and Company, one of the biggest import firms in New York, gaining what one business associate later called "a first rate mercantile education."

In 1833, he sailed for China as supercargo aboard the ship *Commerce,* plunging through heavy seas around the Horn and stopping at several ports along the western coast of South America. He was twenty-four. At Canton he was offered a junior partnership in the new firm of Russell, Sturgis and Company of Boston and Manila. In 1840, at thirty-one, he would become a senior partner with Russell and Company, by then the largest American firm in the China trade. The object of every partner was to gain a "competence"—$100,000—before returning home. Warren Delano would earn at least two, one with each of the trading companies he served.

The China trade was already a century and a half old when Warren arrived in Canton. Britain was the dominant power, but American ships had been competing with her since 1785. Tea and silk were the chief Chinese commodities, for which the Americans traded an odd assortment of foreign goods that included sheets of tin from New England mills, beaver and fox pelts, sandalwood logs stripped from the forests of Hawaii, and ginseng, the man-shaped root that grew wild along the Hudson and which the Chinese believed held aphrodisiac powers.

The politics of the trade were complex and sometimes treacherous. The Manchu emperor at Peking believed that the Americans and other foreigners were *Fan Kuei*—barbarians—tribute-bearing vassals unworthy even of simple courtesy and pitiful in their desperation for Chinese goods. China, on the other hand, needed nothing from the west. "The Celestial Empire possesses all things in abundance and lacks no products within its borders. There is therefore no need to import the manufactures of outside barbarians."

To insure that his subjects' contacts with these ill-mannered outsiders were minimal, the emperor limited all trade to the port of Canton, and further decreed that the western "devil-ships" had to anchor at Whampoa, twelve miles from the city at the mouth of the Pearl River. Goods were unloaded onto barges for the trip upriver to the quay. There, all trading was done within a tiny enclave, barely one quarter mile square, where Warren Delano and the other traders lived, worked, and stored their goods in a block of thirteen whitewashed factories.

There were still more restrictions. Westerners could not carry arms or gather in groups larger than ten. There was to be no rowing on the river or walking within the city walls of Canton. Foreigners could stroll in the square in front of the factories but could not walk in the gardens on the opposite shore more than once a year, and then only in the company of an official translator. The Chinese were forbidden to teach foreigners their language; all transactions were conducted in pidgin English.

And all dealing was done through one of thirteen Chinese traders, who were held personally responsible for the actions of their foreign associates. This was sometimes a touchy business. Sailors reeling back to their ships from an evening in Hog Lane, the single narrow street of grog shops they were permitted to visit on shore leave, occasionally got into trouble, requiring their Chinese sponsors to pay stiff damages to the imperial viceroy. But it was worth the inconvenience. Houqua, the agent who handled business for most American firms, became probably the wealthiest merchant on earth, said to have compiled a fortune of some $26 million by the year Warren Delano first came to know him.

Delano and his fellow traders lived comfortable if cramped lives at Canton, cut off from the real China that began just a few feet behind their factories, but generally content. Their quarters, furnished with chairs and tables and bedsteads brought from home, were two floors above the guarded godown in which cargoes were stored; in early spring, when Chinese goods were heaped there awaiting shipment, the rich smell of spices and tea perfumed their rooms. There were servants to cook and clean and launder and wait table; each man's desk had a bell with which to summon a snack or a glass of water.

Foreign women were forbidden in Canton. Those few traders whose wives and children had crossed the ocean with them had to be satisfied with summers together at the family compound in the Portuguese colony of Macao, some eighty-five miles down river. But for those willing to risk trouble with the authorities there were the flower boats, moored brothels with gilded balconies on which women hobbled back and forth to emphasize the alluring tininess of their broken feet.

The square in which the traders were permitted to take the air was filled daily with a swarm of cobblers, jugglers, fortunetellers, tailors, musicians—and beggars. There were some 1,000 official alms seekers in Canton, all dues-paying members of the Flower Society of Beggars, and they included a long file of blind men who made their way into the factory square each afternoon, roped together, banging the ground with staves and chanting "Cash, foreign devils, Cash!" When the clamor grew intolerable, a complaint was registered with the militia and the square was cleared with whips.

The Chinese took an amused view of the foreigners, and often turned out in large numbers just to look at them, locked up in their compound. One of Warren's friends, longing perhaps for wide-open spaces back home, brought his horse from Macao and doggedly rode it back and forth across the Canton square every afternoon. The owner of a shop past which the horse plodded daily improved business by hanging a sign which said he had "hired a *fanqui* to ride opposite [my] house for the diversion from five to six every evening"; those who wanted to see the sight in comfort were welcome at his tea stall.

The world inside the factories was hearty, profane, profoundly masculine, and not notably taxing. "Canton was and is and will be . . . a most stupid place," Warren once wrote. Only the promise of profits kept him there, and when his younger brother Edward, just twenty-two, arrived in 1839, it was Warren's fond hope that Ned would not have to stay in China as long as he had.

Business picked up with the going and coming of the trading ships in winter, but the rest of the time there was little to do. Most merchants spent several months relaxing at Macao. But even at Canton, the traders found that a good many of the emperor's strictures could safely be ignored, a few coins in the right hands making all the difference. Though venturing out onto the Pearl River was officially outlawed, for example, Delano and his friends formed a Canton Regatta that raced on its muddy waters every spring. In the first annual races in 1837, his six-oared gig, *The Not So Green,* outpulled its British rivals for the cup.

The high points of the Canton social season for the Americans were the sumptuous banquets held at the home of Houqua on the midriver island of Honam. Houqua was a thin, fragile, sad-eyed man with a wisp of gray beard and an air of unfailing kindness. He wore silk brocade robes and clattering ropes of jade and a silk cap with a bright blue button that denoted his special status. The bohea tea grown on the slopes of his family estate and shipped aboard American ships was said to be among the finest in the world and he was generous toward those who had made him rich. His trading partners all admired him—a portrait of Houqua always hung in the Delano parlor at Algonac—and once when he was being harshly treated by imperial officials one of his old American friends wrote to suggest that he might consider moving to the United States; St. Augustine, Florida, the American thought, might be just the place to start over.

The move would have required a considerable adjustment. Houqua lived in splendor on Honam. At noon on banquet days, he dispatched a fleet of intricately carved houseboats to carry his guests across the water. His home was a dazzling complex of kiosks and ponds and pavilions, walled gardens and shrines and a pillared banquet hall, its marble floor covered with silk, all tended by a silent army of servants. The first course was served in the early afternoon; the last near dawn the following morning. Warren Delano and his fellow New Englanders found themselves seated on japanned chairs, dining on plovers' eggs, sturgeon's nose, and soup brewed from sea slugs while sipping green-pea wine from dainty silver cups.

William Hunter, one of Warren's Canton friends, loved the life. "We pursued the even tenor of our way with supreme indifference," he remembered years later, "took care of our business, pulled boats, walked, dined well and so the years rolled by as happily as possible."

The idyll was abruptly interrupted in 1838. Opium was the cause. Traffic in the drug was the dirty little secret of the China trade, almost universally practiced, almost never discussed. And as an increasingly important Canton trader, Warren Delano was deeply involved in it.

The British controlled the business; perhaps a third of their Chinese revenues came from the sale of opium, though its importation had been expressly forbidden by the emperor since 1729. Massive bribery of local officials made it possible; the drug's compactness and the almost insatiable demand for it among Chinese addicts made it spectacularly lucrative.

The Americans did their best to keep up with the British, but never came close to matching their earnings. Every American firm took part, with the lone exception of D. W. C. Olyphant and Company, run by Quakers opposed to selling opium on principle and derided by the other traders as "Zion's Corner" for their abstemiousness. Warren once tried to put the business in what he saw as the proper perspective for his brothers back home. "I do not pretend to justify . . . the opium trade in a moral and philanthropic point of view," he wrote, "but as a merchant I insist that it has been . . . fair, honorable and legitimate . . . liable to no further or weightier objections than is the importation of Wines, Brandies & Spirits into the U. States." Nor did he deny that opium had an "unhappy effect" upon the Chinese people, and his brother Ned, at least, would witness that effect firsthand. In the autumn of 1844, on the way to India to arrange to buy the season's supply of the drug, he had stopped at Singapore and there visited several licensed dens. "Found smokers in all of them," he noted in his diary. "One man was prostrate under its effects—pale, cadaverous, death-like . . . for when I took his pipe from his hand he offered no resistance, though his eyes tried to follow me." Ned continued with his mission, evidently unperturbed.

Robert Bennet Forbes, Warren's friend and immediate predecessor as head of Russell and Company in Canton, offered still another justification for taking part in the trade: the best seafaring families of New England were involved in it, "those to whom I have always been accustomed to look up as exponents of all that was honorable in trade —the Perkins's, the Peabodys, the Russells and the Lows." There was a huge profit to be made. Others were enriching themselves; Warren Delano and his fellow traders saw no reason not to get their share. Under Robert Forbes's energetic direction, Russell and Company became the third-most important single firm in the opium trade, British or American. As Forbes's successor as head of the company, Warren Delano improved upon his performance.

It was a matter of supply, not scruples then, that kept the Americans from doing even better. The British owned their own poppy fields in India. Their American competitors had to make do with opium bought in Turkey, or to sell the Indian drug on consignment for British or Indian firms.

The mechanics of smuggling were simple. Chinese buyers placed their orders with a Canton trader and paid for it in hard cash. Incoming vessels carrying the drug stopped briefly under the lee of Lintin Island in Canton Bay before proceeding to the official anchorage at Whampoa. Scarlet-painted buyers' boats, called "fast crabs" or "scrambling dragons" by the Chinese, scurried out to meet them, propelled by sixty oarsmen and armed against pirates. An agent of the Canton firm waited on deck to open the chests, weigh out the fist-sized cakes of the drug, and repack them in bags made of matting. Some ships carried as many as 100 chests, each containing one picul or 133 ⅓ pounds, enough to supply 8,000 addicts for a month.

For each chest he processed, the agent received five dollars, plus more if the buyer had dallied too long in presenting his receipted order. Robert Forbes handled this chore himself for Russell and Company and is said to have earned $30,000 in commissions; Warren may have done the same when his turn came.

The Manchus were powerless to stop it, though they despaired over opium's impact on their subjects and worried at the drain the trade made on precious specie. Crackdowns were announced from time to time, but they were mostly shadow plays staged by local officials to please the emperor at Peking. Traders and buyers alike knew that corruption was too widespread for profits permanently to be affected on either side; Warren himself wrote that if the Chinese ever seriously attempted to enforce their laws against opium, "the Foreigners *cannot* by any possibility sell or smuggle the drug into the country."

In 1838 the emperor again declared his determination to crush the opium business, and the viceroy of Canton found it necessary to placate him with a new theatrical gesture. A number of oarsmen from the buyers' boats were seized and publicly strangled. Ordinary opium traffic on the river halted briefly, but the flow of profits continued without a break, the viceroy having quietly chartered his own fleet of junks to ferry the contraband inland until things quieted down again.

On December 12, however, another staged event got out of hand. That afternoon traders sitting on the verandas of their factories noticed a Chinese official being carried into the square in his sedan chair. With him came a battered prisoner and two executioners. The official got down, took his seat beneath a hastily erected tent, and ordered that tea be brought to him while the prisoner was lashed to a wooden cross. The westerners realized that a man was about to be strangled before their eyes.

Several hurried out to protest, led by Hunter, the only trader at Canton who spoke Chinese. The official explained that the criminal was the operator of an opium den and had been dragged into the square to die as an object lesson to all the barbarians who had dared to supply him. Hunter said this was an intolerable insult. There matters stood for a few minutes, the prisoner and his executioners waiting patiently as his fate was argued back and forth. Then a band of British sailors who had just stepped ashore on leave took matters into their own hands. They smashed the cross and used the fragments to beat back the executioners. A small riot began, growing larger fast as the westerners, perhaps 100 strong and possibly including Warren Delano, poured into the square, only to be driven back inside by an expanding mob of angry Cantonese.

Soon some 8,000 Chinese had besieged the factories, hurling rocks and battering at the doors. Warren and his friends helped barricade the back entrances with canisters of coal, and they scattered broken glass out the front windows to make an all-out assault as painful as possible to the barefooted mob. When things seemed darkest, Houqua came to the rescue, persuading the authorities to send in the militia. Russell and Company resolved to withdraw from the opium business, at least for the time being.

There things might have ended had a new imperial high commissioner not just been appointed with orders to stop the smuggling. His name was Lin Tse-hsu, and he was incorruptible. As governor general of Hukwang he had eradicated the narcotics problem in his province by the simple expedient of executing every smoker who refused to turn in his pipe.

He arrived at Canton in March of 1839, surrounded the factories with troops, and declared that the barbarians would stay inside until they turned over to him for destruction all the opium in and around Canton, and further pledged not to import more on pain of the "extreme rigor of the law"—decapitation. Armed junks patrolled the waterfront to bar foreign reinforcements, all Chinese servants were withdrawn and food supplies were cut off, though the resourceful Houqua managed to smuggle in pigs, sheep, and chickens when needed. The entire merchant community was held hostage for opium.

Captain Charles Elliot, the British trade superintendent, tried to negotiate, but he was in a poor position to bargain, and Lin refused to budge. Meanwhile, the imprisoned traders struggled to maintain their morale. They held rat hunts and cricket matches and contests to see who could shinny highest up a flagpole. The Russell men enjoyed roughing it. "We laughed rather than groaned over the efforts to roast a capon, to boil an egg," William Hunter remembered. "We could all clean knives, sweep the floors, even manage the lamps." They were less capable in the kitchen, where, one of them admitted, "no white man had ever been before," and Warren was eventually elected chief cook, displacing Robert Forbes, who had blistered the toast and served ham and eggs which even he confessed "bore the color and consistency of dirty sole leather."

Elliot was finally forced to capitulate, surrendering 20,280 chests of opium to the Chinese. The men of Russell and Company gave up an additional 1,540 chests, which they had been holding on consignment for others. All of it was ceremoniously dissolved in water, further diluted with salt and lime, then sluiced into the harbor, after it was suggested to the spirits of the sea that they get out of the way of this unavoidable desecration. It took 500 workmen to finish the job, and when one man tried to save a morsel for himself he was beheaded on the spot.

The British traders then withdrew from Canton—first to Macao and then onto their anchored ships—waiting for London to dispatch an expeditionary force to punish the Chinese. It arrived in June of 1840 and the Opium War that followed, bloody but sporadic, lasted nearly three years.

During that time the Americans continued to trade at Canton, and Warren Delano was never busier. As senior American merchant, he served as vice consul, oversaw the Russell accounts, and also acted as agent for the absent British. Profits soared and opium continued to be carried inland, 8,000 chests of it in 1839 alone.

Americans were not directly involved in the fighting, and Warren and Ned were ambivalent as to who they hoped would win. They sympathized with the Chinese for wishing to defend their homeland, especially when rumors reached them of atrocities, including widespread rape, committed by British sailors ashore. "I truly wish that John Bull would meet with one hearty repulse," Ned wrote, "for why should he enter their peaceful habitations and commit the horridest brutalities upon the women?" On the other hand, official Chinese hauteur had angered the Americans just as much as it had the British. "Great Britain owes it to herself and to the civilized world (in the West)," Warren wrote early in the conflict, "to knock a little reason into this besotted people and teach them to treat strangers with common decency."

Still, if they were not combatants, the war came very close to the Delano brothers. Shortly after the British fleet arrived, it imposed a blockade on Chinese shipping at Canton. The Chinese reciprocated with a counterblockade of their own. Only hours before it was to go into effect, a British ship, the 900-ton *Cambridge*, slipped into Whampoa from Singapore. After she was unloaded, her captain, seeing no way to return safely to sea, sold her cheap to Warren. He renamed her the *Chesapeake*, but before she could enter Russell's service, Commissioner Lin himself asked to buy her. Delano was in no position to argue, and she was sold to the Chinese navy—in fact she *was* the Chinese navy, except for a handful of junks hastily fitted out for battle. The Celestial Empire had never seen much need for sea power.

The ship was towed to the mouth of the river. Her prow was painted with crimson dragon's eyes, bright streamers emblazoned with the Chinese characters for "courage" flew from her masts, and her decks were lined with every imaginable sort and size of cannon, each conveniently surrounded with its own casks of gunpowder. A crew of 400 men lived aboard.

The blockade stayed in effect for seven months while skirmishes were fought elsewhere at sea and intermittent talks yielded no concessions on either side. British patience eventually wore thin. Two ancient fortresses guarded the mouth of the Canton River. On January 7, 1841, at 9:30 A.M., warships moved in on both citadels simultaneously. Five hundred Chinese died in the bombardment. Not one British sailor was seriously injured. The British now anchored. Three smaller forts were all that stood between them and Canton itself. They could be taken any time the talks broke down.

Ned and a friend were rowed out to one of the ruined forts the next day. "What horrid butchery!" he wrote, and described "the burned body of a Chinaman. Some sailors had put a bamboo in his mouth surmounted by a Chinese scroll."

A few days later, the Delanos were returning to Canton aboard a dispatch boat after a brief visit to Macao. Identifying themselves as Americans they were allowed to pass among the tall British warships that now filled the river's mouth, even though they carried an arsenal of weapons in plain view on deck—swords, two double-barreled shotguns, two single-shot pistols, and a brace of Colts, each with five revolving barrels. These offered protection against pirates, but also allowed the brothers to take a shot from time to time at the ducks that sometimes lighted among the river islands.

Their boatmen acted as loaders and later in the day, while one of the shotguns was being put back onto the deck, it went off. Two

Chinese collapsed, streaming blood. One died within five minutes, his face, neck, and chest riddled with buckshot; the other was slightly wounded in the scalp. Their angry companions refused to row further until every weapon aboard was emptied into the water. That done, the dead man and his groaning companion were carried below and the boat continued on toward the factories. The accident, Ned wrote, had the effect of "saddening our hearts and therefore our dinner was not eaten with that good relish with which it ordinarily is."

Word of the incident reached Canton ahead of the dispatch boat, and the dead man's family rowed out to meet them just offshore. When the widow saw her husband's bloody corpse, Ned wrote, she "set up an ugly howling and wailing." Warren offered her $150—"in charity," Ned said—but she was not content with that and "after humbugging for two or three hours, she accepted $200" to keep quiet about what had happened. Ned thought Warren had been too generous; after all, the dead boatman had been happy to work for $1.50 a month when he was alive. Later, when an excited trader whispered to Ned that he had heard a rumor that foreigners had shot two Chinese somewhere on the river, Ned assured him "it is all nonsense."

On February 2, the British paddle steamer *Nemesis* approached the refitted *Chesapeake* which Warren had sold to Lin a year and a half earlier and which now floated empty at anchor, its crew having fled. A single Congreve rocket arced across the water and landed among the powder barrels on deck. The ship disintegrated with an explosion so daunting that Ned saw its "sudden and brilliant light" from the factory twelve miles away.

Exactly one month later, on March 2, a British assault on the city itself seemed imminent and the Prefect of Canton begged Warren as the senior foreigner left in the factories to go to Whampoa and intercede on behalf of the Chinese. Warren refused to take sides, but agreed to do what he could as a neutral party. The British commander was cordial but unyielding.

In a letter to his brother Joseph back home, Warren told what happened to him on his way back to Canton on the eighteenth. The "cowardly Chinese let go a shot at my boat," he said, "which passed some thirty feet over our heads, two men jumped overboard, two or three threw themselves in the bottom of the boat, and roared like squalling babies." (The ancient cannon in the Chinese forts were rarely accurate, since they could not be made to swivel; to hit something, Chinese gunners had to wait till it slid into view, then hope it stayed there until the charge could be touched off.)

His boat now floating helplessly, Warren was towed ashore. Chinese troops marched him three-quarters of a mile into the city "to the wondrous astonishment, admiration and gratification of the gaping multitude, the gallant soldiers informing those we passed of the terrible conflict which had taken place." He was brought before "His Excellency, the Commissioner Yang, a decrepit looking man at the age of 74 years, with bleared eyes and deaf as a haddock." The old official inspected his clothing, "took my hands, examining them carefully and *smelling* them, asked me to unbutton my shirt-bosom and show him my hide, which I did, and then pronounced me a good man, an excellent man, one of the best he had ever known, and seizing a lousy ragged dirty soldier who stood within three inches of His Excellency, said I was 'all the same as he.' "

Warren got back to the factory in time to watch from the roof as the British shelled the last three Chinese forts, then headed toward shore. A few shells were lobbed over the factories and into the city before the longboats landed, driving the other traders to take cover. Warren Delano alone stayed on the roof to watch.[3]

Opium helped make Warren a wealthy man. Neither he nor his descendants were proud of that fact. He kept his business affairs to himself. Years later, one of his sons remembered "how strictly he complied with the admonition not to let his right hand know what his left hand was doing." In a family fond of retelling and embellishing even the mildest sort of ancestral adventures, no stories seem to have been handed down concerning Warren Delano's genuinely adventurous career in the opium business.

In 1879, thirty-three years after he left Canton, when both he and Robert Bennet Forbes were old and important men with fortunes hoarded from a dozen other industries, Forbes wrote his old partner asking him to write down all that he remembered of his early years in China. Forbes was requesting each of the old Russell partners to do the same—some 100 men in all—and hoped to compile a detailed and anecdotal history from their collective reminiscences. Warren responded with a brief and colorless outline of his Canton career without mentioning his part in the drug traffic. Other former partners were still less cooperative. One worried that any account based on the fading memories of old men would exaggerate the parts played by some

3. The Chinese were never a match for Britain, and when the war ended in the summer of 1842, the emperor was forced to open five new trading ports and cede Hong Kong to the foreigners. Opium was not mentioned in the Treaty of Nanking, but Hong Kong provided a convenient new storage and distribution center for the trade.

partners and ignore those of others. Several old Russell men wanted no part of any history. Such a book would be "intrusive," one wrote.

Even Robert Forbes began to have second thoughts. "The only thing I fear," he told Warren, "is that in giving a sketch of the causes and effects of the opium traffic and our imprisonment I may say too much."

Forbes's projected history of Russell and Company was never published.[4]

In January of 1843, Warren Delano set sail for New York. He had been in China for nine years and had built his fortune. Home leave was long overdue. He arrived in the spring, visited his family at Fairhaven, and then took his two sisters on a long slow carriage ride through Massachusetts. At the home of his Canton friend John Murray Forbes at Northampton he met a Forbes cousin, Judge Joseph Lyman, who invited the Delanos to his home that evening.

The Lymans, too, were members of a distinguished old Massachusetts family, not wealthy but intellectually rich. Northampton was smaller then, and mostly made up of farmers who looked upon the Lymans fondly but with something approaching awe. They owned the town's first piano and taught their children to play it, and they ordered the latest books from Boston and read them aloud to one another in the evenings. Eminent men and women often stayed with them. The judge was an influential Federalist and Whig whose friends included John Quincy Adams and Daniel Webster. His second wife was Anne Jean Robbins, also of strong Yankee stock.

They were an unfailingly gracious couple, but formidable. Their friend Ralph Waldo Emerson wrote that he had never seen "so stately and naturally distinguished a pair." Mrs. Lyman was especially impressive, "a queenly woman, nobly formed . . . made for society, with flowing conversation, high spirits and perfectly at ease." The Lymans often had distinguished guests, Emerson remembered—sometimes twenty of them at a time for breakfast—but "none came or could come . . . who surpassed the dignity and intelligence of the hosts."

4. Robert Forbes did append a terse chronicle of the firm, including a list of its early partners and their terms of service, to the later editions of his *Personal Reminiscenes.* But it is skeletal and bloodless, not at all what he originally had in mind. The Russell men's responses to his questionnaire are filed among his papers at the Massachusetts Historical Society in Boston, Massachusetts.

It is interesting that when writing his brief memoir of life at Canton, Warren Delano left out his own involvement with opium entirely, but went out of his way in a footnote to absolve Houqua of ever having owned a chest of the drug.

Source: Delano Family Papers (hereafter DFP), FDRL.

It was not the judge and his wife who interested Warren that evening, however. It was their youngest daughter Catherine Robbins Lyman, just eighteen, dark-eyed, cultured, shy, and good-humored. He was newly rich and at thirty-three ready to start a family.

We know little of their courtship except that it was brief. Warren was committed to return to Canton before the first of the year. Catherine's parents liked him. "We have from the first been delighted by him," Mrs. Lyman wrote. "He has such a composed and dignified air for a man of business, such a quiet and sensible mode of expressing his rational opinions, that . . . there can be nothing but pleasure in his society."

The difference in their ages was no barrier to marriage. Catherine was accustomed to living in a patriarchal household. Her father was twenty-one years older than his wife, who reverently called him "Judge Lyman" even at home. His opinions became hers. Mrs. Lyman never contradicted him, Catherine's sister once wrote, and was the ruler only of "the kingdom of her own mind."

Catherine had evidently modeled herself after her mother. She, too, was kind and deferential, "lovely in her character," her mother wrote, "never out of temper, and always ready to oblige to any extent that her friends can claim." Her readiness to oblige would be tested many times during her marriage; it was never found wanting.

Her engagement to Warren Delano was announced in midsummer and they were married at Northampton on November 1. On December 4, the newlyweds sailed for China aboard John Bennet Forbes's sleek new *Paul Jones.* With them went Warren's younger sister Deborah. The voyage was calm and relatively brief—just 104 days. The *Paul Jones* was the first ship in the China trade to have its own ice house aboard, and according to its proud builder, the Delanos became "the first Americans ever to eat canvas-back ducks and mutton off the Cape of Good Hope." They had enough ice left over at Canton to present chunks of it along with crisp New England apples to Ned as gifts.

Catherine Delano had not wanted to go to China. It seemed impossibly remote. "I feel it is my duty to go," she told a friend, yet "it seems almost dangerous to undertake such a thing. . . . I hope I shall have the courage to the last." But she liked Macao when she got there. The harbor and its hillside covered by white houses with white shutters reminded her of Nahant, she said, and Arrowdale, her husband's big house on the fashionable Ridge was magnificent. "I am the happiest person living," she wrote home to Northampton shortly after she had settled in.

The Delanos stayed in China for three years. Warren continued to run Russell and Company, increasing both its profits and his own with each successive season. Their domestic life was more difficult. Arrowdale burned, taking all their possessions with it. They lived in the Canton factory after that. Some restrictions on barbarians had been lifted and they were even legally permitted to visit the old city of Canton itself. Popular feeling against the *Fan Kuei* still ran high after the Opium War, however, and Warren insisted Catherine stay within the compound. She acquiesced, though she admitted to her mother that it sometimes made her feel like a prisoner.

A baby girl was born in 1844 and named Susan. She died before her second birthday, in the spring of 1846; her body was eventually brought home to Fairhaven for burial. For a time after the infant's death, Warren feared for Catherine's sanity; she had been "queer" ever since the tragedy, he told Ned that summer, and he was afraid she might kill herself in her grief. She seems to have steeled herself after a second daughter, Louise, was born later that same year; the baby fell ill, recovered, but was always frail.

Toward the end of 1846 the Delanos returned to America to stay. Warren threw himself into business with what one friend called "his accustomed vigor and . . . great force," investing his new fortune in a host of likely ventures—New York waterfront property, railroads, copper mines in Tennessee and Maryland, land and anthracite coal in Pennsylvania, where a mining town was named Delano in his honor. He never entirely abandoned the China trade, building and owning several clippers, and when gold was discovered in California it provided him with a whole new market for his cargoes. His ship, the *Mint*, built with Robert Forbes and the Swedish engineer John Ericsson, was the first American paddle steamer on the Sacramento River.

Both Warren and Catherine had been raised in small New England villages in homes that were comfortable but not opulent. Their new and growing wealth now dictated a style of living altogether novel and enticing. They first bought themselves a five-story Manhattan town house at 39 Lafayette Square, one of nine unusual Greek Revival dwellings designed by Ithiel Town and Alexander Jackson Davis. These were called "Colonnade Row" because all nine were linked together by a common porch and a cornice supported by twenty-eight lofty Corinthian columns. The house itself was grand, inside and out, with marble mantelpieces, coffered plaster ceilings and massive doors of mahogany hung on silver-plated hinges.

So was the address. Their neighbors included the writer Washington Irving; John Jacob Astor, now nearing eighty-four but still the wealthiest man in America; and Warren's younger brother Franklin, who had married Mr. Astor's granddaughter Laura Astor just two years earlier. He too had been in the shipping business but had recently "retired" at thirty-one to live off his wife's immense trust fund. While Warren had had to buy his house, Franklin's had been free, a token of the old man's fondness for his granddaughter. William Backhouse Astor, Laura Delano's father, lived just across the street. He had also been generous to the young couple, giving them as a wedding present a handsome country seat at Barrytown, twenty miles north of Hyde Park. It was an old Dutch farm called "Steen Valetje" and adjoined his own sprawling estate, Rokeby.

Warren Delano wanted a country place, too. He now had a city house but as one of his children wrote, "he looked forward to a *home* in the country." Back in 1825, when he had been a boy of sixteen, his father had sailed with him up the Hudson to Albany to witness the impressive ceremonies that inaugurated the Erie Canal. But it was the scenery, not the celebration, that had remained with him, the gleaming span of the river and the imposing houses of the wealthy that could be glimpsed through the trees along its high banks. He had promised himself then that he would someday live in one of them himself.

For three summers the Delanos rented an enormous granite Greek Revival house at Danskammer Point, a rocky promontory that jutted far out from the river's west bank, six miles north of Newburgh. Three more children were born during these years: Deborah (known always as Dora) in 1847; Annie in 1849; and in 1850, Warren III (who died in infancy).

Meanwhile, Warren searched for a place of his own to buy. In 1851, he found it four miles downriver, a sixty-acre fruit farm with a modest brick and stucco house and handsome views of the river and the Hudson Highlands. He named it "Algonac."

More than half a century later, on June 15, 1905, Sara Delano Roosevelt received a cable from her son Franklin and his new bride, Eleanor, who had sailed for England on their honeymoon aboard the RMS *Oceanic*, eight days earlier. The telegram was datelined Liverpool, the newlyweds' landing place.

Its message consisted of a single word: "Algonac."

Mrs. Roosevelt knew instantly that all was well. Algonac was a code word within the family for good news; for everything that made one feel safe, tranquil, protected.

That had been her father's intention. To an extraordinary degree he sought to keep his growing family from unpleasantness of any kind. Algonac's setting high above the river provided a natural sanctuary, and the architect and landscape gardener whom he hired to improve his new house and grounds shared fully his love for at least the illusion of isolation.

Andrew Jackson Downing, just thirty-six, was already one of the best-known builders in America. A slim, dark-eyed romantic, steeped in the Gothic novels of Sir Walter Scott, he had written several hugely influential books on "rural architecture," urging an end to the Classic revival—which he derided as "the Greek temple disease"—in favor of a pseudo-Gothic style he thought better suited to American ideals and atmosphere.

When Warren Delano approached Downing, the architect was busily laying out the grounds for the U.S. Capitol, the White House, and the Smithsonian Institution in Washington at the personal invitation of President Fillmore. He found the time for Algonac, nonetheless; he was a local boy, the son of a Newburgh nurseryman, with a special fondness for designing fine houses in his native valley. When he planned a home on the river, he once wrote, he tried always to achieve that "accessible perfect seclusion" which is "one of the most captivating features in the life of the country gentleman whose lot is cast on the banks of the Hudson." It was his aim always that when one of his houses was completed and stood surrounded by suitable gardens at once beautiful and picturesque, "one might fancy himself one thousand miles from all the crowded and busy haunts of men."

Downing designed three kinds of rural homes: farmhouses for those who actually worked the soil; cottages meant for gentlemen of modest means (those whose households required no more than two domestics); and villas, or country houses, "requiring the care of at least three . . . servants."

Algonac was emphatically a villa.[5] It was to have a permanent staff of ten, with additional temporary help hired as needed. Downing

5. Downing's English-born collaborator, Calvert Vaux, did a lovely watercolor rendering of Algonac as it would look when redesigned; it is now on display in the Dutchess County Room of the FDR Library.

greatly enlarged the existing house, facing it south instead of east to take full advantage of its view of the broad busy stretch of the river known as Newburgh Bay. He added the big square tower and deep verandas, and designed a compatible gatehouse along with barns and greenhouses, and stables with arched windows and brick courtyards, across which Warren Delano's horses came and went with a pleasing clatter.

Because the Delanos wanted to be able to make their home at Algonac the year round, trees and shrubs suitable to each season were planted throughout the grounds, a rich profusion of evergreens for winter, selected maples, elms, beeches, locusts, oaks, and flowering species from China for the warmer months. At Downing's instruction, the shady green lawn that sloped down toward the river was mown "into a softness like velvet."[6]

Downing was a moralist as well as an architect and gardener, believing that it was to houses such as those he designed "that we should look for the happiest social and moral progress of our people." But he was not doctrinaire, and he did not believe in ostentation. "There is . . . something wonderfully captivating in the idea of a battlemented castle," he warned in his *The Architecture of Country Houses,* "even to an apparently modest man who thus shows to the world his unsuspected vein of personal ambition by trying to make a castle of his country house. But *unless there is something of the castle in the man* it is very likely, if it be a real castle, to dwarf him to the stature of a mouse."

Warren Delano was never dwarfed. His great energy made Algonac go. The big high-ceilinged rooms were crowded with evidence of his enthusiasms. The entrance hall was hung with armor and paintings he had brought back from China. Pieces of fine porcelain and curiously carved jade were displayed behind glass cabinet doors and along the mantel. Guests left their hats and shawls on a round Chinese marble-topped table at the foot of the sweeping central staircase. Even the Delanos' bedstead was Chinese and inlaid with mother-of-pearl.

6. Algonac was one of Downing's last projects. On July 28 of the following year he boarded the steamboat *Henry Clay* on his way to New York. He did not know that over the protests of her passengers her captain was racing a rival steamer, the *Armenia.* Off the New Jersey Palisades a boiler overheated and her canvas cover caught fire. Within moments the boat was in flames. Downing was last seen alive at the rail, urging calm and tossing deck chairs down to passengers floundering in the water. His body was not found until the next morning. Some sixty persons died, among them Nathaniel Hawthorne's sister Louisa and Mrs. Bartlett, the wife of James Roosevelt's old Poughkeepsie schoolmaster.

The family—Warren, Catherine, and their three children—moved to Algonac in 1852. With them came several servants and two unmarried relatives, Warren's sister Sarah and his brother Ned, now home from China and without much initiative of his own. Later that year, another boy was born and given his dead brother's name, Warren III.

And there, two years later, on September 21, 1854, Sara Delano was born. She was the seventh child (and the fifth to live); there would be four more before she reached her teens. She was named for her resident aunt. There had been talk of giving her a middle name, Philippa, in honor of her ancestor Philippe de la Noye, and her grandfather Delano was relieved when her parents thought better of it. "Plane Sarah," he wrote, "is decidedly better." The final "h" was dropped from her name, too, so that she and her aunt could be told apart in family correspondence, and when there was still confusion she became Sallie. (Obeisance to the founder of the American Delanos would be paid in 1857, when a second son was named Philippe.)

Algonac was a sunny, loving place in which to grow. Sara tottered after her older sisters and brother, watched them climb the apple trees she would soon climb herself, grew "more cunning every day," according to her eight-year-old sister Dora.

Her mother was warm and sympathetic, devoted to her children, tirelessly willing to read aloud to them from improving works. She was "very angelic," Sara once said, "almost too good, and never could deny us anything. And she never disciplined anything in her life!"

She worshipped her husband, just as her mother had worshipped her father, and was unwilling ever to seem to make the simplest decision without consulting him. And she taught her children to revere him, too.

Her husband was "a dominant character," one of his sons wrote, accustomed to planning the lives of everyone around him. The servants did his bidding and those who did not meet his standards were quickly replaced. And the other adults in the family also relied upon him—Ned, Aunt Sarah, and Nancy Church, his unmarried cousin known to all as "Nannie," who came to Algonac to stay in 1860.

Warren Delano's authority was loving but absolute. He rarely spanked his children. Even in her old age, Sara was proud that he had *never* spanked her. The children were expected to keep a respectful quiet when he was home. "We were not afraid of him," Sara remembered, "but if we were quarreling or doing something we shouldn't in the room in which he was writing, he would say 'What's that? Tut, Tut,' and we would immediately stop."

Bad news was never discussed in front of the children. Looking back, Sara marveled at the way her parents "carefully kept away . . . all traces of sadness or trouble or the news of anything alarming." Their lives were "tranquil," she said, "unmarked by adult emotions."

No one was to complain. When one of the children grumbled about the weather one rainy day, their father said, "Nonsense. All weather is good weather." And no one was ever to be alarmed, a lesson Sara learned early. At four she fell against the sharp corner of a cabinet in the drawing room, deeply cutting her scalp. Bleeding and frightened, she ran to her father. He washed the gash and then, fearing that there would be a scar if he waited for the doctor to ride out from Newburgh, he told her to be brave, gripped her between his knees to keep her from squirming, and sewed the wound shut himself, using a needle and fine thread. The pain was excruciating, but Sara never moved or cried out. It was wrong to worry others.

It sometimes seemed as if Algonac was its own peaceful country. Warren Delano was its chronicler as well as its creator. He and his wife took the time nearly every evening of their long lives together to note in near-obsessive detail everything that had happened that day within their realm. They left almost nothing out. The pages of the Algonac diaries, thousands of them, include the names of callers who came to the door; what everyone gave everyone else for Christmas; the symptoms and progress of every illness large or small suffered by family members or the servants; the butchering of every pig and the arrival of every kitten born in the barn. Precise temperatures were recorded, morning and night. There were meticulous lists of all that was bought or planted or picked; notes on the appearance of the first asparagus and katydid, interspersed with newspaper clippings that had provoked discussion over dinner. And there were other clippings, too, news stories of floods and fires and drownings, the death notices of far-off friends and relatives—reports of the dreadful things that happened to those unfortunate enough to live beyond Algonac's borders.

Nothing that affected a Delano was unimportant.

The Lymans had been a close, cohesive family, but the fierce sense of unity fostered by Warren Delano seems to have been a legacy of his father, Warren the First, whose clannishness approached xenophobia.

When Sara and the other grandchildren went to visit him at Fairhaven as they did nearly every summer, they took the Fall River Line steamer, carrying a picnic hamper so as not to have to eat restaurant food, and traveling on the night boat to avoid having to stay in a hotel. "It would never have occurred to our parents to take us to a hotel in this country," Sara once said.

A servant met them at the dock and drove them and their trunks and carpetbags to the family home, where their grandfather waited on the steps. The old captain was an imposing figure in a black frock coat, leaning on a gold-handled cane. His son Ned had once called him "impregnable." He was tall, massive, jut-jawed, and utterly bald except on public occasions when he insisted on wearing a tousled and unpersuasive black toupee to which no one in the family dared object. His wife, short and fat in a white lace cape and black silk dress, stood next to him. She was his second wife, sour and sensitive to slights and heartily disliked by all her husband's children, who never called her anything but "Mrs. Delano." The grandchildren called her Grandmama, anyway.

She greeted her guests, then gave orders to her butler that every piece of baggage was to be opened in the back yard and each article of clothing taken out, unfolded, and thoroughly shaken because, Sara remembered, "she never knew otherwise what might be brought into the house."

The homestead was enormous and filled with mementos of its owner's career at sea. A high stone wall enclosed it, and tall oaks shaded the lawn, "magnificent trees," said a local reporter, "which seem to belong to an ancient family." The Delano coat of arms hung above the door, and Sara and her brothers and sisters would come to think of Fairhaven as "a family shrine" all of their lives.

It stood on a shady village street along which other children lived. This was a great novelty for the young Delanos, raised in the country in the midst of their secluded estate, but they were not expected to make friends. Sometimes as a special treat they were allowed to walk unaccompanied to the post office, a block and a half away. "It was the most exciting thing we did," Sara recalled at eighty. "I still have a thrill when I go there."

On sunny afternoons they went bathing—not swimming—in the quiet water near their grandfather's wharf, changing into their bathing costumes in one of his warehouses, "just our family."

In later years, a friend asked Sara why she thought she and her brothers and sisters had been so scrupulously kept apart from other children. She wasn't sure. She guessed that "grandpapa was rather hoity toity . . . he had a large family and lived for himself and for them." No one else mattered very much; no one else was needed.

His son, Sara's father, felt that way, too. He had "the patriarchal spirit," Sara said, "he cared little for outsiders, but would do anything for his own family."

Her sister Dora once put it in more positive terms. The Delanos of Algonac were "a united family," she said. She had seen other families whose members seemed to care more for other people than for their own, but "as I look back we always cared most for each other."

In the late summer of 1857, Algonac was nearly destroyed by an intrusion from the outside world which even Warren Delano could not keep out. Panic hit Wall Street, sparked by the abrupt failure of the giant Ohio Life Insurance and Trust Company, but further fueled by the legacy of years of wild overspeculation in railroads and real estate. Market prices were halved overnight; specie payment was suspended for a time; thousands of businesses closed over the next three years; hundreds of thousands of men were thrown out of work.

One by one, Warren Delano's investments soured. Unlike James Roosevelt, who would ride out a similar crash sixteen years later, he had spread his fortune far too thin. For two anxious, sobering years he slid steadily toward financial ruin. He cut back spending, sold off his town house on Colonnade Row, even tried to sell Algonac but could find no one able to meet his price. All of this was kept in the privacy of the Delano bedroom or discussed with relations in the parlor after Sara and the other children were safely in bed. They knew only that their parents sometimes seemed tense.

In January 1860, Warren Delano was fifty and faced with bankruptcy after thirty years in business. He resolved at last to return to China, to Hong Kong this time, and re-enter the trade which had made him so rich so fast when he was young—tea and opium.[7]

7. The Roosevelt and Delano families were silent about the sources of Warren Delano's fortune. The word "opium" does not once appear in *Gracious Lady,* Rita Halle Kleeman's semi-official biography of Sara Delano Roosevelt.

During World War II, Westbrook Pegler wrote at least three columns excoriating FDR as a hypocrite for accusing others of living off ill-gotten gains when the activities of his own grandfather Delano—"an old buccaneer"—had allowed him and his wife to enjoy "to the utmost

Warren's sudden decision appalled Ned, who would have to fend for himself while Warren was away. "It seems the height of folly," he wrote to his brother John, "to abandon so much that is beautiful and attractive for the monotonous life on the 'ocean wave' to be followed

. . . luxury and riches derived from the degradation and wretchedness of the Chinese people. . . . Certainly with their special interest in the family history [the President and Mrs. Roosevelt] must have come upon the evidence long ago that they were living richly on the profits of a slave traffic as horrible and degrading as prostitution."

The White House did not respond, but Daniel W. Delano, the distant but admiring relative who wrote *Franklin Roosevelt and the Delano Influence,* was indignant. "This charge has no foundation in fact," he wrote. "[Warren] Delano's opium dealings were legitimate and no records exist of any transaction that, by the widest stretch of the imagination, could be construed as lacking in honesty." Mr. Delano's motives in dealing in opium during the Civil War through "legitimate trade channels" were patriotic: he was working to obtain "huge cargoes of the much-needed drug" for the care of the Union wounded at the front. To believe that Warren Delano's drug dealing was illegitimate, Daniel continued, "would be to dishonor the memory of President Abraham Lincoln and his integrity. . . . President Lincoln, knowing Mr. Delano personally and having a high regard and the utmost respect for him, appointed him his special agent in China. . . . While serving in this capacity, Mr. Delano brought back to America the first treaties we had with that country."

This defense has itself little foundation in fact:

1. It entirely ignores Warren Delano's participation in the opium business during his first sojourn in China (1833–1846), when his devotion to the Union was clearly irrelevant.

2. The importation of opium was never legal in Chinese eyes; its "trade channels" were never "legitimate."

3. While Warren Delano may have helped obtain the drug for the War Department during the Civil War—presumably at a profit—the major market for opium even then remained what it had always been: the craving of hundreds of thousands of Chinese addicts.

4. We do not know whether Lincoln knew Warren Delano, or even knew *of* him. Daniel Delano offers no evidence that he did. Nor is there any trace of a link between the two men among the voluminous Delano papers at the FDRL, and it seems unlikely that a family so history-conscious would have mislaid the proof if there had ever been any. Nor is there documentary evidence that Warren Delano was ever Mr. Lincoln's "special agent" in China. He was U.S. consul at Hong Kong for a time, a post that went automatically to the most senior American merchant on the island; he had held it for the same reason at Canton during the 1840s.

5. Finally, the first U.S. treaty with China was the Treaty of Wang Hsia, signed at the end of the Opium War in 1844 and carried home by the man who negotiated it, Caleb Cushing.

Precisely what Warren Delano's children thought privately of their father's career in the opium trade may never be known. But there may be one suggestive clue. Perhaps in part as expiation, his youngest son, Fred, volunteered to serve in 1927 as a member of a three-man League of Nations commission that investigated the drug traffic in Persia (now Iran); the poet Archibald MacLeish served as his assistant. The commission urged that a railroad be built to allow commodities other than opium to be hauled out of the mountains to the ocean. The Trans-Iranian railroad was the result, 865 miles of twisting, climbing track that linked the Persian Gulf to the Caspian Sea. Even before it was completed, the Shah Riza Pahlavi had ordered himself a private parlor car with fittings of rosewood, silver, and gold. The opium flow never even slowed.

There is no record anywhere of what FDR knew or suspected about his grandfather's career, but Eleanor Roosevelt was evidently privately bothered by Pegler's charges. When she visited Hong Kong in 1953 she talked them over with a knowledgeable British merchant and reluctantly concluded that "the Delanos and Forbeses, like everybody else, had to include a limited amount of opium in their cargoes to do any trading at all."

Sources: Frederic A. Delano (hereafter FAD) Papers, FDRL; *Time* magazine, January 3, 1938; Eleanor Roosevelt, *On My Own,* page 131.

by an enervating existence on a barren island on the coast of China—and that, too, under British rule!"

It must have deeply troubled Catherine, too, now pregnant for the ninth time. Somehow she who had always deferred to her husband would have to run Algonac without him. She would manage. When there was no man upon whom to lean she always found within herself the will to go on. Years later one of her sons would write that her example had taught him that "firmness of character is often disguised by gentleness, yielding upon [nonessentials] and only asserting itself when conditions demand a firm attitude."

Sara would learn that lesson as well. So, eventually, would her son, Franklin.

For her, however, then just five, her father's sudden departure was terrifying and inexplicable. Without warning, the center of her family's life, the big capable man whose love and attention mattered most to her, had simply vanished.

All she could know was that he had gone to a place unimaginably far away, and that no one could tell her when he would come back. For the rest of her long life she would suffer from an exaggerated fear of being apart from those she loved.

The family was separated for three years. Her mother did her best to keep the children cheerful. Uncle Ned and Aunt Sarah and Cousin Nannie all helped. But Catherine must often have been distracted by her loneliness (however skillfully disguised), by the noisy demands of little Philippe, and by those of the still-newer baby, Catherine or "Cassie," born that first spring.

School occupied some of Sara's time. She was now old enough to join the older children in the made-over breakfast room where Cousin Nannie taught them their lessons while they sat on straight-backed chairs to improve their posture. So did dancing lessons at a nearby estate. And when the Civil War began she joined the women of the house in sewing clothes for the soldiers at the front, and was very proud when she sent off her first muslin shirt with its sewn-in label, "This shirt was made by a seven-year-old girl."

But Sara grew solemn nonetheless, introspective, quiet. She was not to worry others. But there was at least one vivid clue to how she felt. When her father's letters arrived from China and after her mother had read them aloud to the family, Sara carefully soaked off the stamps and saved them. Each one offered fragile, brightly colored proof that he still existed somewhere, that he still cared.

When she was an elderly woman, Sara Delano Roosevelt spent much of her time at Springwood sitting in a tiny densely furnished room just off the big entrance hall. She called it her "snuggery," and from it, surrounded by numberless mementos of her crowded life, she could keep an eye on everyone who came and went from her house. Always near at hand was a small oval tintype of her father, made not long before he returned to China. In it Warren and five-year-old Sara are sitting on his lap. Sara's head rests on her father's shoulder; his long arm and big hand hold her close.

"There was no one like my father," Sara told a friend when she was in her late seventies. Neither her husband nor her son ever quite measured up to her memory of him. That conviction was perhaps inevitable, cemented before she reached the age of six by her father's enforced absence and her dreamy secret child's longing to be reunited with him.

By 1862, Warren Delano's fortunes had improved, not enough to permit him to come home, but enough for him to arrange passage on a clipper, the *Surprise*, and send for his family to join him at Hong Kong.

Again, Catherine did what he wished without complaint. "I suppose it was altogether terrifying to my . . . mother to give up her beautiful home and its peaceful security for perhaps the rest of her life," Sara said later, but if she felt anxiety or resentment she masked it from the children. Algonac was leased to Warren's old Canton friend, Abbot Low, the owner of the *Surprise*, and she resolutely marched her children aboard at New York on June 25.

The voyage would be a family adventure, the greatest of Sara's childhood. Seventy-five years later she liked to entertain her great-grandchildren at Hyde Park by singing the chanteys the sailors sang as they raised the sails:

> Down the river hauled a Yankee clipper,
> And it's blow, my bully boys, blow!
> She's a Yankee mate and a Yankee skipper,
> And it's blow, my bully boys, blow!

The seven Delano children ranged in age from Louise, now sixteen and chronically ill, down to Cassie, just two and known to the rest of the family as "the posthumous child" because she had been born while her father was away. Sara was seven. With them went Cousin Nannie and two nurses.

Catherine Delano kept a detailed journal of the trip. There is not a word of complaint in it; perilous sea voyages of 128 days were just another part of her job. Even the prospect of attack from a Confederate privateer did not faze her. The captain was alarmed when a steamer appeared on the horizon not long after they got under way, she noted, but she herself "was perfectly cool and not at all frightened." (It turned out to be a friendly British vessel.)[8]

The children and their nurses were constantly seasick. It snowed one day off Madagascar, and registered 126 degrees on deck in the China Sea. Sara developed chilblains; Cassie suffered from heat rash. It rained for days and Catherine had to keep the children entertained below deck while the ship pitched and plunged through heavy seas. There were other long stretches when the clipper rested motionless in the water, becalmed. The captain was often "very discouraged," Catherine noted; she herself never admitted that she was.

Some of the younger children were obstreperous. Warren clambered all over the ship; Cassie was "perpetual motion" whenever she could get free of her nurse's arms. Sara remained cautious and sober, did as she was told. Her name appears less often in her mother's diary than those of the other younger children.

She and Philippe were closest, and she often led him by the hand. Together they climbed into the sailmaker's loft almost every day, "decidedly a resource," their mother wrote, not knowing that the old sailor's chief attraction was his ability to jab needles deep into his callused thumb without apparent pain.

One morning Sara and Philippe were gazing drowsily into the water when the ship glided past a huge green sunfish, basking on the surface, twelve feet across from fin to fin. Sara shouted, and a sailor snatched up a harpoon and drove it into the great fish's back. It was

8. This incident provided another example of Franklin Roosevelt's imaginative version of his family history. The President must have known what really happened. He had seen three separate and nearly identical accounts of it—in his grandmother's log, found and copied for him by his Uncle Fred Delano; in the captain's log itself, obtained for the FDR Library, and in Rita Halle Kleeman's *Gracious Lady*.

Still, he was unable to resist making more of it than there was. On April 18, 1942, he wrote to Felix Frankfurter that the *Surprise* had "passed the Confederate commerce destroyer 'Alabama' in the night but [was] not seen."

Source: Max Freedman, *Roosevelt and Frankfurter*, page 656.

hauled on deck and hacked open: scores of little silver fish spilled onto the bloody deck.

The voyage was not all arduous or exotic. Captain Ranlett did his best to make his passengers feel at home. The adults read aloud the novels of James Fenimore Cooper and leafed through back numbers of the *Atlantic Monthly*. The children studied French, sang "Bonnie Doon," and danced the Virginia Reel around the new piano they were taking out to Macao.

On the Fourth of July, the captain fired thirteen guns in honor of the original states and let the older children touch off a fourteenth for luck. A special frosted cake appeared at tea, and, after dark, skyrockets were set off on deck. Then, while Captain Ranlett played the organ, passengers and crew joined in singing "national airs," the thin homey sound of "Yankee Doodle" drifting out across the black surface of the alien sea.

The Delano children got their first glimpse of Hong Kong on the morning of October 31, a blue-gray smudge on the horizon, where their mother had told them their father lived. Shortly after ten, standing at the rail, Sara saw a small vessel moving purposefully toward them. It was the family houseboat, a dozen Chinese sailors straining at the oars.

At the helm, urging his men on, sat her father.

Sara never forgot how he looked at that moment, "all dressed in white . . . very tall and good-looking, with his side-whiskers and moustache, coming very quickly up the side of the ship on a ladder the sailors had let down."

He sprang to the deck of the *Surprise* and lifted her into the air in his great arms.

Sara and the rest of the family were carried up to Rose Hill, the new home her father had readied for them, in what her mother called "a cavalcade of [sedan] chairs."

"I feel very oddly," Catherine wrote that evening, "to be again a *fanqui.*"

Rose Hill was a vast house of whitewashed stone with a big walled garden that crowned the summit of a hill. The large rooms with their lofty ceilings and tall shuttered windows were filled with dark English furniture and Chinese curios. Below the house, down a broad flight of stone steps cut into the rocky slope, was a grassy natural shelf on which the family gathered in the late afternoon to watch the older children and their friends play lawn tennis. Below them spread the blue harbor and beyond, the high green hills of the Chinese mainland.

If there had been no junks among the boats that darted back and forth across the water, Sara might have thought herself gazing down onto Newburgh Bay from Algonac.

Again, Warren Delano had managed to create for his family an exclusive world. As much as possible, China was simply ignored. Nannie taught the children their lessons just as she had at Algonac; their father even had a set of little straight-backed chairs built for them just like the ones back home. Sara studied French and practiced the piano, and she and Warren made crayon drawings of tall-masted ships and American flags, pasting them along with the words to hymns, including "Thank God for the Bible," onto the pages of an old account book on which the number of chests of opium entering and leaving Chinese ports had been carefully recorded.

There were Chinese servants everywhere, of course: cooks, gardeners, waiters, stable boys, watchmen, chair bearers. And on warm evenings a man sat behind a delicately painted screen in the dining room, gently pulling the rope that moved the big muslin punkah back and forth above the table to create the sticky semblance of a breeze.

But the servants were expressly forbidden to teach Sara or the other children a word of Chinese for fear they would learn unsuitable words. Every morning two tailors sat on the veranda talking together as they did the family mending. One day Sara asked a friend, the daughter of a missionary who had spoken Chinese from infancy, what they were saying.

"Oh, perfectly dreadful things!" the little girl said. "Let's play in the other room."

There were diversions—boat rides to Macao or up the Yangtze River, with fireworks on the Fourth of July, banquets for the Russell employees to mark the American holidays. But for Sara her father remained the greatest diversion of all. "Papa is going to shave in a little while," she reported at age nine to an aunt back home. "He is just beginning . . . Papa is at his bath!"

Hong Kong was a crown colony, and most of the foreign community was English, commercial rivals of Warren's firm and sympathetic to the Confederate cause. This last did not endear them to Warren, who once told Ned how he thought Robert E. Lee should be treated once the war ended; Lee should be hanged, he said, and his bones hung with those of Jefferson Davis "150 feet above Richmond and let them rattle to every North wind that sweeps down from New England during the next 100 years, or until New England forgets her duty to God and American liberty."

He was delighted when Sara and Warren decorated their pony cart with American flags and bunting and drove it proudly to the weekly horse races at the Happy Valley course. Russell and Company had its own section in the stands, and Warren took the races very seriously. So did eleven-year-old Warren III, and one bright afternoon at Happy Valley he astonished his parents by secretly volunteering to ride a notoriously skittish horse, "Reindeer," and winning his race against a field of veteran jockeys.

Comic relief was provided each week by the "Chinese Scramble," in which untrained grooms were coaxed into riding against one another for a handful of coins. Years later, Sara returned to Hong Kong and reported back to her father that the scramble had been a disappointment. "The Chinese rode very well," she said, "and everyone says it is not as amusing as it was in the old times when the boys did not how to ride and would often fall off. Now none are willing to ride unless they ride well."

Sara spent three years at Rose Hill, during which the last two Delano children were born, Frederic in 1863, and Laura the next year. In 1864, seven-year-old Philippe fell dangerously ill with a malady his frightened parents called "brain fever" and which left him subject to seizures for the rest of his life.

As soon as he had recovered enough to travel, the Delanos decided to send him, Sara, and Warren home. China was too dangerous for young children. Annie, now fifteen, was appointed to care for them on the journey; she put her hair up, Sara remembered, as a sign of her new status as a surrogate parent. William Forbes, a junior partner with Russell and company to whom Dora was now engaged, provided an escort.

The family was separated again. The children's journey home included an overland passage across Egypt. Aunt Sarah and Uncle Ned, now grown immensely fat, met them at the New York dock. Sara and Philippe were to remain in their charge for two years. Warren was sent off to boarding school. Most of Sara's time was spent in their stern but indulgent grandfather's home at Fairhaven. While she was there her step-grandmother died. She demanded to see the body. Her nurse tried to dissuade her but she was adamant. The memory of the darkened chamber and the sight of the old woman—"so long and thin and drawn and still"—haunted her all her life.

Few of her letters from this period survive. She must again have sometimes felt isolated and apart, but no hint of that intrudes in any of them. She was not to worry people. On April 10, 1865, she wrote to her father that the Civil War was over. "I am so very happy! All the bells of town are ringing and they are firing the cannon near the house!"

Wealthy again at the war's end, and unable to return to Algonac until the Lows' lease ran out in 1867, Warren now toyed with the notion of raising his family in even greater isolation than that afforded by his Hudson River aerie. "I have for some years past had in mind a plan of European residence and education," he told Ned. He would first sell Algonac, then "take the whole family down to the youngest to Europe [and] seek out a fine *old* country residence in a hilly country where woods abound and where saddle horses are good and cheap." An estate in the Pyrenees would do nicely. "I should want it to a *great* degree if not entirely isolated from our countrymen or others who would speak English habitually, and I should want to organize my household as to combine the real comforts and proper luxuries of life with a system of order and regularity of studies, duties, exercise and recreation." It was American snobs he said he wanted most to avoid, "pretentious, boasting," the sort of people "that will disgust the world with what they call Yankees." So great was his dislike of them that he felt "almost inclined to do what might be considered equally snobbish and in our retreat *sink* for the time being our name of Delano and write ourselves 'de la Noye.' "

Instead, he rented an opulent apartment in Paris, overlooking the Bois de Boulogne.

Sara spent most of the next four years abroad, the first in Paris, where she celebrated her twelfth birthday in September of 1866 and attended her sister Dora's wedding to Will Forbes at the American Church the following spring. There was a wedding breakfast afterwards to say goodbye to the bride and groom as they set off for China and Rose Hill, which would remain their home for all their married life.

That evening Sara fell ill. It turned out to be rheumatic fever, and she spent nearly five weeks in bed, often in great pain but outwardly always cheerful, and apologetic when she could not help crying out as the bedding was changed. This was to be the only prolonged illness in her long life, made more memorable by the reeking sulphur baths which the French doctor prescribed. The long tin tub was brought to the building each day lashed to the roof of a horse-drawn cab, then carried upstairs to the Delano apartment. There Sara was immersed in the hot solution, everything of gold or silver having first been removed from the room to prevent tarnish from the fumes.

The Paris Universal Exposition was held in the French capital that year and Sara was allowed to sit out on the balcony on warm days wrapped in blankets and watch as one by one Europe's leaders clattered past on their way to and from the grounds. The Empress Eugénie was an almost daily passerby. Czar Alexander II of Russia came, too, and so did Emperor Wilhelm I of Prussia, accompanied by his prime minister, Count Otto von Bismarck, in a splendid uniform.

The Delanos moved on to Dresden and rented a house for the winter, just as James and Rebecca Roosevelt had done the previous year. Mr. Delano had not entirely abandoned his scheme of "European residence and education," at least for his children. Sara attended a local school for young ladies where she studied German and music. Many of her classmates were Americans, daughters of other wealthy families spending the season on the Continent. Maggie Carey, Sara's best friend, was one of them. Her mother was an Astor, the sister of Aunt Laura Delano, with a summer house at Beacon, just across the Hudson from Algonac. Now they had a house in the same neighborhood, and after school the two girls could walk together to the Zwinger Teich to skate, whirling for hours to Strauss waltzes played by a band in overcoats on an island in the center of the frozen pond.

Most of the family went home at last to Algonac in the early summer of 1868, but Warren and Annie stayed at Hanover with Uncle Ned and Aunt Sarah, who would spend the next two years in Europe watching over their brother's offspring. Sara attended finishing school in the nearby village of Celle, living in the home of the burgomaster's daughter. Summers were spent with her aunt and uncle, the remainder of the first summer on an island in the North Sea, all of the second in the Harz Mountains. A continuing flood of fond and cheerful family letters helped fend off homesickness.

In May of 1869 a letter arrived from Algonac whose sadness could not be disguised: Louise, Sara's eldest sister, had died at twenty-three. It had not been entirely unexpected. She had been ill off and on all her life, and her father wrote that death had come as a blessed release from suffering. But it was shocking nonetheless, the first death among the

Delanos of Algonac. There would be five more in the next few years.

On Louise's birthday in 1870, Sara was given her watch as a precious souvenir. By then Sara, her brother and sister, and their aunt and uncle had all returned to Algonac. They sailed for home in June of that year aboard the *Westphalia,* the last steamship to leave a German port before the Franco-Prussian War began.

At first Sara simply enjoyed being part of the family routine again. "Life was very regular at Algonac," she remembered. "Friends visited us; no large parties, just relatives and friends who came one or two or three at a time." The family still attended Unitarian services in Newburgh nearly every Sunday, and when weather or illness prevented it, Mr. Delano presided over household prayers in the library. The Delanos had adopted the old Lyman custom of reading aloud, and Sara recalled that "most of the standard literature . . . came to me in that delightful easy way and we took turns reading while others worked." Sara rode in the summer, sleighed in the winter, played whist in the evenings. There were visits to Fairhaven and to Steen Valetje at Barrytown, the splendid turreted home of the Franklin Delanos.

Life at Algonac remained the same, but Sara had changed. She was a young woman now: tall, stately, still reserved, at home in French and German. The younger children were a little intimidated by her. Fred remembered that when they all gathered in the schoolroom each morning she blocked out their chatter with her "determined hands" over her ears, while making her grown-up way through a six-volume history of the world.

In January of 1873, her father wrote Warren, "Sallie attended her first *great* city party . . . and Mrs. Carey reports . . . that she looked very handsome (No doubt of it) and received much attention, which I hope will not turn the dear little pussy's head." Another "grand affair" was coming up, for which Sara "will be dressed by Aunt Laura and very handsomely, and we shall feel a good deal of interest in hearing how she gets through the *ordeal,* for such it is to a novice fresh from country life."

Sara bore up well, and each winter thereafter spent several weeks attending balls and cotillions and dinners with one or another of her New York friends—Maggie Carey, Bamie Roosevelt, or Nelly Blodgett, daughter of the varnish king with whom the James Roosevelts had sailed for England in 1865. Sara was a bridesmaid at Maggie Carey's wedding to an elegant diplomat, Alphonse de Steurs, the

Dutch chargé d'affaires. The groom, Sara told her parents, was "the nicest foreigner I have ever met," and the most handsome.

She and her sisters attracted many suitors, "an avalanche of young men," their father once wrote. One especially enthusiastic visitor fell in love with four of them in turn—Annie, Sallie, Kassie (who now insisted on spelling her nickname with a "K"), and Laura. He would have kept at it indefinitely, Sara thought, had the supply of sisters held up.

There was brisk competition among the girls. A Newburgh neighbor had three sons, the most courtly and handsome of whom Mr. Delano nicknamed "the Marquis of Salisbury." All four sisters vied for his attention. "The Marquis is very attentive," Annie wrote to her brother in triumph one spring day. "He took me for my first rowing lesson on Tuesday, and yesterday he came for Marianne (her maid) and me. We were out two hours. The shade under the bank was charming . . . Poor Sallie is off for Irvington."

"Pretty ears are all Dora *needs* to be perfect," Sara once wrote to Warren with sweet malice, and when Sara's glowing complexion was remarked upon (as it often was), Kassie liked to say loudly, "We do believe Sallie paints" just to annoy her.

Sara never got overtly angry, just more dignified, a fact which greatly amused her father: "Sallie had a presentiment that she would do something wicked," he wrote on a spring evening in 1876, "and accomplished the feat in the afternoon." One April Fool's Day, Kassie was sitting quietly in the music room when Sara glided past, after a walk in the garden, resplendent in a red silk dress and a hat with a long green feather. "I am going to take a bath and change my clothes," she announced. "Then I shall come down to practice and I hope I may have this room to myself."

Kassie waited until she was confident her sister's bath had begun, then rang the doorbell and sent a servant upstairs with the calling card of a handsome and much-admired West Point cadet, known in the family as "the Pilgrim father" because of his frequent references to his Massachusetts lineage. Sara dressed again as fast as she could and appeared in the doorway a few minutes later, a bit flushed but smiling welcome.

Her sister sat grinning on the sofa. "It is I who have the honor of calling on you, Miss Sallie April Fool," Kassie said, rising and bowing deeply.

Sara strode from the room without a word.

In matters of the heart as in everything else, Sara's father's word was law. He had begun to fail physically. In 1870 he lost the sight in his left eye when the retina became detached. Two years later, striding along the aisles of a New York dry goods store in search of winter supplies, he stepped blindly to the left and fell to the bottom of an elevator shaft. His hip was shattered. He was brought home in agony, remained in bed for thirteen weeks, managed to get around the place on crutches, seemed fully recovered, then fell again and, further weakened by lumbago, had to settle for a cane.

All three of the most important men in Sara's life became invalids. She would consider it her duty to care for each of them in turn.

On his sixty-eighth birthday in 1877, her father pronounced himself "Age 50 above the shoulders, *86* below." Still, his grip on Algonac and the lives of all who lived there never loosened. He sent some suitors away, prowled the parlor when his daughters entertained, decided whose invitations could be accepted and whose must be turned down.

Dora had to wait to marry until Will Forbes had earned his $100,000 competence as a Russell partner. Annie, too, fell in love with a Russell man, a heavyset earnest young clerk named Frederick Hitch. He came from a fine family but had entered the firm with no funds of his own. Warren insisted that there be no wedding until Hitch, too, had become a wealthy man. Fred and Annie may have discussed marriage as early as 1865, when she was only sixteen. If so, she loyally waited for him for nine years; they were not permitted to marry until the autumn of 1877.

Mr. Delano was no gentler with the private lives of his sons. When young Warren was sent away to school he was bombarded with his father's admonitions and advice. The boy was never to put on airs or dress better than his schoolmates; he must not borrow money or stay awake past ten, and when he slept had to keep the window open four to twelve inches. He should not be tempted to drink "or *taste* even, wine or beer. . . . Touch not tobacco." In fact he was to "*Do* nothing, *touch* nothing, *say* nothing, that you will not do, or touch, or say in the presence of your father, your dear mama, or your loving sisters. Do nothing in secret that you would not do in the light of the sun."

Later, when his son was studying engineering at the Lawrence Scientific School at Harvard, there were social directives as well: "I want you to call on Mr. [Henry Wadsworth] Longfellow [the venerable poet and an old friend of the Lymans]. First dress yourself properly for the occasion and . . . have as much conversation with him as Mr. Longfellow appears to have the time and inclination to bestow upon you and to help you to talk you may refer to your voyages to China and back."

Warren was a genial, handsome young man, bearded and athletic —"nothing short of a demi-god" to his younger brothers—as determined as his father but at least initially more playful. At Harvard he had applied his engineering skills to hoisting a big wooden top hat onto the head of the figure that surmounts the Soldiers Monument, sixty feet above the Cambridge Common; it took the combined forces of the police and fire departments two hours to knock it off again.[9]

He was graduated in 1874, hoping to travel west as a mining engineer. His father had other plans for him, however, and he went to work instead as superintendent of one of Warren Delano's enterprises, the Union Mining Company, digging coal and shale from deposits near Mount Savage, Maryland, and making firebrick from the local clay.

While still at Harvard he had met and fallen in love with Miss Jennie Walters of Baltimore. Her brother was a classmate of Warren's and had introduced them. She was both beautiful and unusually well educated, attending classes at Harvard and living with other young women in the home of Professor James Bradstreet Greenough, a

9. Mr. Delano's parental reactions were not always predictable. He was evidently amused by young Warren's Harvard prank, but four years later, when his youngest son, Fred, took part in something similar but on a much smaller scale, he was outraged. Fred was thirteen in 1878, a boarding student at the Adams Academy in Quincy, Massachusetts, when he and several other boys rigged up a miniature cannon so that it would go off loudly but harmlessly on the second floor of the school after everyone was in bed. Dr. William Everett, the headmaster, was "a highstrung, nervous man," Fred recalled many years later, and interrogated all sixty boys as to who had been responsible. "When it came my turn, he asked if I knew anything about the incident. I could not say that I did not. . . . I said that I did, but refused to tell who had a hand in it." All the other boys denied knowing anything at all. As a result, the headmaster put Fred on a train for home that afternoon. His father met him at the Newburgh depot "in great distress," and when they reached Algonac not even his mother was allowed to speak to him. "There was no suggestion of sympathy on anyone's part. I was treated as a disgraced boy." He was kept in his room. A servant brought him his meals. This went on for several weeks while his father and Dr. Everett carried on a long anguished correspondence about the boy's future. Finally, he was allowed to go back to school for his final examinations.

Years later, after Warren Delano died and Fred was cleaning out his father's desk, he found a packet of more than a dozen letters dealing with this incident and its aftermath and was astonished to discover that Dr. Everett had proposed only a short suspension; his father had urged expulsion. The boy was "forever disgraced," he had written. "He even went so far," Fred remembered, "as to say that if he were to rear another family, he was inclined to think he would seek a home among the Chinese, because in China the sons of the family could be depended on and honor their parents and live up to their standards."

Source: An unpublished autobiographical sketch by Fred Delano, kindly provided to me by his grandson, Frederic D. Grant, Jr.

champion of women's education who later helped found Radcliffe.

Her father forbade her to marry. William Thompson Walters was a curious man. He had organized the Atlantic Coast Railroad Line, made himself many times a millionaire, and compiled one of the finest collections of French art in America. Major works by Delacroix and Corot, Millet and Gérôme covered the walls of his big house on Mount Vernon Street; and he traveled to Europe to pick up more so often that two large galleries had eventually to be added to hold the overflow. A diminutive man—under five feet tall—and unshaven rather than bearded, he introduced the giant French percheron horse to America, and he had grown increasingly eccentric since his wife's death in 1862.

Jennie was his only daughter, and whenever she was at home she managed his cluttered household as best she could and acted as hostess to his infrequent guests. So far as he was concerned she was not to marry Warren Delano or anyone else; life without her would be intolerable. When she protested that she was truly in love, he ordered her not to see her admirer or even to write to him for two years. If she defied him he would cut her out of his will, bar her from his home.

She stuck to her resolve. Her father stopped speaking to her, and they lived together for months in what Mr. Delano called "that ill-regulated mansion," picking their way among "the groups and piles of works of art" in total silence. Warren's father was sympathetic to his plight. The ban on correspondence was "an unreasonable course," he said, but he warned against doing anything hasty. "Be patient, prudent," he warned, or there would be "a more or less violent severance of relations with Mr. Walters, for which neither Jennie nor you are prepared."

Tempers cooled, although Mr. Walters was never fully reconciled to the marriage, and in May of 1875 the young couple announced their engagement to their closest friends. They were married in July at a country church not far from the Walters' country residence. Warren's family almost did not attend, Mr. Walters having stubbornly refused to invite them until the last minute, and the wedding itself was understandably subdued. Only a handful of friends and neighbors came. The Delanos sat alone in their pew. After the ceremony, Mr. Delano noted, the bride and groom "left the church together, followed by W. T. Walters, my family, and the audience, [who] without congratulations or demonstrations of any kind, dispersed."

The marriage was solid and affectionate in spite of its strained beginning, and in 1877 the young Delanos had a son. He was christened Warren Delano IV in the presence of his proud grandfather at Algonac, just moments after Annie married Fred Hitch.

Sara Delano was known all her adult life for the strength of her will. But in its first real test her resolution proved weaker than Jennie Walters' had been.

Sara had her share of suitors but so far as we know seems to have taken only one seriously, Stanford White—whom she and everyone else then called "Stanny." His aunt, Mrs. Laura Fellows, lived nearby, and he and his older brother, Richard, had been frequent summer visitors at Algonac over the years. They took the Delano sisters sailing, accompanied them on picnics, played croquet with them across the smooth lawns. But in the summer of 1876 the old friendship between Stanford White and Sara may have flared into something more.

White was twenty-three that year and a whirlwind, tall and thin with bristling red hair, freckles, a flaring mustache, and bright intense eyes. He slammed doors, never walked when he could run, boomed out things like "Thunder and guns!" and "Gin and seltzer!" when he got excited (which was often), and liked to whistle airs from *Don Giovanni* when there was even a moment's lapse in the conversation. Music was just one of his enthusiasms; he also loved sporty clothes, fine horses, fishing, architecture, and art; he carried a sketchbook under his arm and had a way of pronouncing a Hudson Valley sunset "bully" and rushing outside to capture it on paper in rapid sure strokes of watercolor.

He evidently fascinated Sara. He appalled her father, who called him "the red-headed trial." To him Stanford White must have seemed everything unwanted in a son-in-law. He was noisy, intrusive, overconfident, unreliable, and without prospects. There was nothing wrong with his Massachusetts family. His grandfather had been a wealthy clipper merchant, but steamships had put him out of business, and young Stanny's father, Richard White, was a foppish aesthete reduced to piecing together a living writing reviews of music and literature. Worse, Stanny himself had hoped to be an artist, giving it up at seventeen only when the painter John La Farge told him that in art there was precious little prestige and still less money. For some five years now he had been one of several badly paid draftsmen in the office of the eminent Boston architect H. H. Richardson and—though Warren Delano may not have known of it—he had also begun a lifelong series of affairs with women who were, as a member of his family later said, "not of his class." He spoke loud and often of striking out soon on his own, but Sara's father had little reason to believe him. As a husband and provider, Stanford White seemed a terrible risk.

One afternoon at Algonac, Mr. Delano came upon Sara unwrapping a huge basket filled with flowers White had sent her. "I suppose those are from the red-headed trial," he said. "Remember that I don't care for that at all."

But Sara evidently did care for White; she may even have loved him. It is impossible to measure the depth of their feelings for one another in that reticent age now so long ago. No letters between them survive. But if she was in love, she must have been deeply torn. In her desire to please and placate her father, she was her mother's daughter; but she was her father's child in her determination to have what she wanted, and she did not want to give up Stanford White.

The decision was put off. Dora and her husband had been home on leave and were now about to make their way back to Hong Kong. Sara was evidently told to go with them and see what time and distance might do to her infatuation.

She was away for nine months. She visited England, where she first savored English country life at the home of Will and Dora's friends, watched the races at Ascot, and heard Prime Minister Gladstone and Lord Beaconsfield—Benjamin Disraeli—speak at Westminster. Half a century later, in 1929, she took several of her grandchildren to see George Arliss in the film *Disraeli.* When the gaunt, hawk-nosed actor appeared on the screen, she startled the children by hissing loudly, "But he *is* Beaconsfield!"

At Hong Kong a smitten British officer sent her a beautifully carved ivory fan. Dora intervened in her father's absence, reminding Sara that, like Stanford White, the young man was without sufficient means to be a proper suitor. Sara sent back the gift with a note gently suggesting that it might better be sent to the officer's sister.

At Paris on her way home the following spring, Sara took a long walk in the Bois de Boulogne and stopped to pick a bouquet of the daisies and buttercups that grew there beneath the ancient trees. It all reminded her overwhelmingly of Algonac. "Dear Papa," she wrote that night, "sometimes I feel I would do anything for a little talk with you."

Time had done its work. She had come around. Her father's approval still meant more to her than her own independence or the bright promises of Stanford White or any other man.

She returned home that summer. White paid a visit to Algonac on the evening of September 16. Whether he saw her then or only spoke to her father we do not know. But he never called again.

Seven years later, on February 7, 1884, White married Bessie Springs Smith of Smithtown, Long Island. He had by then become one of the most celebrated and prosperous architects in America. Writing in the Algonac diary that evening, Warren Delano tersely noted: "Mr. Stanford White is married today."[10]

Sara met James Roosevelt three years after she gave up Stanford White. She was twenty-six. Her devotion to her father had not diminished, and she now shared the running of the household with her mother, hiring servants—and firing them if they displeased her. But Dora and Annie were already married. So was Maggie Carey. If she did not marry now she might never get another chance. None of the objections her father made to White could fairly be made against Mr. James. He was in many ways very like her father—far closer to his age than hers, sober, wealthy, self-assured. We cannot know precisely what she felt for him then, but for someone so devoted to her father, so accustomed to doing what he wished without question, those similarities must have mattered. In a sense, Mr. James may have been the next best thing.

10. Dr. Nona Ferdon, in her pioneering unpublished thesis, *Franklin D. Roosevelt: A Psychological Interpretation of His Childhood and Youth* (page 145), reports that "in confidential conversation with a recognized Roosevelt scholar" living in Cambridge, Massachusetts, in 1970, she was told that "Stanford White was the only man Sara Roosevelt ever loved." The scholar was Frank Freidel, who was told the story by a member of the Delano family.

This was clearly an exaggeration, but Sara's friend and biographer, Rita Kleeman, provides some suggestive evidence that there was a thwarted romance. On page 83 of *Gracious Lady* she notes that Stanford White, "a magnificent looking boy with a shock of flaming red hair" was a frequent caller at Algonac. On the same page she tells of "one red-haired young man who was exceedingly attentive" to Sara. Her father disapproved of this suitor, calling him "the red-headed trial," and eventually had her send him away. Warren Delano's disapproval "ended it for Sallie," Kleeman continues, "for she still thought that her father knew more than any one else in the world and that whatever he said was right."

Since Sara herself must have been the source of both these stories, I suspect she may have told her friend rather more than she had meant to reveal about her relationship with White and that either then or later the two women agreed to separate the two anecdotes out of respect for the memory of Mr. James. It should also be remembered that Warren Delano was not wrong about White's reliability as a husband, as Sara and the world learned in 1906, when he was murdered in the presence of his former mistress by her deranged husband. Sara may well have told the story originally to Mrs. Kleeman more as an example of her father's perspicacity than as a romantic tale about herself.

Further evidence is provided by the Algonac diaries which record White's frequent visits to Algonac in the summer of 1876 and none at all after September 16, 1877. My account also helps explain Sara's otherwise curiously sudden decision to accompany Will and Dora Forbes back to China in 1876 and her very short stay at Rose Hill. After taking nearly six months to get there, she started home again in less than a month.

The wedding day was set for October 7, but preparations for it did not absorb the family's attention as fully as they might have that summer. Cousin Nannie Church, who had taught all the children their lessons, had died suddenly the previous January. Sara, her mother, and her sisters all still wore mourning dress when Mr. James first called at Algonac. Then, on August 11, just a few days after Sara's secret had been revealed to family and friends, and several days before news of the engagement appeared in the newspapers, Aunt Sarah died at Algonac of cancer. Mr. James accompanied the family to the burial services at Fairhaven and there was introduced to a host of Delano cousins. Mr. Delano was pleased, of course, that Roosevelt "devotes himself to Sallie who in her turn is absorbed in thought of him," but was privately gleeful when his worldly future son-in-law seemed "a little surprised at the luxury and comfort surrounding the old home."

Sara had greatly loved the aunt for whom she had been named, and out of respect for her memory the scale of her wedding was considerably reduced. Only 125 close friends and members of the family were invited.

It was a splendid afternoon, the wooded shores above the river brilliant with autumn. Guests arriving from New York were met at the Newburgh ferry landing and driven to Algonac in a fleet of Delano carriages, the *New York World* reported, and "many of the villagers and residents in the pretty country cottages on the roadside turned out to do honor" to them as they passed.

The Algonac gardeners had draped the parlor walls with ropes of ivy, and an alcove had been "metamorphosed into a floral chancel" with ferns and palms and wild flowers. Family and guests watched as Sara swept to her place beneath a canopy of blossoms, tall and regal in a gown of white brocade, her bridegroom's wedding gift of five strands of pearls around her neck.

Mr. James took his place beside her in a morning coat, his gray side-whiskers freshly combed. And there, shortly after three o'clock, they exchanged their vows.

Many years later, a guest remembered that several elderly women in the back of the room "were crying that such a lovely girl should marry an old man."

Sara dutifully became a Roosevelt when she married Mr. James. Even the manner of her journeying from her father's house to her husband's seemed designed to make that clear. She emerged from Algonac after the wedding beautiful in a black hat and going-away gown of mourning black and gray. Mr. James helped her into the Delano victoria waiting beneath the porte cochere, then took his seat beside her. Michael French, the Algonac coachman, snapped his whip and the couple spun off down the gravel path. It was precisely four-twenty by Warren Delano's pocket watch. Beyond the gate they turned north toward Hyde Park. At Milton, roughly halfway home, they drew up alongside Mr. James's liveried coachman and his T-cart, waiting under the trees. Mr. Delano's victoria returned empty to Algonac; his daughter rode on to Springwood in the Roosevelt carriage, Mr. James himself holding the reins.

The Roosevelts spent what Sara recalled as "a happy month" together at Hyde Park before embarking on an extended honeymoon in Europe. They rode together each morning, their horses' hooves scattering drifts of leaves, and on sunny afternoons Mr. James rowed them up and down the river. In the evenings they often dined with neighbors or with Mr. James's mother and his brother's family at Rosedale. Years later, John Roosevelt's daughter Ellen recalled that whenever she knew Aunt Sallie was coming to dinner she asked to be allowed to stay up long enough to catch a glimpse of her—"so tall and slim and lovely in a dress of dark velvet."

Sara had little to do that month except to be lovely and affectionate. The Algonac housekeeper had come up before the wedding to arrange the bride's things in the bureau drawers of her new bedroom. Springwood was still managed by Elespie, just as it had been in Rebecca Roosevelt's day; a cook and housemaid carried out her orders.

Reminders of Rebecca were everywhere, and Mr. James did not encourage change. He seems to have hoped to recreate as precisely as possible the life he had led with his first wife. If Sara ever resented this, she did not openly object. Like her father, her husband had the right to have his home precisely as he wished. He did not, for example, much enjoy the traditional Lyman and Delano custom of reading aloud; Sara gave it up and played bezique with him every evening they were alone together, just as Rebecca had.

Still, Sara remained a Delano. She and her father saw to that. During the first month of her marriage she went home twice to Algonac while James was in New York on business, and twice her parents visited Springwood. Throughout their married life the Roosevelts journeyed to Algonac or Fairhaven whenever the Delanos gathered: Christmas, Thanksgiving, birthdays, and anniversaries. If Mr. James disliked being so subsumed by his wife's family he left no record of it.

Both Roosevelts traveled to Algonac for several days toward the end of their first month together and there witnessed a giant Republican torchlight parade in honor of James A. Garfield and Chester A. Arthur, Mr. James's old acquaintance from Union College. The presidential contest was especially bitter that year, and it must have been a somewhat strained occasion. Mr. Delano had contributed heavily to Garfield's campaign. Mr. James liked Arthur well enough, but he had loyally backed the Democrats while again declining their nomination for Congress. We know that he watched with his in-laws as the Republicans paraded through Newburgh with their placards and flares, and can only assume he was embarrassed for his party when, from the darkness, local Democrats began pelting the marchers with eggs and bottles.

Mr. James voted his convictions at Hyde Park on Election Day, November 2. Garfield and the Republicans won, and Mr. Delano's pleasure in their triumph was tainted only by the stubborn Democracy of his own servants. "All my Irish employees from French down," he told his son, "not only voted the Irish ticket but show signs of such anger at the result that another week will probably see 3 or 4 of them discharged from service."

The Roosevelts sailed for Europe aboard the *Germanic* five days later. Uncle Ned, Laura, and Sara's parents all came to New York to say goodbye. "Sallie sad going off," her father noted, "but bears it bravely enough." They spent ten months abroad, together but rarely alone, visiting a multitude of friends and relatives then living on the Continent and in England. Will and Dora Forbes spent three weeks with them in Rome, and the Roosevelts stayed for a time with the Franklin Delanos at Geneva. The whole Algonac family met them in Paris, where Mr. Delano had hired an entire floor of the Hotel du Rhim for a month-long reunion; James patiently took Sara's mother and sisters to the Opera in the evenings and for long drives in the Boïs de Boulogne in the afternoons.

In Spain, James nursed Sara through a brief illness and bought her an old lace mantilla to cheer her up. "James too devoted to me," she wrote in her new diary. They gazed together into the glowing pit of Mount Vesuvius while "burning stones fell all around us," and visited Ghent, where Sara showed James the coat of arms of her remote ancestor, Jehan de Lannoye, carved in the cathedral wall. At Scheveningen in Holland they bought an old Dutch clock and ordered a massive sideboard built for the Springwood dining room, made up of carved medieval panels.

On Sunday morning, August 21, 1881, the Roosevelts attended services at York Cathedral in England. "I nearly fainted, giving James a little fright," Sara confided to her diary that night, "but the feeling passed over." She was nearly four months pregnant, and it was time to sail for home.

The Roosevelts settled back into life at Hyde Park to await the baby. The Delano seamstress came to alter Sara's dresses. Mr. James surprised her with a Chickering grand piano on their first anniversary. Friends came and went.

Sara's Uncle Ned had died suddenly of a heart attack aboard his yacht, while they were still abroad. She was again in mourning. Then her brother Philippe fell ill. He had grown into a tall, slender young man, gifted and outgoing but always delicate, and a special favorite of Sara's. His father had sent him to Cambridge, Massachusetts, to study the year before—he wrote with zest and wit and could recite long passages of prose or poetry after a single reading—but repeated seizures drove him home, and a male companion was hired to remain with him day and night. Then, on December 10, he suffered a massive seizure. Twenty-four more followed over the next forty-eight hours. He died on the morning of December 12.

The Roosevelts hurried to Algonac. Philippe was to be buried in the family plot at Fairhaven, but Sara was far enough along in her pregnancy, her father wrote, so that it was thought "not quite safe" for her to accompany the family. Mr. James stayed behind with her at Algonac and helped care for Warren Delano IV, her older brother's four-year-old-son. "It is a comfort to have Baby Warren," she wrote, "and though my thoughts are in Fairhaven, I have to be happy with the baby. We take him to drive and to the farm to see the animals and James tells him splendid stories."

CHAPTER 3

THE VERY NICE CHILD

"In thinking back to my earliest days," Franklin Roosevelt once wrote, "I am impressed by the peacefulness and regularity of things both in respect to places and people. Up to the age of seven . . . Hyde Park was the center of the world." He almost failed to occupy that world at all. His mother's pregnancy had gone smoothly enough, but the birth itself when it finally came nearly killed her and her son. Precisely what went wrong we do not know.

"Sallie's troubles began," Mr. James wrote, at seven-thirty on Sunday evening, January 29, 1882. The contractions continued all night, growing more frequent and intense. Mrs. Carrie Lee, a trained nurse, was at her side. The baby was long overdue; Mrs. Lee had been living at Springwood for two weeks, waiting for this moment. At dawn Mr. James sent for Dr. Edward H. Parker of Poughkeepsie. He arrived at nine-thirty, stamping the snow from his boots.

The morning inched past, and then the afternoon. Mr. James moved from window to window, staring out at the empty white landscape and trying not to hear Dr. Parker's exhortations to bear down or Sara's answering cries of pain. The baby would not come.

Toward evening the doctor came downstairs long enough to tell him that things looked grave. At seven, Sara's mother arrived from Algonac; her son-in-law, pale and grim, met her at the depot with the alarming news.

By eight o'clock, Sara lay exhausted. She had been in labor for more than twenty-four hours. In the hope that at least the mother might be saved, Dr. Parker administered chloroform. Mrs. Lee was sure the baby would be born dead. And when he finally slid into the world forty-five minutes later, it seemed she had been right. He was a big baby—"he weighed 10 lbs. without clothes," Mr. James noted later—but he was blue and eerily still. Dr. Parker lifted the infant from the bed, placed its small mouth to his own, and began to blow into its lungs. The baby took one shuddering breath, another, and then began a thin angry reassuring squall. Sara did not hear it.

When she had finally recovered consciousness and seemed out of danger, her weary husband scrawled a note to his sister-in-law, Ellen Roosevelt. Dr. Parker dropped it off at Rosedale on his way back to town: "I have only a moment to write you that Sallie has a bouncing boy; poor child, she has had a very hard time."

That hard time may have had much to do with the extraordinarily powerful bond between mother and son that was forged during the first moments of Franklin Roosevelt's life and remained intact until the last instant of hers. Sara spent a month in bed recovering from her ordeal, and later that spring suffered what seemed to be a relapse that greatly frightened Mr. James. Dr. Parker came to see her often, and it seems likely that he advised her it would be wisest not to have more children.

The fragility of life was evident all around her. She herself had nearly died. So had her baby. Uncle Ned and Philippe were gone. And on February 12, just twelve days after her son's birth, little Warren Delano IV, who had been such a comfort to her during her brother's funeral, died at Algonac of typhoid fever and was buried beneath one of the great trees that shaded the lawn.

Her baby's well-being became the central object of her life. She would not have a second chance.

She would never fully trust her boy to anyone else. "At the very outset he was plump, pink and nice," she recalled. "I used to love to bathe and dress him, although I took the responsibility of lifting and turning him rather seriously. I suppose all young mothers are a little fearful in the beginning of dropping their babies, and in that respect I was no different from the rest. Still, I felt . . . that every mother ought to learn to care for her own baby, whether she can afford to delegate the task to some one else or not."

That kind of delegation was the rule among mothers of Sara Roosevelt's class, and the love of a nurse was often a substitute for the maternal love then being lavished elsewhere. Young Winston Churchill, for example, eight years older than Franklin Roosevelt, was ignored at first by his beautiful but self-obsessed American mother and actively disliked by his erratic father. The devotion of his nurse, Mrs. Everest, meant nearly everything to him. "Mrs. Everest it was who looked after me and tended all my wants," he wrote. "It was to her I poured out my many troubles." Her photograph hung in his bedroom until he died.

Sara Delano Roosevelt would brook no such rival. Mr. James hired an English nurse for the baby a few days after he was born; she proved overly intrusive and was dismissed. Dora Forbes found another one two months later. She was Scottish, Sara wrote, "a good and experienced woman and very gentle," named Helen McRorie. She would stay for nine years and be called "Ellen" by the older Roosevelts and "Mamie" by her charge.[1]

The baby's own name had been a problem. By naming Rosy after himself twenty-eight years earlier, Mr. James had broken the Roosevelt tradition of calling eldest sons alternately James and Isaac. He now wished to return to it in honor of his late father. Sara thought Isaac a dreadful name. She wanted instead to name the baby Warren Delano Roosevelt after her own father, and Mr. James acquiesced.

The death of his first grandson had kept Mr. Delano from seeing his second for more than a month, but on March 9, the old man finally drove up to Hyde Park and declared himself delighted. The baby was "a beautiful little fellow—well and strong and well-behaved," he wrote, "with a good-shaped head of the Delano type." He was pleased, too, that Sara wished to name her son for him but suspected that the mourning parents of Warren IV might find a new Warren in the family hard to bear. He volunteered to see if he couldn't persuade his son to permit it nonetheless. If Warren's wife, Jennie, objected to

1. In 1934, while visiting friends in Canada, Sara Delano Roosevelt paid a call on Ellen McRorie, then long retired and living in a home for the elderly at Hamilton. "She is 89," Mrs. Roosevelt reported to her son in the White House, "and has a wonderful memory. We had a good talk and she remembered *everything* about you and even asked about nearly every member of the family. In sitting by her and talking I got accustomed to the change in her (very thin and frail), but the same fine old *deep set* eyes. She cannot *see* well, but tho' she only saw me dimly she knew my voice and felt that I had not changed much. [Mrs. Roosevelt was herself then eighty.] When you speak over the radio the nurse tells her and she listens to you and *lives* in the thought of you. She told little stories of how [Elespie] tried to spoil you and never could say no, but you were such a 'good boy' and only sometimes full of mischief. I told her that I felt that her fine sterling qualities had helped you always and given you a wonderful *start.*"

Source: Roosevelt Family Papers, FDRL.

hearing another child "called a name so dear," he wrote, all that he had to do was say so. But he and Jennie should keep in mind that "this is not a Warren Delano but for some time will be 'baby Roosevelt,' and he is really so fine a child, and so distinctively Delano in form, that he will not physically at least discredit the name." Sara had proposed an alternative—Franklin Delano, after her rich childless uncle—but, her father continued, "the idea that might be suggested that this name is given with some idea of possible advantage to come from the wealth of Uncle Frank deters."

Warren wired back that neither he nor Jennie could endure having another child in the family named Warren so soon after their great loss. "We are disappointed," Sara wrote, "and so is Papa, but of course there is nothing to say." And so, on March 20, in the small heated chapel not far from St. James, the baby was christened Franklin Delano Roosevelt. There were two godfathers, one from each side of the family: Will Forbes (too plagued by gout to attend) and Elliott Roosevelt, who, had he lived, would have eventually become the baby's father-in-law as well. Nelly Blodgett, Sara's girlhood friend, was the godmother.

Sara never entirely abandoned her wish to identify her son with her father. When the Roosevelts made their first pilgrimage to the Delano house in Fairhaven that summer, Franklin was put to bed in the same hand-carved hooded cradle in which his grandfather had slept seventy-three years before—but facing its foot so that he would not bump his head. Warren Delano eventually had seventeen grandchildren; none of the others was ever permitted to sleep in his old cradle.

Looking back on Franklin Roosevelt's boyhood, Sara's sister Dora once said that "he was brought up in a beautiful frame." Certainly everything about his infancy seemed calculated to make him feel loved. His mother constantly carried and held him. She fed him at her breast for nearly a year—and she fed him at the slightest sign of hunger. "Baby went with us" became a cheerful litany in the pages of her journal. His parents took him everywhere—for carriage rides along the Hyde Park roads, to visit friends in New York, to the homes of neighbors, to Fairhaven again for his first Thanksgiving, where every member of his mother's clan signed a tribute to him as "one member of the Delano family" who "although the last to arrive in the world would . . . not prove one of the least in merit."

He returned joy for joy. He "crows and laughs all the time," his mother wrote, and his grandfather agreed. Franklin was "a very nice child," he assured his brother for whom the baby had been named," . . . that is, always bright and happy. Not crying, worrying, infractious."

Sara recorded nearly every detail of his development, and she noted as well the tributes paid to him by her visitors. Mrs. Theodore Roosevelt, Sr., spent a week at Hyde Park during which, Sara wrote, "we admired Baby" constantly; and in a letter to her son Elliott, this mother of one future President left a vivid picture of the warmth and security in which a second would be brought up: "While the nurse took her breakfast I held your dear little godson and enjoyed him *intensely*. He is such a fair, sweet, cunning little *bright* five-months-old darling baby. Mr. Roosevelt is *very proud* of him and Sallie devoted and looks so very lovely with him, like a Murillo Madonna and infant. The place is looking very lovely. My windows are open as I write and I see the lovely view up the river. . . . Sallie and I have seen each other . . . several times this morning, tho' we do not breakfast together until 11 A.M.—Enticing little trays of tea, coffee or cocoa and toast and cheese to our rooms at Eight O'Clock and you do as you please until 11. . . . Mr. R. rows and sails and attends to his place . . . James is devoted to the soft innocent baby."

Uncle Franklin and Aunt Laura visited, too—"a great event," Sara noted—and "gave baby a Russian silver gilt cup, saucer and spoons."

At five months, Franklin was put into short skirts, "as he liked to kick and feel free to move about." He had cut two teeth by the end of his first summer, but his mother worried that he was "rather too thin, not as fat as a baby ought to be"; he would, in fact, remain remarkably slender until middle age. By November he was trying "to imitate Budgy [Mr. James's white spitz] and the cats and manages to say a semblance of papa and mama." That same autumn he was taken to his first adult party on a nearby estate. "Baby wanted to dance," Sara wrote. "I could hardly hold him." In May of 1883, Franklin walked unaided for the first time and "was quite proud of his accomplishment."

Franklin had the bad luck to have been born at the height of the fever of sentimentality kindled in American mothers' hearts by Frances Hodgson Burnett's novel *Little Lord Fauntleroy*. In emulation of its precious hero, Franklin's mother kept him in dresses and long curls until he was nearly six. Then she dressed him in Scottish kilts and highland caps, and finally—reluctantly—permitted him to wear miniature sailor suits. Through all of this, he yearned to put on pants and shirts as did other boys, and to have his hair cut short. His mother resisted as long as she could. "I still think to this day that he looked very sweet," she wrote in 1933, "his little blond curls bobbing . . . as he ran as fast as he could whenever he thought I had designs on combing them." When they were finally shorn—"Oh, long before they should have been"—she wept and gathered up the remnants from the floor for safekeeping.

Constantly in the company of his adoring, watchful mother, his father, and of Mamie and Elespie, Franklin was at first painfully shy with anyone else, even with the friendly servants who worked at Springwood. "When I made the rounds of the house each morning he would go with me," his mother recalled, "trotting along and chatting over his small affairs. But when he reached the kitchen he was always stricken dumb. He could hardly be prevailed upon to step over the threshold, so shy was he, and he hid safely behind me when he did, hanging his head and rolling his eyes at the fat, good-natured French cook who tried to coax him out with little broken English endearments. He would not speak a word, though, and always seemed relieved when he left that strange and for some reason awe-inspiring territory."

The briefest separation from his mother was frightening. In December of 1883, not yet two, Franklin was left for a day at Algonac with Mamie and his grandparents while his parents attended the New York wedding of his godfather, Elliott Roosevelt, and the beautiful Anna Hall. Franklin searched frantically for his mother, unable to believe she could have left him behind. He finally found her jacket hanging in the nursery and buried his face in it, Sara was told, crying, "Mama! Mama!"

Three years later, when Franklin was four, the elder Roosevelts took a rare trip without him, traveling to Mexico in Mr. James's private railroad car. Mexico was thought unhealthy for a small child, and Franklin was left behind again at Algonac. His parents were gone three months. Franklin did not overtly betray his apprehension; he may already have learned that unpleasant emotions were best kept to himself, that "a very nice child," in his grandfather's words, was "always bright and happy." But he spent hours alone playing with a hobby horse he named "Mexico," and when his mother and father returned at last and his mother got into the wagon at the Newburgh ferry landing, he climbed up beside her, stood on the seat, and "without crying or laughing or speaking," held on to her "like a little soldier" for all of the two-mile ride to Algonac. Franklin was "perfectly blissful at seeing us again," Sara wrote. "He showed great feeling."

It seems curious that FDR remembered Hyde Park as "the center of the world" during his first seven years, for even then the restive Roosevelts rarely stayed at home for long. Mr. James had never let Rosy's upbringing interfere with his own love of almost ceaseless travel; Franklin would not alter it either. In 1884, for example, when the boy was only two, the three Roosevelts spent just four months out of twelve at Springwood, traveling often to New York City and living for most of the year in England.

From the time he was three, Franklin spent almost every summer on Campobello, a slender rockbound island, ten miles long, in Canadian waters just off the coast of Maine, on which his father had built a big comfortable seaside cottage. Mr. James had first been attracted to it by the splendid sailing offered by Passamaquoddy Bay; but old friends were also buying land and building summer houses there—Mr. and Mrs. James Lawrence of Groton, Mr. and Mrs. Russell Sturgis of Boston, Mr. and Mrs. Alfred Pell of Highland Falls, New York. And there was a plentiful supply of the sons and daughters of local fishermen willing to help make life agreeable for the summer people. Franklin's earliest memories of Campobello were fearful. Wild cattle were allowed to roam the island unmolested, and FDR remembered running from them in terror. But he soon learned "they were perfectly harmless," and life on Campobello, with its walks and picnics and yachting excursions, became a part of the serene cycle of the Roosevelts' year.

It was not so much Hyde Park, then, as what it stood for that stayed with FDR. Just as Algonac symbolized for Sara Delano Roosevelt the tranquillity and comfort provided by her big loving family, so Springwood came to stand in her son's memory for the love and approval showered upon him by his parents there, and wherever else they took him.

On Easter morning in 1885, Franklin and his parents were on their way home from England aboard the steamship *Germania,* two days out from Liverpool. Franklin was three. The ship had been tossed by heavy seas all night, and Mr. James had just come back to the cabin from breakfast with the captain to say that Sara should not take Franklin on deck. The ocean was too rough. At that moment the ship seemed to plunge beneath the sea. Everything went dark and the Roosevelts could hear the steerage passengers shouting in terror.

"We seem to be going down," Mr. James said.

"It does look like it," Sara remembered answering. James went above to see what had happened. Franklin and Sara watched from their berths as water began to trickle in from underneath the cabin door. After what seemed a very long time, Mr. James returned. The ship was foundering. A great wave had broken over her, washing one sailor overboard, ripping five lifeboats from their davits, tearing a hole in the bulkhead of the ladies reading room directly above their cabin. One woman had been lifted off her feet by the rushing water and hurled against the opposite wall; her clothing caught on a coat hook and she hung there, shrieking, until other passengers cut her down. All the pumps were going. The stewards were bailing with pails, but the captain could not be found.

There was a steady rush of water above their heads now, and the trickle beneath the door had become a deepening pool, sloshing back and forth with every new wave that slammed into the helpless ship.

"I never get frightened," Sara said years later, "and I was not then." But as the water edged up the cabin wall and wet the hem of her fur coat, she took the heavy garment down from its hook and wrapped it around her son.

"Poor little boy," she said to her husband. "If he must go down, he's going down warm."

A bright toy floated on the surface of the rising water. "Mama! Mama!" Franklin shouted. "Save my jumping jack!" Sara leaned out from her berth to save him, too.

The *Germania* did not sink. The captain—who had been knocked senseless and wedged beneath a sofa in the chart room by the first wave—resumed command. The water never reached the boilers, and the battered ship was finally able to make her way back to Liverpool.

But the assurance offered by his father's imperturbability, his mother's warm coat, and the sight of his mother reaching down to rescue his bobbing toy were among Franklin Roosevelt's earliest and most comforting memories.

So far as we know, only one other untoward event marred the placid surface of Franklin Roosevelt's first seven years. Unlike the close call aboard the *Germania,* it seems permanently to have affected him.

President Roosevelt was about to begin his biweekly press conference on December 14, 1933. As reporters crowded into the Oval Room to take their places before his big cluttered desk, he lit a cigarette. A cascade of glowing ashes fell onto his suit and startled him. Slapping at the sparks, he tried to joke away his obvious alarm. "Every President is used to playing with fire," he said. "You won't burn up. When I was two years old I was discovered on the floor playing with matches. Perhaps that was a prophecy." The conference went forward.

But FDR was in fact deeply afraid of fire. Since almost nothing else seemed to frighten him—he had not even ducked when a madman fired several pistol shots at him in Miami in 1933—those closest to him often wondered about it. Most probably came to agree with his eldest son, James, who believed that his father had "developed a dread of fire" after he had been afflicted with infantile paralysis in middle age. FDR's immobility may have intensified his fear, but the dread itself predated his crippling by many years. Its roots are unknown, of course, but it is interesting that when the President saw sparks smoldering on his clothing his mind rushed back to his second year. He may have played with matches then and been caught at it, as he said, but there is vivid evidence that year of a far more shattering encounter with fire.

On Saturday, July 19, 1884, Fred and Annie Hitch returned to America from China. Sara, Mamie, and Franklin, then two, hurried down to Algonac to greet them. Only one Delano child still lived at home: Kassie had left to marry Charles A. Robbins the spring after FDR was born, and twenty-year-old Fred, a Harvard junior, was off in the Pennsylvania coalfields learning the anthracite business as his father had directed.

Laura Delano at nineteen was perhaps the loveliest of the Delano sisters; even Sara liked to wash and brush her long silken hair. And she adored her nephew; there is a photograph made at Algonac earlier that summer in which she lies on the grass in a flowered dress, her body curved protectively around Franklin, beaming at him as he peers at the camera.

"She is a good deal of a little witch," her father had written when Laura was a small girl, "and don't like to study. . . . She is wilful, daring and persistent but loving and affectionate—*and she knows it*, beautiful." He alternately indulged and tried to discipline her, and his fondness sometimes took curious forms. When her dog died, he took it to a Newburgh taxidermist who promised to "mount his skin and give back to Laura the portrait of 'Tip' in a sitting posture."

She looked especially lovely the evening the Hitches came home, Sara remembered, standing in the Algonac doorway as their carriage drew up, wearing a summer dress of white muslin with a deep pink sash. A homecoming dinner followed—the Hitches had returned to stay—and the next day the whole family was to attend church together.

All were getting dressed at nine o'clock the following morning when they heard an explosion followed by a scream. Both came from Laura's room on the third floor of the tower. She had been wearing a thin wrapper as she heated her curling irons over an alcohol lamp; somehow, the lamp was knocked over. Burning alcohol sprayed her robe. Her door banged open, her horrified father wrote later, and "Laura flashed down the stairway a cloud of fiery flame." Fred Hitch happened to be standing in the hall and tried to stop her, but she brushed past him, screaming in her panic. He snatched up a woolen rug and ran after her, out from under the porte cochere and onto the green oval of lawn around which the driveway coiled. There, Sara wrote, he "caught her . . . and managed to lay her down" and smother the flames. Sara herself raced behind with another rug, "but I wonder Fred could catch her for she *flew.*" "The household followed," Mr. Delano recalled, "and with oil and cotton and blankets sought to alleviate the agony of the sufferer who was at last got into the house and upon her bed."

The doctor was called and came within half an hour. A nurse was summoned from New York City. Laura was given morphine. But nothing could be done. Only her lovely face and neck were untouched by the flames. She did her best to mask her pain. Like Sara, she had been taught not to worry others. Laura was "brave and patient [and] courageous," Mr. Delano wrote, "reassuring everyone"—especially her father—that 'I am young and strong and shall get all over this.' " She was concerned that news of the accident not upset her brother Warren's wife, Jennie, now pregnant again. She fell into a coma late in the day and died early the next morning.

Five of Warren and Catherine Delano's children were now dead. "All is mystery," their grieving father wrote.

We do not know how much of all this Franklin knew or consciously remembered; he is not recorded as having ever mentioned Laura Delano's terrible death. Mamie presumably sheltered him from all that she could. But he may have seen his aunt's fiery plunge down the stairs, and he could not have missed hearing her screams. The hours that followed were his first experience of sorrow.[2]

Franklin Roosevelt was sixteen months old in the spring of 1883 when he was taken to a Poughkeepsie portrait studio to be photographed with his father for the first time. The slender little boy, wearing curls that do not yet quite reach the lace collar of his dress, perches a little nervously on Mr. James's shoulder; one small fist holds a tired rose; the other rests on his father's head, ready to grasp his hair. On the little finger of the big broad hand that steadies him is a bloodstone ring. FDR would later wear that ring on his own left hand every day of his adult life. And when the air around Hyde Park first turned crisp and cold in the fall, he liked to dress himself in a brown tweed suit before setting out in his automobile to survey the woods and fields that

2. Roosevelt's early fear of fire got plenty of firsthand reinforcement. There were at least three small but frightening fires at Springwood during his youth. On January 16, 1899, he and the farm superintendent had to tear up part of the floor in the parlor to drown a blaze in the cellar beams, and just a few weeks later at Groton School, he helped man a bucket brigade that tried without success to save the burning stable. It was "a horrible scene," he told his parents, "the poor horses . . . lying under the debris with their hide entirely burned off and fearfully charred," all because "*there was no back door.*" At Harvard in 1901 he watched the two top floors of Trinity Hall burn out of control, and later campaigned hard for dormitory fire escapes as editor of the *Crimson.* When he and his mother enlarged Springwood in 1915 he insisted that the new walls be fireproof. (Sixty-seven years later, in 1982, that decision was credited with having helped confine still another potentially devastating blaze largely to the attic.) Even so, as late as 1944 FDR was still so worried as to how he might get out of his bedroom in case of fire that Eleanor Roosevelt commissioned a young serviceman with architectural training to draw up plans for a curious chute arrangement down which the President could slide unaided; the record is unclear as to whether it was ever built, but the drawings for it are filed with the Secret Service Papers at the FDRL.

Another fire razed Algonac itself in 1916. It was rebuilt by the Delano family (minus its handsome tower), then sold after Frederic Delano's death in 1946, and its lands divided up among developers. The reconstructed house remains on Susan Drive in the Newburgh suburb of Balmville, and the driveway still twists around the grassy oval on which Laura fell in flames, and passes beneath the porte cochere from which Sara and Mr. James drove away to start their lives together. But the once-splendid views of the river are interrupted by the foliage and tract houses that have grown up over the intervening years, and the house and its big old trees now seem oversized for the site on which they stand. When the author paid an unannounced visit one summer afternoon in 1983, an elderly maid with a European accent answered the door. She was unaware of any of the history that had happened in the house.

had once belonged to his father. That suit, too, had belonged to Mr. James, made for him in Scotland half a century before, and later altered to fit his son.[3]

These were only the outward signs of FDR's affectionate memories of his father, and perhaps of a desire to emulate him as well. Franklin and his father had eighteen years together, but because Mr. James died before his son was fully grown, and because he was so much older than his wife, he has often been portrayed as a sort of fond but distant grandfather, preoccupied and frail. That impression is only partly accurate; Mr. James was never distant, and for the first half of their lives together, at least, he and Franklin were vigorous and almost inseparable companions.

"Franklin never knew what it meant to have the kind of respect for his father that is composed of equal parts of awe and fear," Sara Delano Roosevelt wrote, perhaps remembering the intimidating presence of her own father. "The regard in which he held him, amounting to worship, grew out of a companionship that was based on his ability to see things eye to eye on mutual tastes, and his father's never-failing understanding of the little problems that seem so grave to the child who is faced with them. His father never laughed at him. With him, yes—often. They were such a gay pair when they went off on long rides together. But Franklin's tragedies became his father's woes, and I've often marveled at his success at stifling a very natural merriment over some of our son's minor disasters."

Mr. James was fifty-four when his second son was born, thickening at the waist and subject to various ills; still, he did his best to act far younger, and seems to have spent even more time with Franklin than he had with Rosy. Even Franklin's nickname for his father—"Popsy" —implied more intimacy than awe. Mr. James passed on intact his own fondness for the outdoors. He loved trees, for example, knew their

3. To FDR, his father's old suit evidently represented frugality as well as filial loyalty. In 1938 he wrote to a Scottish friend about it: "In 1878 my father had a tweed suit made in Edinburgh—that was four years before I was born. He wore the suit constantly until his death in 1900. I inherited it and wore it steadily until 1926, when I passed it on to my boy James. He still has it and wears it in the winter time when he is in the country. A good example of Scotch craftsmanship aided and abetted by Dutch thrift."

At FDR's own death, the ring he and his father had both worn was willed to his son James, who wears it on the little finger of his right hand.

Sources: FDR to Arthur Murray in Elliott Roosevelt, ed., *FDR: His Personal Letters, 1928–1945*, II, pages 781–782; interview with James Roosevelt.

varieties, would allow none to be cut unless they were dead or diseased, and he made sure his son felt the same way.

He took the boy sledding before he was two, taught him to ride and row and skate and man an iceboat and, when the time came, to shoot as well. Sometimes he overdid it. Tobogganing with Franklin in 1888, "dear James strained his knee," his wife noted, "and I had to call the men to drag him up the hill."

Despite that uncharacteristically careless moment, Mr. James was good at all these things, and he sought lovingly to impart his easy mastery to his son. By the summer of 1888 he had taught Franklin at least the rudiments of sailing his big yacht; there is a photograph made off Campobello that summer in which the little boy tensely holds the wheel in a stiff breeze; the wheel is nearly as tall as he, but at six Franklin Roosevelt is already at least momentarily in command.

Horses were still at the center of Springwood life. One of Franklin's most vivid early memories was of watching workmen build his father's splendid new stables in 1886; its tower stood three stories above his mother's rose garden and was topped with a copper weather vane boldly marked with James Roosevelt's initials.

At four, Franklin was riding out each morning with his father, just as Rosy had thirty years before, while Mr. James directed the work on the place. His men tipped their hats to their employer, and to Master Franklin riding next to him on his fat Welsh pony, "Debby." By the time he was eight, wearing tall boots and a sailor suit, he rode well enough to accompany his father on a twenty-mile ride to Algonac without tiring.

To a small boy, Mr. James's daring must have seemed heroic. The Great Blizzard of 1888 buried Springwood in snow. The Albany Road was obliterated and food in the big house ran low. Franklin never forgot watching through the front window with his worried mother as his father mounted "Doolittle," his favorite horse and the last of his trotters, and set out into the white silence in search of supplies. The big horse sank to its shoulders, but Mr. James urged him slowly forward up the long invisible driveway, across the road, as far as the gate to the Roosevelt farm. There he was met by his farmer, John Irving, who had shoveled his way along the top of the stone wall, and handed over a sack containing milk, eggs, cheese, and a pair of chickens, enough to get his employers through until his men could clear the roads.

In the autumn, the Dutchess County Hunt often met at Hyde Park.

Mr. James was an organizer of the club, and hunt breakfasts were sometimes served at Springwood. Women and children in carriages waited along the road to watch as the long line of riders rushed past them in the distance, coursing across the fields and jumping the fences behind their yelping hounds. Young Franklin ached to ride alongside his father and one year disobeyed his parents and took after the hunt, arriving at the kill with his pony in a lather. His father ordered him home, less because he had been disobedient than because he had overtired his mount. There were always rules to be observed, even when amusing oneself.

Mr. James's air of benevolent but unquestioned authority extended well beyond Springwood. In fact, everywhere Franklin was taken throughout his boyhood, his father seemed set apart, in charge: to the village of Hyde Park, where Mr. James had been supervisor and now served as head of the school board; to St. James Church, where he was senior vestryman and collected the offering each Sunday; to the Hudson River State Hospital, just down the road on the site of his old home, Mount Hope, where he acted as unpaid manager. Here his son saw him genuinely rattled for almost the only time in his dignified life. While inspecting the wards, Mr. James had come upon a harmless but persistent old woman who believed herself Queen Victoria; she chased him down the corridor under the delusion that he was Prince Albert, come to take her home to Windsor.

When Franklin traveled with his father beyond New York—as he and his mother often did—they rode in Mr. James's private car, the *Monon*, with its separate bed and sitting rooms fitted out in brass and mahogany, and were waited upon by a deferential black cook-porter named William Yapp. Even the tracks of the Delaware & Hudson and the Louisville, Albany & Chicago over which the *Monon* clicked belonged to Mr. James, in a manner of speaking; he was a director of both lines and would eventually become their president. The Roosevelts traveled to Canada several times, stopping to inspect the handsome steamboats the Delaware & Hudson indirectly operated on Lakes George and Champlain, and they went west to the up-and-coming port of Superior, Wisconsin, where Mr. James had invested heavily in a business block and row of town houses called "Roosevelt Terrace," in the apparent hope that Superior was about to eclipse Chicago.

At age seven, in August of 1889, Franklin was again taken to England. "The dear little man" was running a temperature when the

Adriatic set sail, his mother noted, and did not feel at all well; but Dr. Parker had assured her that the boy had simply picked up a slight fever while swimming in the Hudson; a sea voyage would be just the thing to "break it up." Two days out, the ship's doctor diagnosed typhoid fever. The special care and treatment Franklin then received (and which both he and his parents evidently assumed was his due) must have heightened his sense of his family's importance, and of his own. The ship's captain gave him his own "large airy room on deck"; his mother never left it during the crossing except to change her clothes, and once to attend church services, praying for "darling Franklin" while "his dear papa and Ellen" watched the patient. At Queenstown, the captain wired ahead to have his own cousin, a Dr. Gemmell, and a trained nurse meet the boat at Liverpool. Sir Thomas Ismay, founder of the *White Star* line and an old friend of Mr. James, dispatched a special tender to ferry Franklin ashore. A carriage took the pale little boy on his mattress to the doctor's own home, where he lived for several weeks, receiving round-the-clock attention. The captain of the *Adriatic* came to call; Sir Thomas sent fresh flowers daily; his partner sent fresh milk.

Franklin got better slowly. His temperature fell. He graduated from "cold boiled milk" to "chicken tea" to bread and milk laced with a little port (which he told his mother was deliciously "fruitful"). He played with paper cutouts and a basin filled with toy ducks, and by November 5 was well enough to travel with his parents to Pau, where he and Mr. James rode together each morning, Franklin on a small pony named "Coquette" whose frenzied gallop precisely matched the pace set by the gentle canter of his father's big horse, "Gigi."

In 1892 and again in 1893, the Roosevelts would journey to Chicago, to visit the site of the World's Columbian Exposition. Even there they were treated as important personages; Mr. James was an alternate commissioner to the fair from the State of New York. On their first visit, when Franklin and his father and mother stepped down from the *Monon,* FDR recalled, "a delightful old gentleman with one of those flowering bell-shaped coats and a whip in his left hand, and a shiny black top-hat on his head stepped forward and . . . said to my father, 'How do you do, Cousin James.' Well, he was a Roosevelt, too . . . the head of one of the livery stables of those days, and dressed accordingly." Candidate Roosevelt told this tale to a Chicago crowd during the 1932 presidential campaign in order to create some sort of historical link with his midwestern listeners, but the point of the story within the Roosevelt family, of course, had originally been amused wonderment that so unexalted a man could be even a very distant cousin.

The company his mother and father kept, at home and abroad, and to whom Franklin was routinely introduced, offered further proof of their social standing. By the time he was ten, he had met Mark Twain; Dom Pedro, the exiled emperor of Brazil; Queen Victoria's daughter Helena, the wife of Prince Christian of Holstein; and the Duke and Duchess of Rutland.

In the winter of 1887, the Roosevelts spent eight weeks in Washington. Mr. James's friend Grover Cleveland had been elected President in 1884, the first Democrat in twenty-eight years, and Roosevelt money had helped. In gratitude, the President offered Mr. James several diplomatic posts abroad, all of which he declined; even appointive office was not for him. But the family's sojourn in the capital provided "two months of very gay, pleasant life," Sara noted, "constant dinners and charming people. Everyone has been charming to us, and even Franklin knows everybody."

Toward the end of their stay, Mr. James took five-year-old Franklin to the White House with him to say goodbye to the President. The massive, weary chief executive placed his own huge hand on the boy's head. "My little man," he said with utter seriousness, "I am making a strange wish for you. It is that you may never be President of the United States."

Sara Delano Roosevelt was once asked if she had always thought her son would grow up to be President. "Never, oh never!" she answered. Her ambition for him had been loftier, she said: "The highest ideal I could hold up before our boy—to grow to be like his father, straight and honorable, just and kind, an upstanding American."

All her long life, Sara would pour her formidable energies into making sure Franklin reached that goal. At some unknown date before her husband's death in 1900, she destroyed her journals for the years 1884 to 1887. No one now knows why. It has been suggested that the Roosevelts had adopted sexual abstinence as the only certain way to avoid a second and possibly fatal pregnancy, and that some evidence of the marital strains that decision is likely to have caused might have found its way onto the otherwise uniformly discreet pages of the diary.[4]

Certainly no one observing the Roosevelts together could detect any difficulty. The artist Felix Moscheles spent several weeks at Springwood working on a portrait of Mr. James; his wife wrote that "they are a most attractive couple, so cultivated and refined—and, a thing I love to see, always—devoted to each other."

In any case, something happened then which she did not wish to remember. We may never know what it was, but if it did imply a loss of intimacy between her and her husband, that might offer an additional motive for Sara's undiminishing absorption in the life of her son. Still young and beautiful and energetic in her early thirties, but married to a much older man whom she could still revere but no longer physically love, she may have found an emotional release in directing the life of the little boy who still depended on her.

No moment of Franklin's day was unscheduled or unsupervised. Up at seven. Breakfast at eight. Lessons from nine to noon. An hour in which to play, then lunch and more lessons till four. Two more hours to play games of which his mother approved. Then supper at six and bed by eight. Day after day.

There was no such thing as privacy. His mother oversaw everything, followed him everywhere. Staying at Algonac one weekend, he wrote an exultant letter home to his father: "Mama left this morning, and I am to take my bath alone!" He was then eight and a half years old, and had never bathed by himself. Nor is there any reason to think his mother did not reappear at his tub-side when she got back. It was a parent's mission, she said, to keep a child's mind "on nice things, on a high level."

Within the rather special limits of the life they led, Sara and Mr. James did their best to teach their son self-reliance and responsibility. He was not given an allowance except when traveling; "money was never discussed at home," his mother explained, and besides, "living

4. Dr. Nona Ferdon proposed this explanation for the missing journals in a letter to me in 1983. She may well be right, but it should be pointed out for the record that the privacy of Mrs. Roosevelt's diaries was always relative. The Roosevelts (like the elder Delanos) sometimes took turns noting events; Mr. James, for example, alone kept the diary for several weeks after FDR was born and took over again later that spring when Sara became ill. Thus an indiscretion in its pages, particularly one touching upon the most intimate relationship between them, would seem surprising. After her husband's death, Mrs. Roosevelt evidently discussed the missing pages with her son, still a freshman at Harvard, for on January 18, 1901, she wrote to him, "You were right. Why did I destroy any [of my journals], bad as they are, the record of dear papa's life!"

as we did in the country there was little opportunity for spending it . . . all his books and toys were provided for him." But before he could have his first pony or the red setter "Marksman," a gift from his uncle Warren Delano and the earliest in the succession of big rangy dogs that romped through his boyhood, he had to promise to feed and care for it himself.

And he was expected always to evidence the breeding and good manners of a gentleman; it was the mark of his class, an example he owed to those less fortunate than himself. An Englishman who had taken afternoon tea with his own daughter and young Franklin at a German hotel remembered all his life the polite gravity with which the little American insisted on paying for their treat.

Raised among adults without rivals his own age, it was assumed that he would act like an adult, would exhibit what his mother called "a kind of kinship with older people" that other children, handicapped by clamorous brothers and sisters, found impossible to achieve. Children, she believed, "had pretty much the same thoughts as adults"; all they lacked was a large enough vocabulary with which to express them. Literature would provide that. She had seen no need to supervise Franklin's reading, his mother once explained; Springwood was filled with good books—and, besides, he had access to no others. But she read aloud to him daily, and was irritated whenever his attention seemed to wander. *Swiss Family Robinson,* the story of a shipwrecked family whose survival depends on the virtue and omniscience of its patriarch, was the special favorite of both mother and son; she read it to him twice.

Hers was a loving, even adoring autocracy, but an autocracy, nonetheless. And the very gentleness with which it was administered smothered even the possibility of natural boyish rebellion.

Franklin displayed his first recorded sign of resistance at three, aboard the British ship that brought the family home after the *Germania* nearly went down. Sitting with his parents at luncheon in the dining salon, he raised a tumbler to his mouth as if to take a drink and instead bit off a large jagged chunk of glass. His mother fished the shard from his mouth, marched him out onto the deck, and hurled the fragment into the sea. For days afterward, she said later, she was haunted by the thought of what might have happened had it "punctured his little windpipe."

"Franklin," she asked when she was sure no harm had been done, "where is your obedience?"

"My 'bedience," said the little boy, "has gone upstairs for a walk." And to prove it, when he and his mother had returned to the table, he picked up a second glass and pretended to bite off another piece.

He was not physically punished for this breach of good behavior; his mother thought it merely "impish." Nor was he ever spanked for any other, so far as we know. "We never subjected the boy to a lot of don'ts," his mother wrote, "and while certain rules established for his well being had to be rigidly observed, we were never strict merely for the sake of being strict. In fact we took a secret pride in the fact that Franklin instinctively never seemed to require that kind of handling."

Disapproval or the threat of it was the gentle but effective weapon that kept him in check. His mother was never angered by what he did, just disappointed; she needed to tell him only how he had let her down and, worse, how sad his busy father would be to learn of it, to have him promise to mend his ways. And when he needed to be spoken to about some indiscretion, his mother always took pains to chastise him out of the hearing of others. "Any fault-finding I needed to do had to be conducted when there was no possibility of being overheard, either by Ellen . . . or Elespie. . . . They worshipped him blindly and would not admit, even over our protests, that their little charge could be improved upon. I remember coming to Elespie one day when I had been brought some rather disquieting accounts of Franklin's behavior, and saying, 'Elespie, I hear our boy has been misbehaving.' 'They tell me,' she hedged, 'that he has faults, but I cannot see them.' "

The servants indulged him even when he climbed the back stairs to their rooms to play Old Maid. If they won he would lose his temper, his mother admitted, and could only be calmed when his opponents would agree to "remove the stigma of the name, the meaning of which he did not even comprehend at that time."

"They would always give him his way," his mother continued, "but not so his 'Mummie,' who took quite another view." When he was four, she recalled, and she was playing with him a board game called "Steeplechase," she won twice in a row. He demanded that she turn over to him "your horse; it's a better horse." She gave it to him, rolled the dice—and won again. "This crowning humiliation was not to be borne, and he sulked in furious silence. Quietly I picked up the toys and told him in as firm a tone as I could muster that, until he learned to take a beating gracefully, he could not play any games again. I dare say I was thought rather a hard disciplinarian at that time, but it was the last indication anyone ever saw of a lack of sportsmanship in Franklin."

Mr. James seems to have been content to leave what little disciplining was needed to his wife, though he did sometimes think she "nagged" the boy too much, and was privately amused at the seriousness with which she took her maternal role, calling Sara "The Mother" in at least one letter to his son some years later.

At eight, Franklin would try again to assert his independence. Sara told the story:

"One day . . . we noticed that [Franklin] seemed much depressed and bound, do what we would to amuse him, not to be distracted from his melancholy. Finally, a little alarmed, I asked him whether he was unhappy. He did not answer at once, and then said very seriously 'Yes, I am unhappy.'

"When I asked him why, he was again silent for a moment or two. Then with a curious little gesture that combined entreaty with a suggestion of impatience, he clasped his hands in front of him and exclaimed, 'Oh, for freedom!'

"It seems funny now, but at the time I was honestly shocked. For all he was such a child, his voice had a desperate note that made me realize how seriously he meant it.

"That night I talked it over with his father. . . . We agreed that unconsciously we had probably regulated the child's life too closely. Evidently he was quite satisfied with what he did with his time but what worried him was the necessity of conforming to given hours.

"So the very next morning I told him that he might do whatever he pleased that day. He need obey no former rules nor report at given intervals, and he was allowed to roam at will. We paid no attention to him, and, I must say, he proved his desire for freedom by completely ignoring us. That evening, however, a very dirty, tired youngster came dragging in. He was hungry and ready for bed, but we did not ask him where he had been or what he had been doing. We could only deduce that his adventures had been a little lacking in glamour, for the next day, quite of his own accord, he went contentedly back to his routine."

And his mother returned determinedly to hers.

Thereafter, he would be free only in his imagination, commanding a phantom ship from a crow's nest made of nailed-together boards jammed into the branches of a tall hemlock just outside the rose garden, or trying to construct a raft on which he hoped to sail across the Hudson. (It sank three feet from shore, to his mother's quiet amusement.) But Franklin did find one way in which at least to seem to be on his own. One afternoon he climbed into the top of one of his father's giant trees and sat there gleefully silent while darkness fell, watching as the servants and his worried mother called for him from far below.

Saturday, May 17, 1884, had been an unusually crisp spring day at Hyde Park, and when Franklin, Mamie, and his mother hurried across the south lawn early that evening, they were warmly dressed. A gently curved path was always kept open through the woods, and the party of three moved along it as fast as Franklin, not yet three, could manage. A big bracketed red house stood at the end of the path, and a tree-lined avenue ran back to it from the Albany Road and formed an oval before the front door.

A small crowd was already waiting there when the Roosevelts arrived, and just as they reached the front steps they heard the cheerful blast of a coaching horn and turned to see a handsome four-in-hand turn into the white gates and start down the avenue toward them, gravel spattering from beneath its bright red wheels. Two matched bays galloped in the lead; behind them came a pair of dapple grays. The swaying coach itself was white, its details and undercarriage painted scarlet. Several gentlemen in green cutaways and tall gray hats sat on top. One of them, Franklin saw, was his father. But as the coach thundered closer, he saw that the driver was familiar, too. He, too, wore a gray hat; his red-brown mustache was waxed, his beard neatly sculpted. He held the reins with one yellow-gloved hand, and with the other expertly flicked a long whip here and there to make his teams wheel, then slow, in perfect tandem. As soon as the lathered horses came to a complete stop, he handed the reins to a liveried groom and bounded down, tearing off his gloves to shake hands with Franklin and his mother.

This was Rosy—James Roosevelt Roosevelt—Franklin's dashing, exuberant half brother, who lived part of each year with his wife and two children in the house next door to Springwood. He was one of the dozen best amateur coachmen in America; all of his passengers except Mr. James were fellow members of the Coaching Club of New York who were to spend the weekend with him at Hyde Park.

Rosy is mostly forgotten now, and even during his lifetime many thought him a showy relic of an earlier age; Eleanor Roosevelt once dismissed him as "a terrible snob." But he was a fond, avuncular presence throughout much of Franklin Roosevelt's youth, and he provided his far younger half brother with a vivid and instructive example of what wealth without ambition could make of a man.

In order to understand what FDR became, it is helpful to understand what he might easily have been instead.

By the time Franklin was born, Rosy had become very rich indeed, a leader of the most extravagant sporting segment of New York society. That society had changed greatly since his father was a young man. The old Knickerbocker families had begun to be eclipsed by new clans with new money. The Vanderbilts were prominent among the newcomers; so were the Whitneys and the Belmonts. But the greatest of these—and the first—were the Astors. The Roosevelts and Delanos were well off. The Astors were rich beyond imagining. John Jacob Astor, the German-born founder of the fortune, had been cunning, avaricious, and crude. "He ate his ice cream and peas with a knife," a visitor remembered, and when he had finished his meal he wiped his greasy fingers on the tablecloth. Society never interested him at all, and in his old age, when he grew bored at one of the ostentatious occasions his many descendants liked to arrange, he would sometimes remove his chewing tobacco and with it "absently trace watery patterns on the window pane." What did interest him was making money, first from furs and then from rents on great chunks of New York real estate. He may have been the first true American millionaire, and when he finally died at eighty-four in 1848, he had amassed some twenty million untaxed dollars—a sum one obituary writer termed "as incomprehensible as infinity," but which his son and grandsons multiplied many times.

By the early 1870s, precisely who belonged in society and who did not had become a matter of serious concern for the wealthy and well connected of New York. Where once there had been only John Jacob Astor, the new age of railroads and steel and speculation had created scores of new millionaires with wives and offspring eager to be recognized. Clearly, society would have to change with changing times, but how to separate the right sort of newcomer from the merely aspiring?

Caroline Schermerhorn Astor, wife of William Astor and granddaughter-in-law of the founder, took it upon herself to decide. She had four daughters who would soon be of marriageable age, and she was determined that they encounter only the proper sort of suitor. Her own resolution and her complacent husband's money helped make her *the* Mrs. Astor, final arbiter of New York and Newport society for nearly forty years, but she could also call upon the promotional and social skills of Ward McAllister, a mincing social climber from Georgia who took the planning of cotillions and table settings with immense gravity. It was his shrewd notion that Mrs. Astor give a subscription ball each January, to which a select group of twenty-five "Patriarchs" would each invite five gentlemen and four ladies. The Patriarchs' good taste and good judgment would insure the proper mix of exclusivity and realism, Knickerbockers with the newly wealthy. "We wanted the money power," McAllister explained years later, "but not in any way to be controlled by it." In this way his patroness would at once "create and lead society."

The Patriarchs' ball was held in the art gallery of the turreted Astor mansion at Fifth Avenue and Thirty-fourth Street. The room held just 400 guests, a limitation McAllister successfully turned to advantage. "Why," he told the press, "there are only about 400 in fashionable New York society. If you go outside that number you strike people who are either not at ease in a ballroom or else make other people not at ease."

Guests' wraps were taken by servants dressed in blue livery faithfully modeled after that worn at Windsor. Mrs. Astor greeted visitors standing before a full-size portrait of herself and covered with diamonds, so many and so blinding that one visitor thought she resembled an animated chandelier. The walls were banked with orchids and other exotic flowers, and on a balcony above the waltzing guests a full orchestra played, also dressed in Astor blue.[5]

James and Rebecca Roosevelt had often attended these evenings and others only slightly less splendid at Mrs. Astor's, and Mr. James for a time had been one of the trusted Patriarchs. Rosy went to Mrs. Astor's, too, and there is a studio portrait of him dressed for a fancy dress ball held there in March of 1875. In it he wears the powdered wig, ruffled shirt, dress sword, and silk hose of a member of the court of Louis XIV. He seems a somewhat sturdy courtier, thick-calved and ungainly to the modern eye, but his mother thought "he looked so handsome."

Helen Astor, Mrs. Astor's second-oldest daughter, evidently

5. The Astors' rather special sense of their own place in the world was nicely pointed up in March of 1881, when Theodore Roosevelt found himself dining next to Mrs. John Jacob Astor IV, Mrs. Astor's daughter-in-law. Word had just come of the assassination of Czar Alexander II of Russia at the hands of revolutionaries. Mrs. Astor was especially upset, TR remembered. "Mr. Roosevelt," she said, "they are attacking *us* all over the world."

Source: TR recalled this exchange in a letter to his sister Bamie, August 20, 1887. Theodore Roosevelt Collection, Harvard.

agreed. Rosy had met her while still a student at Columbia College. It is easy to see what Helen Astor offered him. She was attractive (if somewhat solemn) and gloriously rich. Rosy worked hard to win her. He was taking "Miss Astor" for long carriage rides at least four years before they became engaged in 1876.

What she—or her mother—saw in him is somewhat harder to assess. He came from a fine old family, of course, and would provide the Astors with a link to Knickerbocker New York, and he had perfect manners and a great deal of charm. "He was always having a good time, always smiling," a cousin remembered, "very much in demand wherever he went." But he had no plans to support himself. The sheltered, timid little boy who had slept in his parents' bedroom until the age of ten and been terrorized at first by his one brief brush with school in Dresden, had grown up utterly unprepared to make his own way outside Springwood's friendly walls. All his life he would hide his hypochondria and his fear of ordinary people and of competition in the everyday world behind an elegant, affable façade. He was bright enough, graduating from Columbia with honors in 1876, and he expected to go to law school, but, like his father, he had no real wish or need to practice. Nor did business interest him much. What Rosy liked most was enjoying himself. He had adopted most of his father's more extravagant enthusiasms—blooded horses, yacht racing, riding to hounds, hunting and fishing in Scotland, English country life—but without Mr. James's sobering sense of responsibility. Marrying into the Astor family would insure that he could afford always to do all these things, and more.

He and Helen were married at Grace Church in New York in 1877. Mr. James, then still a widower, attended with his mother and other members of his family, but the newspapers focused on the Astor women and what they wore. The bride, though hung with jewels, was easily outshone by her mother in a Worth gown of lace and silk brocade. "The shoulders and bosom were literally armored with diamond pins and pendants," one reporter noted; other large stones flashed from her arms, ears, fingers, throat. "Her jet black hair was arranged in puffs," the newspaper continued, "and on either end of each puff were rosebuds of large diamonds." One thousand guests were later served refreshments at the Astor residence.

In addition to the income on a trust fund of $400,000, Helen brought to the marriage a Fifth Avenue mansion of her own, but when they were not abroad, she and Rosy would spend most of their time at the relatively modest "Red House" adjacent to Springwood, lent to them by Mr. James. Like his own father, James Roosevelt always wanted his sons close by.

Mr. James had become a grandfather before he married Sara Delano. Rosy and Helen had a son in 1879; he was christened James Roosevelt Roosevelt, Jr., but was almost always called "Taddy." And in September of 1881, while Sara was still pregnant with Franklin, they had a second child, a daughter, whom they named Helen for her mother.

Rosy was given a mostly honorary position with the Astor real estate office; the real work of collecting rents was performed by sterner hirelings. He went to the office fairly often, a member of the family recalled, "to pick up his mail." He had his charities. For forty years he would be a trustee of the Cathedral of St. John the Divine in New York, and he was for a time an officer of the Downtown Relief Bureau, which acted as "almoner among the worthy poor in the distribution of moneys which men in the hurry of business would otherwise give to the unworthy."

The rest of the time—*most* of the time—he was free to do as he pleased, and he was pleased to do very little. His life was even more peripatetic than his father's; living in England or Scotland and later in Bermuda always suited him better than living at home. And it was in England that he developed his fascination for coaching, the aristocratic hobby that came to occupy most of his waking hours and made his Hyde Park arrivals and departures so dramatic.

Coaching was an enormously expensive exercise in selective nostalgia. By the 1870s, railroads had replaced stagecoaches for serious travelers on both sides of the Atlantic. But in England, the Duke of Beaufort, the Marquess of Blandford, and other gentlemen of leisure had revived coaching as a sport. Its discomforts were forgotten—the brutal lurching ride over rutted roads, the mud, the bad food served in smoky inns. Aristocratic coachmen reveled instead in the manly camaraderie coaching trips fostered, the considerable skill required to handle four spirited horses at a fast clip over country roads, above all, the opportunities it offered for gorgeous display.

An Astor, Colonel De Lancey Astor Kane, was one of the first important American whips; he imported a celebrated English coach, the *Tally Ho,* in 1876 and personally drove it daily that spring from the Hotel Brunswick on Madison Square to Arcalarius' Hotel at Pelham Bridge in Westchester County and back again. Theoretically at least, anyone with $2.50 could ride along, and for an additional half dollar could sit on the box behind the elegantly tailored driver. The sight of the gleaming canary yellow coach clattering past, a liveried guard blowing his long brass horn, fascinated the public. It was the fashion then to "ape the English," one member of society recalled, and the Coaching Club of New York was established that same year, ostensibly "to encourage four-in-hand driving in America," actually to provide English-style amusement for fashionable young gentlemen who liked horses and had nothing better to do.

For men whose wealth did not come to them through actual ability or effort—for young Belmonts and Vanderbilts and Whitneys and Havemeyers—coaching provided a kind of mastery in which they could take pride. An anonymous American coachman who signed himself "an old whip" captured something of coaching's appeal: "What other sport can stand beside it? As the coachman looks down from the box, holding well in control the four blood horses, checking the least of their caprices, giving full play to their strength, what general regarding the raging battle, what statesman compelling the votes of his party, has a sense of personal authority like his? At his side sits a friend, aiding, counselling, or learning; or it may be a lady, relieving the strain of his work with her pleasant prattle. Behind him are the merry spirits of the party, chatting, joking, or breathing with full lungs the serene air of spring. . . . So the landscape passes by: the fields and the lanes and the hedgerows in blossom; and the travellers can scarcely believe that it is anything but a dream."

When Rosy joined the club in 1881, he was already a veteran of the back roads of France and Italy as well as England, and he took it all with great and uncharacteristic seriousness. He drove in the annual Club Meet, a procession of members' carriages through Central Park and down Fifth Avenue; his wife sat next to him, her hat and dress coordinated to complement the colors of his coach. Thousands of ordinary New Yorkers lined the avenue to watch the coaches pass; squads of mounted police kept the buggies and gigs of curiosity seekers from getting too close. There were drives to Jerome Park to watch the races, to Newport, and to the country seats of club members. For four seasons, Rosy and several friends ran their own daily public coach from New York to Pelham—and one year even managed to make a profit, if one didn't count in the cost of grooms or equipment.

An infinity of rules had to be observed. "It is hardly necessary to say that a man when driving should always take off his hat to a lady of his acquaintance," wrote Rosy's friend Fairman Rogers in his encyclopedic *Manual of Coaching*. "It is in bad taste merely to raise his whip in place of so doing. If he has not hands enough to spare one for his hat, he should continue to practice driving until he can find one." In winter, there were repainting and repairs to the coach to be seen to, and the latest equipment to be ordered: the finest whip handles, for example, "rabbit-bitten hollies"—saplings on which the teeth of wild rabbits had left distinctive patterns. And at least once a year Rosy traveled north to farms in Vermont and Maine, where he stood in the snow and bargained for the next season's horses, twenty at a time.

His coaching, along with the stag stalking and salmon fishing that added variety to his crowded year, left him little time to act as father to his children, and each was affected by his frequent absence. Whenever his family was at Hyde Park, Taddy and Helen played with Franklin. One Thanksgiving at Springwood the children presented an after-dinner tableau; all three were then steeped in gory English history, and Franklin and Taddy portrayed the Little Princes in the Tower, noisily expiring beneath pillows held by Helen. She was high-spirited and tomboyish, more interested in tobogganing than dolls, and she and Franklin got on well.

He and Taddy did not. Taddy was three years older, heavier, faster, stronger—everything an only child like Franklin would find disquieting in a competitor. But something also really seems to have been wrong with him. He was sometimes uncontrollable, at others oddly withdrawn. He was unable to concentrate on his studies; one tutor thought him "very backward." His father believed him only "very shy and wanting in confidence." Alice Roosevelt, the daughter of Cousin Theodore, once complained to Franklin that Taddy could not be stopped from pulling her hair.

Relations between the neighboring Roosevelt households were always correct and sometimes cordial but also a little reserved, perhaps complicated by the fact that Sara and Rosy were the same age. She, at least, must have sometimes seen her son and Taddy as rivals for her husband's affection. In that competition, she found Taddy wanting. So did Mr. James. He did not quite approve of the frivolous life Rosy and Helen Astor led, and he thought he saw evidence of its bad effects in his troubled grandson.

What Rosy needed was serious work, something he might accomplish on his own and feel good about. His father tried to provide it for him. When, in 1887, President Cleveland asked Mr. James to serve his government abroad, he had turned him down. But he had countered with a request of his own: Might Rosy be appointed first secretary to the American legation in Vienna? It would not violate family tradition against public office, since he had himself served unofficially under James Buchanan in the London embassy many years earlier. Rosy was fluent in both German and French, had always been a loyal Democrat, gave handsomely to the Cleveland campaign, and could help pay embassy expenses from his wife's fortune. Besides, the boy needed something to do. Cleveland agreed.

The *Poughkeepsie News* reported that Rosy's New York friends were astonished by the appointment: " 'Politics, did you say?' said a member of one of the 5th Avenue clubs. 'Why, I never knew Rosy to cast a vote. In fact, I don't think he ever troubled his head about it. But he is a splendid fellow, for all that.' "

Rosy's first experience of gainful employment did not go as smoothly as he or his father had hoped. Relations with the U.S. minister, General Alexander T. Lawton, were cordial enough. Lawton, an Atlanta attorney and businessman who had been badly wounded at Sharpsburg fighting for the Confederacy, liked Rosy, seeing in him "a gentleman by birth, education, position and habits, and possessed of a temperament and social facilities" ideally suited to the diplomatic life.

Nor were Rosy's duties onerous. A clerk handled all the paperwork, leaving the first secretary free to interview applicants for visas, find out what had happened to the minister's subscription to the *Atlanta Constitution*, give and attend formal dinners, and advise visiting Americans on the niceties of local custom. "When going to receptions, parties, etc.," he told one newcomer, "it is always necessary to take a servant with one to hold coats, wraps, etc., as there is never any cloakroom." Plenty of time was left over for Rosy and Helen to fish nearby streams for trout and to take long drives around the city in their four-in-hand.

Still, he was not happy. His table silver had arrived from England "badly scratched and rubbed" for one thing, and because General Lawton had asked him to take up his post as soon as possible after his Senate confirmation in February, 1888, he had not been granted the customary three-week transition period for travel. "This necessitated my presence in Vienna during the whole of the most trying season of the year," he complained to his superior in late August, "and forced the residence of my family in one of the suburbs instead of any of the more healthy country resorts further afield." Unless he was given sixty days' leave in which to travel to England and breathe "its more bracing air" before enduring another Austrian winter, "I shall consider myself *at perfect liberty to resign my position.*" The leave was granted, and Rosy spent the autumn with his family in England, shooting grouse and driving a brand-new blue-and-yellow coach with wheels striped in yellow and black.

He was still there in November when he got the dispiriting news that the Democrats had lost the presidency. Benjamin Harrison would take office in March, and Rosy's job would presumably end shortly thereafter. Mr. James hoped he would stay on—it was so heartening to see him holding down a responsible position—and wrote to the Republican Secretary of State designate, James G. Blaine, asking that Rosy be retained at Vienna. His son was not pleased. He *wanted* to resign, he told his father, for "If I stayed, say for a year, under the Republicans, I should be 'neither fish nor fowl' at the end of that time. . . . By Resigning . . . I am in a *very much better* position with our party, should they come in again in '92."

As to what he would do in the meantime, he was not sure. "I want so much to feel that I may have something to do when I get home," he told his father, ". . . as I don't want to get back to the old rut I was in before I came here." Mr. James tried to create a job for him with West Superior Steel, and Rosy seemed pleased: "A moderate position of that kind would suit me exactly, where the responsibility would not be too great." But the firm was doing too poorly to add another executive.

The new American minister arrived that spring. He was Frederick D. Grant, the youngest son of the late Ulysses S. Grant, and not Rosy's sort at all. "The Grants are *pretty bad,*" he told his father, "tho' I must say very civil and accommodating to us." He was more blunt when describing them to his mother-in-law, Mrs. Astor: "He [Fred Grant] is very much like his father, without the brains but just as common. She is rather pretty but western and provincial. The last sort of people who ought to have been sent here!"

In August, after writing a reassuring note to his successor as first secretary—"It is considered quite enough here if a Secretary's wife has a fiacre . . . as long as she has a footman in livery on the box"—Rosy left Vienna for a short stay at Karlsbad. With him went his family, three servants, eleven trunks, and twenty-three crates. He was thirty-six years old and again without anything much to do, but he was not overly concerned. Before going home to Hyde Park in the fall he thought he might leave the children at Heathfield, his estate near Ascot, and undertake a long coaching trip to the west coast of England.

Franklin was an only child, but he cannot really be said to have been lonely. Other children besides Helen and Taddy came to play at Springwood. Some were his cousins, the sons and daughters of his mother and father's siblings, but there were unrelated playmates, too. Like him, most were the offspring of the Hudson River gentry, those fifty-odd well-to-do families whose elaborate country seats lay scattered for miles along the wooded bluffs on the eastern shore of the river. Many were interrelated; all were well-to-do and devoted to what Sara Delano Roosevelt once called "living life as it should be."

Their lovely stretch of the river even had its own suitably aristocratic tramp, a genial eccentric named Henry Madison. Although he was hugely fat and his tattered clothes were tenuously held together by safety pins, he claimed to be the nephew of President James Madison, and his air of genteel refinement forbade him even from speaking to the other tramps he met along the road. According to FDR (who remembered him well from his boyhood), Madison wintered each year in Florida, courtesy of Chauncey Depew of the New York Central Railroad, whom he apparently amused, and whose residence in Peekskill he always made a point of visiting.

But each summer for more than twenty years he came north again to eat his epicurean way from Garrison to Rhinebeck, calling at the back doors and sampling the larders of some of America's wealthiest men. He was an annual guest in the Springwood kitchen, spinning tales of his travels for Franklin and the servants in exchange for a good meal. In fact, Hyde Park was one of his favorite stopping places. North and south of there, hospitable kitchens were often separated by several hungry miles, but in Hyde Park the great estates bordered one another, and one hardly had to walk at all to get to the next feed. Approaching town from Poughkeepsie along the Albany Road, Madison would first visit the Roosevelts. But just next door—less than 200 yards further north—was Bellefield, the big white home of state senator Thomas Jefferson Newbold, who, like his old friend and neighbor Mr. James, was a Democrat and therefore an anomaly among the river families.

Just beyond the Newbold house, set back from the road in the midst of a vast English-style park, stood Crumwold, the still more impressive home of Colonel Archibald Rogers, a Standard Oil official who had married into a wealthy local family. His Romanesque castle with its seventy rooms was said to have cost $300,000 to build—a sum less startling even for that time when it was remembered that Mrs. Rogers earned a thousand dollars a day in interest on her legacy alone.

The tiny village of Hyde Park itself next provided Henry Madison with a few hundred yards in which to walk off luncheon at Crumwold. The newspapers of the day invariably called it a "hamlet"; it was a crossroads community, just a handful of modest houses, a hotel, and several small stores, including three butcher shops that provided venison, game birds, and other exotic meats for the tables of the well-to-do. Down along the riverbank, hidden from Madison as he heaved his way northward along the road, were the railway depot and a boat landing where supplies ordered by the estate owners could be brought ashore.

From Henry Madison's specialized point of view, perhaps the most appealing Hyde Park mansion was also the last to be built. At the northern edge of town, on the site of the house built by Dr. Isaac Roosevelt's old mentor, Dr. Hosack, Frederick W. Vanderbilt had constructed for himself a full-fledged Renaissance palace with fifty-four rooms in 1898. He furnished it with tapestries and coffered ceilings and whole rooms of carved paneling ripped from the homes of European royalty. Best of all, its staff of seventeen household servants included a chef trained in Paris.

Franklin's closest boyhood friends lived on the estates closest to his own: Archie Rogers, Jr. (just Franklin's age), and his younger brother, Edmund; and pretty Mary Newbold (also his age), who lived right next door at Bellefield. He did not choose them as other children choose their playmates; they became his friends, his daughter Anna once explained, simply because they "just happened to be there."

Franklin played with both Rogers boys, but Archie was his favorite. He rode his pony along the forest path to Crumwold to see him almost every day. Together they dug a tunnel beneath the snow, sailed wooden boats on the river, and learned their ABC's from a governess in the Crumwold tower schoolroom. At seven, in March of 1889, Franklin wrote to Archie from New York: "We are going to see Barnom's Circus and it is going to march through the streets and we are going to see it. . . . Send love to Edmund."

The following December, Archie was dead of diphtheria. There is no mention of the death of her son's closest friend in Sara Delano Roosevelt's journal (nor is it marked in either her own book, *My Boy Franklin*, or in *Gracious Lady*, her semi-official biography for which she supplied most of the information). In the Delano tradition, unpleasantness of any kind, even simple grief, was best forgotten or kept to oneself. Archie Rogers' death must have affected Franklin. It offered vivid, frightening proof that life was not always as secure and untroubled as Springwood made it seem. But, as with the death of his Aunt Laura, there is no record of his ever having spoken of it to anyone.

There were other small visitors, but even Franklin's friendship with children of whom his parents approved was strictly regulated. None ever spent the night with him at Springwood, for example. "I never should allow a small boy to visit a friend over night, especially in the same town," his mother once explained. "It is always a mistake."

Isabel and Hasseltine Whitney, two small and well-bred sisters from Paterson, New Jersey, were several times imported for the day to play with Franklin. A cousin remembers being told that they had not looked forward to their visits to Hyde Park. Franklin was "very spoiled," they reported to their mother; "he did not like to share his toys or books." To be fair, their memories may have been curdled by subsequent dealings with FDR as President. Many years later, when both sisters had grown old, their parents died within weeks of one another, subjecting them to a doubled inheritance tax which they thought unjust. The Whitney sisters had long since lost touch with their playmate and they disapproved strenuously of his politics, but Isabel, the eldest, now wrote to Roosevelt in the White House, reminding him of their old acquaintance and asking for an appointment. FDR, to whom all such early contacts always remained important, agreed to see her and listened patiently as she told her story. When she had finished, he told her that he was terribly sorry, but not even the President could alter a law enacted by the New York State legislature. There was nothing he could do. The Whitney sisters would have to pay their taxes. Isabel rose to her feet. "You were always a nasty little boy," she shouted, waving her cane, "and now you are a nasty old man!"

Franklin was sometimes permitted to play outdoors with the children of his parents' employees, but his proper relationship with them had been fixed as early as Christmas Eve in 1884, when, not yet three, he had first helped hand out gifts to the people who worked on the place and their children, who were permitted to come into the parlor once each year to gaze at the tall tree lit with candles. He was especially friendly with the stable boys, his mother remembered, because they shared his love for horses. But both Franklin and his playmates always understood who was ultimately in charge. Once, watching from the piazza as he told a companion precisely how their fort must be built, his mother urged him to let the other boy give the orders some of the time.

"Mummie," he replied, "if I didn't give the orders, nothing would happen!"[6]

Two small boys, sons of one of the Roosevelt farmers, were sometimes allowed to bobsled with Franklin and his father, shouting with pleasure as they hurtled down the steep slope behind the house. But each time they reached the bottom, it was the brothers' task to haul the bobsled back up the hill again while the two Roosevelts came along behind, unencumbered.

In summer, copperheads sometimes sunned themselves in the Springwood gardens and along the stone walls that separated the fields. Mr. James worried that Franklin might be bitten, and offered his employees' children a shiny new quarter for every dead snake they showed him. The same two boys who had pulled the bobsled spotted a snake, killed it, and carried its thick bronze body up to the house. Mr. James paid up, and they scurried off to find another. When no snake showed itself in two days of hunting, it occurred to the oldest boy that displaying the original corpse might win them another quarter. It worked a second time, but "Old Mr. Roosevelt eventually got wise," a descendant remembered, when the original snake "got kind of dry," and he imposed a new rule: Henceforth, the snake had to be left behind after each reward.[7]

There were other boys in Hyde Park, of course, most of them the offspring of the men and women who worked on the great estates that lined the Albany Road. They reflected the hiring preferences of their parents' employers. The Rogers family, for example, usually hired Scandinavians. Mr. James favored Scots. His brother John once advertised his blunt requirements: "Germans and Scandinavians highly

6. This familiar story, first told by FDR's mother and repeated by many of his biographers, is often cited as an early sign of his instinct for leadership—and of the willingness of his peers to grant it to him. But his playmate was not a peer; he was "a little boy on the place," in Mrs. Roosevelt's words, an employee's son, and presumably well schooled in the realities of power at Springwood.

Source: Sara Delano Roosevelt, *My Boy Franklin,* page 26.

7. Like FDR, one of these boys was actually born in Springwood itself. His father and mother lived there—in the servants' rooms—and watched over the house one winter when the Roosevelts were in New York. Their son grew up to be a plumber and eventually moved to Brooklyn.

Source: Nancy Fogel interviews, FDRL.

thought of; Irishmen rejected; blacks not considered." The village children had their own brutal hierarchy. Boys and girls from outlying farms were called "monkeys," and Staatsburg, the district from which many of them came, was "the zoo."

In summer, the whistle of the steamboat *Mary Powell* was the signal for town boys to leap on their bicycles and pedal down to the riverfront to dive in and ride the swells that slapped against the landing. When the shad ran in the spring, the same boys hurled nets from rocks just off shore near the depot, then threw their wriggling silver catch over their shoulders to their sisters waiting with buckets on land. Later, the fish were salted and stored for the winter months, when boys and girls alike bundled themselves against the wind and picked their way along the snowy roads to school.

Franklin's contacts with this rough and tumble childhood world were tenuous and fleeting. When his father rode into town to inspect the public school—sitting in the back of the room, a former student recalled, his riding crop across his knees, and listening gravely as the pupils recited—Franklin waited outside with the horses.

One day at age five or six, driving with his parents along Noxon Street in Poughkeepsie, he saw three small boys playing with a pet rabbit in their front yard. He asked his father if he might be allowed to pat the rabbit. The carriage stopped, and Mr. James called the boys over with their pet. Franklin was delighted. Might he buy the rabbit? Mr. James asked. "Oh, no, sir," the eldest boy answered. "We can't sell them, but we will give your little boy two, as we have more." A box was found, and the two rabbits went home to Springwood in Franklin's lap. The boys were named Moore, their sister wrote to remind President Roosevelt many years later. He was sorry not to remember them, FDR responded, but "I do remember the rabbits."

His first seven years at Springwood had taught Franklin Roosevelt that his parents were important people and that, as their son, he was important, too. He had learned as well that the world was for the most part a sunny congenial place, and he had every reason to believe that his own future would be bright with pleasures, only lightly alloyed with duties.

When the three Roosevelts went sleighing, the sleek vehicle lined with wine-red velvet in which they rode had been a gift from Czar Alexander II of Russia to his friend Napoleon III, the emperor of France. Mr. James had bought it at auction in Paris after the Commune for fifteen dollars, and the silver trappings that now sparkled on the harness bore the Roosevelt crest.

Franklin sat by himself in the back, where the Empress Eugénie had once ridden as she glided through the Bois de Boulogne; his mother and father rode side by side up front to shield him from the cutting wind.

CHAPTER 4

THE LOVING CONSPIRACY

On November 1, 1890, Sara Delano Roosevelt admitted to her diary that she had had "quite a busy morning." The Dutchess County Hunt was to have its hunt breakfast at Springwood that afternoon, forty guests in all. Charles Anderson, the Roosevelts' new English butler, was in charge; he was an able organizer, despite his blue glass eye, which, one visitor remembered, had an "electric effect on children." And Sara's sister, Annie Hitch, had come up from Algonac the night before to help.

Everything was ready when the riders pounded up to the house at twelve-thirty, exhilarated and hungry from the morning's chase. Sara showed them to the sideboard in the dining room where the steaming food was laid out: oatmeal, baked potatoes, mutton chops, griddle cakes, rye muffins, coffee, and tea. No one could have told that anything was wrong.

But something was. Mr. James was not there. He lay in bed upstairs, too ill even to greet his guests. Two weeks earlier he had returned from a week-long business trip to West Superior, Wisconsin, and experienced what he and Sara both thought only a chill while driving out to dinner. But pains in his chest had sent him home later in the evening, and he had been ill off and on ever since. His doctors were at first uncertain what the matter was. He had always been susceptible to back pains, which he and they attributed to some sort of kidney trouble, and for which he had often taken the waters in

Europe. And he also suffered from frequent indigestion. But this was different. The pain was in his chest and so severe that simple breathing was often agony.

He had suffered a mild heart attack; the sharp recurring pains were angina pectoris. Mr. James was just sixty-two, and would live on for ten more years. But he would never be fully well again. That fact altered almost every aspect of life for the Roosevelts, with profound and lasting impact on the development of Franklin's personality. Mr. James had always been his active, good-humored companion, as well as his father. Now, increasingly, he would be an invalid, someone to be cared for, not played with or relied upon.[1] The boy's strong impulse to be what his grandfather Delano had called "a very nice child . . . always bright and happy. Not crying, worrying, infractious" was now intensified by the very real danger that to worry or annoy his father was to risk further weakening his damaged heart. From 1890 on, Franklin and his mother were brought still closer together as conspirators in a loving plot to keep Mr. James alive and well.

His role in that conspiracy sometimes demanded a startling degree of stoicism. Once, while traveling with his parents aboard the *Monon*, a steel curtain rod fell onto his forehead, cutting him deeply. Though blood poured down his face, terrifying his mother, Franklin, then just nine, insisted that Mr. James not be told, asking instead for a cap to put on to cover the wound. He spent the rest of the day wearing the cap and standing outside on the observation platform.

Much later, at fourteen, he was playing with a friend on the shore at Campobello, taking turns batting pebbles out into the water with sticks. His companion's stick slipped from his hands and smashed into Franklin's mouth, splitting his lip, breaking one tooth, and chipping another. He made his way up to the house but would answer his mother's questions about what had happened only in monosyllables. She knew something was seriously wrong and finally demanded that he open his mouth. The nerve of the broken tooth hung down, ex-

1. Mr. James's failing health did not diminish his unquestioned supremacy within his home. Sara may have controlled her son, but her husband—like her father before him—controlled her. He was not to be challenged on matters of what he considered principle. When the three Roosevelts visited the Chicago World's Fair for the first time in 1892, Sara encountered her girlhood friend, Maggie Carey in the lobby of the hotel. They had not seen each other for years, and Sara was eager to get reacquainted. But in the intervening years Maggie had shed her first husband for a second, causing a newspaper scandal. Mr. James forbade their meeting. There were words between the Roosevelts. "James feels so strongly on the matter," Sara wrote in her journal, "that I give up seeing Maggie again! It is not easy to make up my mind!" Mr. James made it up for her; she and her old friend did not meet.

Source: SDR Journal, FDRL.

posed and throbbing. Again Franklin had suffered in silence as long as he could rather than cause alarm. Later that day, his mother noted proudly, he endured the extraction of the nerve "without fuss."

Before 1890, European travel had been a pleasant diversion for the Roosevelts. After Mr. James's heart attack they thought it a necessity. Salvation, they came to believe, lay in the warm saline waters that bubbled up naturally from several ancient springs on the northeast slope of the Taunus Mountains in the Rhineland town of Bad Nauheim. It was an old city with a thriving new industry. In 1859 a local physician had published a treatise which alleged that heart patients could be helped by a carefully supervised sequence of warm baths in the carbonated waters of one of the Nauheim springs. Thousands of sufferers believed him.

The Roosevelts were first sent to Nauheim in May of 1891 by a London specialist. They would return with Franklin four times, and come a fifth time on their own. Their first visit there, with its unstated but unmistakable air of anxiety, was made still more difficult for Franklin when fear prevented his nurse, Helen McRorie, from coming along. She was ill herself, and the prospect of an ocean crossing alarmed her. "The parting from her was really terrible for darling Franklin," Sara wrote, "his good devoted 'Mamie' for nine years, all his life in fact." But he did his best to hide his sadness.

Nauheim was a quiet resort compared to Karlsbad or Baden-Baden, but well enough appointed for all but the most extravagant visitors. The Roosevelts usually stayed in the same suite at the Villa Britannia, a big expensive well-staffed hotel whose other guests were mostly Britons. Anderson sometimes came along to see to the Roosevelts' further comfort.

The keys to a successful cure were regular habits and patience. "Do not become impatient; remain, drink, bathe, and you will succeed," one German doctor wrote. The Roosevelts dutifully complied. Drinking the waters of one spring was said to ease indigestion; daily baths in the waters of another healed the heart. Mr. James did both. He rose early every morning, made his way to the vast colonnaded *Kurhaus* and joined one of the long, slow-moving lines that shuffled toward the octagonal fountain that stood in its vaulted center. Sara always kept him company. Each patient held his or her own porcelain cup, and when the fountain was finally reached, a hearty young woman in a cap and white apron turned on a burnished tap and filled the cup with eight ounces of warm salty water. "You hate it savagely for the first day or two," one patient wrote, but soon get used to it. Some sufferers were encouraged to go back for as many as four refills, with fifteen-minute intervals between drafts. To "promote absorption," gentle strolls were prescribed through the adjacent park filled with flowering horse chestnut trees, weeping willows, and formal beds of blossoms; a full orchestra played Chopin and Mozart to make the time go faster.

Then followed an hour's promenade before breakfast. German patients generally ate together in the garden. The Roosevelts and their English friends walked back to their hotel to dine; according to Mr. James, it was Sara who objected to "feeding with German swine." An hour or so later, Mr. James went to one of the three bathhouses that accommodated some 1,000 patients a day. There, an attendant helped him into his own marble tub filled with dark orange water, naturally heated to 99 degrees. His bath lasted fifteen minutes—more than that was thought counterproductive—during which millions of tiny white bubbles of carbonic gas formed on his skin. These bubbles and the pleasant tingling sensation they produced were said to "dilate blood vessels, relieve the heart and circulatory system, improve blood supply. . . ." Certainly the warm, naturally buoyant water in which weary aching limbs moved with renewed ease lent the anxious patient a sense of euphoria and peace.

In any case, Mr. James came to believe that these baths were keeping him from invalidism, fending off death. Sara and Franklin believed it, too. And when the time came many years later for Franklin to put his faith in the restorative power of mineral waters, it is not surprising that he did so with such energy and hope.

The rest of each day was devoted to eating (moderately, and with as little consumption of fat as possible), leafing through *Punch* and the London *Times*, provided free in the *Kurhaus* reading room, going for graded walks in the park, and, if Mr. James was feeling especially well, making short excursions up the wooded slopes of nearby hills. Every effort was made to keep the patient from worries of any kind. "Do not trouble your mind with business affairs," one physician urged; even "excessive letter writing" was thought "decidedly pernicious" because the excited thoughts it inspired hampered sleep. After-dinner card-playing was also discouraged, and the Roosevelts' nightly game of bezique had to be played in secret. In any case, they were in bed beneath feather comforters by ten every evening.

No amount of Mozart or bright flowers could disguise the fact that the German baths existed to treat the desperately ill. Many of the men and women who lined up each morning with Mr. James to drink the waters were perfectly healthy, or seemed so. Some, like Sara, were merely accompanying the sick; others were taking the treatment as a preventative. But, as one visitor to Karlsbad wrote, "also you see . . . a sadly larger percentage of invalids, such as no kind soul could look upon without a pang. . . . Here are half-crippled sufferers, with pallid ghastly faces, limping to the springs on crutches, and looking as if their next step will be into their graves." The same was true at Nauheim. Some patients were not even well enough to stand; friends or servants carried them on pallets or pushed them in wheelchairs. Faces noticed one morning might not be in line the next.

Sickness and the vivid possibility of death surrounded Franklin at Nauheim, day after day. He knew that he was never to worry his father. Nor must he appear to be worried himself. He is not known ever to have spoken of the sights he saw at Nauheim, but he must have deliberately set out not to notice what was happening all around him, not to allow himself ever to be seen to be frightened or repelled.

"Life here," one visitor wrote, "is simple and quiet to the last degree," just what unwell adults needed, perhaps, but it cannot have held much interest for a lively little boy.[2] Few other children stopped at Nauheim, and of those present, most were ill themselves. Franklin befriended at least one of these that first summer, a pale English boy, smaller than himself and confined to a wheelchair, who spent several hours each day listening to music in the garden. His name was John Percival Droop, and many years later he remembered that the big American boy had been "very kind" to him all season, and when the Roosevelts were about to leave that September, Franklin had given him a storybook and signed its flyleaf with a confident flourish that might have seemed remarkable in any other nine-year-old: "To Percy from his friend, Franklin D. Roosevelt."

Franklin did his best to entertain himself. He had a bow and arrows and played Indian alone in the park, and he sailed a wind-up boat his father had bought for him at Cologne back and forth across its pond. And he learned to swim. Mr. James was not well enough to teach him,

2. Another patient at Bad Nauheim during the summer of 1892, the second season Mr. James and his wife and son spent there, was Livy Clemens, Mark Twain's wife, then suffering from both a heart condition and from goiter. With her was her eighteen-year-old daughter, Clara, who recalled that her father had christened the place "Bath No-Harm." "Certainly," Clara wrote, "not much benefit was evident from this cure, and the spot was none too cheerful. . . . There was nothing to do but walk through the valley."

Source: Clara Clemens, *My Father Mark Twain*, page 113.

so a friend, Sir Cameron Gull, did so in Spartan British style, tying a rope around the boy's waist and throwing him into the pool suspended from a stout pole; whenever he stayed under too long he was pulled up till he got his breath back, then plunged in again.[3]

Perhaps in part just to give him something else to do, his parents sent him to the local *Stadtschule* for six weeks that summer, just as Mr. James had enrolled Rosy in public school in Dresden twenty-six years earlier. If Franklin was frightened by his first contact with public education, as his half brother had been, he let no one know of it. The school director, Christian Bommerscheim, praised his "assiduous zeal" to his parents, and said that he had made "brisk diligent progress" in all his subjects. Years later, when FDR had been elected President, Herr Bommerscheim told a reporter that he had been "an unusually bright young fellow. He had such an engaging manner, and he was always so polite, that he was soon one of the most popular children in the school." It seems likely that the director meant that he had been popular with his teachers; they were adults, after all, and Franklin knew how much value adults placed on manners and unbroken amiability. But it seems unlikely that he was especially admired by his classmates. He was a year younger than they, less than fluent in their language, and dressed daily in a blue sailor suit at his mother's insistence. In any case, neither he nor his parents seem to have taken the experiment very seriously. His mother thought it "rather amusing, but I doubt if he learns much," and Franklin himself was dismissive when describing the exotic experience to his young cousins Muriel and Warren Robbins back home: "I go to the public school with a lot of little Mickies and we have German reading, German dictation, the history of Siegfried, and arithmetic . . . and I like it very much."

No "Mickies" are known to have come to his room to play, and although he returned several times to Nauheim with his parents, he never again went near the school.[4]

3. When the time came for his own children to learn to swim, FDR repeated this terrifying technique. Louis Depew, his mother's chauffeur, usually held the pole; but sometimes Roosevelt himself took charge, shouting encouragement all the while. "It really was a wretched way to teach you to swim," his eldest son recalled, "but it was the way Father had learned and—traditionalist that he was—it was the way he was going to teach us."

Sources: Roosevelt and Shalett, page 48; and Dows, *Franklin Roosevelt at Hyde Park,* page 99.

4. Some of Roosevelt's biographers have made a good deal of the political impact upon him of his early trips abroad, and when it suited the needs of the moment FDR did, too. The bellicose emperor Wilhelm II had been on the throne for just three years in 1891, but already every German schoolboy was receiving instruction in map reading and military topography—or so

When the Roosevelts left London for Pau after Franklin's bout with typhoid in 1889, a Miss Buckingham had accompanied them. She was his first governess and would remain only until the family began to make its way home again the following spring. At least seven more governesses and tutors followed over the next ten years.[5]

Franklin liked some better than others, but knew always that none was permanent. Like the boy they were hired to teach, governesses and tutors looked to his parents for their authority; neither Franklin nor his teachers ever had any doubt as to who was ultimately in charge. They were there to teach him what he needed to know, to answer his questions, to help him make his way. When one moved on, another would appear, in turn to be displaced. He may have been sorry to see one or another of them go, but it was all part of the natural scheme of things. They were there for him; he would outlast them all.

He was not notably rebellious. He knew that his parents wished him to study, so he did. But he was not a rigorous student, either, and it never took much to get him out of anything he found unpleasant.

Roosevelt said he remembered. In fact, he stated in 1933 (and again in 1945) that his own introduction to that discipline in the classroom at Nauheim had given him his first glimpse of the German potential for aggressive militarism. He did not, however, bother to mention that he was studying maps when he wrote to his cousins about his studies at the time, nor did his schoolmaster list topography among the subjects his American pupil studied while in his care.

His earlier remarks about the Germans proved embarrassing in October of 1939, when President Roosevelt was trying hard to maintain a public posture of strict neutrality. That month the columnist Harlan Miller wrote two lengthy and laudatory pieces on FDR's understanding of foreign affairs, placing special emphasis on his boyhood trips to Europe. Not surprisingly, Roosevelt found Miller's conclusion—that "No other American president has ever entered the White House with such an intimate knowledge of world politics and international stresses"—"essentially accurate."

But Ernest K. Lindley, a veteran journalist and early Roosevelt biographer who generally admired FDR, found Miller's columns a bit much. Roosevelt had a built-in anti-German bias, he suggested, recalling for his readers his own conversations with Roosevelt, in which FDR "had made it plain that he did not look back upon Germany with the same friendliness that he felt for Great Britain and France." The President was indignant, and dictated a long cutting letter which he wanted Steve Early, his press secretary, to send out over his own signature. Lindley's story was "essentially inaccurate," he said, and the notion that he had ever thought less of Germany than Britain or France was "deliberate falsification." "As a matter of simple fact," he said, "I did not know Great Britain and France as a boy, but I did know Germany. If anything, I looked upon the Germany that I knew with far more friendliness than I did Great Britain or France."

He *did* know Britain and France, however, and if he preferred Germany he successfully hid that view from his parents, whose own scorn for Germans was unrelenting.

Sources: FDR's letter to Lindley and supporting documents, Stephen T. Early Papers, FDRL.

5. Franklin Roosevelt's governesses and tutors and their dates of service: Miss Buckingham, 1889–90; Miss Gerver, 1890; Miss Reinsberg, 1890–91; Mademoiselle Jeanne Sandoz, 1891–93; Miss Alice Clay, 1893–94; Mr. Foley, 1894–95; Mr. Arthur Dumper, 1895–96.

Source: SDR's journals, FDRL.

The smallest scratch on his finger—"a bobo," his sympathetic mother called it—was enough to put off piano practice; he skipped church often enough, pleading illness, that his father joked about his "Sunday headaches" but let him stay home anyway.

In Paris, on their way home after Miss Buckingham returned to England, the Roosevelts heard of another English governess with an excellent reputation, a Miss Gerver, then living in Vienna. Mr. James sent for her and she was hired. Within a day or two, however, Sara wrote that she did not believe Miss Gerver "suitable"; in fact, "I do not believe I can stand her."

"We always had people taking care of Franklin," she explained years later, "who . . . gave him a great deal of time with us alone. It was evident from the outset that this companion had no such intentions. We were never without her, but it seemed to bother Franklin much less than it did me. On several occasions I asked him whether he liked his governess, only to have him say, 'Oh, she's all right.' "

Sara continued to resent her, however, and when the time came to decide whether she would return to Hyde Park with the family, she pressed her son hard for his honest opinion: Did he really like her?

"I think she's perfectly awful," he said finally. "In fact, I have a name for her. I call her the long-legged duckling."

Then why had he said she was all right?

"Because," he answered, "I thought after Father had gone to such trouble and spent so much money to get her, it wouldn't be right for me to complain."

Miss Gerver did not come to Springwood.

The governess who stayed with Franklin longest was Mademoiselle Jeanne Sandoz, a French-speaking Swiss whom his parents hired in 1891. She was just nineteen and barely five feet tall, but energetic and experienced, having already cared for five Scottish children. She was one of several applicants who filed through the Roosevelts' London hotel suite to be interviewed that fall, and Franklin himself had helped choose her. "Mama, take that one," he had whispered loudly enough so that she overheard him. "I like her. She smiles all the time." She was in fact remarkably cheerful and enthusiastic; when things were going especially well she liked to say all was "superfine, splendide et pas chere."

Franklin may initially have thought her an easy mark; at nine, he was nearly as tall as she. "Franklin works well enough," she told his parents in her first report, "but his obedience outside of class leaves much to be desired." She turned out to be a shrewd judge of the dynamics of power at Springwood. To Franklin's mother, whom she always thought "*très formidable,*" she said she was sure he would distinguish himself, and she seems to have known by instinct that the best way to bring the boy into line was to appeal to his fear of letting his parents down. "Your father is wasting his money," she told him one day, "and I am wasting my time. I shall leave you." Thereafter, the two became "fast friends," or so she recalled forty years later.

Franklin's exercise books show that he and Mademoiselle Sandoz studied the Bible and catechism daily, along with arithmetic, science, geography, poetry, music, history (ancient, European, and English, but not American), as well as English and German. All but the last two were taught in French, and when Franklin and his teacher dined together that is all they allowed themselves to speak. He almost always received a "*très bien*" in history; his conduct was often "*mal.*"

Later in her life, Mademoiselle Sandoz became interested in a number of causes—the Social Gospel, spiritualism, the League of Nations—and it has been suggested that she sought to inculcate an enhanced sense of social conscience in her young charge. If she did, it does not seem to have taken. In an essay on ancient history he could not contain his amusement at her earnestness:

"The people of Egypt were divided into 3 classes: the Priests, the Warriors and the work people. The land was divided between the Warriors, the Priests and the Kings and each had a 3rd of it. The working people had nothing. They lived in the porches of the temples or in little straw huts. The kings made them work so hard and gave them so little that by wingo! they nearly starved and by jinks! they had hardly any clothes! So they died in quadrillions!"[6]

6. The theory that Mademoiselle Sandoz somehow implanted in her young pupil, the seeds of his social conscience is partly based upon an apparent misreading of a letter FDR wrote to his old teacher from the White House in 1933. It reads in part: "I have often thought that it was you, more than anyone else, who laid the foundation for my education." The very next sentence suggests strongly, however, that all the President meant was that she had helped him master French: "The lessons in French which I began at that time have stood me in good stead during all these years, and here in Washington it is a great pleasure to be able to converse with the members of the Diplomatic Corps in a common tongue." Two years later he wrote her again, enclosing a photograph of himself and paying the same cordial but limited tribute to the impact of her teaching: "I think it will interest you to know that it has been the greatest possible help to me to be able to speak French—not only during the war days when I was in France and Belgium, but also here in Washington where I meet so many foreigners and diplomats who cannot speak English."

Whatever impact Mademoiselle Sandoz may or may not have had on Franklin, the fact that she had been his teacher was important to her family long before he became President. One of her nieces wrote to FDR in 1935 explaining that all through her childhood "I heard of the

He was fond of Mademoiselle Sandoz and liked to try out jokes on her: "What animals are always ready to travel? Answer: Elephants. They always have their trunks with them." And she liked to recall the Roosevelts' visit to West Superior, then still mostly mud, with pine stakes marking out the projected streets. A new corridor rug had been laid in the settlement's only hotel, and electric sparks crackled from it with every footstep. "How Franklin ran up and down that corridor," she remembered, "making me run with him until I was breathless."

But he was not notably respectful. When the Roosevelts traveled to Europe in 1892, he slept in the berth above hers and woke her each morning by dangling a string down onto her face, and when she fell from the family toboggan and bruised herself badly, even his mother was momentarily displeased at his attitude: "Poor little Mlle Sandoz. . . . Franklin seems to think it a rather fine joke."

Her predecessor, a thin unsmiling German named Miss Reinsberg, had fared worse. One afternoon while she was downstairs, Franklin slipped into her bedroom and spooned a double dose of effervescent powder into the chamber pot beneath her bed. When she used the pot during the night and the powder began to bubble and hiss, she rushed down the hall and awakened Mrs. Roosevelt to tell her of the alarming symptom she had suddenly developed. His mother never figured out what had happened—or so FDR always maintained—but Mr. James did, and the boy was summoned to the smoking room for a solemn talk with his father. Franklin confessed, and Mr. James, struggling to keep from laughing, dismissed him, saying, "Consider yourself spanked."

Since Miss Reinsberg eventually suffered a nervous breakdown and had to be hospitalized, and Mademoiselle Sandoz returned to Europe to marry in 1893, FDR liked to say that he had driven one governess to the madhouse and the other to matrimony.

Again, it was not his teachers but his parents who molded their son's personality and character; his mother and his father who instilled in him at least the rudiments of responsibility toward his community. Both the Delanos and the Roosevelts took seriously the ancient notion

remarkable youth whom [Aunt Jeanne] had taught at Hyde Park, and for a long time there was a photograph of him in my father's stamp album, a photo that was most delightful to our eyes, for my brothers wore overalls and their feet were bare. But now and then Father would let us see the boy with such fine clothes, and such neat hair. 'A fine young gentleman,' my Father would remark. 'And don't forget that a Swiss woman was his teacher, and a Sandoz.' "

Sources: Constance Drexel, "Unpublished Letters of FDR to His French Governess," *Parents' Magazine* XXVI, September 1951, PPF 119, FDRL.

of "noblesse oblige." "One can be as democratic as one likes," Sara once told her son, "but if we love our own, and if we love our neighbor, we owe a great example."

The Delanos of Algonac were once credited by a local newspaper with being the wealthiest family in Newburgh, "or at least the most liberal." Even the retiring Catherine Delano helped raise funds and gather food for the needy, and her husband contributed to Booker T. Washington's work for black education and uplift in the south. Sara remembered seeing Washington at Algonac, welcomed onto the piazza though not into the parlor. And when her sister Annie Hitch came to live in the old house after her father's death, she became a tireless force for good in her city. She presented Newburgh with a park and served as president of the Associated Charities, for which she coined the new and enlightened slogan: "Not alms, but a friend." Old-fashioned charity was no longer enough, she argued; instead, "we must furnish work to do away with pauperism." She was so much admired that the local Elks made her a full-fledged member, the first woman ever so designated.

After Mrs. Hitch died in 1926, an old friend recalled her work among the city's least fortunate: "How often have I seen her step into her automobile at the door while old Peter, her chauffeur, put in after her half a dozen of the well-known Algonac baskets, filled with fruit and flowers. No need to tell him where to go, as passing through the city, he stopped at various humble dwellings. Here, notwithstanding her lameness, he helped her up the steps carrying the baskets, and voices of children could be heard, 'Here she comes. Here comes our Mrs. Hitch.' "

Sara Roosevelt's own efforts were less strenuous. She dispatched food, clothing, and cheering bouquets to the sick, paid faithful visits to former servants and their families in time of need, and supervised a sewing class at the Hyde Park School.

In a remarkable address delivered before the St. James Guild toward the end of his life, Mr. James offered his own earnest views of a citizen's responsibilities toward himself, his family, and his community. The theme of his talk was "Work," and its first half was indistinguishable from the complacent preachments of other wealthy men of his day, a hymn to the virtues of toil, integrity, and thrift. Hard work was the key to success: "There is not so much to *luck* as some people profess to believe. Indeed, most people *fail* because they do not deserve to succeed.

"Extravagance," he continued, was "the pervading sin among all classes of people, rich and poor alike; you see it everywhere, in your public buildings, in your churches, in the streets, on the backs of your wives and children, display in dress, in furniture, in equipage, in entertainments, in marriage—display in funerals . . . Go to your towns and cities and see the velvets and silks sweeping the streets, the men with their fast horses and extravagant habits, families in their brown stone and marble fronts, all for show and fashion, how many do you think can afford it?" (It is hard not to think that the show and fashion of Rosy's life were on his father's mind when he wrote these words.)

He asked his listeners to think back to the days of their childhoods when people lived sensibly within their means. "No man has any business to live in a style which his income cannot support or to mortgage his earnings of next week or of next year, in order to live luxuriously today. The whole system of debt is wrong when we anticipate or forestall the future." The thing to do was save. Ten cents a day would do for a start. "Try it—begin tomorrow. . . . The curtailment of any selfish enjoyment will do it, a cigar, a paper of tobacco, a glass of beer."

But Mr. James's travels had taught him that abstemiousness alone could not solve the problems of the truly desperate. "In all countries and all ages," he told the Guild, "there have been more workers than work." He had himself seen what life was like in the squalid, crowded tenements of New York, Paris, and London, "many of them containing more people than this whole village." In Shepherd's Court in London's East End, he had climbed tenement stairs to see a single room that measured just three lengths of his cane one way and four the other in which lived an entire family of ten. The floor was rotten and full of holes; water ran down the walls and dripped from the ceiling. The St. Giles district was still worse; here, the poor huddled beneath the street in cellars, "dozens of them, you can see their open mouths luridly lit by the fire and candle light below. These possess no windows and the only way in which light and ventilation can be conveyed to the inhabitants below is through a hole in the pavement." He had clambered down a ladder, "several feet below the sewage and gas pipes," and found there "half a dozen nearly nude and hideously dirty children, a man toiling by the flame of a candle, a woman lying ill abed, all in this pestiferous and dingy den."

Exhortation would not rescue these desperate people. "Help the helpless!" Mr. James concluded. "Here is *work* for every man, woman, and child in this audience tonight. The poorest man, the daily worker, the obscurest individual, shares the gift and the blessings for doing good. It is not necessary that men should be rich to be helpful to others. Money may help, but money does not do all. It requires earnest purpose, honest self devotion and hard work. Help the poor, the widow, the orphan; help the sick, the fallen man or woman, for the sake of our common humanity. Help all who are suffering. Work then for your daily support. Work for your wives and children. Work for fame and honor. Work for humanity. Work for your Lord and Master.

"Man is dear to man; the poorest poor long for some moment in a weary life when they can know and feel that they have been themselves the fathers and dealers-out of some small blessings;—have been kind to such as needed kindness—for that single cause that we have, all of us, one human heart."

We do not know precisely when Mr. James exhorted his fellow parishioners, and so cannot say whether Franklin was present at St. James to hear him. But his father's views must have been as familiar to the boy as was the setting in which they were delivered.

From his earliest days, St. James and the dignified, restrained Episcopalianism it fostered embodied religious faith for Franklin Roosevelt. As a small boy, he only learned that there was "another church in the village besides my own" when an elderly Methodist couple invited him into their home for a slice of gingerbread. The wine-red silk of the cushions on which he sat between his parents in the Roosevelt pew, the rhythm of the responses, the beauty of the language, the singing of the choir (all his life he loved to sing hymns; "Art Thou Weary, Art Thou Languid, Art Thou Sore Distressed" was his favorite), the genteel exhortations of the rector—all provided him with solace, comfort, continuity. So did the church itself. He had been baptized in its chapel; his father and half brother were vestrymen and senior wardens—as he would be when the time came.[7] The walls and

7. FDR remained committed to his boyhood church to the day of his death, first as junior vestryman and vestryman, then as senior warden. Vestry meetings were sometimes held at Springwood after he was stricken with polio, usually on Saturday or Sunday afternoons. Even during the worst days of World War II these often went on into the early hours of the morning. "They *never* seemed to end," said Mary Newbold Morgan, FDR's childhood friend who remained his next-door neighbor after her marriage to Gerald Morgan, a former journalist, sometime businessman, and fellow member of the vestry. No detail of St. James's operation was too small to hold the President's attention. He fretted over church investments, suggested the precise wording of historical plaques, and sought to reduce the size and number of the family memorial tablets that he felt cluttered the walls. In 1941, when the church treasurer resigned, FDR nominated a candidate of his own. "What would you think of the young man who runs the drug store [Raymond Hill]?" he wrote to Morgan. "He seems to be up and coming. He is a violent Republican!" (*footnote continued on next page*)

windows were covered with memorial plaques honoring old friends from Hyde Park's most prominent families.

His faith always remained simple and unshakable. Much later in his life, Eleanor Roosevelt asked him whether he and she shouldn't refrain from trying to impose their own religious convictions on their children; wouldn't it be better to leave them free to make up their own minds? FDR was astonished at the suggestion. His children would be trained as he had been, as Episcopalians. "But are you sure that you believe in everything you learned?" she asked. "I never really thought about it," he said. "I think it is just as well not to think about things like that too much."[8]

Nor, so far as we know, did FDR ever seriously examine his own apparently irresistible compulsion to collect things, a compul-

---

Sources: Interview with Gerald Morgan, Jr.; President's Secretary's File (PSF) 154, FDRL.

8. The sources of Roosevelt's apparently unquenchable optimism and self-assurance will always remain to some extent mysterious. His sturdy religious faith must surely have been one of them, however, and some biographers have placed especially heavy emphasis upon it. Rexford Tugwell, for example, believed that his faith developed strongly during adolescence. "This belief in and reliance upon a fatherly God to take the place of the earthly father who was retreating into the shadows of age became so settled and fixed in his life as never again to be questioned . . . ," he wrote. "The secret of his unassailable serenity and his easy gaiety lay in this sense of oneness with ongoing processes of the universe and his feeling of being, as Emerson said, in tune with the infinite." Always, Tugwell writes, when Roosevelt was about to undertake something new, he would "ask all his colleagues in it to accompany him . . . in asking for divine blessing on what they were about to do. It must be remembered that one who asks and feels that he receives support in this manner, and with sincerity, cannot, even in his own estimation go disastrously wrong. If an error is made it is an understandable one and nearly always unavoidable in the sense that no one could have done more."

Kenneth S. Davis goes still further. Roosevelt, he writes, "believing absolutely in God the Father and Jesus Christ as the Son of God; believing that God, caring for each individual human being, was infinitely kind and good as well as all-wise and -powerful; believing or *feeling* that history was a working-out of divine purpose, that every truly fundamental historical force was a manifestation of divine will—believing all this, he must and did believe that history, though it had at any given extended period of time a tidal ebb and flow, had in the long run a surging flow in one direction. It was away from polar evil toward polar good. This was the essential progress, from worse to better, a progress that was inevitable because it was God's will. As a chosen one, he himself was an instrument of progress, a special agent on earth of divine beneficence. But *only* an instrument. *Only* an agent . . . By his religious faith and his self-conception in terms of it (his sense of his role in history) he was required actively to seek great power—the greatest earthly power. But he never did so with the feeling that he himself would *become* the power he exercised, or even that it would become his personal property, to be used in service of his purely personal will. It was assigned, imposed from on High. It remained God's. And the ultimate responsibility for his use of it was therefore also God's. This conviction enabled him to act, often, as if he were possessed of what Spengler called a 'dreamlike certainty' of decision."

Surely religious certitude helped FDR make hard decisions—and to sleep soundly once they were made. But the basic question remains unanswered. How did he first become persuaded that he was what Davis calls "a chosen one"? *Who* chose him? Religion helped confirm his sense of himself, but the real answer to that hardest of biographical questions, I believe, lies not at St. James but down the Albany Road, within the walls of Springwood.

Sources: Tugwell, *The Democratic Roosevelt,* pages 31–32; Davis, "FDR as a Biographer's Problem," *The American Scholar,* Winter, 1983/84.

sion first felt during his boyhood but from which he was never free.

In 1938 he announced plans to have built at Hyde Park a library to house his personal and presidential papers and his various collections. The repository was to be constructed with private money—some 28,000 people eventually contributed to the building fund.

But the land on which it stood—just outside his mother's rose garden, at the western edge of his father's hayfield—would be deeded to the nation. Eventually, most of Springwood would be given to the federal government "to be maintained for the benefit of the public."

It was an unprecedented notion; Roosevelt's thirty predecessors had been content to scatter their papers among libraries and descendants all over the country, and his enemies inevitably saw in it evidence of megalomania. The journalist John T. Flynn compared FDR to "an Egyptian Pharaoh" who wished to transform his estate into a "Yankee Pyramid." But Roosevelt faced an unprecedented problem. His ability to communicate directly with the millions of ordinary citizens he called "my friends" had loosed a torrent of mail on the White House. Four thousand letters addressed to him arrived daily in 1940, for example, more than ten times the number that had come to Herbert Hoover. And the vast expansion of federal responsibility and power over which he so cheerfully presided yielded an equally vast growth of federal paperwork. The Franklin D. Roosevelt Library would one day contain forty-five *tons* of documents.

But just as important was Roosevelt's own inability to throw anything away. He was a self-confessed pack rat. "I have destroyed practically nothing," he admitted, and the result, even he knew, was "a mine for which future historians will curse . . . as well as praise me." This was in part an inheritance from the Delanos, who seem to have believed that nothing they wrote or received or simply owned was unimportant, precisely because it had passed through their hands. His mother helped inculcate that attitude, reverently saving his childish drawings and letters, his books and best-loved toys. But in Franklin Roosevelt it became almost obsessive. At one time or another he seems to have collected everything. The thousands of physical objects he left to the library are in some ways more revealing than his voluminous but circumspect papers; they constitute "a very conglomerate, hit-or-miss, all-over-the-place collection," he once said, "on every man, animal, subject or material."

His stamps were his best-known collection, well over a million of them in 150 matching albums. His physician, Admiral Ross T. McIntire, who saw him nearly every day in the White House, estimated that FDR spent at least 2,140 hours poring over these bright bits of paper during his dozen busy years in the White House. But stamps were only part of Roosevelt's variegated hoard. There were also some 15,000 books—2,500 volumes on the American Navy alone, hundreds more on the history of Dutchess County, but also children's books, children's books in *French,* miniature books, first editions, books with lavish illustrations. His collection of naval paintings and prints alone included some 1,200 items, plus thirty-seven leather-bound albums filled with photographs of naval vessels, each carefully captioned in his own bold, slanting hand. There were groups of English political cartoons, drawings by George Cruikshank, and some 200 fully rigged ship models, so many that the White House staff despaired of ever keeping them all dusted. Even Roosevelt's presidential desk was thickly forested with scores of miniature donkeys and elephants and Scotties.

This headlong enthusiasm for hobbies and collecting seems to have begun very early but to have intensified after 1890, when, with his father forbidden to overexert himself and increasingly distracted by concern for his own failing health, Franklin found himself with still more time to spend on his own.

The first letter he ever wrote—at age five and inevitably addressed to his mother—had included two surprisingly detailed drawings of sailboats. He came by his lifelong love of ships and the sea naturally. His father and half brother were enthusiastic yachtsmen, but his mother attributed her son's enthusiasm directly to "my own love of ships and distant horizons. . . . The Delanos have always been associated with the sea," she explained, and "I have always been a great believer in heredity."

She and her father took turns telling Franklin stories of seafaring; so did his nurse Mamie, tales so exciting that he wasn't entirely sure he believed them, but always asked for more. His frequent visits to the Delano homestead at Fairhaven were voyages into maritime history. From the old stone wharf built by his great-grandfather he could gaze out at the masts of a score or so of old whalers still at anchor in New Bedford harbor. His grandfather gave him a battered sea chest in which the boy carefully kept a collection of family relics: a button from a naval officer's coat, said to have been shot off in combat; a miniature brass cannon; his great-uncle's sailor hat worn in the War of 1812. And on his own in the cluttered attic he uncovered a set of whalers' logs. They were bound in canvas, "with stenciled whales in the margins," Roosevelt remembered, "the speaking of other ships, the total of the catch, the visits to Fayal, to the Falklands, to Unalaska . . . Here was a tale."

He sailed toy boats, carved and collected miniature ships, read naval history with special attention to the works of Admiral Alfred Thayer Mahan, and rejoiced when in 1891 Mr. James took delivery of the *Half Moon,* a fifty-one-foot sailing yacht with an auxiliary naphtha motor. She had her own uniformed captain and three-man crew, of course, but Franklin often took the wheel. He was still more pleased at sixteen when his father presented him with his own twenty-one-foot knockabout; he named her the *New Moon* and sailed her almost daily every summer at Campobello, learning to navigate the rocks and tides and treacherous currents of the Bay of Fundy.

His mother was largely responsible for introducing him to stamp collecting, too. Her own collection, begun when she was five and pining for her distant father, had long since been passed on to her brother Fred. He, in turn, had greatly enlarged it before losing interest; and when he presented it to his ten-year-old nephew in 1892, it was already comprehensive enough to make most adult collectors envious. Franklin spent evening after evening adding to it, pasting new stamps into albums and making careful notes on the pages, studying their designs, wondering about the countries from which they came. Not even his mother's nightly reading aloud could interrupt him. Once, annoyed at his apparent inattention, she demanded that he tell her what she had just read. He repeated it back almost verbatim, explaining that he would be ashamed of himself if he couldn't do two things at once.

Birds interested him almost as much. He had collected eggs and nests as a small boy; one little girl, invited to Springwood for an Easter egg hunt, recalled that Franklin had arrived late, emerging slowly from the woods and inching his way across the lawn, a brilliant blue robin's egg cupped in his small hands. Soon eggs and nests no longer satisfied; he wanted to collect the birds themselves, and at ten he began asking for a shotgun. His mother thought this a dreadful idea—the boy was much too young—but his father agreed, presenting him with a gun on his eleventh birthday. With it came a set of rules: There was to be no shooting during the mating season; nesting birds were off-limits; only one member of each species was to be collected.

That shiny new gun meant many things to Franklin. It helped him create a collection of stuffed birds, first of all. But ornithology, in turn, licensed him to kill, to affect things directly on his own and out from under his mother's anxious love. He became an "insatiable" hunter, she wrote, and something of his passion survives in a composition he dashed off for Mademoiselle Sandoz in 1893. The subject was "Guns and Squirrels." "Many Mamas," it read in part, "think guns are very dangerous things & think they will go off without cartridges or without being cocked, but if properly handled they are not dangerous. Some boys if they saw a solitary squirrel would cock both barrels & on killing him with the first, would probably forget that the other barrel was cocked & should he touch the trigger it would go, bang! . . .[9] It is great fun shooting [squirrels] and it is not very easy to get a shot at them while sitting still; when they fall they bump their heads on the ground three times before they die. The old ones hold on to the branches & try to hide when wounded. I have fired at a squirrel 5 times & when he fell counted 31 shots in his body!"

He kept a day-by-day tally of his kills: "Shot a Pine Finch. The bird was alone in a small pine tree, and he appeared very shy. Had great difficulty in shooting him. . . . Shot a Barred Owl at 5 PM in Newbold's Gully." He skinned his own birds and did his best to mount the first few, though his mother said the effort made him turn "quite green." But when it was clear that he would never warm to this redolent hobby he was allowed to send his trophies off to professional taxidermists in New York and Poughkeepsie. By the age of fourteen he had shot and identified more than 300 different species native to Dutchess County.

His mother was proud of his skill and industry. She lined bookshelves and mantelpieces with his mounted specimens and eventually had a glass-fronted case built for them in the entrance hall; a big dusty harrier hawk hung from a wire in front of it. The birds greeted guests right through the presidential years, the labels beneath their claws written out in FDR's boyish hand.

9. His own mama evidently feared this with good reason. On April 14 of the following year, while Franklin was walking with her and his current governess, Miss Clay, his gun did go off accidentally. The pellets buried themselves harmlessly in the ground. And at some point later in his hunting career, Mr. James took his gun away from him for a time because the boy had carelessly fired it in the general direction of some people walking along the Albany Road.

Source: SDR diary, FDRL.

Ornithology won him the admiration of other adults as well. His grandfather Delano made him a life member of the New York Museum of Natural History, and when he was fifteen its bird department gratefully acknowledged his gift of ten carefully prepared pine grosbeak skins. And it helped him overcome his early shyness. Traveling in England with his parents, he was desolated when a business appointment in London forced them to cancel a planned visit to Osberton-in-Worksop, the Nottinghamshire seat of Cecil Foljambe, the Baron Hawkesbury, one of England's most knowledgeable bird fanciers, whose collection of mounted birds was unmatched outside of museums.

"Mummie, can't I go without you?" Franklin begged.

"You mean you'd visit people you had never met?" she answered, genuinely surprised.

"I'd go anywhere to see those birds," he answered. His parents allowed him to take the train alone, and the elderly baron and the eleven-year-old American ornithologist spent the afternoon together talking about birds and gravely examining the glass cases. At day's end, the baron insisted on sending his housekeeper to escort Franklin back to London on the train. "This must have been a great blow to his pride," his mother wrote, "for he considered himself quite grown up and self-reliant." But of course he did not show it.

In hunting, as in everything else, his assumption was always that things would work out well for him. One day he strolled into the house from the river side and asked for his gun. His mother asked why he wanted it.

"There's a winter wren up in one of those big trees down there," he said. "I want to get him."

His mother unlocked the cabinet in which the gun was kept. "Why do you think the wren is going to oblige you by staying there while you come in and get your gun?"

"Oh," said Franklin, shouldering his shotgun. "He'll wait."

He returned a few minutes later, his weapon in one hand, the warm dead bird in the other.

Even Franklin's genuine ornithological accomplishments were evidently not enough for him. Perhaps too much emphasis on the importance of being grown up beyond his years had made him dissatisfied on some level with what he could do on his own; he must have known within himself that whatever his admiring parents and grandparents might say, his work could not really compare favorably with that of adults. In any case, in the spring of 1896, when he was fourteen, he contributed a short article on birds to the third issue of *The Foursome,* a homemade children's magazine compiled at Tuxedo Park for the family by his cousins Warren and Muriel Robbins. The essay is called "Spring Song," and while its source is unknown, much of it appears to be plagiarized. The ornate yet chatty style gives it away; it is written in the voice of a weary adult hack, not an adolescent: "Listen, the bugler has come!" it begins. "A few shrill notes and a trill, and we see our friend the Song Sparrow. In quick succession the Robins and the Bluebirds arrive. This is the advance guard. A few days more and Black Birds appear. Hear their juicy note, which reminds you of strawberries and cream, but venture too close and they will be off with a cheery 'Can't catch me.' " The ending is even more elaborate: "The Peabody Bird[10] or White Throated Sparrow comes at this time, and he will stay with us until driven southward by the cold, when, sitting on a fence rail, he bids us 'Farewell.' "

No one seems ever to have found him out, and his mother proudly kept this effort alongside his far clumsier authentic boyhood writings. Perhaps appropriating the words of others did not present a problem for his conscience; like tutors and toys, they were at hand for his use.[11]

The hobbies that consumed Franklin Roosevelt as a boy seem at first to have been remarkably diverse—sailing and the sea, collecting stamps, the shooting and classification of birds. Yet they may all also be seen as reactions to his mother's fond but unyielding efforts to control him. Squinting down the barrel of his shotgun or gripping the *New Moon*'s wheel, he was in charge. His decisions made things happen, his alone, and not his mother's. Collecting and classifying, too, fostered independence, a quieter kind perhaps, but just as determinedly defended; in arranging his birds or stamps he was able to order a world of his own, one in which his mother was only an interloper.

In all of these activities, Franklin pleased himself while pleasing adults. Other children did not matter much, and we know little of how he conducted himself when thrown together with them. He knew few other children, and only a tiny handful of those he did know left even brief memoirs of their time together. But one early friend's detailed

10. This interpolation was probably an inside joke, a reference to the Reverend Endicott Peabody, founder and headmaster of Groton School, to which both Franklin and Warren Robbins would go.

11. At the risk of pushing the evidence too hard, it may not be accidental that FDR became the first President consistently to call upon ghostwriters to help him express himself.

account of her first encounter with him reveals in miniature how he would always confront the world.

One winter morning in 1892, Miss Huybertie Pruyn of Albany was told she would have a visitor. Her mother said that a Mr. and Mrs. Roosevelt of New York were coming for the night and were bringing with them their ten-year-old son, Franklin. Bertie was fourteen and not enthusiastic. She was to be nice to the boy, "polite and helpful," even though he was much younger than she, her mother added, for "he is bound to have good manners." Bertie was unmoved, and when she spotted her young friend Erastus Corning III, known as "Ratty" across the street, she told him about the priggish little stranger who was on his way. Ratty sympathized. "I can settle him for you," he said, packing a snowball with his gloved hands. "I can trip him up so he won't know what happened and then wash his face. He's probably a New York sissy."

The Pruyn family sleigh jingled around the corner. Mr. James and Sara sat in front, wrapped in bear rugs against the cold. Franklin, slender and small, sat in the back. "Ratty and I stood there with our sleds," Bertie recalled. "I am sure we did not look any too cordial." Then, "almost before Owen the footman could jump off the box to open the sleigh door," Franklin leaped down, held out his hand, and asked, " 'May I go coasting with you?' He took us completely by surprise," Bertie remembered. "We forgot our inhospitable plans and . . . ran for the toboggan slide. Our guest was no sissy. He soon showed us he knew more about all kinds of coasting than we did, and he turned hand-springs down the slide."

Franklin Roosevelt already knew at ten the power of his charm to disarm, that the best way for him to overcome his own insecurity was to act always as if it did not exist.

Later, Bertie and Franklin had supper together in the pantry; their parents were to dine at eight. "We were good friends by this time in spite of the difference in ages—he was old for his age and I was young for mine," she wrote. "I suggested we hurry up and get out by the play-room door to the garden before I was caught to do my lessons. It was a lovely evening and the slide in fine condition. After we had coasted awhile, our old laundress Mary O'Mara stopped . . . on her way to her room over the laundry [and] said 'Sure, 'tis too bad for ye to be leading that little boy in the paths of sin—keeping him out of bed this time of night, poor lad.' "

The City Hall bell tolled nine o'clock. Franklin said he was supposed to be in bed—that his mother would be sure to go upstairs after dinner and find he was not there. "I said I, too, was supposed to be in bed," Bertie remembered. "I got 50 cents a week if I was prompt —but we cannot go in now. The dinner party is over. They are going into the Conservatory. We must get the ice cream. We went down the outside cellar stairs and through the blackness of the cellar with only the glow from the furnaces to give a faint light and make the shadows look blacker. I did not think [Franklin] was frightened when I told him to wait by the inside stairs while I went to loot the ice cream. In my moccasins no one could hear me, and luck was with me. . . . The silver platter of ice cream was on the dumb waiter which had been sent down from the pantry and, more luck, there was also a platter of cakes. I rushed back with them, almost falling downstairs in my . . . hurry. We carried our loot into the garden."

The tall girl and her new friend sat on their slides taking turns eating, the lamplight from the conservatory windows glittering on the snow, their delight doubled because they could look inside while they spooned in the stolen dessert and watch their unsuspecting parents sipping madeira. When they had eaten all they could, they left the platter on a sled for the family dog to lick and crouched down by the garden gate to hurl snowballs at the ankles of churchgoers tramping home from evening services.

After a time they heard Bridget the cook shouting, "What has she done with the platter? Is it coasting on it, they are? Sure, the poor little boy will be sick with the goings-on. And the dog is eating off the silver." Then Mr. James began calling for Franklin from the dining-room piazza. "There was nothing we could do," Bertie remembered, "but to go in and receive . . . mild scoldings as to the lateness of the hour."

Later, when his mother came upstairs to see if he was well tucked into bed, she said she hoped he'd had a good time. He had, he told her, but the maid had said he had been "lured into the paths of sin" and he wanted to know what that meant. Answering his question might have proved embarrassing, and so his mother pretended not to hear him and said good night.

Bertie would much later marry Charles Hamlin, a member of the Federal Reserve Board, and she often saw FDR, in Washington and elsewhere. Once, riding with her in a White House elevator, he recalled that snowy evening in Albany. He had never been so frightened in his life, he confessed, as he had been while waiting alone in that cellar for her to steal the ice cream.

On a cold November evening in 1892, ten-year-old Franklin was asleep in his brass bed in his big room at the top of the Springwood stairs when he heard strange music—"Yankee Doodle," rattled and shrilled on a snare drum and piccolo. He ran to the window to see a parade of farm wagons turning into the long driveway, accompanied by men carrying torches. Hurrying downstairs in his nightshirt, he joined his father and mother on the porch. It was election night, and Grover Cleveland had been returned to the White House. Friends of Mr. James had gone to Poughkeepsie for the returns, then raced back to bring the glorious news. "Yankee Doodle" had been the agreed-upon signal that the Democrats were back in power—"the sweetest music I ever heard," Mr. James said—and all the Democrats in town had turned out to celebrate. One farmer, seeing Franklin shiver from cold and excitement, leaned out from his wagon to hand him a buffalo robe. The boy wrapped himself in it, he remembered at another Springwood victory celebration many years later, "and had a perfectly grand evening."

A Democratic triumph was almost always good news to the Roosevelts, but this one meant more than usual. Mr. James expected that it would greatly improve the prospects of his latest scheme to make himself a still richer man. He had helped form the Maritime Canal Company of Nicaragua during the 1880s. Its aim was to link the Atlantic and Pacific by scooping out a navigable canal that would run through Lake Nicaragua in direct competition with a French effort directed by the builder of the Suez Canal, Ferdinand de Lesseps. Mr. James had helped lobby Congress for its incorporation during the winter the Roosevelts spent in Washington in 1887, and had looked on as his friend President Cleveland signed it into law. The French project had conveniently failed since, and preliminary construction on the American canal had begun in 1890, but millions of additional dollars would be needed. It was Mr. James's fond expectation that Cleveland could be counted upon to help obtain them.

Then there was the matter of Rosy's stalled diplomatic career. The Republican victory four years earlier had forced him to leave his post in Vienna, and he had been drifting amiably ever since. Cleveland's election prodded him to action. He had contributed $10,000 to the

Democratic campaign. Now he wished to be made American ambassador to Belgium. His old chief at Vienna, General Alexander Lawton, wrote a dutiful recommendation to the President on his behalf. Understandably, it placed heavier emphasis on Rosy's geniality and good manners than his skills. The ambassadorship went to someone else, but the following autumn Rosy was offered the post of first secretary of the London embassy.

He was in many ways a natural choice. He already lived much of the time in England; many of his closest friends were Britons; and with his increasing corpulence, his waxed mustache, and graying well-barbered beard, he even bore a remarkable resemblance to the leader of the fashionable sporting set in which he already played a prominent role—Edward, Prince of Wales, himself. Nor would the first secretary's duties unduly interrupt his pleasures. There was a rush of work each spring when flocks of ambitious young American women and their mothers arrived in London determined to attend the Queen's Drawing Room, and it was the first secretary's delicate task to pick and choose among them. But otherwise there would be plenty of opportunity for him to drive and shoot and follow the races at Epsom, Ascot, and Newmarket Heath.

Mr. James, Sara, and Franklin visited Rosy and his family at their country seat near Ascot on their way home from Bad Nauheim that October. Sara noticed that Helen Astor Roosevelt, Rosy's wife, seemed ill and "thin." She spoke personally with the family physician, who said Helen's liver was at fault; it was sluggish and only a regimen of determined horseback riding could jar it into working properly again.

Shortly after they had returned to Hyde Park a cable came from Rosy saying that Helen had fallen "seriously ill." James and Sara offered to return at once to England, but Rosy wired back that the doctor had grown more optimistic: "Do not come."

Mr. James was deeply wounded by this, and when on November 12 another cable arrived saying that Helen had died, he refused to consider sailing for England. "James is unwilling to offer to go again," Sara noted in her journal, "as he thinks Rosy does not want us."

Rosy was in "an agony of grief," he said, but there were practical matters to be dealt with. He had his wife interred in the Episcopal cemetery at Ascot, and was later infuriated to receive a bill for fourteen pounds for a temporary grave marker, double the usual amount "on the grounds of being a non-parishioner." He would bring her remains home to Hyde Park for burial behind St. James the following June.

Meanwhile, who would help care for his motherless children? Who would act as his hostess at the formal dinners his new position would inevitably require him to give? Who would now intercede for him with the big quarrelsome Astor clan?

His answer was the same one that other troubled Roosevelts of his generation fell back on: Bamie. Anna Roosevelt was still unmarried in 1893 and physically handicapped, but rocklike in times of crisis. As soon as word came of Helen's death, she offered to come to London and help out. Rosy gratefully accepted. It was an extraordinarily generous offer. "You are an angel, as usual," wrote her friend Mrs. Henry Cabot Lodge, "to go & take care of all the poor forlorn things of the world." And even Bamie, with all her energy and eagerness to aid the members of the family, might not have made it had she not had a secret objective of her own.

Mr. James, nearly twice her age, had once been in love with Bamie before he met Sara Delano. Now Bamie, in turn, had become interested in his eldest son. Neither she nor Rosy was young anymore—both were thirty-eight—and each was in need of companionship. Bamie knew she was not beautiful, but perhaps the time had come when Rosy might be encouraged to overlook those shortcomings in favor of her warmth, intelligence, and spirit. She would go to London, become Rosy's hostess, and hope to become his wife.[12] Sara and Mr. James visited her in New York as soon as they heard of her plans and were puzzled by her determination. "She seems to *want* to go," Sara wrote in her diary.

She went, and within a few days of her arrival had dismissed the beautiful young French governess Rosy had just hired for his daughter, explaining that she was "unsuitable" for the household of a widower, and replacing her with a British nanny with reassuringly white hair. Bamie was an immediate social triumph, so gracious, adept, and charming that the ambassador himself, former Secretary of State Thomas F. Bayard, made her the unofficial hostess for the entire embassy. Nor did she ignore Rosy's special problems. She stood by him when he went to court, seeking to force the Astor trust to raise his children's annual allowance of $30,000 from their mother's estate of $1.5 million. The suit backfired, to Rosy's intense embarrassment; instead of raising the allowance, the New York Supreme Court judge cut it in half, declaring

12. In this she evidently had the backing of her brother Theodore. Rosy was "a dear good fellow," he told her when Rosy visited him briefly in Washington in 1894. "It was a real pleasure to see him and have a long talk about you, and his own affairs and everything. I like him so much."
Source: Theodore Roosevelt Papers, Harvard University.

that children "should be brought up to prudence and moderation rather than to extravagance and the gratification of every luxurious desire." And when a venerable employee of the Astors died and Mrs. Astor and her son Jack demanded that Rosy resign his post and hurry home to New York to take his place, he refused, then put Bamie "in charge of the negotiations" with the Astors. She proved so steely a negotiator that Mrs. Astor angrily accused her of being "biased," interested in keeping Rosy abroad only for "her own benefit." Rosy indignantly denied the charge in a letter to his mother-in-law; it was "quite unjustifiable, as you must know."

But it was not entirely unjustifiable. Bamie did hope to hold him in London for her own purposes. What she did not know was that Rosy's future as a diplomat was not all that kept him there. Sometime during his London years he had secretly acquired a mistress, a lovely soft-spoken woman named Elizabeth Riley, and called "Betty." She was the daughter of a rural clergyman and was a clerk at Harrods department store when he met her. At some point in early 1895, Bamie evidently found out about her existence and learned that Rosy was genuinely devoted to her—though marriage then seemed out of the question.

All this she evidently kept to herself, and shortly thereafter, to the astonishment of her entire family, she announced her engagement instead to Navy Commander William Sheffield Cowles, ten years her senior, a portly, placid man from Connecticut, with a gray walrus mustache. She would come to call him "Mr. Bearo." They were married in London; Rosy gave the bride away. Despite everything, he and Bamie remained friends all their lives.

Meanwhile, the children needed attending to. Helen was just twelve when her mother died, but now doing well under the care of Bamie and her new English governess. Taddy, at fourteen, was more problematical. If he was to attend college as his father hoped, he needed preparatory training, but Rosy thought him too delicate for any of the English public schools to which the sons of his British friends went; he was too far behind in his studies and had too little "self-reliance." What the boy needed, Rosy said, was to go to a school in his own country where he could learn among the right sort of "personal influences to strengthen his character."

Those influences, that character-building, were the stock in trade of the Reverend Endicott Peabody, founder and headmaster of Groton School at Groton, Massachusetts. He was a man of immense personal magnetism—tall, sandy-haired, athletic, with a steady blue gaze and a deep voice of astonishing resonance, and he came from a sturdy, well-connected old Salem family. His father was a partner in the American-owned London banking firm of J & S Morgan & Co., and young Endicott—"Cotty" to friends and family, though never to his boys—had been educated in England, first at Cheltenham College, then at Cambridge. While in England he had been so moved by the majesty and ritual of the Church of England that he had abandoned the chaste Unitarianism of his fathers and began to dream of becoming an Anglican clergyman. He tried to make a go of banking when he got back to the States but found it unsatisfying, and finally entered the Episcopal Theological Seminary at Cambridge, Massachusetts.

His first church had been at Tombstone, in Arizona Territory. He had arrived there, in fact, windburned and covered with dust from a six-hour ride on top of a swaying stagecoach on January 29, 1882, at about the time Sara Delano Roosevelt was going into labor at Hyde Park. Tombstone was then a wide-open mining camp—what little law there was grew from the pistols of the Earp brothers, Wyatt, Morgan, and Virgil—but Peabody managed to thrive there, holding services every Sunday in the courthouse while persuading the townspeople first to pay for and then to build a permanent church, the very first Episcopal church in the territory. Peabody liked the town, and it liked him. The *Tombstone Epitaph* noted with pleasure that in him they had "a parson who doesn't flirt with the girls, who doesn't drink beer behind the door, and when it comes to baseball, he's a daisy."

But he had larger plans. He wanted to marry his lovely first cousin, Fanny Peabody, back in Massachusetts, and then with her at his side to create a church boarding school for upper-class boys. Once Peabody's mind fixed on an objective, few could resist him. He returned to New England and laid energetic siege to his father's wealthy friends, J. P. Morgan among them, and in early 1883 was rewarded with a gift of ninety acres of farmland near the tiny Massachusetts town of Groton, thirty-five miles north of Boston, along with enough money to begin to build. (Fanny Peabody held out a little longer; she and the rector were married in the summer of 1885, just after Groton's first academic year had ended.)

Franklin Roosevelt had been enrolled for Groton before its foundation had been dug. Although there was already a direct family link—Theodore Roosevelt was married to Peabody's cousin Alice Lee—Mr. James and Sara apparently first learned of the young rector and his school during their initial visit to Campobello in the summer of 1883. Their friend James Lawrence was an especially enthusiastic trustee—it was he who had deeded land for the school; he and his wife lived just down the road—and one evening after dinner, seated before a roaring fire in the inn where both couples were staying, he conveyed his enthusiasm to the Roosevelts. Groton was to be unique among American private schools, he said, headed by an Episcopal clergyman and run along the enlightened lines laid down by the great British headmaster Dr. Thomas Arnold of Rugby, where Mr. James had once considered sending Rosy. The worst abuses of other English schools—fagging, flogging, snobbery—would be outlawed. Instead, as Peabody's prospectus explained, "every endeavor [would] be made to cultivate manly, Christian character, having regard to moral and physical as well as intellectual development." The student body was to be small—there would be just twenty-seven boys in the first entering class—so as to retain what Peabody called "the family aspect," and they were all expected to attend the school for six straight years, beginning at the age of twelve.

Even though opening day was more than a year off, Lawrence said, prominent men were already signing up their sons so swiftly that there might soon not be room for more. Peabody's personality had won them over; that plus the importance of the school's trustees and the fact, as Peabody's friend Frank D. Ashburn wrote, that many wealthy fathers were then "privately disgusted with the bringing up of well-to-do boys of that period. They thought them spoiled ladies' men tied to women's apron strings, and heartily welcomed the chance to send their sons to a place where the boys had to stand on their own feet and play rough-and-tumble games."

The Roosevelts were at first a little amused at their friend's unexpected zeal, Sara remembered many years later, but they heeded his warning and placed Franklin's name on the waiting list right away.

Now, ten years later, Rosy wrote to Peabody from London, asking that Taddy be admitted, too. It would be hard for him to part with the boy, he said, but it had been his late wife's "strong wish and desire" that Taddy be sent to Groton to learn "application, self-confidence and thoroughness."

The rector somehow found room for Taddy, linked as he was to both the Roosevelts and the Astors, even though it meant that the boy would begin his studies toward the end of the second form rather than at the beginning of the first.

That decision would have an unforeseeable but important impact on Franklin's future.

Mr. James met the pale, forlorn fourteen-year-old at the dock on March 31, 1894—August Belmont, Jr., the sportsman son of the Roosevelts' old friend, had brought the boy home from England—and Sara saw to it that he went to the dentist and helped him pack his belongings. Both elder Roosevelts escorted him to Groton and left him there, weeping and lonely, to try his best to catch up with his new classmates before vacation began. Rosy returned briefly to Hyde Park in June with his wife's remains, and after the burial behind St. James and a short consultation with his superiors in Washington, he sailed back to England with Taddy for the summer.

When Taddy returned to Groton the following September, still "looking very badly," according to Sara, and bitterly homesick for his distant father from whom he rarely heard, Franklin should have gone with him. He was twelve that fall, the customary age at which boys entered Peabody's care; in fact, in later years, the headmaster proved reluctant to take any boy who could not begin his studies in the first form.

But at some point between the day Franklin's parents placed his name on the Groton rolls and the autumn of his twelfth year, they had decided to forestall his leaving home for two more years. He would enter Groton in 1896 at fourteen, not twelve; in the third form, not the first.

Precisely why, no one now can say. Tradition holds that it was his mother who could not bear to part with him so soon. But it seems likely that Mr. James, too, wished to hold on to him as long as he could. They were equally devoted to the boy Sara once called "*our* especial treasure." And just as her fondest wish for her son was always that "he grow to be like his father," his father continued to consider the manner in which he himself had been raised the proper pattern for bringing up Franklin. Mr. James himself had been nearly fourteen when he had left home for the Hyde School at Lee, Massachusetts, after all, and like his old schoolmaster, the Reverend Alexander Hyde, Endicott Peabody was a New England clergyman; like him, too, he offered his pupils a church-oriented education in a homelike atmosphere. Each evening both the rector and Mrs. Peabody said good night to every individual boy. After Groton, Franklin would continue on to college and then to law school, just as Mr. James and Rosy had.

Evidence that this was how Mr. James reasoned came the following year, when Franklin expressed a tentative wish to attend Annapolis and then to become an officer in the Navy. It is almost the only known instance in which he risked a direct confrontation with his father. Mr. James took him aside and spoke to him "man to man," FDR recalled. It would simply be too cruel for an only son to be away from his parents as much as a naval career would require, his father explained; instead, college and the law would provide him with the right sort of preparation for any kind of work a gentleman might be called upon to perform.

Franklin may have been deeply disappointed—he would never get over his love for the sea or his romantic feeling for the Navy—but he backed down fast. He knew he must not irritate his ailing father with further argument, must seem always to surrender cheerfully.

At about the same time that Rosy first wrote to Peabody seeking a place for his son, Mr. James was writing to him about Franklin. His latest governess, Miss Alice Clay, was not working out. She had come to Hyde Park from London in the autumn of 1893 when Franklin was eleven, and, while "a perfect lady," she was simply not up to the job of thoroughly preparing "a bright boy" for Groton. Besides, though Mr. James did not say so explicitly, he seems to have felt it was time for the boy to experience more steady male companionship. With himself no longer able to accompany Franklin in the more rugged forms of play, the boy was on his own more than his father liked. John Griner, one of the Springwood workmen, had taught him simple carpentry, which he seemed to enjoy, and there were always pets to care for and play with. Franklin would later recall lazy afternoons spent lying on his stomach in the grass, eating wild strawberries or, with his dogs, futilely stalking the woodchucks whose warrens pocked the big hayfield in front of the house.[13] But time was passing, and Mr. James wondered whether the rector could recommend someone: "a New England man," if possible, "a *gentleman* . . . one who could inspire respect and . . . be my boy's companion." "Have we in this country," he asked, "any men with the culture and training of Englishmen, combined with the standard character of the American gentleman?"

13. FDR remembered the Springwood woodchucks fondly during the dedication of his library in 1941, asking that their descendants be permitted to occupy the estate in perpetuity. And so, in the spring and summer and early autumn they may still be seen almost everywhere on the old estate, poised at the entrances to their burrows, then plunging underground in fat anxious flurries if you draw too close.

Peabody's reply is lost, but not long thereafter the Roosevelts did hire a tutor, a young man named Foley—who did not work out either. Mr. James angrily dismissed him within a few months when he failed to return on time from a holiday.

The man who finally filled the Roosevelts' demanding bill was Mr. Arthur Dumper, who arrived at Springwood in September of 1895. He was a handsome, vigorous young master of Latin and mathematics at St. Paul's School—Mr. James had learned of him from Henry A. Coit, the headmaster of St. Paul's, whom the Roosevelts had met on shipboard coming home from Europe that summer—with a Phi Beta Kappa from Kenyon and plans to become an Episcopal clergyman. Dumper stayed with Franklin until he entered Groton the following autumn, accompanying the Roosevelts to Bad Nauheim and providing just the sort of masculine comradeship Mr. James had planned. He and Franklin bicycled together, played tennis and golf, hunted birds, and tracked animals through the Hyde Park snows. Dumper eventually rose within the church to become the first dean of Trinity Cathedral in Newark, New Jersey. He was always reticent about his days with the Roosevelts, his son recalled ninety years later, but he had admired Sara—"the power in that house, by then"—and he had genuinely liked Franklin, though he always found the buoyant but apparently haphazard way in which his pupil went at his lessons alarmingly "unorthodox."

Infirmity and old age, rarely discussed but ever present, now prevailed at Algonac as well as Springwood. In the spring of 1891, Russell and Company, the firm that had twice made Warren Delano's fortune in the China trade, suddenly and unexpectedly failed. The old Delano home at Macao had to be sold off, and Annie and Fred Hitch, now jobless, came home to live at Algonac. Later that year, making his slow way upstairs, Mr. Delano somehow lost his footing and fell, shattering his good hip. Thereafter, he had to settle for life in a wheelchair. In December, while the bone was still knitting, word came that his brother Franklin—the rich Uncle Frank after whom FDR was named—had died of a heart attack at his villa near Monte Carlo.

Still, the old man struggled on, sustained by his fond family. Franklin and his mother—and less often, Mr. James—called regularly, and his grandson often recited verse for him or delivered boyish talks on local birds while Sara stood by proudly. In 1889, Mr. Delano celebrated his eightieth birthday, and the assembled family gave him a specially bound parchment booklet of pen and ink renderings of scenes from the nearly nine decades of his life: his leaving Fairhaven for the city as a boy; his and Catherine's voyage to China; Algonac itself, sheltered by its big trees. Three years later he insisted on attending the World's Fair at Chicago, a servant wheeling him among the exhibits. He was "thrilled" at all he saw, his son Fred recalled, and by "the fact that he had in his long life attended the opening of the Erie Canal and witnessed the entire span of . . . railway development."

Nor did he or his wife ever let their age or frailty erode their dignity or their affection for one another. A servant brought a note to Warren one summer morning toward the end of his wife's life:

> Dear Warren,
>
> Will you meet me at the front door to take a drive in the new phaeton which I have bought as a birthday gift for you?
>
> I am waiting for you,
>
> Your affectionate,
> Katie

The Delanos celebrated their fiftieth wedding anniversary in November of 1893. The whole family reassembled at Algonac. Sara and Mr. James gave the couple a gold-plated muffineer, Franklin offered a letter opener with a gilt handle, but perhaps the old couple's favorite gift was a tray engraved with a view of the Lyman house at Northampton, Massachusetts, in which they had been married half a century before.

Even in her last weeks, frail from the cancer that would finally kill her, Catherine Delano insisted on being brought downstairs in a rolling chair and taken into the library, where Warren sat waiting for her, trapped in a wheelchair of his own. Nearby hung portraits of them both, painted in their full vigor just before they sailed for China as newlyweds. "Though gasping and panting for breath," a visitor remembered, "she would always be thinking of something pleasant to tell him." One morning, the same visitor overheard Warren ask her how she was.

"Rather good for nothing," she answered.

"I am, too," her husband said.

"But, Warren, we were a rare young couple once."

Warren wheeled himself into her bedroom on the evening of February 9, 1896, to say good night, just as he had for years. She was asleep when he approached the bed, but she opened her eyes when he leaned forward to kiss her.

"Good night dear," she murmured. "Good night, goodbye, darling."

She died in her sleep the following morning.

That summer, the last before Franklin was to go off to Groton, he returned to Bad Nauheim with his father and with his mother, once again dressed in mourning. Arthur Dumper came, too, and in his company the boy had several adventures of which he later loved to tell. In London, where they went first to consult Mr. James's physicians, he and Mr. Dumper set out one afternoon to visit the bird collection at the South Kensington Museum, only to find the doors closed. The Prince of Wales himself was inside, dedicating a new wing. Only those with invitations could get in; the general public was barred for the day. Neither at fourteen nor later did Franklin Roosevelt ever consider himself part of the general public. He strode up to the uniformed guard and gravely presented his engraved gilt-edged life membership card in the New York Museum of Natural History. The guard examined it and then, no less gravely, ushered the young scientist and his older companion inside.

Later, while Mr. James and Sara took the waters in Germany, Franklin and his tutor took three or four short bicycle trips through the countryside. It was the boy's very first experience with handling money on his own; each day he was given four German marks—then about a dollar—with which he was expected to feed and house himself overnight. His parents were both pleased and surprised to find that he came home each time with change to spare.

They were still more pleased at how Franklin handled himself when on his own. He and Mr. Dumper had found themselves under arrest four times in one busy day of bicycling—for picking cherries along the roadside, for wheeling their bicycles into a railroad depot, for riding into Strasbourg after dusk (it was then forbidden to enter "a fortified city of the Empire, on, with, or in a wheeled vehicle after nightfall"), and finally, for the inadvertent slaughter of a panicky goose that had thrust its long neck between the spokes of Mr. Dumper's front wheel. Franklin's good German, his self-assurance, and his well-honed skill at disarming adults with charm got him and his companion out of all but the last violation without a fine. The police official before whom they were brought at Strasbourg was so taken with the young

American that he served him and his friend wine and cake before letting them go—or so FDR liked to remember. They did finally have to pay five marks to the angry owner of the goose, however, even though Franklin always maintained the bird had really "committed suicide."

All the Roosevelts knew that things would never be quite the same again for any of them once Franklin left for school in September, and Sara sought to keep him close for as long as she could. Before returning to Hyde Park, she took Franklin with her to Bayreuth for several days to hear Wagner's entire Ring Cycle. Franklin developed a cold and high fever on the way. She dosed him with the laxative Castoria—her customary curative for anything that went wrong—and had him sleep in her hotel room until he felt better. He was a patient onlooker at the opera. "Franklin really appreciated it much more than I thought he would," Sara wrote proudly to her sister Dora. "He was most attentive and rapt . . . and always sorry to leave, never for a moment bored or tired."

The day of separation grew closer. The Roosevelts returned home to Springwood in early September. Mr. Dumper left for the seminary. Sara carefully supervised the packing of Franklin's belongings, and the two spent one last long day together. "We dusted his birds," she wrote that evening, "and he had a swim in the river. I looked on and with a heavy heart."

The next day, September 15, the three Roosevelts boarded their private railroad car and set out for Groton. Franklin remained "dry-eyed and resolute," his mother said, though "white-faced," and he greeted the rector and his wife with his usual good manners. Nor were there tears when he finally took leave of his mother and father. They wanted him to stay at this school, therefore he would stay. His real feelings remained hidden, but Sara confided hers to her diary: "James and I feel this parting very much," she wrote. "It is hard to leave my darling boy."

CHAPTER 5

GETTING ON VERY WELL WITH THE FELLOWS

In some ways, the setting of Franklin's new school must have seemed familiar to him. Like Springwood, Groton's red brick buildings stood surrounded by an immense grassy clearing edged with deep forest which tilted down toward the bank of a slow-moving river, the Nashua. Like Springwood, too, the school was built near enough to town to provide pleasant walks on crisp fall afternoons, but not so close as ever to be thought part of it. At night, only the scattering of far-off village lights beyond the trees reminded Groton boys that there was another world outside the school.

But there the resemblance ended. Every other aspect of life at Groton would prove profoundly different from anything Franklin had known before. Accustomed to the admiring company of adults, he had now to make his lonely baffling way in an entirely new world of suspicious, intolerant schoolboys. "I shall be anxious to know how you get on with the boys," Sara wrote a few days after leaving him at school. "It is a great change to be with so many of all sorts."

Franklin's new schoolmates were "of all sorts" only in a severely limited sense, of course. Groton was already one of the most exclusive schools in the country; nine out of ten of its students came from families listed in the social registers of Boston, Philadelphia, Newport, or New York. Like Franklin, they had been brought up in wealth and comfort—even luxury—and Groton's deliberately Spartan atmosphere required a considerable adjustment for all of them.

Franklin was led to his new quarters in Hundred House along a wide bare corridor, its woodwork stained dark brown. "Durable but in no sense sybaritic," one graduate remembered. He spent his first night, and most of his school nights thereafter, in one of the twenty-four claustrophobic cubicles—six by nine feet, with just room enough for a bed, bureau, and chair—that lined both sides of the dormitory hall. There was no closet; clothes were hung on pegs. No pictures were permitted on the whitewashed walls. There was a curtain rather than a door, because the rector frowned upon too much privacy for adolescent boys; it led only to trouble.

The change was too much for some. Peabody found one new arrival, the son of a Manhattan millionaire, weeping on his first day of school. What was the matter? he asked. "Sir," the boy answered between sobs, "sir, there are no carpets on the stairs."[1]

But the boys were given few opportunities for brooding. "Perhaps the most noticeable feature of life at Groton is that it is very busy," an early master wrote. This, too, was part of the rector's plan. "The curse of American school life is loafing," he once said. "The tone of loafers is always low. . . . The best thing for a boy is to work hard . . . to play hard . . . and then, when the end of the day has come, to be so tired that he wants to go to bed and go to sleep. That is the healthy and good way for a boy to live."

The crowded day was punctuated by bells. The first woke the school at six forty-five, and the boys in each dormitory rushed with their towels to a big common washroom lined with black soapstone sinks and taps that ran only cold. This first stop of the day may have been the most unsettling for Franklin during his early bewildering days at Groton. Every boy was expected to take an icy shower each morning. Accustomed to warm languid baths in the big clawed tub upstairs at Springwood—his only tubside companion had been his mother, years before—he now found himself surrounded by two dozen pushing, shouting naked boys, waiting together in line to suds themselves with big slippery cakes of ordinary yellow kitchen soap. "I can never smell that soap without recalling again the first misery of a new boy," one graduate recalled, "the crowding pressure, the weight

1. Another wealthy Hyde Park boy who attended Groton some years after FDR had moved on recalled how hard it had it been for him to adjust to the school. "Life on an estate," he told me, "was the most abnormal way in the world to grow up. Imagine it for yourself: always having maids and governesses, never seeing the inside of a public school, knowing no one else in town, unable to cope with the tough, real world outside. It's a wonder how any of us grew up half sane."
Confidential source.

of numbers, the incessant chatter and clatter, remorseless and unending. One could not escape, could not get back inside of oneself."

A second deep clang of the bell came at seven-thirty, sending Franklin and his schoolmates, now scrubbed, combed, and dressed in suits and ties, racing downstairs to breakfast. The day's schedule was fixed and rigid. Morning chapel began at eight-fifteen, the rector himself booming out the lesson. There were classes from eight twenty-five till noon; dinner, with each boy in his assigned seat (Franklin sat next to the only other new boy in his form); then more classes, sports, a second frigid shower, supper, evening study in a common study hall under the eye of one of the masters, evening prayers, and the final nightly ritual of shaking hands good night with the headmaster and his wife.

Studies were the least of Franklin's worries. He had been well prepared and within a month of his arrival stood fourth in his class of nineteen. His father, "who was so anxious for him to study well," was very pleased; and except for some trouble with Greek in his second year, Franklin never had serious academic difficulty. He displayed "more than ordinary intelligence while at Groton," Peabody once said of him, and took "a good position in his form but [was] not brilliant."

This last was not necessarily criticism. Brilliance was not highly prized at Groton; athletic distinction and Christian character always came first. "I am not sure I like boys who think too much," the rector once admitted. "A lot of people think of a lot of things we could do without"; and when a proud mother introduced her son to him as precociously bookish, he told her not to worry: "We'll soon get *that* out of him."

Like most boys, Franklin yearned both to excel at school and to fit in, but he was ill prepared to do either. More than most boys, he had been the object of universal admiration and affection—from his parents and grandparents, of course, but also from his father and mother's friends, his nurses, governesses, and tutors, from the doting servants at Springwood and Nauheim and Campobello. It had been the natural order of his childhood world that he be liked by everyone, and he worked almost desperately to replicate that world at Groton. His inevitable failure to do so confused and frustrated him. "I always felt entirely out of things," he admitted to one close friend many years later, and to his wife he would confess that something had gone "sadly wrong" at Groton.

At first he set out to do what he had always done so successfully

—please the adults in authority. Ten days into his first term he announced to his parents that he was setting out to win the punctuality prize, even though "it will be hard work, as one lateness will spoil it." He did win it at Prize Day at the end of the year—and would win it twice more before he was graduated—but it was a hollow triumph. To be always in his seat, pen poised and apparently eager to learn, when the bell rang at the beginning of each class may have won him the respect of his teachers, but it did nothing to help make him popular with his classmates.

Nor did the fact that for eight long months he earned no "black marks," the penalties for minor infractions of school rules that other less well behaved boys piled up routinely. He did not get his first one —for talking in class—until mid-May of the following spring. "I am very glad of it," he told his parents, "as I was thought to have no school spirit before."

Franklin's mother was powerless to ease his adjustment to the unforgiving conformist world of schoolboys. It probably never occurred to her that a Roosevelt and a Delano would ever find it hard to win acceptance. Roosevelts and Delanos accepted or rejected *others.* The way for him to win friends, she wrote, trying to be helpful, was to "exert all your good kind instincts in relation to those about you."

Other obstacles barred the way to the universal popularity he sought. He was slight for his age, weighing barely 100 pounds, and he spoke with a distinctive accent gleaned unconsciously during summers spent abroad and which the other boys thought affected and altogether too "English." His manners were thought overly refined, too. He had to be told to stop bowing from the waist when he said good night to Mrs. Peabody each evening; a simple bob of the head was a more suitably American sign of deference. His sense of isolation was further intensified because his parents had been unable to part with him until two years after all but one of his classmates had entered the school. "The other boys had formed their friendships," he would tell Eleanor Roosevelt, and he had remained "always a little the outsider."

Finally, there was the humiliating presence of Taddy, now in the fourth form and universally unpopular. He was a "queer sort of boy," one of Franklin's classmates recalled, "much made fun of by his classmates," and when they found that the new boy was related to him they inevitably derided him as "Uncle Frank." Franklin was brave about it —"I would sooner be 'Uncle Frank' than 'Nephew Rosy,'" he wrote home—but it made his time at Groton still more trying.

Very little of his painful struggle for acceptance made its way into his relentlessly cheerful letters home. "I am getting along finely both mentally and physically," he had reported in the very first of these, setting the tone for all those that followed. At his parents' insistence, he wrote at least two letters a week for four years, and if he forgot to mail one even for a day his mother and father telegraphed the headmaster to make sure he had not fallen ill. There are only the gentlest hints of trouble in any of them. To his "Dear Papa and Mama," Franklin continued to present a uniformly sunny picture of people and events, the world of the "very nice child, always bright and happy," that his grandfather Delano and his mother and father had always insisted that he be.[2]

Sara would have been still less serene had she known how Franklin had really been greeted by his schoolmates. One day early that first term a group of older boys from the fourth form trapped him in a corner of the corridor and ordered him to dance, jabbing hard at his ankles with hockey sticks to make sure he stepped fast enough. Franklin did better than that. Refusing ever to seem a victim, even to himself, he pirouetted and toe-danced in apparent high spirits as if he were part of the fun instead of its object. No one sensed his fear. "He did what he was told," one eyewitness recalled, "with such good grace that the class soon let him go."

He got off easy. New boys often faced far worse humiliations. Fagging was strictly forbidden at Groton, but a strict and unyielding hierarchy based on seniority was firmly in place. Sixth-form boys were made prefects and helped the masters keep order. Younger boys were not to associate with older ones, had in fact to step off the narrow boardwalk that led from one building to the next if upperclassmen were seen coming the other way. Even brothers of different ages were expected to stay away from one another. A few years later, when Moncure Biddle of Philadelphia took pity on his homesick younger brother, George, and occasionally walked to town with him or brewed him a cup of cocoa, his classmates denounced him as a "queer"; rather than further risk their scorn, he stopped speaking to his brother at all.

Older boys were encouraged to keep an eye out for newcomers who failed to conform to the school's unwritten standards of behavior —who seemed too "fresh" or insufficiently excited about football or

2. His later personal letters—thousands of them written over forty-five years—are almost equally bland, revealing as little as possible of the emotional life of the man who moved the pen. Even most of those intended for his wife, Eleanor Roosevelt once admitted, were just "letters to be letters."

just lacking in the proper "tone." And when necessary, they were called upon to administer stern correctives. Newcomers like Franklin secretly quailed at the prospect of undergoing either of the school's two traditional forms of punishment: "bootboxing" and "pumping." The first of these was the mildest, usually inflicted by the older boys without the masters' knowledge. The miscreant was made to fold himself inside the small airless locker in which he kept his footgear while the other boys sat and pounded on the closed lid.

Pumping was dreaded more, imposed before the entire school with the tacit sanction of the rector and only after a solemn, drawn-out ceremony that made its cruelty all the more excruciating for the victim. Francis Biddle, who entered Groton the year before FDR left it and who would much later become his Attorney General, remembered how it was done: "Immediately after evening prayers the senior prefect would ring the bell and announce that the sixth form wanted to see the offender *immediately* in his study. A little boy got up, walked to the door in front of the whole school, who watched him and wondered what he had done—or tried not to look at him. They waited there in silence. No one in the big schoolroom was allowed to move, while behind the closed doors in the senior prefect's study he was lectured, told that he was not behaving like a Groton boy, dismissed—and as he walked out of the study the fourth formers [usually led by the brawniest football players] seized him and rushed him down the back stairs to the cellar, where he was turned upside down and held under the gush of a faucet—the water power was excellent—until he had almost fainted. . . ." Having suffered all the initial sensations of drowning, still retching and gasping, he was then asked if he fully understood the seriousness of his offense, and if he failed to be properly enthusiastic in his apologies or not fervent enough in his promises to do better, the onlookers would chant "Shut him up! Under again!" and the tap was turned on a second time. "The victim," Biddle continued, "half-drowned and dripping, found his way back to his bedroom alone. . . . I still vividly remember that moment of black suspense which hung over me, over all the younger boys, when the rector walked out after prayers, and the senior prefect announced that the school would remain seated: *Was it to be me?*"[3]

It was never Franklin. He was neither bootboxed nor pumped.

3. The rector was nothing if not impartial about pumping. Theodore Roosevelt, Jr., was pumped twice with Peabody's approval, just three weeks before his father was sworn in as Vice President of the United States; and his own son, Malcolm Peabody, also once underwent the ordeal because of his allegedly poor "tone."

Eleanor Roosevelt contended that his sense of isolation at Groton had helped foster her husband's sympathy for outcasts. If it did, it was in retrospect. At the time he did all he could to identify as closely as he could with the majority against the misfits. Within two weeks of his arrival—and in the same letter in which he vowed never to be late to class—he was writing scornfully of Moncure Biddle, then an unhappy member of the second form, as "quite crazy, fresh and stupid, he has been bootboxed once and threatened to be pumped several times." Again a month later: "Poor Biddle has been sent to bed for being saucy to one of the masters. . . . I found it necessary to chastise him yesterday, but he is just as fresh again today!"

The next fall he reported, "You will be pleased to hear that George Cabot Ward Low (O! law!) has been pumped, & a pretty sight he was! He left off swaggering immediately!"[4]

Athletic distinction was central to real success at Groton, and football, wrote a school historian, "was the Groton game *par excellence.* . . . Instinctively," he added, the rector "trusted a football player more than a non-football player, just as the boys did." Football, Peabody believed, ". . . is of profound importance for the moral even more than for the physical development of the boys. In these days of exceeding comfort, the boys need an opportunity to endure hardness and, it may be, suffering."

Franklin's enthusiasm for the Groton football team was all that the rector could have hoped. An early letter home began:

> Hurrah, Hurrah, Hurrah
> GROTON
> 46
> St Mark's
> 0
>
> I am hoarse, deaf and ready to stand on my cocoanut! OUR team played a wonderful game. . . .[5]

4. Francis Biddle reacted much the same way. Pumping's special savagery was entirely lost on him while at school; he was just grateful it was never done to him, and glad to be among the punishers instead of the punished. "I was not shocked by it, only frightened. . . . I had no sense of shame or regret, but on the contrary knew the thrill of exercising mob justice and the excitement which communicated itself to me as I struggled to be in the center of the crowd that was handling its victim."

Source: Francis Biddle, *A Casual Past,* page 172.

5. His admiration for Groton athletes was wistfully adolescent. On the backs of group photographs of the football teams he carefully noted the name and weight of every player.

But his playing skills were something else again. He had almost never been on a team of any kind before he first ventured onto the Groton football field, and he was far too spindly to do well. He was quickly assigned to the second-worst of eight graded schoolwide squads; even at that, his mother worried both that he might be injured facing boys as big as Taddy in the line, and that he "not have the *misfortune* of hurting anyone."

He was little better at baseball, and in his first season found himself on "a new team which is called the BBBB or Bum Base Ball Boys," which was made up of "about the worst players in the school." During its game against a marginally more skilled team called "Carters Little Liver Pills," he managed to get hit hard in the stomach by a line drive, he told his parents, "to the great annoyance of that intricate organ, and to the great delight of all present."

Mr. James, perhaps worried that his boy was too delicate, insisted during Franklin's second year at Groton that he take six boxing lessons from a former professional on the staff. He dutifully jabbed and shuffled through them, then took part in a single two-round fight against a boy named Fuller Potter in front of the assembled school. Both combatants left the ring "with bloody noses and cut lips," he reported, but Potter was judged the winner. Franklin professed not to be surprised, since "this is the third year [Potter] has boxed, and even then we were quite close."

Franklin was better at other individual sports, but they all counted less with masters and boys alike—at tennis and golf and at the high kick, an obscure event peculiar to the school. A tin pan was suspended from the gymnasium ceiling and raised by measured stages after each contestant had tried three times to touch it with his foot. By the time the finalists competed it hung high above the heads of even the tallest boys, and in order to reach it each in turn had to leap into the air, kick high, and then crash helplessly back to the hard floor. In the spring of his first year, Franklin managed to outkick all third-form competitors, reaching the pan at seven feet three and a half inches—"two feet over my head," even though "at every kick I landed on my *neck* on the left side so . . . that the whole left side of my body is sore and my left arm is a little swollen."

Franklin expressed no overt anger at having been sent away to Groton. "I am getting on very well with the fellows," he wrote home that first October, when he clearly was not. But there is a curious undercurrent to his letters from school through all of the four years he spent there, a litany of complaints about minor ills and injuries that must have constituted a subtle and perhaps unconscious revenge upon the overly anxious parents who had made him attend. In his first year alone, he claimed to have dislocated a finger ("my hand looked like a large ball"); cut his eyelid ("I think from a shoe heel"); endured a "whack" on the nose and another on the head; nursed a bruised "tail" and injuries to his neck and arm (which he expected to continue to hurt "for two months or so"); experienced a painful "gumboil [abscess] which feels about three feet in diameter"; *almost* fallen from a canoe; and struggled with a series of sniffles for which his worried mother regularly sent him bottles of castor oil.

Athletic injuries were badges of adolescent honor, proof that he was not shirking and could endure pain as well as his classmates could, even if he was unable to outplay them. And he always described them in breezy, apparently carefree terms, hedged around with exhortations not to be overly alarmed: "You need not worry about my getting drowned, as there is always a master there in a canoe to watch us." But it also seems obvious that he wanted his mother and father to know at least something of what he was going through.

Franklin did finally win an athletic ribbon at Groton, as manager of the baseball team in his final year. He worked hard at it—though he considered managing a "thankless task," a colorless round of rolling the diamond, readying equipment, making sure the players turned out for practice—and was pleased when his team beat their traditional rivals, St. Marks, 7 to 6. "All my work is over & over successfully," he wrote home, "& there has not been a single complaint." But there was little individual praise for him, either; the players got the glory.

His mother was proud of his athletic accomplishments, just as she was proud of everything he did, but Franklin was not fooled. He knew that, try as he might, he would be remembered at Groton, in the rector's own words, as "athletically rather too slight for success."

Some sense of the depth of Franklin Roosevelt's disappointment at not having done better in the arena that counted most at his school may be seen in the fact that he later felt compelled to lie about it, telling a newspaper reporter in 1911 that he had been "quite a boxer" at Groton, and confiding to his friend Henry Morgenthau in 1939 that while his doctors thought he had trouble with his sinuses, the real trouble was that he had twice broken his nose playing football at school.

Groton was undeniably Endicott Peabody's creation, the red brick embodiment of his rugged, demanding creed. But other masters, too, influenced Franklin and his fellow students. Two had been there from the very beginning—the Reverend Sherrard Billings and William Amory Gardner.

Billings was three years younger than Peabody, a short, black-bearded, voluble cleric known to the boys as "Mr. B.," "Beebs," or "the Little Man." He taught Latin, coached football, and took care of the small details of Groton life for which the headmaster had no time. He was enormously popular with the boys. It was he, not Peabody, whom they carried on a chair around the victory bonfire every time Groton beat St. Mark's; they brought to him questions and complaints they would never have dared discuss with the rector. Billings preached in chapel from time to time—more eloquently than Peabody, some students said—and admitted to an occasional troubling doubt, to the great relief of at least some graduates. He led the choir (in which Franklin sang soprano his first year and tenor his last), and he conducted the singing of the Groton nonsense song "Blue Bottle" at the annual School Birthday, waving a carving knife instead of a baton.

For him, good form was essential in everything. "He never ceased to insist that there is a correct way of doing things," wrote a former student, "whether of speaking, or shaking hands, or parsing a Latin sentence." And he believed that no boy should be graduated who had not first been infused with the responsibilities of citizenship and an interest in public affairs. To that end, he introduced compulsory debating, a discipline to which Franklin took with eager enthusiasm. He may have been only a passable athlete and a slightly better than average scholar, but he had been encouraged to talk since infancy and to discuss public affairs with his parents and their friends. His first public speech was a two-minute extemporaneous address on a topic close to his father's heart, the continuing need for a Nicaraguan canal. Mr. James, who had himself been an able debater in college, took a keen interest in all the debates that came after, supplying his son with fat envelopes of newspaper clippings bearing on his assigned topics—the importance of a bigger Navy, for example, and the case against the annexation of Hawaii—and urging him not to memorize but rather to learn to speak his mind without notes.

William Amory Gardner—"Uncle Billy Wag" to the boys—was something of an anomaly at the school. On the surface he seemed to be everything a Groton man should not be. A rich Boston orphan, he had been raised in the huge art-filled home of his flamboyant aunt by marriage, Isabella Stewart Gardner, and he was a lifelong bachelor, shrill and utterly unathletic. It was said that when he played bridge—his favorite game—he had to stand up and hold his heart out of sheer excitement. And he cultivated a wealth of eccentricities of the sort tolerated only in academics and the very rich. He knitted and wore luridly colored woolen socks, once greeted a visiting clergyman wearing just a pair of fur bedroom slippers, and built for himself a mansion on the school grounds called "The Pleasure Dome," complete with a stage, a swimming pool, squash courts, and a maze. Here every Sunday afternoon he served the boys cake and "google," a sticky-sweet drink that came in two colors and one flavor—lemon.

His unconventionality spilled over into the classroom, often to the rector's despair. He taught Greek but had a hard time keeping to the task at hand. Once, a student remembered, "we hit a passage in the *Iliad* which mentioned dogs. Wag was off like a bloodhound. He told us about dogs, which led to architecture in Belgium, the canals of Holland and New York State, various methods of burying the dead, famous epitaphs, the Battle of Thermopylae, Aegean steamers, and the unreasonableness of publishers. As we left the room he chanted after us in Greek the twenty-line assignment."

Arriving at another class, he found that the boys had placed his chair on top of his desk, just to see what he might do. He climbed up without a word and lectured from there, breaking suddenly into a hopping dance of mock rage when he discovered the boys had not done their homework. The class roared and Peabody appeared in the doorway to chastise Gardner yet again for disrupting the school. As usual, Gardner offered to resign; as usual, the rector refused to hear of it.

Gardner's wealth was clearly an asset to Groton. His fortune built both the small Tudor-style chapel in which Franklin first worshipped and the majestic Gothic edifice that replaced it and was dedicated during his last year. But the rector's fondness for him went far deeper than that. Gardner was in fact a superb teacher, able to convey a richer sense of the world outside the school than any of the other masters. "Let the best men," he once wrote, "if they are to teach physics and chemistry, be men who know a good deal about Homer, Beethoven, Dante, and Velasquez. If they are to teach classics or history, let them know something of business, trigonometry, how long it takes a hen's egg to hatch. . . ."

For a boy with a mind like Franklin's—eager for knowledge, fond of unconnected facts, disinclined to rigor or abstraction—Gardner was a reassuring kindred spirit. He was Franklin's favorite teacher. "I can learn better & quicker with him than anyone else," he told his parents.[6]

But it was Endicott Peabody himself whom Franklin professed to revere. "As long as I live," he wrote from the White House in 1934, "the influence of Dr. and Mrs. Peabody means and will mean more to me than that of any other people next to my father and mother." In paying such public obeisance to the rector, he was in part simply being a true son of Groton; he felt about Endicott Peabody pretty much the way most of the rector's boys had come to feel by the time they left his care. It is hard after nearly a century to see just what it was about this tall, plain-spoken, plain-thinking educator that so drew the boys to him. Not all were so drawn, of course: W. Averell Harriman once told his father, "You know he [Peabody] would be an awful bully if he weren't such a terrible Christian"; and the artist George Biddle dismissed him as "an almost great man" whose stale tenets rewarded conformists and hypocrites and stifled the truly creative.

He could certainly be forbidding. Six black marks accumulated in a single week meant a private interview with the rector. It was that certainty, rather than the penalties he might impose, that kept most boys in line. His customary greeting to those unlucky enough to be summoned to his study was "Are you looking for trouble, boy? *Well, here I am!*" Franklin never felt his wrath, but just the remote possibility of it was unnerving. "After dinner today Mr. Peabody called the choir into his study and we expected a big talking to," a relieved Franklin once reported to his parents. "But he surprised and delighted us by saying that he had decided to let the choir go to Southboro' for the game next Saturday."

And he was sometimes simply absurd. Of all the many sins a good Christian must avoid, "impurity" was by far the worst, so far as the rector was concerned, and by it he sometimes seemed to mean sexual feeling of any kind; he certainly meant any sexual feeling outside of marriage. He was for many years vice president of the New England Watch and Ward Society. He barred the works of Voltaire from the

6. "Many-sided men," FDR told an interviewer in 1932, "have always attracted me. I have always had the keenest interest in five men . . . of comparatively modern times." They were Thomas Jefferson, Benjamin Franklin, Napoleon, Theodore Roosevelt, and Count Rumford. (The last of these is little remembered today; he was Benjamin Thompson [1753–1814], an American-born genius who combined careers as soldier, statesman, essayist, scientist, and inventor and became a count of the Holy Roman Empire. The drip coffeepot is said to be one of his inventions.) All five pursued political careers while maintaining the broadest possible variety of other interests—precisely as Roosevelt himself sought to do.

Source: Lindley, *Franklin D. Roosevelt: A Career in Progressive Democracy,* pages 336–337.

Groton library and would not let his boys read Kipling's *Stalky and Co.* because he thought the English boarding school it described was substandard; and he once expressed the impatient wish that Christmas vacation might be canceled because those boys who attended the theater while at home too often came back to school discussing "not the merits of the character portrayed, not the problems presented, but *the beauty of the actresses.*"

"The rector preached directly at us when he talked about impurity," Francis Biddle recalled, "and though he never said what he meant he looked into our eyes as he towered above us from the chapel pulpit, beautifully white and clean and healthy and manly, searching out our hidden secrets." In an effort to smother even the possibility of impurity among his boys, the most responsible ones were sometimes assigned to elevate the tone of schoolmates suspected of harboring unsavory thoughts or indulging in solitary pleasures. Franklin and his closest friend, Lathrop Brown, were asked to "reform" such a classmate for a time, sticking close to him even when he walked to and from chapel.

But Peabody could be fond as well as furious, amused as well as puritanical, a stern but benevolent substitute father to all his boys. He strode into Franklin's life breathing vigor and certainty, just as the boy's own father was growing frail and increasingly querulous. (Mr. James had in fact overexerted himself just bringing Franklin to school and had to be helped home and kept in bed several days to recover his strength.) As one who had spent his whole boyhood as part of a loving and inseparable triumvirate, life on his own at Groton was doubly difficult for Franklin. No Groton boy struggled harder to get close to the austere rector—or to his more warm and understanding wife. He was a faithful weekly guest for tea at "Mrs. Peabody's Parlor," and when in his fifth-form year he was appointed one of two head "mail niggers" whose task it was to sort the mail, he was especially delighted, he told his parents, because "the 2 head niggers take breakfast with the rector twice a year during the term."[7]

[7]On the general topic of racial equality, turn-of-the-century Groton reflected all the contradictions of its time. The word "nigger"—to denote those who did life's dirty work—was used without a thought. There were also "chapel niggers" who readied the chapel for daily services, and "express niggers" who wrestled trunks and delivered packages. Peabody himself, who believed "that the Anglo-Saxon race should be the predominant one for the good of the world," invited black spokesmen such as Booker T. Washington and fund raisers from Hampton Institute to address his boys. The favorite songs sung by Groton boys included "The Battle Cry of Freedom," "Marching Through Georgia" and "De Leader ob Company B," which begins: (*footnote continued on next page*)

Miss Liza Jackson loves a coon who belongs to Company B.
He longed to be a soldier in the army.

Perhaps the closest Franklin ever came to the rector while at school was during the fifth form, when Peabody offered a sequence of lectures to prepare him and several other boys for Confirmation. Candidates met with him once a week in his dark study. Burning logs flickered and snapped in the fireplace. Peabody sat behind his desk, a lamp softly illuminating his long earnest face, as he outlined the tenets of his simple, even primitive faith. His convictions were unsullied by doubt. He had little interest in theology, no patience with skepticism. A boy once had the temerity to ask him why he was so sure of immortality. "Why," he answered in genuine astonishment, "the Bible states clearly that Christ assured us of life immortal."

Franklin never raised a difficult question. Already steeped in the serene Episcopalianism of his father and St. James, he followed the rector's admonitions with special seriousness. He was more slender than his fellows, less well equipped than many to make his way on his own, and impelled to conceal all the roiling thoughts and stormy yearnings of adolescence both by childhood training in reticence and because of his schoolmates' uneasy scorn for genuine intimacy. Peabody's brand of confident Christianity provided a safe harbor.

It also served to reinforce the self-assurance and optimism that had been bred into Franklin by his father and mother. Peabody exuded an easy assurance that would one day find its echo in FDR's own. "It used to bother me when I made mistakes," the rector once said, "and I wasted a lot of time fretting. Now I have learned that if one does the best he can in the light of all his available knowledge and judgment, then . . . there is no use grieving over it. I do the best I can under the circumstances and go on to something else. One thing at a time, that is the great thing."

In his 1945 inaugural address, FDR adopted Peabody's own confidence in the future as his own: "I remember that my old schoolmaster said, in days that seemed to us then to be secure and untroubled: 'Things in life will not always run smoothly. Sometimes we will be rising toward the heights. Then all will seem to reverse itself and start downward. The great fact to remember is that the trend of civilization itself is forever upward; that a line drawn through the

---

He said a Gen'ral Jackson he was bound fo' some day to be.
Said he, a shot or two would never harm me.
Miss Liza, she was powerful mad, said she, Mr. Coon, you makes me sad.
If a great big bo-doo ball hits you
It'll neber stop a-going till it goes right froo.

middle of the peaks and valleys of the centuries always has an upward trend.' "

In any case, Franklin was confirmed not long after his sixteenth birthday in the winter of 1898. Bishop William A. Lawrence of Massachusetts performed the ceremony in the Groton chapel with Sara and her sister Dora Forbes proudly looking on. Mr. James was not well enough to come, and Taddy was not present. "You ask if Taddy is to be confirmed," Franklin had written to his parents some weeks earlier. "No such happy thing, and altho' he went into one lecture, he has not been in since, & is as far from the Good Path as ever."

The Good Path led Franklin to join the Groton Missionary Society, headed by Sherrard Billings, that same year. He and Lathrop Brown were made responsible for seeing after Mrs. Freeman, an indigent eighty-four-year-old black woman, the widow of a Union drummer, who lived in a tiny house just off the school grounds. Whenever it snowed, they plunged through the drifts to dig her out and make sure her chickens were fed and that there was enough coal for her stove. Franklin thought her "a dear old thing," and from time to time thoughtfully provided her with old copies of *Punch.*

Franklin also accompanied members of the society each week as they set out by wagon to conduct evening services at schoolhouses and small churches in the surrounding villages. Franklin was the organist —he could "play four hymns fairly decently," he said—and on his first expedition through a howling March blizzard he and his friends found that they greatly outnumbered the congregation—one small boy and the man hired to light the stove.

The missionary society also sponsored a summer camp for poor boys held each summer on Lake Asquam in New Hampshire. Franklin twice served two-week stints on its "faculty," helping the campers learn to swim and canoe and sail. They were from the slums of New York and Boston. "Only the poorest and raggedest are allowed to come," the *Grotonian* assured parents who had complained that some of the very first arrivals had seemed suspiciously well fed and clothed. There were pickpockets among them, petty thieves, and would-be tramps. The aim was twofold—"to bring a little sunshine and pleasure" into the campers' drab lives, and to combat snobbery among Groton boys. The summer camp, said a school pamphlet, taught "fraternal feeling for those who, with all the difference of environment & education, are yet moved by the same hopes & fears & temptations as they. The ultimate equality of human beings is impressed in a way not likely to be forgotten in the years when these members of the faculty become men in the community." This last did not always work smoothly. "The boys readily make friends with the faculty," the *Grotonian* reported at the end of one season, "and work fairly well, but the faculty felt no confidence in their honesty or truthfulness." Nonetheless, the Groton camp did provide Franklin with his first fleeting contact with the poor.

Sara thought all this missionary activity splendid. "It will interest you in doing for others," she wrote to him; "nothing is so helpful to ourselves as doing for others and trying to sink all selfishness."

But mere unselfishness was never enough for Endicott Peabody. He had a far grander vision of the role his boys should play in American life. One of his motives for establishing his school had been the hope that it would turn out young men capable of bringing its high ideals to the reform of government. "How distressing the political outlook seems to be!" he had told a friend in 1894. "One looks almost in vain for men who are willing to serve their country. Those who are not for themselves seem to be hopelessly bound to their party interests, and the country comes in a certain last. . . . It makes me feel like chucking up everything and making a desperate charge in Politics."

He never dared do that, but he did make certain his boys got a hefty dose of current events. Each was required to take part in school debates; every issue of the *Grotonian* included an article on a political issue—"Degeneration in American Public Life," "The Silver Question," "Civil Service Reform." Prominent reformers were invited to address the boys. In his first year alone, Franklin heard Jacob Riis, Booker T. Washington, and a delegation from Hampton Institute—"a quartet of negroes, & a negro lawyer, & an Indian soldier, and one paleface," he reported—who so impressed him that he donated fifty cents to their cause and wrote home for permission to subscribe a second half-dollar.

Theodore Roosevelt was another favorite chapel speaker. He was the man the rector pointed to most often as his exemplar of the gentleman in government. He and Peabody were friends and mutual admirers. The rector had offered the young TR a position on the Groton faculty in 1884, and all four of Roosevelt's sons would eventually attend his school. Theodore Roosevelt's vigorous views on the obligations of young gentlemen mirrored Peabody's own. "You are not entitled, either in college or after life, to an ounce of privilege because you have been to Groton," he told the graduating class one year. Rather, Groton boys were to be held to "an exceptional accountability. Much has been given you, therefore we have a right to expect much from you. . . . I was glad to hear the rector when he asked you to be careful not to turn out snobs. Now, there are in our civic and social life very much worse creatures than snobs, but none more contemptible."

"If some Groton boys do not enter political life and do something for our land," Peabody once wrote, "it won't be because they have not been urged."

Franklin would take less urging than most. Nor did he have any trouble identifying closely with his Cousin Theodore. Just as the obligation of service had first been bred into him by his parents, so had admiration for TR. Twenty-three-year-old Theodore Roosevelt had made his maiden speech in the Assembly chamber in Albany just six days before Franklin was born, and as the boy grew he watched the spectacular rise of the man his mother called "your noble kinsman" with pride and even awe. The Hyde Park and Oyster Bay Roosevelts were then still linked by warm family feeling as well as blood, and as a boy, Franklin had visited Sagamore Hill several times, doing his best to keep up as TR led his tireless brood up and down a tall sand dune; the contrast with his own aging father must have been vivid.

The single documented instance of open boyhood defiance of his parents was sparked in the late spring of 1897, when from far-off Nauheim and for reasons now forgotten, his mother declined an invitation from Cousin Bamie for Franklin to spend the Fourth of July at Oyster Bay. Franklin was coldly furious: "I am very sorry that you refused Cousin Bamie's invitation for the 4th and as you told me I *cd* make my own plans and as Helen [Roosevelt] writes me there is to be a large party & lots of fun on the 4th, I shall try to arrange it with Cousin B. next Wednesday. Please don't make any arrangements for my future happiness." When Bamie and Helen visited Groton a few days later, Franklin told them he would come for the holiday, in spite of what his mother had written.

The next day, Theodore Roosevelt—newly appointed assistant secretary of the Navy—himself arrived at the school to speak about his term as president of the Board of Police Commissioners in New York. "After supper tonight," Franklin told his parents, "Cousin Theodore gave us a splendid talk. He kept the whole room in an uproar for over an hour, by telling us killing stories about policemen and their doings in New York." TR, too, invited Franklin for the Fourth, and he again eagerly agreed to come. "I have accepted Cousin Theodore's invitation," he told his distant parents, "and I hope you will not refuse that too." When the time came, he went.

All three Roosevelts proudly followed newspaper accounts of TR's exploits in Cuba, and when he and his Rough Riders returned to march in the great victory parade, Sara and Mr. James stood in the crowd to cheer him as he passed. The Roosevelts were again all in his camp when he ran for governor of New York that autumn. Family loyalty —plus his own fierce disapproval of what he called "the silver craze" among the Democrats—persuaded Mr. James to disavow his own party in favor of a Roosevelt and the Republicans. Sara and Mr. James attended a crowded rally at the Metropolitan Opera House. "There were 3000 people jammed in," Mr. James reported; "we had a box"; Rosy was "afraid to go," because although he, too, planned to vote for TR, he did not want to be seen cheering a Republican in public for fear it would hurt his future prospects with the Democrats.

FDR wrote that he and all his schoolmates were "wild with excitement" at the news of TR's victory, and his parents were almost as pleased. "Hyde Park gave the Colonel [an] 81 majority," his father wrote. "Last spring the Democrats carried the town by 91, so we think we did very well by our cousin."

Franklin's admiration for Theodore Roosevelt turned to emulation in 1899. When a Boston oculist told him he should wear glasses for his nearsightedness, he took it upon himself to order two sets of lenses, one mounted in a gold-rimmed pince-nez precisely like that the colonel had worn up Kettle Hill; he only rarely wore the other pair.

To be related to Theodore Roosevelt was a mark of distinction at Groton. To be related to Taddy remained a hideous embarrassment, daily agony for a boy like Franklin who yearned so fiercely for social success. Their names were constantly being confused; in his second year, Franklin was assigned the same cubicle in which Taddy had lived the year before. "Worse luck!" he wrote home. Taddy skipped lectures (preferring to "Loaf," according to Franklin), did not study, slipped away from school—and always got caught. On his way back to school one year he forgot his health certificate. Returning with Franklin from a ski trek to town on a winter Sunday afternoon, he dropped an entire bag of oranges one by one along the way, and the two boys had to retrace their tracks through the snow to pick them up. Many years later, Mary Newbold Morgan, Franklin's childhood playmate and lifelong neighbor, told her son that Taddy had always seemed to her "dim-witted, inconsequential . . . his only topic of conversation . . . what his pair of socks had cost him." There began to be talk, too, of secret drinking. Mary's mother had whispered that the cause was "the Astor taint," a genetic flaw which was supposed to produce an unfortunate eccentric every other generation or so.[8]

Sara shared some of her son's scorn for Taddy, and she sometimes worried about his influence on Franklin. "Do not let Taddy persuade you that [choir singing] is a bore," she wrote one year, "for he is no judge. Many things in life bore him and he will lose a great deal by having such ideas but cannot help it." But she also felt sorry for him. Such ideas she clearly believed were inherited from his father, whose preoccupation with amusing himself she always found trying.

The Democrats lost the White House again in 1896, and by the following spring, Rosy was once again without anything to do.[9] Even

8. The shaky basis for this theory was probably John Jacob Astor's eldest son, John Jacob II, who lived most of the time in what one observer called "a state of mental stupor," emerging from time to time to compose idiosyncratic verse. His father built him a house at Ninth Avenue and Fourteenth Street in New York City, where he lived to be seventy-seven under a doctor's constant care, taking daily walks in the specially designed walled garden that shielded him from the gaze of passersby.

Source: Cowles, page 51.

9. The Republican triumph would have put Rosy out of a job in any case, but his years at the London embassy had not proceeded as placidly as he had hoped. He was skilled enough at the social side of diplomatic life, but in the summer of 1895 a genuine international crisis threatened war between Britain and the U.S. and made stringent demands on Rosy's skills as a political tactitian.

The border between British Guiana and Venezuela was the somewhat unlikely cause. In 1886, Britain had suddenly declared that some 30,000 square miles of what had once been generally considered Venezuelan territory now belonged to the Crown. The dispute festered for nine years, neither side yielding an inch. Most Americans sided with Venezuela, and in July of 1895 the U.S. Secretary of State Richard T. Olney sent an official note to London demanding that Britain submit to arbitration and declaring her in violation of the Monroe Doctrine. The British prime minister, Lord Salisbury, answered in effect that Britain's quarrel with Venezuela was none of America's business. The impasse took four years to resolve peacefully.

Meanwhile, Ambassador Thomas F. Bayard—who had been President Cleveland's Secretary of State during his first administration, and whose personal relations with Olney were anything but cordial—was suspected in Washington of being too malleable in his dealings with the British. To circumvent him during the crisis—and to impress upon the British America's seriousness of purpose—Olney secretly made Henry White his unofficial agent. White was Rosy's predecessor as first secretary, still living in London and intimately acquainted with British statesmen. Rosy was quietly instructed to make the official embassy cipher book available to White whenever clandestine messages needed to be passed to or from Washington.

This betrayal of his chief made Rosy uneasy—Bayard was an old friend and fellow sportsman who had been one of his sponsors for the London post—but he agreed, asking only that White "not inform me of the nature of his communications."

Rosy evidently lacked something as a conspirator and was quickly found out, so that for nearly two years he and the ambassador spoke to one another as rarely as possible. "I am not having an easy time with Mr. B. by any means," he complained to Olney, "and my position is a difficult one, as he resents bitterly any nonagreement with his policy and ties my hands at every step."

It was an awkward, painful business, and when Cleveland left office in March of 1897 and both Rosy and the ambassador lost their positions, Rosy wrote Bayard a sad note trying to make amends: "I write . . . to say goodbye and tell you that I am sorry to have differed with you as I have but can assure you it has not been through unfriendliness but purely as a matter of so, he rarely communicated with his troubled son at school, and late that May Taddy wrote Bamie to ask her if she knew where Rosy was: "I have not heard from my father for over a month," he said, "and have no idea of his whereabouts. Our paper said he had sold all his horses and had started for Paris. The papers are . . . more informed on the subject than we are."

He had, in fact, gone to Marienbad to take the cure for one of his many elusive illnesses before coming home to Hyde Park in the late summer. There, Sara confided to Franklin that "brother Rosy" occupied himself with "an extraordinary tricycle with a machine part electric and part naphtha with which he rides all over the country. It is very useful as he has no horses yet and it *amuses* him! This is only a side remark for *you alone.*"[10]

Taddy was almost pitifully grateful for any attention from anyone. When Sara sent him an Easter card, Franklin reported, "he told me that you were much kinder to him than his own family." Bamie, too, did her best to provide the warmth and support that Rosy's children needed but got only sporadically from their father, but even she could only do so much, and when she and Commander Cowles had their only child, W. Sheffield Cowles, Jr., in 1898, Franklin wrote to his mother, "I fear Helen and [Taddy] will be rather left in the cold."

Franklin had no such fears for himself. The wrench of separation had been at least as great for his parents as it had been for him, and they never ceased to worry about him; every detail of his life at school absorbed them. It was cool in Hyde Park the day Sara and Mr. James returned from leaving Franklin at school for the first time. "I hope you have put on your flannels," his mother wrote to him that evening. "Do

---

judgment. My feelings toward you are only those of kindness and regard." Bayard evidently did not respond.

Sources: Rosy's letters to Olney and Bayard are among his papers at the FDRL. The murky story of the Venezuelan crisis is told from various points of view in Alan Nevins, *The Life of Henry White;* Charles Callan Tansill, *The Foreign Policy of Thomas F. Bayard: 1885–1897;* Henry James, *Richard Olney and His Public Services.* (Rosy himself cooperated with James in writing this last volume, as two letters from James to him attest, FDRL.)

10. Sara's private impatience with her husband's firstborn was shared only with Franklin. In Rosy she saw displayed all the weaknesses she and Mr. James had worked hard to insure would not affect their boy—frivolousness, hypochondria, fearfulness, ostentation. It seems clear that she thought him an unworthy heir to her husband's name and reputation. But there were limits even to the confidences between mother and son, and at least once Franklin went too far. When Rosy was operated on for hemorrhoids in 1898 and seemed to take forever to recover, Franklin made schoolboy jokes about it in his letters home: "What a time you must have had with Brother Rosy! I hope it won't recur annually like a sort of bloom in the spring!" Sara was not amused, and Franklin apologized to her for having been too vulgar. Rosy's "temperament is not exactly conducive to bearing pain," he added, comfortable in the shared knowledge that his was.

not catch cold. It would be so trying for you and put you back, and then I should be so anxious." She felt as if he would walk back into the house at any moment, she added. "It makes me miserable to go to your room and to look at your clothes and things."

Sara kept each of his letters in her pocket, she told him, and read them over and over whenever she was alone; she also corrected his spelling and supplied words his schoolboy haste sometimes made him leave out before filing them away for the future. Sara thought about him constantly, visited Groton often (with and without Mr. James), asked her sister Dora's brother-in-law Charles Forbes to paint a portrait of Franklin, dusted his stuffed birds herself ("as I dare not trust it to anyone"), agonized with him over having his teeth straightened, exhorted him to dress warmly and drink milk each evening ("*please* never omit it"), to take his cod liver oil, to be especially careful playing football, and to be "sweet with Taddy. I want him to be fond of you." And when he needed shoes she sent him a new pair, serenely sure that they would fit: "You see a mother's eye can always see *inwardly* the size of the child's foot and everything about him!"

Franklin dutifully agreed to all his mother's strictures, and he asked that his parents send him photographs of themselves for his desk—a standard one of Mr. James, but of Sara "the little picture of yourself in the little heart-shaped frame on my bureau." Although his letters were always addressed to both of his parents, they were really meant mostly for her, and as his father's health deteriorated, increasingly filled with concern that Mr. James not become overtired. Franklin told her everything about his life at Groton that he thought she would like to hear, and kept to himself nearly everything disappointing, awkward, ambivalent.

He and his mother were more and more on their own now, and he fantasized that he, not Mr. James, had become her protector. When she was knocked down by a Manhattan bicyclist in front of Bamie Roosevelt's brownstone, she was not seriously hurt, "tho' rather nervous," but her sixteen-year-old son was enraged. "I am so sorry you were knocked down by that horrid bicycle," he wrote home. "I would have given anything to have been there, as the bicyclist would have been the jarred party instead of you, and he would have found out that I took a few boxing lessons last winter."

Franklin's parents worried most about his health. Perhaps because he had so rarely been exposed to other children and the standard diseases of childhood before going away to school, he seems to have been susceptible to every Groton germ. He suffered not only from frequent colds and chronic sinus trouble, but also from prolonged sieges of measles and mumps, for each of which he was sent home to Hyde Park for several weeks of his mother's loving care.

But Mr. James's health continued to come first with her. The winter of 1897–98 had been a grim one for Sara. All three of the most important figures in her life had fallen ill and she had to nurse them all. When Franklin arrived home for Christmas, he found his father in bed, pale and enervated from yet another heart attack. His grandfather Delano had already sent word that he was no longer up to presiding over the traditional family dinner at Algonac; a week later he developed pneumonia. Franklin himself came down with indigestion, spent several days in his room, and was late returning to Groton.

Back there on January 16, Franklin got word from his father that his grandfather was growing steadily weaker: "It is only a matter of hours." The old man died the following day. Sara had been at his bedside, helplessly watching as the father whom she very nearly worshipped slipped away. "I could think only of 'Peace, Perfect Peace,' when I saw the beautiful calm face," she wrote in her diary when it was over. "Franklin loved and admired his grandfather. We are thankful he is old enough to remember him always."

Whether or not Franklin understood the full depth of his mother's feelings for her father, he knew she needed to be comforted. "To my darling Mama," he wrote that evening. "You can never imagine how deeply grieved I was to hear that my darling grandfather had passed away. I know you are heartbroken, but we must remember that he has gone to a better place than this earth, and will be far happier there. . . . I only wish I could have been near you in our great trouble." He was excused from school two days later to attend the funeral and stood alongside his mother at the Fairhaven graveside.

Still recovering slowly from his Christmas illness, Mr. James had been too frail to attend. He needed to rest, Sara thought, and then should return to Nauheim as soon as he was able to travel. She hated to leave her boy behind; they had all planned to go to Germany together in July, just as they had in earlier summers. But this was an emergency; "*nothing* but James' health would induce me to cross the ocean without Franklin!" Her son understood her concern and urged his parents to go on without him: "Papa must not put off going."

Before she left, Sara wrote directly to the rector with instructions as to how her son was to be cared for should he fall ill in her absence:

"I trust sincerely that Franklin will keep well, but I must beg that in case of any illness he may have a room alone. When he is ill he needs sleep and rest and quiet which with his nature is impossible if he is in a room with other boys."

The elder Roosevelts set sail for Europe accompanied by a maid in late April of 1898, just a few days before the war with Spain began. That event—about which Franklin and his schoolmates, he said, were "wildly excited"—helped inspire one of the most commonly recounted—and least plausible—of all the stories from his childhood. Within hours of the declaration of war, Franklin, Lathrop Brown, and another classmate had decided to run away together and join the fighting—or so FDR always claimed. The Navy was recruiting young men at Long Wharf in Boston, just thirty-five miles away, but to make their way there the boys first had to find a way to leave the school grounds without being seen by the masters. A pieman who visited the school twice each week peddling cookies and cakes and pies to the boys provided the answer. Franklin and his friends bribed him to allow them to ride off the school grounds inside his wagon. On April 28 they were all set to climb aboard—sometimes FDR liked to say they *were* aboard—when they developed the burning throats and racking chills of scarlet fever, then raging through the school. They went instead to the Groton infirmary.

FDR often told this tale with extravagant embellishments, hinting that he and his companions had planned to join Theodore Roosevelt in Cuba rather than enlist in the Navy, though TR himself was still a civilian when Franklin fell ill, and more than a week away from resigning his post at the Navy Department. But even the basic story has all the earmarks of fiction. It seems unlikely that any sane pieman, dependent for his living on regular access to a steady supply of hungry Groton boys, would have risked the headmaster's anger—let alone possible criminal charges—by agreeing to spirit away three of his students, and especially not in exchange for the very modest sort of bribe three schoolboys could manage to put together out of their allowances. Nor does it seem possible that a boy like Franklin, so consistently concerned about the danger of alarming his ailing father, would ever have seriously considered going into combat against his parents' wishes.

Like so many of FDR's family stories, this one seems to represent what he *wished* had happened rather than what did. Perhaps he and Brown did discuss going off to war in a moment of boyish patriotism, but for FDR to claim that they ever actually tried to make such a break seems to have been still another example of his desire to remember his basically placid boyhood as having been eventful and adventuresome.[11]

But if the aborted Cuban adventure was largely imaginary, Franklin's illness was all too real, and terrifying to his far-off parents. They first learned of it on May 2 in London when two cablegrams arrived, one from Annie Hitch, the other from Rosy. Franklin had suffered a "slight attack scarlet fever"; "no anxiety whatsoever." His mother and father were not reassured. "James is so upset," Sara wrote, "that I dare not show how I feel." But when a cablegram came the next day from Peabody himself saying that Franklin was recovering nicely, she added, "I am so anxious for James to take his cure that I encourage him to stay and *not* go home." They pushed on fearfully for Nauheim.

The Roosevelts arrived there on the sixteenth and had just settled into their hotel—Mr. James had been put to bed—when a cablegram arrived saying that Franklin had developed "inflamed kidneys." Sara woke the maid and together they repacked their trunks. Mr. James was told the bad news in the morning and all three set out immediately for home.

The eight-day ocean voyage seemed endless. Sara spent most of it in her cabin, and when the *Teutonic* nosed at last into the New York dock on May 25 and she spotted Fred and Annie Hitch and Franklin's godmother, Nellie Blodgett, in the crowd "all so cheerful in expression . . . my nerve gave way with relief" and she wept.

She and Mr. James reached Groton the next day to find "darling Franklin very thin and very white but better." Because of the danger of infecting her husband, Sara wrote, "I have to choose between going in to him and staying in and deserting James or merely seeing Franklin thro' the window and being with James. As the infirmary is full and F's room has 2 other boys and 2 nurses in it, I decide not to go in."

Instead, she stood on a box placed beneath the window and later spent hours reading aloud to him from the top of a rickety stepladder, much to the amusement of Mr. James. Sara saw nothing funny in it. "Franklin loved to see me appear over the window ledge," she remem-

11. Evidence for the runaway plot is scant and confusing. Not a word of it appears in Sara Delano Roosevelt's journals. It first appeared in print in Ernest K. Lindley's early biography, *Franklin D. Roosevelt* (page 52), and its source must have been FDR himself. Versions of it also appear in Sara's *My Boy Franklin* (pages 42–46) and in Rita Kleeman, *Gracious Lady* (page 196). Finally, FDR himself told the story to "a Broadway columnist" (probably Walter Winchell), from whose account it is retold on page 10 of *The Real FDR*, edited by Clark Kinnaird. Curiously, all three of these accounts attribute the plot's fizzle to measles—which FDR suffered from in 1897, a full year before the Spanish-American War began—rather than to scarlet fever.

bered, "and, at first sight of me his pale little face would break into a happy albeit pathetic smile."

When he was well enough, she took him home to Springwood, where he was cared for by the same nurse who had looked after Warren Delano in his final illness. Sara never forgot how proud she had been when the nurse told her that Franklin constantly reminded her of his late grandfather. There could be no higher praise.[12]

When Franklin returned to Groton to begin his final sixth-form year in September 1899, things seemed at last to be going his way. Taddy had moved on to Harvard. "For several years he was extremely troublesome," the headmaster had written of him in what was a remarkably pallid college recommendation. "He is occasionally eccentric and difficult to deal with. He *has* a conscience . . . [but] I do not feel sure of him." He was gone in any case, and Franklin looked forward to a year without him.

Like almost half his classmates, Franklin was chosen to be a dormitory prefect and proved kind and helpful to the new boys, whom he now loftily called "infants" or "the kids." He was awarded one of "the five best single studies," too, a real room at last, for which his mother sent him an embroidered sofa cushion and a framed engraving by Doré. And partly because the rector had seen fit to award this prized room to him, he was fairly confident he would soon be made a senior prefect, one of the nine or ten boys whom Peabody believed displayed the highest qualities of leadership in the school and with whom he conferred daily.

He managed to make the second football squad as well and—though he rarely left the bench during games—wrote home exultantly: "Football bruises, afternoon teas, lack of sleep, gossip & engagements come thick and fast . . . a glorious time."

The younger boys all admired him. George Biddle, three forms behind Franklin, remembered him as "gray-eyed, cool, self-possessed,

12. Sara knew her boy well, and her warning to the rector that Franklin not be expected to recuperate peacefully in a room with other patients turned out to have been fully justified. He had been quarantined with two other boys when he first fell ill. All three had been making "satisfactory progress," she said many years later, "until one of them—I'm afraid it was Franklin—put a highly nefarious plan into action. Their nurse, a waddly, good-natured soul, used to make frequent trips into the ward . . . and no sooner was her back turned than they would hitch on to her starched skirts, and, with her first move in the opposite direction, send the beds, which were on casters. shooting across the highly-waxed floor. This performance, repeated at frequent intervals, so aggravated Franklin's condition that he was soon in the throes of a relapse."

Source: My Boy Franklin, pages 42–43.

intelligent . . . [with] the warmest and most friendly and understanding smile." His younger brother, Francis, then in the still more lowly second form, recalled Franklin simply as "a magnificent but distant deity."

And he continued to be admired by those older than he. At Campobello he supervised the Golf Club course, often won tournaments competing against older players, and was thought so mature, energetic, and responsible at eighteen the following summer that he was asked to be both secretary and treasurer. (Even his mother thought this too much responsibility for her son and urged him respectfully to decline; he accepted instead, and when she offered to help with the paperwork, gently refused that, too, insisting on handling it all himself.)

His charm and energy made younger boys look up to him and delighted adults, but with boys his own age—the constituency he sought most eagerly to please—he was still not really popular. "They didn't like him," Eleanor Roosevelt once told an interviewer. "They had to give him a certain recognition because of his intellectual ability. But he was never of the inner clique."

He may have known more than most boys about the bigger world beyond Groton, but they knew far more than he about being boys.

His demeanor had a lot to do with it. The easy charm and cordiality that so pleased his mother and delighted his parents' friends—bright, eager, offhand, instinctive—seemed artificial to many of his contemporaries—studied, smooth, even oily. And there was more to it than that. One classmate recalled that by the end of his time at Groton, Franklin had also "developed an independent cocky manner and at times became very argumentative and sarcastic. In an argument he always liked to take the side opposite to that maintained by those with whom he was talking. This irritated the other boys considerably."

But that attitude itself may have been born of frustration, a means of expressing anger he otherwise repressed. Sarcasm was a natural weapon for an intelligent, bewildered, articulate boy who believed he was somehow being victimized, cheated of the exalted status that everything in his upbringing had taught him would be his by right. If he was not doing as well as he believed he should, others must be at fault. He could not be.

That pattern seems to have been established early, in the autumn of his second year at school, when he failed an examination in Greek, then delayed telling his parents about it, finally informed them (claiming he "forgot" what had happened for a time), while accusing his teacher of having been unjust: "Not only was the paper unfair but the marking was atrocious and altho' I got about .50 the old idiot Abbott refused to pass me as is customary when one almost passes." (Mr. James found this failure "too provoking" in his single documented instance of even mild irritation with his boy. Franklin must do better or be put back, he warned, and "imagine, my son, FDR, stepping down to a lower form!" But his father could not stay angry with him long; the rest of his letter concerns the doings of a new puppy and the flattering things visitors had said about the new portrait of Franklin, now hung on the Springwood landing.)

Such excuses, perhaps put forward as much to convince himself as to persuade his parents, would blanket his shortcomings wherever they occurred at school. According to him, the boys who outran or outboxed or outkicked him were invariably too experienced or too big to have provided fair competition; if he slipped in the academic standings it was because of the arrival of two "horribly clever" new boys. And if he thought distorting the truth would go undetected, he did not hesitate to try that, either. He told his parents he had "tottered in" fourth in a field of 100 boys who took part in an all-school six-mile paper chase in his sixth-form year, knowing that the *Grotonian* would list only the first three finishers in its columns; and when that magazine rejected his plan for an article on the Dreyfus case, he reported that it had been because "they had one [on the same subject] about a year ago"—although they had not.

Many years later, some of Franklin's classmates, distrustful of him and hostile to his presidency, would charge that FDR had lacked "sincerity of purpose" even at Groton; perhaps it was excuses and exaggerations like these they had in mind.

The sixth-form play scheduled for February of his final year seemed to Franklin to offer a chance for real distinction at school. The seniors were to present W. S. Gilbert's musical farce *The Wedding March—An Eccentricity in Three Acts.* Franklin first tried out confidently for the second male lead—"in which I appear constantly, have little to say but *lots* of acting"—but failed to land it. Then he auditioned for a female lead. He had nearly reached his full height of six feet one and a half inches now and sang tenor, not soprano, in the choir, but he was still so slender as to seem almost willowy—the school doctor had prescribed a daily snack of crackers and an egg milk shake to add weight—and like many boarding school boys of his time he seems to have been intrigued by the possibility of such a masquerade.

(In 1898 he had sent home photographs of that year's class play so that his parents could see for themselves "what good girls boys make!") But a friend of his, Kerr Rainsford, got the part. "It seems hard," Franklin wrote, "as there are so few girls and I am sure I could do as well as Kerr. As it is now, I doubt if I get a good part at all, and [the director] is being bullied by his Boston friends (!) to give *them* all the best parts."

He had abandoned hope when—"joyful news"—the boy slated to play a country bumpkin called Uncle Boppady fell ill with rheumatic fever and Franklin was asked to fill in. "I suppose it is criminal to rejoice," he wrote home, "but I can't help it! I've got his part and it's one of the best of the play!!!!"

Nothing in his Groton years so excited him as his part in this production. Letter after letter flew home, filled with requests for old clothing from which to compile a costume (two big boxes of his father's discards were eventually dispatched to Groton) and pleas that no one be told anything about the play in advance: "Remember, *Mum's* the word. Impress the importance of it on Papa, as it would spoil *everything to have it known!*" Sara and Mr. James traveled to Groton to see one performance and were so pleased they stayed over to see their boy again the next night. "Franklin acted and sang well," Sara noted, and the *Grotonian* concurred: "Uncle Boppady is deaf and Roosevelt imitated very cleverly a deaf man's voice. . . . Roosevelt did very well and looked like an old print in his beginning of the century costume."

Franklin's pleasure in his triumph lasted less than a month. The rector himself, whose "tyrannical way" Franklin had already denounced to his parents at least once, passed him over for senior prefect in late March. He was bitterly resentful. "Three more prefects made today," he wrote home, "but I'm glad not to be one after the choice. Harold Peabody (what a swipe), Jack Minturn!!! & Harry Markoe who is all right. Everyone is wild at the Rector for his favoritism to his nephew, but the honor is no longer an honor & makes no difference to one's standing."

In fact he was still upset by it weeks later, talked it over with his mother over Easter vacation, and when he returned to school for the last time in April she was still doing her best to comfort him. "Do not worry over *certain* things," she told him; "life is full of that sort of thing and we must be above caring. Only keep up your position and character and let *no one* make you feel small, go ahead your own way, and be kind to every one if you have the chance, and be humble minded to your superiors in years and to your parents who live for you and in you."

Excitement over the coming year helped blunt his disappointment during his final weeks at Groton. Like all but two of his classmates, Franklin would go on to Harvard. He and Lathrop Brown had agreed to live together in Cambridge, and while boating on the river discussed how they would arrange their college rooms. They had already put down a deposit on a suite in Westmorly Court, a private and exclusive dormitory on Mount Auburn Street.

But as graduation neared, Franklin grew nostalgic, too. In gratitude for their victory over St. Marks, the rector and his wife took the baseball team and its manager on a special picnic; all "had a roaring good time," Franklin said, eating their lunch spread out on the grassy summit of a hill while admiring "the most glorious view." In the annual Memorial Day parade to the Groton village cemetery, he led a company of boys, all wearing straw hats, dark jackets and white trousers and marching in careful cadence to the music of the school's fife and drum corps. American flags flew overhead in the warm spring sun, and Endicott Peabody himself rode at the front on a huge white horse.

And on Prize Day, June 24, Franklin was given the prize for having written the best essay in Latin, a forty-volume set of Shakespeare. Mr. James had not been well enough to attend, and Sara had not dared leave his side. But, she wrote, "I can see it and *feel* it all." "You may imagine I feel rather tickled," Franklin reported home. " 'The strife is o'er, the battle won!' " he continued. "What a joyful yet sad day this has been. Never again will we hold recitations in the old School, and scarce a boy but wishes he were a 1st former again. . . . I can hardly wait to see you but feel awfully to be leaving here for good."

In later years, FDR would rarely pass up an opportunity to heap praise upon his old school and its headmaster. The rector performed the marriage ceremony that united him with Eleanor Roosevelt. FDR saved every one of the forty-odd birthday postcards Peabody sent him over the years, dispatched all four of his own sons to Groton—making sure they entered the school properly at twelve, not fourteen, and, like Mr. James, sometimes providing them with material with which to win their debates. The President lobbied hard to have the rector awarded an honorary degree from Cambridge, his English alma mater, in 1935. Peabody, he told the American ambassador to London, was "the unquestionably outstanding private school Headmaster in the United States." And he invited him to officiate at private religious services on the eve of each of his four inaugurations as President—not, as one cynic suggested, because Peabody was "a nice old man who needed a ride on a train," but out of unfeigned affection and respect. "I count it among the blessings of my life," he once told the rector, "that it was given to me in formative years to have the privilege of your guiding hand and the benefit of your inspiring example . . . for all that you have been and are to me I owe a debt of gratitude which I love to acknowledge."

And Peabody returned the favor, defending the President against bitter criticism from his former schoolmates. He was duty-bound to vote for Hoover in 1932, then believing him the "abler man," but FDR's victory did not displease him. That spring, Franklin Roosevelt, Jr., had been elected senior prefect at Groton—his father had been delighted, especially when his son had told him that the only way FDR could equal that feat was to be elected President—and at six in the morning following election day he was asleep in his study at school. The light snapped on. "Roosevelt, wake up!" The rector stood in the doorway in his long white nightshirt. "Yes, sir," Franklin, Jr., said, blinking back sleep and swinging his feet onto the floor. "Your father was elected President of the United States yesterday," Peabody said. "The first Groton student to be so honored and very much in the tradition of Groton School." He left the room without another word, but he was always for Roosevelt after that, a little gingerly about specific New Deal policies, perhaps, but strenuously vouching for his former student's sincerity and religious conviction, and persuaded that FDR's actions had helped immeasurably to "save this country from the serious attacks made upon it by extreme radicals."

When the New York alumni gave the rector a dinner at the Union Club on his eightieth birthday, he closed his remarks by saying, "I believe Franklin Roosevelt to be a gallant and courageous gentleman. I am happy to count him as my friend." Not one of his hosts clapped.

Yet, as was so often the case with FDR, things were not quite as they seemed. He had not always admired the rector while actually under his care, and in later years he liked to tell schoolboy stories that cast the old man in a less than flattering light. "From the president's conversation," his aide William Hassett noted in his diary, "[I] have always gained the distinct impression that he liked Peabody better in the years after Groton than when he was a boy there. I guess that has been the experience of more than one schoolboy."

But FDR was in fact different from all of Peabody's other schoolboys. He alone had become President of the United States, and perhaps in his pleasure in that unique distinction lies the secret of his relentless public fealty to the rector. Franklin had not been well liked at Groton. Nor had he achieved there the status he had expected would be his, or grown as close as he would have wished to the headmaster and his wife. Worse, he knew that his old schoolmates knew it. Now, as President, he was able to do what none of them could do: summon the rector to his side and bask publicly in his authentic if belated approval.

In the spring of 1934 he agreed to attend the school's fiftieth birthday celebration. For the rector's sake, even the President's most adamant opponents among the alumni agreed to treat him more or less affably, as just one of the more than 400 graduates on hand for the great occasion. But it was not made easy for them. When the President's motorcade, led by a squadron of Massachusetts state police on motorcycles, turned in from the highway and Roosevelt's big open Packard pulled up in front of Hundred House, there was a patter of applause from the assembled guests, but Mrs. Peabody could not contain her genuine pleasure. She rushed down the steps ahead of her more reserved husband and threw her arms around the President before he could be helped from his car. "Franklin, dear boy," she exclaimed as she kissed him. "I am *so* glad to see you!"

Worse was to come. At the last moment, the rector decided that all his guests should have the honor of meeting the President, and a receiving line formed up in front of the headmaster's residence. A good many alumni were privately appalled. One of the most exercised was the Wall Street broker Fuller Potter (Groton '01). Franklin Roosevelt's political career both mystified and angered him. He had after all outboxed Franklin in 1898, had been the star second baseman on the 1900 team Roosevelt had merely managed, and had found FDR's election as governor four years earlier simply an embarrassment to the school. No true Groton man would ever have allied himself with Tammany. "I can't understand this thing about Frank," he had said then. "He never amounted to much at school."

Embarrassment had changed to anger over the intervening four years. FDR's ascendancy to the nation's highest office would have seemed a bad joke were it not so dangerous, a calamity as serious as the Crash of 1929. The new President's decision to close the banks, he believed, had been just a hint of the Bolshevik-style revolution the malleable new President's sinister advisers were trying to bring about, and there had even been muttering among his friends of the need for assassination. Potter had forbidden such talk in his own house. He would not sink to "That Man's level, at least not that far down," he said; besides there were "other ways of handling the problem," as he planned to demonstrate publicly if FDR dared attend the Groton anniversary.

Potter's vehemence had so alarmed his son Jeffrey, then himself a Groton student, that he gently suggested it might be best if his father stayed away. His father said no; he would come. He owed it to the rector to be there. (His feelings about Peabody had not changed since he had done so well against St. Marks by keeping in mind each time he came to bat how much a Groton triumph would mean to the rector.) But he would not be afraid to show just how he felt about Franklin Roosevelt. "You know how hard I have always played," he told friends, "and I'll take care of it my own way."

Several of Potter's friends winked and patted him on the back as he and Jeffrey joined the end of the reception line. Some wished him luck. One told him, "Don't let us down." He stood very straight as the line moved slowly forward, his face pale, fists clenched. Jeffrey was terrified at what his father might do and was not reassured when he looked ahead and saw that the Secret Service men were "in just the wrong place—too far away to stop [his father] but near enough to catch him." He closed his eyes as they edged along, and began to pray.

They reached the bottom of the steps. The school bell rang. And at that instant the boy heard the President "shouting Father's name—and his *first* name at that. . . . There was laughter behind us. The President called to him to come up here and give him the hand that won the St. Marks game."

Jeffrey opened his eyes and looked up to see his father—now "looking small but smiling"—squeezed in between the old headmaster and the big grinning man who had at last become his prize pupil.

CHAPTER 6

UNDER THE INFLUENCE OF HIS MOTHER

Sara Delano Roosevelt took a photograph of Franklin and Mr. James on the porch of their Campobello home sometime during the summer of 1900. In it, father and son sit together in the sun on a rustic-style seat made of unfinished tree limbs, both dressed warmly against the chill sea wind. Franklin is taller than his father now, and sits with a newspaper across his lap, slender and a little solemn in sweater, coat, and tie, his hair parted precisely in the center. Mr. James wears a straw skimmer and sits up as straight as he can, but he is clearly very frail—too weak even to make his way back to Nauheim. His carefully tailored tweeds hang loosely on his thin shoulders. His neck no longer fills his collar, and some sort of deep discoloration has stained the whole right side of his face.

This was to be the last summer the three Roosevelts would have together.

Mr. James had suffered two major disappointments in the past few years. First, the Nicaraguan Canal project—the third and last of his schemes to make himself immensely rich—finally collapsed in 1899, superseded by the canal to be built across Panama. He took the news with his usual equanimity about business matters; it had been a gamble and gambles did not always pay off. Nothing irreplaceable had ever been at risk. But he had been genuinely saddened in the autumn of 1898 when his big yacht, the *Half Moon,* mysteriously blew up and sank as she was being towed up the Hudson to Hyde Park. "She was in all her details and auxiliary power a creation of my own," he told Franklin, "as no boat was ever built like her. . . . I am so disheartened." Franklin had been saddened, too, and worried over the disaster's impact on his father's health. He offered to sell his knockabout, the *New Moon*, to help pay for a replacement, a gesture which Mr. James gently refused but thought wonderfully "unselfish."

He still did his best to maintain the standards that had always been so important to him. Shortly after Mr. and Mrs. Frederick Vanderbilt moved into their monumental villa on the site of Dr. David Hosack's old house in Hyde Park in 1898, a servant had brought to Sara at the dining-room table a hand-written note from her new neighbor.

"Mrs. Vanderbilt has invited us to dinner," she told her husband.

"Sallie, we cannot accept."

"But she's a lovely woman," Sara answered, "and I thought you liked Mr. Vanderbilt."

He did, Mr. James said; they had served on the same boards of directors together and got along well. That was not the point: "If we accept we shall have to have them at our house."[1]

He was still capable of rallying his spirits. The way his new eighteen-ton auxiliary schooner was being fitted out soon absorbed him, and Sara had given him a fine new saddle horse named "Bobby"—"a beauty, only five years old and kind and gentle . . . Kentucky-bred."

But there had been growing signs of fretfulness as well. A quarrel with a neighbor over a few feet of beachfront had made him threaten for a time never to return to Campobello. The servants sometimes made him peevish, and when he learned that Todd, his latest English butler, had quietly answered an advertisement for a new position, he

1. FDR loved to tell this story, always prefaced by a plea that Mr. James not be misunderstood: "He was the most generous and kindly of men, and always liberal in outlook. . . . My father was no snob."

Relations with the Hyde Park Vanderbilts were polite—Sara and Mrs. Vanderbilt even became friends—but the Roosevelts continued privately to think of their neighbors as gaudy newcomers, overly anxious to impress. William Hassett recorded a tale that both Rosy and the President enjoyed retelling. Rosy had once been Mrs. Vanderbilt's dinner guest. "At the appropriate time the dinner was halted. The butler, in full livery, approached and called out in solemn tones, 'A cable from King Edward.'

" 'Dear old Knollys,' said Mrs. Vanderbilt. 'How lovely of him [reading]. He's thanking me for my birthday greeting to the king.' " Even Rosy found this evidence of intimacy with the royal family stirring—until he was invited back again for dinner and the whole tableau was restaged for him by his forgetful hostess, word for word.

For his part, Frederick Vanderbilt found FDR's Democratic politics abhorrent, and during the presidential years, his chauffeur had standing orders that when the master arrived at the Poughkeepsie depot he was to take a roundabout route through the city to avoid passing the new post office FDR had ordered built. Just the sight of it could spoil Mr. Vanderbilt's weekend.

Sources: Hassett, pages 124–125, 88–89; confidential source.

fired him instantly. "It all rather upset Papa," Sara had told Franklin, "and I am *very* sorry simply for the reason that Todd is so unusually clean and respectable, a thoroughly gentleman's servant." He had felt bad leaving their service this way, Todd had told her, though with Mr. James now so often ill he "found our work more than he could do 'with justice to himself.'" Franklin had urged his father not to worry: "There are plenty of good butlers in the world."

Other things had come to bother Mr. James, things about which he had never complained before. The village boys, for example, who "make Hyde Park a disgrace to a Christian community by their *baseball* matches on Sunday. Last Sunday morning," he had written to Franklin at school, "there were 300 on the grounds, men, women and girls in wagons and on bicycles from all parts of the county. I am going to have it stopped."

Increasingly, too, there had been thoughts of his own death. On the eve of Franklin's seventeenth birthday, Mr. James had written, "Do you realize that you are approaching manhood and next year, when you begin your university life, you will be away from the safeguards of school and will have to withstand many temptations? . . . But I always feel your character is so well formed and established I have no fear as to your future career, and I often reflect that your dear mother will outlive me and will rely upon you to take care of her when I am gone."

In the same mood, he called his granddaughter, Helen Roosevelt, into his private, wood-paneled smoking room on her eighteenth birthday. "I wondered what I had been up to and whether I was going to get a scolding," she remembered many years later. He unlocked a drawer in his desk and took from it "a little round leather box, very worn," and pressed it into her hand. "You're eighteen now," he said. "These are your grandmother's jewels and they've been put away for a long time. . . . I want you to have them." His eyes filled with tears; Rebecca Howland Roosevelt had been dead for almost a quarter of a century. Meanwhile, Sara did all she could to take care of Mr. James, with Franklin's active help. The fond conspiracy between her and her son to keep his father alive had drawn them still closer, for all the physical distance that now separated them. Nearly every letter Franklin had written home during his last months at Groton urged that his father not be allowed to worry, not try to go to the Delaware & Hudson offices in Manhattan, not overdo. "*Private,*" Sara had written to him that spring. "When we go to Campo I am anxious to prevent

Papa from using his 3rd floor room, on account of the stairs. . . . You might suggest in one of your letters a *little later* that you would like to have that room." Franklin had complied a week later, saying that he found his old room insufficiently "cozy" and would welcome a change.

The new Roosevelt yacht, *Half Moon II,* arrived at Campobello on July 16, her deck gleaming, the three-man crew in crisp uniforms with her name embroidered on their caps and blouses. Mr. James was delighted with her. It was his seventy-second birthday. Franklin was away finishing his two-week stint at the Groton camp, so Sara and his father celebrated alone together aboard ship. Mr. James's physician had advised him to carry brandy with him at all times as an emergency stimulant for his heart, so Sara—who normally disapproved of drinking anything stronger than wine—gave him "a *very* small pocket flask" of silver, engraved with his initials.

Franklin returned from camp the next day with his friend and future roommate, Lathrop Brown, and the four of them went for a two-day sail up the Bay of Fundy to Saint John on the New Brunswick coast. It seemed like old times at first, but only at first, for it was soon evident that Mr. James "was not very well," Sara noted in her diary, "and I was so afraid he w'd be really ill that I slept not at all." (Both she and Mr. James must have remembered that Rebecca had suffered her final heart attack on board another Roosevelt yacht.) The family got home safely, but never again dared sail together far from shore or for more than a few hours.

Mr. James was only sporadically well for the rest of the summer. He spent long drowsy hours in the sun on the veranda looking out across the bay on which Franklin and his young friends sailed every afternoon. Sara usually sat with him, ready to tend to his needs, both waiting eagerly for their son's return each evening with cheering stories of all he had been doing. He won the golf tournament again that August, despite the herds of oblivious sheep that constituted such an unpredictable hazard on the Campobello course. The players, FDR recalled, "simply had to aim well over their cropping heads, shut their eyes and hope for the best." There were domino parties and dances and taffy pulls, and one evening Sara managed to leave her husband's side long enough to act as hostess for a "young dinner" for Franklin and seven of his friends.

The Roosevelts left Campobello for Hyde Park in early September, stopping in Boston for a few days so that Franklin and Lathrop—with a good deal of supervision from Sara—could order carpets, furniture, and drapes for their four-room suite in Westmorly Court. They all stayed at the Touraine Hotel, and as they left the city for home, Mr. James told Sara he had so enjoyed it that "we must go there often and see Franklin."

They had one more week with him at Springwood before he was scheduled to begin his freshman year at Harvard. Mr. James rode around the estate on Bobby—a groom had to lift him in and out of the saddle—and pronounced his gentle new horse "*perfect,*" according to Sara. Rosy returned from Europe on September 21, just in time to help celebrate her forty-sixth birthday. "My dear James surprised me with a cake and candles and sapphire sleeve links," she noted with pleasure that evening. Three days later, Franklin took her for a long quiet canoe ride on the river, and on the twenty-fifth he set off for college.

Sara thought this "a great step!" though in many ways it was a modest one. To a remarkable extent the world to which he was going was the same as that from which he had only recently emerged. There was to be sure, little sign of the rigorous austerity so favored by Endicott Peabody in Franklin's Westmorly suite; he and Lathrop Brown would live in comfort at Harvard, as suited preparatory school graduates residing in one of the four exclusive residence halls—Westmorly, Randolph, Clavery, and Russell—that lined Mount Auburn Street and made up what was called the Gold Coast. (Less prosperous students lived in shabby, poorly maintained dormitories within Harvard Yard.) And there were certain self-conscious evidences of worldliness, of which the rector would have disapproved: beer steins suspended from nails framed a doorway and hung here and there on the walls.

But Franklin and his roommate also did their best to transform their suite into a Groton shrine. The walls were hung with Groton pennants and framed team photographs; more school mementos lined the study tables and mantelpieces. And they lived surrounded by their Groton classmates, all but two of whom had entered Harvard with them. Franklin ate breakfast, lunch, and dinner every day at an all-Groton table in a private dining hall—"great fun and most informal," he told his parents—and in the evenings he and Lathrop sauntered down Massachusetts Avenue to a tobacco shop and billiard parlor called Sanford's, where they were sure to find "most of the Groton, St. M[ark's] & St Paul's & Pomfret fellows."

James Roosevelt sits for his portrait in a Paris photographer's studio in 1861. His eldest son, James Roosevelt Roosevelt—barely six but already known to everyone as "Rosy"—stands at his side.

Rebecca Howland Roosevelt (above), James Roosevelt's first wife, and two portraits of their son, Rosy: at twelve (right), fitted out for school in Dresden in 1866, and nine years later (facing page), ready for Mrs. Astor's fancy dress ball in the costume in which his mother thought "he looked so handsome."

Springwood, seen from the south, in 1900: the tiny figure on the veranda is James Roosevelt reading his newspaper.

Algonac, the home of the Delanos, at Newburgh, New York.

The Delano sisters, as they looked in the autumn of 1882: (standing, left to right) Laura, Sara, Kassie; (seated) Annie and Dora. Facing them is their father, Warren Delano II, photographed at Algonac in 1889, five years after Laura's fiery death; her portrait leans at the right, surrounded by flowers.

James Roosevelt, widower, in 1879.

Sara Delano Roosevelt in Rome on her honeymoon in 1881.

Warren Delano III and IV. It was the sudden death of this small child that prevented Sara from naming her son for her father.

Mr. James and Franklin in June 18

Franklin at four, with the blond curls his mother always thought had made him look "very sweet."

Franklin at five, shorn at last, but now persuaded to wear kilts. This portrait was made in the winter of 1887 in Washington, where Franklin visited the Oval Office of the White House for the first time.

Master Franklin and Mr. James at Springwood in 1891. Franklin rides his pony "Debby"; his father sits astride "Doolittle," the last of his stable of trotters.

Franklin and Fräulein Reinsberg (right), his German governess, on the frozen lawn of Crumwold, the neighboring Hyde Park estate of Colonel Archibald Rogers, in March 1891.

It was with these young men that Franklin identified at Harvard, among them that he was determined to succeed.

In effect he was already a sophomore, his final year at Groton having been the academic equivalent of his freshman year at college. The elective system pioneered by the university president, Charles W. Eliot, required only that first-year students take a handful of basic courses, after which they were free to enroll for pretty much whatever courses they fancied. Franklin and his Groton classmates had all taken and passed advanced placement examinations during their sixth-form year and were therefore allowed to skip the basic curriculum and finish their Harvard course of studies in three years instead of four.

The Harvard faculty roster was filled with distinguished names. William James, Josiah Royce, Hugo Münsterberg, and George Santayana (then still an instructor) were all in the philosophy department; George Lyman Kittredge and Charles T. Copeland taught English; history was in the hands of Albert Bushnell Hart and Edward Channing. Franklin would get to know few of Harvard's finest teachers, and was rarely overly concerned with what anyone tried to teach him. He would miss five weeks of lectures on frontier history by Frederick Jackson Turner, then visiting from the University of Wisconsin, for example, in order to take a Caribbean cruise. The appeal of systematic or abstract thought remained a mystery to Franklin Roosevelt all his life. He maintained an academic average at Harvard just slightly above C and seems to have been interested in his courses only to the extent that they amused him or added to his cluttered store of truly useful knowledge. There is not one word about their content in all his letters home from Cambridge. He had found them all dissatisfying, he would tell his roommate in his final year—"like an electric light that hasn't any wire. You need the lamp for light, but it's useless if you can't switch it on." And the stories he later told about his days in Harvard classrooms mostly had to do with pranks, such as the time he and most of the rest of his class slipped quietly out the window after attendance had been taken by a tedious but blessedly myopic lecturer on English history.[2]

2. Franklin did take one course whose title at least promised practical application—English 18: The Forms of Public Address, taught by Professor George Pierce Baker. He was required to write one hypothetical speech every two weeks on an assigned topic. One of Franklin's arguments has survived. The assignment was to write as the northern parent of a Harvard student trying to persuade the parents of potential students from the south to send their sons north to Cambridge as they had before the Civil War. "Is it true, we ask, that the inhabitant of one section of this great nation cannot enter a large university in another section because that institution represents hostility to the ideals and bringing up of that man? God forbid!," he wrote, "Is it true

"It is not so much brilliance as effort that is appreciated here," Franklin wrote at Harvard, "determination to accomplish something." What he hoped to accomplish was to triumph where he felt he had failed at Groton, in the athletic and social standings that mattered most to him and to his peers. From the very first he worked tirelessly to win what he would later call "a large acquaintance," and to remain "always active." He tried out for football his first week. He had reached his full height but was still far too slight for the varsity. He did make "The Missing Links," the lightest of eight scrub teams, however, and was elected its captain. "It is the only one composed wholly of Freshmen," he proudly wrote home on new stationery emblazoned with his interlaced initials, "and I am the *only* Freshman Captain." He signed up along with some seventy rivals as a candidate for the university newspaper, the *Crimson*, too, reporting that "if I work hard for two years I may be made an editor. I have to make out notices and go to interviews so I am very busy." And he joined the Republican Club and marched, wearing a red cap and gown, with most of the members of his class in a "grand torch light parade of Harvard & the Mass. Instit. of Technology . . . into Boston & thro' all the principal streets about 8 miles in all. The crowds to see it were huge all along the route." An icy rain pelted the marchers all evening, but it was worth it. William McKinley of Ohio was the party's presidential nominee; his running mate was Cousin Theodore.

---

that Harvard, the oldest university of the New World, represents only that narrow faction, yes, that increasingly narrow faction of Americans who do not and will not make an attempt to meet the South halfway in their great problem, the Negro? Once more, God forbid!" Northerners, Franklin continued, must be encouraged to "*know and sympathize with* our brothers of the South more and more. . . . You complain that the ignorant black is on the same political footing with yourselves, and we understand it and ask a remedy." That remedy was education, a "crusade against ignorance. . . . And this is why, and this only, that Harvard has done honor to perhaps a half a dozen negroes—men all of them who have given their lives for their race. Yes, Harvard has sought to make a man out of a semi-beast." In that effort, the north needed the south's help. Only by forgetting the bitter past and getting to know one another could north and south "understand each other better, love each other more."

One of his instructors thought Franklin's argument cogent and intellectually persuasive but altogether too bluntly stated and therefore unlikely to "budge firm southern prejudice."

Many years later, FDR told his aide William Hassett that "he withdrew from Baker's class after a few weeks; thought it didn't have much for him. Remembered that he and the professor could not agree on the way to deliver Lincoln's Gettysburg Address. FDR slouched to the rostrum and spoke it in a monotone without gestures. Baker was all for rounded resonant periods with gestures and all the elocutionary tactics."

But FDR did not withdraw from the course. He was, according to one of his instructors, notable for his diligence, "always appearing to give close attention and to take notes." At the end of the year he received a C-plus.

Sources: Rita Halle Kleeman Papers, FDRL; Hassett, page 159; Freidel, *The Apprenticeship*, pages 54–55.

But it was the crowded social circuit that occupied Franklin most consistently. He bought himself evening shoes, a derby, and a new dress suit which "looked like a dream and was much admired," and he sent home for his late Uncle Ned's old pipe and a big ceramic tobacco canister made in the shape of a dog for his desk. There were dances, teas, and dinners in the homes of family friends in Back Bay and Beacon Hill. He accepted a classmate's invitation to shoot ducks at his home near Newburyport. "It is not the pleasure of going with him that induced me to go," he explained, "but the chance to get some good duck shooting which I have never had & to see a new place."

After Harvard beat Pennsylvania at football, 17–5, Franklin reported, "we all, that is about half the college went to the theatre, 'The Monks of Malabar,' and regularly 'rough-housed' the play. They had to lower the curtain half a dozen times and missiles flew all over the place. After it was over, everyone went to the Hotels, I to the Touraine with 3 others, & 9/10 of Cambridge was 'tight'! Lathrop & I remained sober as judges but couldn't get a car back till 2 A.M.!!!!!!" After such evenings, Franklin and his friends slept till noon, then cooked griddle cakes over a chafing dish in their rooms and augmented them with broiled lamb chops, brought to them by a servant.

Clearly, Franklin's life as a Harvard man had begun auspiciously. But one barrier to social success remained stubbornly, maddeningly in place: Taddy. As at Groton, the humiliating existence of his half nephew continued to haunt Franklin and torment his parents. Taddy was no longer at Harvard himself; in fact he had not completed his freshman year. He had acted just as strangely at college as he had in school. Franklin had received alarming reports of him from time to time while at Groton the previous year, and had passed on chaste versions of them to Sara and Mr. James. Taddy had grown his hair long, he told them, looked like a tramp, and "scurried away" when spotted by old schoolmates; he had not gone to classes, had undergone some brutal hazing. "Very funny," Franklin thought, though "rather too much." Taddy had refused to visit Groton with his fellow graduates at first—Sara had urged Franklin especially to invite him: "make him feel welcome. It is a chance to do a kindness, my boy"—and when he finally did come had lost first his hat and then his travel money; Franklin had lent him enough to get back to Cambridge.

But even at that, Franklin had kept some more disquieting news to himself. At the end of his own freshman year, Taddy had been placed on academic probation first for failing to show up for classes, then for not appearing when summoned to discuss his laxness with the dean. When he also did not come home to Hyde Park in early June as he had promised, Sara quietly wrote Franklin to see if he knew whether it was probation or something else that had kept him away.

Franklin wrote back with uncharacteristic vehemence. He had "never heard of such assininity," he said, "everyone up here . . . thinks [Taddy] a fool." Academic probation had nothing to do with his disappearance, he said. "I think I should tell you that Taddy has been off to New York several times without letting anyone know of it. . . . He may be off on a bat now for ought I know. I think the very strictest measures sh'd be taken, but of course Papa must not worry . . . as after all it is no affair of ours." At the very least, Taddy's allowance should be halved.

Sara answered that while she hoped for the best, she feared that Taddy would one day embarrass the family. "I am sorry Taddy has Papa's name if he is not going to grace it," and she wanted Franklin to do all he could to disassociate himself from his half nephew. She and Mr. James had contributed toward a pew in the new Groton chapel. "By the way," she wrote, "will you be sure to have [it] marked with your *full* name, *initials* mean nothing. . . . I wish your full name given. You must see to it. You owe it to your good father and Uncle Frank."

But it had already been too late. Taddy had done more than skip lectures. Beginning the previous March, he had spent much of his time in New York and there found congenial company in the Tenderloin, the city's noxious West Side vice district, where he became known as a young man who could be counted on to spend and drink a good deal before stumbling home to a friend's flat in the early hours of the morning. His favorite stop was the Haymarket Dance Hall on West Thirtieth Street, a big noisy place with gambling rooms upstairs, and so infamous that in order to hold on to its license the management had to fabricate fictitious clubs—"The Piano Tuner's Benevolent Euchre and Whist League," "The Welsh Rabbits"—that supposedly rented out the place each evening for their balls.

Here, sometime that spring, while Franklin was worrying over his part in the sixth-form play, Taddy fell in love—with a Hungarian-born prostitute named Sadie Messinger. She was short and plump but "accounted a beauty of her type," according to one newspaper, with creamy skin and hazel eyes, and she spoke English with a fetching lisp. Little more is known about her. Her father was said to live in Brooklyn; she was variously known as "Dutch Sadie" and "Sadie of the Tenderloin," but she sometimes called herself "Mrs. Gray," claiming once to have been married to a Boston dentist of that name who had abused her. In any case, on June 14, 1900—just a week after Sara had asked Franklin if he knew of Taddy's whereabouts—he and Sadie had driven up to City Hall in a private brougham, applied for a marriage license, and asked to be wed right away. She was at least twenty-five but claimed to be nineteen; Taddy said he was twenty-one, though he was two months shy of it.

The clerk issued the license, idly wondering whether the young man was any relation to Governor Theodore Roosevelt, then sent for a Tammany alderman who happened to be upstairs to perform the ceremony. The Roosevelt family knew nothing of any of this. Rosy, who as usual had gone abroad for the season, had had a letter from his son saying that he planned to go "cruising" with a Harvard friend, Polly Wharton, most of the summer.

The bride and groom spent a long honeymoon at various country hotels, then rented a flat at 124 West Eighty-fourth Street. A furniture dealer was given $5,000 to furnish the apartment. Taddy hired servants and a coachman. On August 21 he celebrated his twenty-first birthday and became the master of half of his mother's huge Astor legacy. His secret seemed safe.

But Rosy returned to Hyde Park later that month and early in October a notice arrived there from Cambridge attaching Taddy's furniture. "Do not mention it," Sara wrote Franklin. "Papa and Brother Rosy feel very ashamed about it." Rosy evidently then decided to look more closely into the life his son was leading. On October 15 he visited the Eighty-fourth Street apartment, accompanied by two lawyers. There was an angry confrontation. Taddy had been a minor when the marriage took place, his father said, and he had not given his consent; therefore, he would have it annulled. Meanwhile, his son was to come with him and be sent away until he regained his senses. Taddy went along meekly.

Two days later, someone—perhaps hoping indirectly to embarrass Theodore Roosevelt, now the vice presidential nominee of his party—tipped off the press. The story was a sensation: BOY MILLIONAIRE WEDS; ASTOR SCION'S BRIDE WON IN DANCE HALL; "I LOVE JIMMIE AND HE LOVES ME," WIFE SAYS.

Sadie seemed eager to talk to the reporters who crowded her door. She told one she had never really married Taddy, adding (perhaps accurately) that he was not the only man who called upon her on Eighty-fourth Street, that in any case she had never been divorced from the cruel Dr. Gray. In another interview she said she had been visited by "one of those swell women from Fifth Avenue" who had claimed to be engaged to Taddie and had gone down on her knees begging her to give him up. "I told her I didn't care who she was. I loved Jimmie and he loved me. . . . Say, I didn't have to marry the whole Roosevelt family, Teddy and all, did I? I'm just as good as she." To still a third reporter she said she had already offered Taddy a divorce only to have him implore her to stand by him. If Mr. Roosevelt, Sr., tried to have the marriage annulled, she warned, she would sue him for alienating the affections of her husband.

The scandal sheet *Town Topics* delighted in the story. Rosy was "nearly frantic," it said, and his mother-in-law, Mrs. Astor, had gone into hiding. "The young man, it has long been known, is 'not all there' . . . the wonder has been that the father did not exercise better surveillance over the boy." One reporter was moved to verse:

The social atmosphere is hot,
As hot as it can be,
And "Jimmie, Junior," has got
Much notoriety;
And at the fame that he has gained
His folks most grievously are pained.

His father's ire and sore distress
Would cause a Jove to wince;
He's uttering words today, I guess,
This journal never prints;
While Mrs. Astor—well, I see
The pallor of the social She.

If things have gone to such a pitch
That his relations find
Young James they must now unhitch,
'Twould surely be more kind
To fill with bliss Dutch Sadie's cup—
In other words to take her up.

Society is passing slow;
It might refresh us, then,
To hear her views of life, to know

Her attitude toward men.
When everything is said and done,
Society is out for fun.

And should morality arise,
As an issue on the side,
And should they raise their saintly eyes,
It cannot be denied
That many social dames there are
Whom, by such judgment, we should bar.

Mr. James was mortified. Nothing remotely like this had ever happened to anyone in his family, or in Sara's. He first heard the news on the eighteenth from reporters who cornered him in the Delaware & Hudson office, and he managed to maintain his dignity under their questioning. He could not deny the story, he said, "though of course I have no idea who the woman can be." His grandson was "a good boy on the whole, though notoriously weak."

He hurried home to Springwood that evening, and there had a serious heart attack two nights later. Sara knew that he had been working too hard. A coal strike and a broken leg suffered by the man normally in charge of the D & H office had required him to spend several days in a row behind his New York desk. But "the dreadful and disgraceful business about Taddy was the last straw," she told Franklin. "Poor Brother Rosy and dear little Helen are terribly upset. Helen knows it all and feels disgraced. . . . Your father cannot get . . . out of his mind the thought that his grandson has been leading a wicked life for months. His marrying the creature brings it before the public, but the sin came first and he has disgraced his good name. Poor Papa suffered so much in the night for breath that he thought he could not live. He talked of you, and said 'Tell Franklin to be good and never be like Taddy.' Then he said, 'I *know* he is good and will be good.' He says he never remembers a disgrace coming to his family before, and it is dreadful to him."

Mr. James "thinks of it when awake and dreams of it when he is asleep," she reported. "It is *too* bad. This is *entre nous* entirely. Poor Helen, pretty hard on her and not very nice even for *you.*"

"The disgusting business about Taddy," an angry Franklin wrote to his mother, "did not come as a very great surprise to me or to anyone in Cambridge. I have heard the rumor ever since I have been here, but in the absence of facts the best course has been silence. I do not wonder that it has upset Papa, but although the disgrace to the name has been the worst part of the affair, one can never again consider him a true Roosevelt. It will be well for him not only to go to parts unknown, but to stay there and *begin* life anew."

Taddy was sent away to Florida, where he lived for a time under an assumed name. The annulment suit never came to court. He and his Sadie remained married, at least officially, until her death in 1940. Rosy disowned them both, a somewhat empty gesture in light of his son's inheritance from the Astors.

Franklin's strange half nephew had made his life at Groton much more difficult than it might otherwise have been. Now the scandal threatened to do the same for him at Harvard. But worse than that, Taddy had done what Franklin's own fantasies must have made him fear that he might do, had actually brought his father to the edge of death.

So far as anyone knows, FDR did not ever see or speak with Taddy again.[3]

Mr. James never really recovered his health. Frightened that he might not survive another harsh northern winter, Sara rented a cottage at the fashionable southern resort of Aiken, South Carolina, sight unseen—"rather small," she gathered, with "only one parlor" and room for just four servants. Still, the sun would warm her "beloved

3. Taddy remained an enigma to the end. His wife is said to have joined him in Florida in 1900, and at some later date the couple returned to the north, to Forest Hills, New York, where they took two rooms above a garage in which he repaired automobiles. They would remain officially married until 1940, although they evidently did not always live together.

He never touched his legacy, would not answer letters of inquiry from the Astor office, which simply continued to reinvest the interest it earned in more and more real estate.

Sometime before 1927, a friend told Bamie Roosevelt Cowles that he had met Taddy in Forest Hills and that he was talking of leaving his entire fortune to the Salvation Army. Intrigued, she invited him to lunch at Oldgate, her late husband's handsome colonial house in Farmington, Connecticut. Before he arrived, the butler took the precaution of locking the liquor cabinet just in case he proved uncontrollable. He needn't have worried. Before they sat down to eat, Bamie asked if he'd like a glass of sherry. No, he hadn't touched a drop of liquor in twenty years.

What had happened to his wife? She no longer lived with him; his life hadn't been what she'd hoped.

What did he do for a living? Nothing just at the moment. He'd developed arthritis from lying underneath cars on the cement floor of his garage and had been told to stop working.

He had no car of his own—too expensive, he said—but he did like to bicycle, and he pedaled every summer up along the Hudson to Hyde Park, past his father's Red House and Springwood, to lay flowers on his mother's grave in the St. James churchyard.

He had made a kind of peace with his sister, Helen, once visiting her in New York and taking her to a restaurant he especially favored—which turned out to be an automat.

Taddy died in 1958 and, true to his word, left $5 million to the Salvation Army.

Source: The account of Taddy's lunch with Bamie was given to me by one of his fellow diners, W. Sheffield Cowles, Jr., as we sat at the polished table around which it all took place.

invalid" there, and it would get him away from the day-to-day anxieties of business and the farm. Franklin was "delighted" with her plan; it would force his father to have an "absolute rest," insure that he forgot for a time about the affairs of "the everlasting D & H." His parents planned to leave for the south in mid-December. Franklin would join them there for Christmas.

In the meantime, Mr. James as always did his best to seem well, and Sara exulted in the slightest hint of improvement. He could not be stopped from going to church one Sunday in late October, because the bishop of New York was to deliver a sermon and confirm fifteen new members. "James handled the plate as usual," she noted in her diary, "but he looked very delicate as he did so."

He had retained his fondness for animals of all kinds, purchasing a small black Pomeranian named "Tip" whose devotion to him was instant and slavish, and he continued to take short, slow rides on Bobby whenever he felt up to it, Sara walking at his side. Nor had he lost his lifelong love of speed. Rosy had now replaced his motorized tricycle with a Locomobile. It ran well enough on level ground, but often stopped halfway up an incline and began to roll backward; whenever his daughter Helen rode with him and this happened, she had standing orders to jump down and hold the light automobile in place until Rosy could get it going forward again. Nonetheless, Mr. James was fascinated with it, and when Sara's brother Warren and his wife, Jenny, came for a visit he insisted on taking his brother-in-law for a noisy, jolting ride to the village and back. "I can see they think James looks ill," Sara confided to her diary that evening. "He is doing too much and still thinks and talks much about Taddy's behaviour."

So did Sara. She demanded to know from Franklin if he knew whether there had been any truth at all to Taddy's story of summer cruising: "Is Wharton *that* sort of boy . . . or was he at home? . . . We know Taddy's cruising was of a very peculiar sort. . . . It is difficult to touch mud and not get soiled," she warned. Franklin must make his college friends "very *slowly*" so as to avoid bad company.

Mr. James suffered still another attack in late November. Franklin was "too distressed" to hear of it and said he would come home at a moment's notice if necessary. Sara sat up with her husband night after night, reading aloud when he wished her to and "giving remedies at regular intervals." Racing up the stairs to bring something to him, she fell and hurt her knee, and so could no longer "run up and down all day." A nurse moved in. Franklin came home for a one-day visit and

Rosy came over from next door for lunch. "James is happy to have his two sons . . . To our surprise, James came down in the lift and sat with us and then he and Franklin and I sat together in the south parlor all the afternoon . . . James very delicate and tired-looking in a velvet coat, but it was sweet just to be together."

The next day, November 27, Sara and the nurse took Mr. James to New York by train, to their apartment in the Hotel Renaissance at 10 West Forty-third Street so as to be nearer to his doctors. He did not improve under their care, had now lost five more pounds, could not sleep. Sara wired for Franklin on the fourth of December. He arrived early the next morning, Sara wrote, "and tried to give me courage. . . . James was so glad." For the next three days Franklin ran errands, sat up with his father, did all he could to comfort his exhausted, anxious mother.

On the seventh, Rosy arrived from Hyde Park, and "when he got there," Sara wrote, "his dear father was quite bright and they made me go down to dinner. I c'd hardly bear it."

At two-twenty the following morning, with Sara, Franklin, and Rosy at his bedside, Mr. James died.

They took him home three days later. As requested in his will, eight of "the men on my place"—the young William Plog among them—were waiting as the special train pulled into the small Hyde Park depot that overlooked the river. Together, they lifted the casket from the train and carried it to the undertaker's hearse, black and gleaming and drawn by two black horses with black plumes on their harness. Franklin, Sara, and Rosy took their seats in the first of several carriages. Friends and grieving members of the Roosevelt, Delano, and Howland families followed along behind as the procession wound its way up the bluff, through the village to the door of St. James.

There was a brief simple service. Three of Mr. James's favorite hymns were sung—"My Faith Looks Up to Thee," "Hark, Hark, My Soul," and "Peace, Perfect Peace"—and then the coffin was slowly carried to the receiving vault in the cemetery behind the church. It would rest there until a permanent place could be prepared for it beside Rebecca Howland Roosevelt, and the twin Scotch granite monuments Mr. James had planned twenty-four years before could be built above them.

"We brought him to Hyde Park and I returned to this house without him," Sara wrote at Springwood that evening. She was numb. Everything looked the same; everything was different.

Franklin did his best to console his mother, saving his own grief for sleepless nights in his bedroom, as he had been taught to do. Sara worried that he would fall ill for want of sleep and tried to "keep him very quiet."

"The days drag on," she wrote. "We have to bear them." Sara and Franklin gathered flowers every morning in the Springwood greenhouse and drove together to the churchyard to place them on "the sacred place." They shared a desultory Christmas and took a long sad afternoon walk together on New Year's Day. "I dread his leaving," she wrote of Franklin that evening. Two days later, he took the train back to Cambridge.

There were other consolations. Tip stayed close at her side. "He seems to understand," she said. The Delanos closed ranks. Her brother Warren came to stay until an attack of typhoid sent him home; anxiety over his illness added to her sense of despair. Her brother Fred came, too, and so did Annie Hitch and Kassie and her two young daughters. The children were "a great pleasure and even seemed to appreciate my misery . . ." she noted, "tho' I tried not to show any sign of it." Dora Forbes sailed home from France to be with her, and they spent long quiet hours together, reading aloud to one another from *Paradise Lost* and the *Divine Comedy.* "They are all good to me," Sara wrote.

Scores of condolence letters arrived, and she saved them all. Arthur Dumper, Franklin's last tutor and now a fledgling clergyman in Cleveland, wrote that "Christian hope [will] bring your consolation." Dr. Schott, Mr. James's physician at Nauheim, expressed his formal regret. A cousin of Mr. James's first wife said she wished she could help in some way, "but Alas! No one can do that except Franklin, for you have him to love and care for." Mrs. Archibald Rogers wrote from Crumwold that she was "inexpressibly sad to think that we will not see the kindly face and sympathetic presence of our dear Mr. Roosevelt about this neighborhood which has known him for so many, many years. . . . God help you and Franklin!" A slight acquaintance whose small son had been introduced to Mr. James while he was visiting Groton during Franklin's siege of scarlet fever recalled how he and her boy "used to walk and talk together. He was so wonderfully sympathetic with a boy, full of interest and the warmth of affection . . . even though he was so much wiser and older. . . . I think it never entered his mind that he was *better* than other people."

An old New York servant named Mary Moore arduously penciled a note as well:

My Dear Mrs Rosevelt,

I went to the renson [Renaissance] this morning to inqire for mr. Rosevelt. I was very much shocked to heer of Your Dear husbandes Death Excep my seincer regret in this our of Triel. . . . If I could doo any thing for you I would bee glad to Doo it.

There were newspaper tributes, too—like his forebears, Mr. James was mourned as a "gentleman of the old school"—and some of the boards of directors upon which he had served sent calligraphed resolutions of regret; the one from the Farmer's Loan & Trust Company was especially beautiful, its borders wound with lilies rendered in gray wash. Sara was "quite overcome" by the Delaware & Hudson's gift—"a high silver vase 2 ft 4 high with two handles . . . with a great salver or deep silver tray, 1 ft 10½ inches across. . . . It has all quite upset me," she told Franklin, "as I can only think of Papa. How little he thought of the feeling he created in others!"

She read over her old diaries in the evenings, angry at herself now for having destroyed some of them, and wondering anew at Mr. James's vigor. "I remember what a delight all the beauty of nature was to him," she wrote Franklin, "and how he could enjoy it even when he fell ill. . . . In all my journals I read how indefatigable he was and how it was never too cold or stormy for him to go out to walk, drive and ride. I was the one who often stayed indoors on account of weather when you were small."

Her own energy and strength had always more than equaled her husband's, however, and as the weeks passed, slowly, gradually, life began for her again. About a month after Mr. James's death she lay awake, she told her son, "and lived over in my thoughts that night four weeks ago and thought of the help it was to me when you, my dear dear boy, came to me and I realized how much I still had to live for, even with your darling father's spirit flown. . . . You need not worry about me for I am all right." She began to ride Bobby around the estate, just as Mr. James had done, seeing to it that the ice was properly cut and stored and arranging sleigh rides for the servants who had been so loyal and solicitous. "I try to keep busy," she wrote, "but it is hard." She dusted and aired all of Franklin's birds, ordered a stained-glass window from England to be installed at St. James in memory of her husband. By the beginning of May she was helping Plog burn caterpillar nests in the trees on the farm, noting firmly that "it ought to have been done in April."

A month later, she was able to bring herself to ask the veterinarian to chloroform Doolittle, the last survivor of the stable of fine trotting horses of which her husband had been so proud. The horse had grown feeble and stiff-legged and was losing weight, "so that I feel he suffers," she told Franklin. "It cost me a good deal of feeling to come to this decision. He was such a pet of Papa's. . . . I hope Bobby may last much longer, and as he is about 5½, he ought to give us years of pleasure." She was again thinking of the future.

All her life, Sara Delano Roosevelt had directed her love and energy into caring for and identifying with a man—first her powerful father, then her loving husband, finally her son. Now she had buried two of them.

She was just forty-six, heavier than she once had been, but still regally handsome, well connected, and wealthy. Springwood was now hers, along with the rest of her husband's sizable estate (except for trust funds of $120,000 meant for each of his sons), and her father had left her an additional $1,300,000. Remarriage might have seemed likely. Two of Sara's own sisters had been widowed. Kassie had already remarried when Mr. James died; Dora would marry again within two years.[4] But Sara is not known ever to have considered life with another man.

4. Both second marriages were in fact somewhat unconventional. Dora and Will Forbes had been married more than thirty years when he died in 1896; seven years later (and to Sara's astonishment) Dora married her late husband's youngest brother, Paul Forbes.

Kassie's first husband, Charles Robbins, had died young, leaving her with two children. Her second husband, Hiram Price Collier, whom she married in 1893, was a divorced man, a former Unitarian clergyman, and would-be author without funds who had just written his first book, *Mr. Picket Pin and His Friends*, an account of life among the Sioux. The Delanos evidently disapproved of this union, at least at first. No mention whatsoever is made of it in the otherwise encyclopedic Algonac diary for 1893. Fred Hitch was then the estate's chronicler.

The Colliers lived at Tuxedo Park, where they built themselves a fine house and he worked away at his writing when he was not engaged in the outdoor sports that were his special enthusiasm. The editors of *Town Topics* savaged him at least twice in print as a feckless adventurer, living off his wife's wealth and oblivious of the scorn of his neighbors. He and his wife, they said, displayed "joy and excitement over their new home and their even newer social recognition [with] childlike ingenuousness. They fairly sweat self-content."

These articles angered Sara. "I am so sorry for dear Aunt Kassie," she told Franklin in 1901, "and considering her family, and bringing up, and beautiful home, it is, to say the least, trying to have any paper speak of her new house as if she had at last risen to opulence. And why can't they let Collier alone when he is leading a good life, and they are a happy family?"

Price Collier—he dropped the Hiram when he began to write—eventually won a considerable reputation as an idiosyncratic travel writer with books such as *America and the Americans*, *England and the English*, and *Germany and the Germans;* and he and his wife spent a good deal of their time abroad. All his works were laced with his firm and distinctly conservative political views. "He stated his beliefs vigorously," an official biographer wrote with great tact. "Some of his characteristic beliefs were in capital punishment, athletics, war, the Kaiser and the House of Lords." He collapsed and died instantly of a heart attack while shooting rabbits on a ducal estate in Denmark in 1913.

Kassie lived on in Tuxedo until her own death, and Sara often visited her there. Both she and her children found themselves adamantly opposed to every aspect of the New Deal. Despite this, Kassie and Sara remained close throughout their lives, their shared Delano heritage too strong ever seriously to be threatened by political quarrels among the children.

Sources: Dictionary of American Biography; Town Topics, May 2, 1901, and March 23, 1905.

A long empty widowhood stretched ahead of her. She would fill it with steady devotion to Franklin. His life would give hers meaning, just as her father's and her husband's had. His successes would be hers.

Even if Franklin had not been genuinely saddened by his father's death, the rigid strictures of what was then called "deep mourning" would have curtailed his social life for six full months. His and his mother's black-bordered letters were now filled with discussions as to what he could and could not decently do. Might he be an usher at a friend's wedding in June? The six months would then just be over. Sara thought he might, and Franklin agreed—"I feel as you do that dear Papa would have liked me to"—but when the wedding was moved back to April he had to decline. If he went to Groton to see the sixth-form play, he promised "to keep in the background as I don't want to see many people," and he would accept his friend Tom Beal's invitation to spend a quiet March weekend at his family's home in Boston only if no other guests were to be there. "I shan't do it if he has a single other person in the house." He could go, Sara replied, adding some words of advice: "I trust, dear boy, that you will take your evening clothes and all nice things, silver clothes brush, etc., in your valise to the Beals, as when visiting a lady's house you should be especially 'au petit soins,' and not get packed in such a hurry [as] to forget slippers, or anything and black gloves, etc., for going to church."[5]

Mother and son kept as close as they could. Each felt responsible for the other. Mr. James's will had appointed Sara Franklin's sole guardian and expressed the wish that he be always "under the influence of his mother." Franklin had been exhorted to care for her after his father was gone. But neither had needed urging; their lives had always been intimately intertwined. Franklin visited Springwood several times that spring, and Sara came to Cambridge long enough to pronounce herself pleased with his rooms. Presumably the beer steins had not yet been hung or had been temporarily removed. She was pleased, too, when he was elected an editor of the *Crimson* and secre-

5. Sara's patrician sense of humor was returning, too. The Roosevelts' New York butler Peter MacCarty wrote her a note resigning his post, and she sent it along to Franklin: "I am sorry to have given you such short notice," it said. "But as I have made a great deal of money in the stock exchange it is very important for me to look after it, consequently I must forfeit my place." She thought this hilarious, worthy of reprinting in *Punch* or the *Crimson* with a change of name. Franklin, too, was "much amused," though he also thought MacCarty "a fool not to keep his good position as he is sure to come to grief some day." He cautioned his mother not to be too hasty in hiring another butler "as we must have a good one."

tary of the freshman glee club, and became stroke on one of the intramural rowing teams, though she also worried that he was trying to do too much. She thought it best that he resign his post as secretary and treasurer of the Campobello Golf Club, for instance: "You know you told me you would do it the first thing after your return to college. . . . Now . . . do try to go to bed early and do not let others keep you up. . . . Try to use your strength of mind and systematize your time a little, especially now with so much more writing." And once a week she sent him by express from Springwood fresh eggs and cream to help keep up his strength.

The question of how best to spend their first summer without Mr. James was a thorny one. Sara thought at first it might be best if they simply stayed together at home at Hyde Park with perhaps a week or two at Campobello. Franklin disagreed; the memories at both places would be too painful. "I don't want to go to Campo, neither do you; I don't want to stay on the river in August, I don't want you to." Alfred Pell, their old Campobello friend and neighbor, had died suddenly in March, leaving a wife and a daughter, Frances, with whom Franklin had played and studied birds in summers past. Why shouldn't all four of them tour Europe together? "We will both enjoy seeing new places & new things and it will take us quite out of ourselves. . . . Read my reasons thro' two or three times & I know you will agree with me."

She did, and in early July, Franklin, Sara, her maid, and Cousin Theodore Douglas Robinson, the son of TR's sister Corinne, set sail for the Continent. They would meet the Pells in Norway.

The Roosevelts spent ten weeks abroad, coming back in late September just in time for Franklin to return to college. They explored the fiords on the cruising yacht *Prinzessin Victoria Luisa,* going ashore from time to time to visit a whaling village or Lapp encampment, to climb a hillside or view a waterfall. Their cabins were vast—forty-four by thirty-six feet—the food and service sumptuous. Steaming into the harbor at Molde, they came upon the German emperor's yacht *Hohenzollern* at anchor, gleaming white against the dark green of the surrounding hills and encircled by its escorts—a cruiser, a naval training ship, and three torpedo boats. Kaiser Wilhelm II himself came aboard their yacht for tea, unsmiling and astonishingly forceful, Sara recalled, despite his withered arm. Later, Franklin, Frances Pell, and Teddy Robinson with some of the other passengers were invited aboard the *Hohenzollern.* Sara and Mrs. Pell watched through field glasses. Franklin and Frances made such a tall, handsome couple, Sara remembered, that even the Kaiser turned to watch them pass. When Franklin returned he brought with him a pencil which he had lifted from the emperor's desk; it had been authentically dented by the imperial teeth.

Later they visited Dresden, and Sara showed her son where she had lived and gone to school as a girl. In Zurich they stayed in the same hotel in which she and Mr. James had stayed on their honeymoon twenty years before. They spent a week with Aunt Laura Delano at the Beau Rivage Hotel on the shore of Lake Geneva. Sara was especially proud that Aunt Laura seemed "so very pleased with Franklin."[6] Then they visited Aunt Dora and Franklin's Howland cousins in Paris. There they learned on September 7 that President McKinley had been shot the day before while visiting the Buffalo Exposition; it was "a very serious wound," Sara noted, but the President was expected to live.

The Roosevelts sailed for home aboard the *Teutonic* four days later, and as they passed the Nantucket lightship on the nineteenth, Franklin noted, they "received news by megaphone: President McKinley died last Saturday." All New York seemed draped in black when they went ashore.

"Terrible shock to all," Franklin wrote. But there must have been excitement, too. Cousin Theodore was now President of the United States.

Not long after he got back to Harvard, Franklin wrote home asking his mother for help. He was very busy writing a thesis for History 10 on "The Roosevelts of New Amsterdam," he said, and the Cambridge libraries seemed to yield little information. Would she please therefore "copy for me all the extracts in our old Dutch Bible & send them to me. Also the old brown genealogy which you have, a pamphlet, & any

6. Laura Delano was a tiny woman—"a little old lady," one relative recalled many years later, "in a black dress up to her chin"—but still formidable and accustomed to being treated as an Astor. She and her late husband had been so fond of the magnificent lobby of the Beau Rivage that they remodeled the foyer of Steen Valetje, their huge home at Barrytown, to resemble it. Once, when the empress of Austria was coming to the hotel for a brief stay, the manager asked Mrs. Delano if she would be willing to give up her usual suite for a few days; she indignantly refused: she had paid for the rooms. The empress had to settle for more modest quarters.

From time to time, small nieces and nephews were sent to stay with her in the frank hope that they and their parents might be remembered in her will. Eighty-odd years later, one niece recalled a trip to Rome with her aged aunt. They were to take a ride together in her brougham one morning, she said, and as they took their seats, "Aunt Laura handed me a small leather bag filled with coins, which I was to throw in the *faces* of the beggars. A terrible affront, I thought." But the little girl hurled them anyway; one did not quarrel with Aunt Laura.

The old woman died in 1901, not long after Sara and Franklin had visited her, leaving behind a vast fortune.

Source: Interview with Laura Chanler White.

other records you have. . . . I must have them as soon as possible." She bundled up all that he had asked for and sent it off.

The thesis survives. "One reason," Franklin wrote, "perhaps the chief, of the virility of the Roosevelts is [their] democratic spirit. They have never felt because they were born in a good position they could put their hands in their pockets and succeed." At nineteen, Franklin was an enthusiastic Roosevelt but an amateurish historian. In fact, the "democratic spirit" of most of his ancestors was hard to discern; they had been perfectly content to keep their hands firmly in their pockets. But if he had inaccurately described his forebears, it was his fifth cousin whom he was really trying to account for. TR's latest triumph provided still more vivid evidence of what a Roosevelt might do in the greater world.

Mother and son were united in their admiration for the new President, and sometimes Sara's enthusiasm outstripped even Franklin's. When TR intervened in the bitter coal strike the following year, the Harvard government student gravely wrote home that "in spite of his success in settling the trouble, I think that the President made a serious mistake in interfering. . . . His tendency to make the executive power stronger than the Houses of Congress is bound to be a bad thing, especially when a man of weaker personality succeeds him in office." His mother would have none of it. "One cannot help loving and admiring him the more for it," she said, "when one realizes that he tried to right the wrong."

"I constantly hear your father's voice saying when he was ill 'Only tell Franklin to be good, to be a good man,' " she wrote to Franklin later in his college career. "He often repeated it and never until the other day in reading Jacob Riis' [biography of Theodore Roosevelt] did I know that Mr. Theodore [Roosevelt, Senior's] last words to *his* son were 'Be a good man.' Is that not a coincidence?" That kind of coincidence, with its clear if unstated hint of succession, must have greatly pleased her son.

His kinship with the President was occasionally an embarrassment to him. He now had to slough off a good deal of kidding about his intimacy with "the royal family," and much that he did came under special public scrutiny simply because he was a Roosevelt. When he and two friends organized a fund drive that raised $336 for the relief of the Boer women and children, who they believed were then being mistreated by the British in South Africa, for instance, he was singled out by the *Boston Globe* for special, fulsome praise: "Young Roosevelt has many of the qualities that have put his [cousin] at the front. He is a hard worker, thoroughly democratic."

Such tributes surely delighted Sara[7]—Franklin always sent the clippings home for her to see and save—but they embarrassed him, made him "excessively 'tired,' " he said, and did him no good among his classmates. Still, in the main, being Theodore Roosevelt's young cousin stood him in good stead at Harvard. He had been passed over for the *Crimson* staff when the first freshmen were picked for it in February of 1901, but he scored a journalistic coup two months later when he learned that the then Vice President was staying overnight at the Boston home of Professor A. Lawrence Lowell. Both Franklin and Teddy Robinson were enrolled in Lowell's course in constitutional government. Hoping to catch at least a glimpse of his cousin, Franklin called the professor's home, asked for the Vice President, and was put right through. TR said he'd be delighted to see Franklin and Teddy, but there was no need for them to come into Boston. The best time would be the next morning, right after Lowell's nine o'clock class, which he planned to address on his experiences as governor of New York; his lecture was being kept a secret to keep the crowds down. Franklin put down the telephone and raced to the *Crimson* with the story. It ran the next morning, and by class time some 2,000 students and curiosity seekers were milling around the doors of Sanders Theater. Lowell was furious, but the Vice President seemed not to mind, and when he spotted Franklin among the 500 spectators who had managed to squeeze inside to hear him, he interrupted his talk to smile and wave a special greeting.

Perhaps a little embarrassed at how easily he had come by the story of TR's lecture, FDR later liked to claim responsibility for a second —and far more impressive—freshman scoop. President Eliot of Har-

7. The *tributes* must have pleased her, but Franklin's affection for the Boers may not have. Mother and son had first gently clashed over their cause during Franklin's last semester at Groton. "Hurrah for the Boers!" he had written home during the siege of Ladysmith, "I entirely sympathize with them." Sara was shocked. She thought the Boers "treacherous. . . . They even disregard a flag of truce *every time!*" And again, "I feel very strongly that the Boers are not a race to do good in the world. Perhaps I am a little bit influenced by meeting on a steamer and travelling with them for three weeks, some dutch and half breeds. I was only a child of ten but I got a horror of the common dutch men with their native and half native families! Then all one reads of their life in the colonies and in South Africa shows them to be 'boors.' Still, I like you to form your own opinions and to look into things more deeply than your Mummy does."

Franklin had responded then with masterful diplomacy: "I think you misunderstand my position in regard to the Boers. I cannot help feeling convinced that the Boers have the side of right . . . and have been *forced* into this war. . . . *However,* undoubtedly now that the war is actually on, it will be best from the humanitarian standpoint for the British to win speedily and civilization will be hurried on."

vard was known to have strong reservations about Theodore Roosevelt, once having denounced him and his ally Senator Henry Cabot Lodge as "degenerated sons of Harvard" for their jingoism; and TR had privately returned the compliment, seeing in Eliot signs of the flabby sentimentalism which he believed "eats away the great fighting qualities of our race." In 1900, however, with the presidential election fast approaching, Eliot had published an article in the *Outlook* which seemed more cordial toward the McKinley-Roosevelt ticket than to William Jennings Bryan and the Democrats.

The *Crimson* editors understandably wanted to find out for whom Eliot ultimately planned to vote. Eliot thought this none of his students' business and refused even to speak to *Crimson* reporters. FDR, who later said he had not known of the president's firm policy of silence, thought the easiest way to discover Eliot's intentions was simply to ask him. He strolled over to the president's residence one evening and knocked. Eliot asked him who he was. FDR identified himself, then blurted out his question: "I came to ask you, Mr. President, whether you are going to vote for McKinley or Bryan?"

Eliot was enraged. "Wh-a-a-t?" he shouted.

Then, FDR recalled, "I realized just what the situation was, and wished the floor might open and let me through to any kind of darkness that would hide me. Still, I had come for news, and I stood there while Dr. Eliot looked me through and through."

" 'What do you want to know for?' he asked finally.

" 'I want to get it for the *Crimson*,' I said."

Eliot finally barked that he planned to vote Republican.

The story appeared in the *Crimson* the next morning, and was picked up all over the country.

FDR told of his brash visit to Eliot's home in vivid detail in an interview with a reporter for the *New York Telegraph* in 1913. It was a good tale, except for the fact that FDR had had absolutely nothing to do with obtaining Eliot's preference for the paper. The intrepid freshman reporter had actually been Albert W. De Roode, who was at the time of FDR's interview with the *Telegraph* a junior law partner in FDR's firm.[8]

Franklin's authentic coup may have owed more to connections and serendipity than to enterprise, and the published story ran just eight

8. In 1932, FDR admitted this, claiming at the same time that he had no idea how the story that he and not De Roode had been responsible ever got started.

Source: Freidel, *The Apprenticeship*, pages 55–56.

lines, but it helped get him elected one of the five new *Crimson* editors picked at the end of the year. Now he hoped that success and the family connection upon which it was partially based would help him achieve what he wanted above all else, an invitation to join Porcellian, the most exclusive of all the exclusive social clubs that epitomized social success at Harvard, the club of which his father had been made an honorary member in 1853 and to which his Cousin Theodore was still proud to belong.[9] As a "Legacy"—a close relative of former members—he knew he would receive especially careful consideration.

The long, convoluted process by which Porcellian members were chosen began in the autumn of the sophomore year, when the oldest and largest of all the clubs, the Institute of 1770, chose 100 men to become members—about one fifth of the class. Institute members were named in groups of ten, the candidates thought most desirable being grouped in the first lot, those thought socially marginal in the last. A certain number of these Institute men were then asked to join a more shadowy fraternity, Delta Kappa Epsilon, known as the "Dickey." From this still more select group, in turn, came the members of the best clubs.

Lathrop Brown was chosen for the Institute before his roommate was. Franklin went home for Christmas in an agony of suspense. Fifty men had been picked and he was still not among them. The holidays seemed endless, alleviated only by his mother's Christmas gift—a handsome new ice yacht, *Hawk*—and by an invitation to attend the ultimate social event of the season, Alice Roosevelt's debut at the White House. He spent three crowded days in the capital, attending formal dinners, a reception at the Austrian embassy, the dance itself, held in the East Room and "most glorious fun," according to Franklin. "The Washington people weren't in it with the New Yorkers & from start to finish it was glorious." There was also tea with Cousin Theodore, lunch at Cousin Bamie's home on N Street (so often visited by her brother that it had become known as the "Little White House"), a second private talk with the President—altogether "something always to be remembered."

Back at college in early January, he found that he had finally been picked for the Institute—"the 1st man on the 6th ten." There then

9. In 1905, when President Theodore Roosevelt wrote to Kaiser Wilhelm II, telling him of his daughter Alice's engagement to Nicholas Longworth, a Republican congressman from Ohio, he could think of no higher praise than to point out that his prospective son-in-law also belonged to Porcellian.

began a week of arduous, sometimes humiliating initiation rites known as "running for Dickey." These held no terrors for Franklin; though he was "about to be slaughtered," he told Sara, he was "quite happy." Everything seemed finally to be going well, and at the end of the week, a full-fledged member of the Dickey, he pronounced himself "nearly used up. Wonderful." The invitation from the Porcellian seemed only weeks away.

The system by which new members were chosen was brutally simple. The membership—sixteen juniors and seniors—sat at a table in their clubhouse, each holding one white and one black ball. The name of each prospective candidate was read out, and after what one member recalls as "much discussion," a formal vote was taken, each man depositing one ball in the wooden ballot box that was passed among them. A single black ball was all that was needed to exclude a candidate, the idea being that every current member must be enthusiastic about every new one: no one considered merely "all right," was ever to be allowed in. Eight sophomores were unanimously endorsed.

Franklin Roosevelt was rejected. No one now knows what tipped the scales against him. It may have been the scandal surrounding Taddy. Perhaps some members had been put off by the same chatty overconfidence that had alienated many of his classmates at Groton. Eleanor Roosevelt once suggested that the Porcellian men had found Franklin too bookish. But whatever went wrong, the secrecy with which the vote was conducted made the rejection all the more difficult to bear: even those who voted did not necessarily know which of their fellow-members had placed a black ball in the box. Franklin felt that the five members who had been his schoolmates at Groton had somehow failed to back him as they should have, that newer acquaintances whose friendly allegiance he had worked hard to win might have proved false. But he could not be sure who they were, could not contest the snub or explain it, even to himself. He knew only that just as at Groton he had unaccountably been barred from the exalted position that his childhood training had taught him should be his without effort. And, still more searing, he had to live with the knowledge that he had been found wanting by the same club that had so eagerly welcomed the two men he had been taught most to revere: Theodore Roosevelt and his own father.

The wound never healed. Fifteen years later, returning from Europe as assistant secretary of the Navy aboard a U.S. battleship and in the entourage of the President of the United States, he told a relative that his failure to make Porcellian had been "the greatest disappointment of my life." (By then his failure had been made still more humiliating: two of Theodore Roosevelt's own sons, Theodore, Jr. and Kermit, had been admitted to the club.) Eleanor Roosevelt would later go so far as to say that the Porcellian rebuff had given her husband "an inferiority complex," but she also believed that like his similar defeats at Groton, it had helped him to identify with life's outcasts.

Again, if it did, that identification came later. To be sure, there continued to be a sober, charitable side to him, more than a hint of substance beneath the glossy gregarious exterior. He still found time at Harvard to serve the Groton Missionary Society, teaching occasional classes and overseeing games at the St. Andrew's Boys Club in Boston, and he joined the Harvard Social Service Society. He was genuine in his wish to do his part to aid the unfortunate, just as his father and mother had always insisted that he should. But his contacts with the poor remained tentative, superficial, and on at least one occasion, frightening.

Running late for a train to New York, where he planned to spend a social weekend, he boarded a streetcar for South Station carrying a heavy suitcase. The streetcar stalled with a broken wheel. With just four minutes to spare, he jumped down and sprinted for the station, still several blocks away. A small Italian boy darted out of a side street in front of him. Both crashed to the ground, the child gasping for air; Franklin's suitcase had knocked the wind out of him. Franklin helped him up, but the frightened boy punched at him. An angry woman stuck her head out of a tenement window and shouted at Franklin in Italian; she was the child's mother. Afraid he would miss his train and unable to calm the boy or even to make his apologies understood, he unfolded a new dollar bill and waved it in front of him. The child struck it from his hand and, his breath now partially returned, cursed him for a rich bully. More heads appeared in the windows along the street. A crowd began to gather, muttering and gesticulating. No one seemed to speak English. Franklin let the crumpled dollar lie in the gutter, picked up his suitcase, and tried calmly to walk away. The crowd followed. He broke into a run. So did they. He ran faster, the suitcase growing heavier with every stride. He considered throwing it away, he remembered many years later, "But I had my dress clothes in it and they seemed at the time too much of a sacrifice to any mob." His train was pulling out when he finally reached it, clambered aboard, and collapsed in the last seat of the last car, his pursuers still shouting and shaking their fists from the platform. It took him several minutes to get enough breath to tell the conductor where he was going.[10]

Franklin kept his bitterness over Porcellian largely to himself. His natural resilience—that ability to seem always "bright and happy" that had characterized him since his Grandfather Delano first described it in infancy—sustained him and helped disguise his unpleasant feelings. Even Lathrop Brown failed to gauge the depth of his resentment. "Franklin was not a typical Club man of his generation," he once wrote. "He had more on his mind than sitting in the Club's front window, doing nothing and criticizing the passers-by. Thus, his not 'making' the Porcellian meant only that he was free of any possible restraining influences of a lot of delightful people who thought that the world belonged to them and who did not want to change anything in it." In any case, Brown concluded, "there was room at Harvard for other clubs besides Porcellian."

There was, and Franklin was invited to join several of them. His membership in the Institute of 1770 made him an automatic member of the Hasty Pudding, and he played minor parts in its annual theatricals. He was also elected to Alpha Delta Phi (known as the "Fly"), the Signet Literary Society and the Memorial Society, devoted to the history of the university; he was on the "first ten" for this club, he assured his mother, and "it is a good thing to make." He served both the Hasty Pudding and the Fly as librarian, buying books for them while beginning a collection of his own at the same time. The same energy that he had once devoted to stalking birds was now focused on discovering treasures in secondhand bookstores. "I went to Bartlett's to see about some Club books," he once happily confessed to Sara, "with the sad result that I invested in a few volumes for myself. They are to be sent home and you can open them. The Smollett is a very nice old edition, as are the Junius letters and Dryden's Virgil." As usual, his mother encouraged him in his enthusiasm. "Your *Morte D'Arthur* came," she told him. "I spent all last evening [poring] over it and opened it gingerly, handled it with care and realized that I was the . . . caretaker of a treasure. The burglar alarm is fortunately in

10. Telling this story to Earle Looker, an early and adulatory biographer, FDR claimed to have learned an important lesson from the experience: "I had bumped into a human situation and I had failed to play my part in it. I remember I said to myself: 'The whole trouble was that I didn't solve the problem. I tried to dodge it by creating a diversion. That doesn't work. I'll never try that again!" This homily, Looker concluded, was "the beginning of wisdom"—though of course FDR was all his life a master of the creative uses of diversion.

Source: Looker, pages 35–38.

perfect order, so if anyone comes to purloin the two volumes, Tip and I shall go for him."[11]

Despite all this cheery bustle, the memory of the Porcellian debacle continued secretly to fester, and there were those among FDR's political enemies who would later charge that a desire for personal vengeance upon the wealthy and exclusive young men who had rejected him at Harvard lay behind many of the New Deal measures that made them denounce him as a traitor to his class. This is a simplistic and remarkably complacent explanation, of course,[12] but the rejection must surely have reinforced Franklin's growing fascination with politics and power. First at Groton, now at Harvard, he had learned firsthand that admission to what his future wife called "the inner clique" was not automatically conferred, even upon a Roosevelt. He became "extremely ambitious," Tom Beal recalled, wanting above all else to become "popular and powerful." He would never again exclusively rely on position and congeniality to get ahead, would no longer depend upon others to notice him; instead, he would do his energetic best to carve out a constituency of his own.

11. Franklin did not tell his mother of his long, fruitless search for a copy of a rare volume he knew his classmates were especially eager to have, Mark Twain's bawdy *1601; or Conversation as It Was by the Social Fireside in the Time of the Tudors.*

12. For the record, all but three of the sixteen Porcellian men who turned Franklin down became bankers, brokers, corporation lawyers or manufacturers; of the eight admitted to the club from his class, all became bankers or brokers.

FDR himself was fond of tracing the motivations of his political opponents back to youthful confrontations. He once told Walter Trohan of the *Chicago Tribune,* for example, that the reason Trohan's employer, Colonel Robert R. McCormick, so disliked him was that when both were students at Groton he had stolen McCormick's girl at a dance. (McCormick labeled this "another of Franklin's shallow lies.") And in 1942 FDR claimed that Arthur A. Ballantine had "hated me ever since" he defeated Ballantine for the presidency of the *Crimson* forty years before. Ballantine became an eminent Republican attorney and served as undersecretary of the Treasury under Herbert Hoover and (briefly) under FDR. His own short reminiscences of Roosevelt at Harvard are rueful rather than openly hostile. "As I watched [FDR's] extraordinary career," he wrote, "there were times when I wished that Franklin Roosevelt had managed to spend more time in college on some of our excellent instruction in economics and government."

And the President never tired of jokes about the fury his actions stirred among conservative clubmen. A favorite concerned four millionaires, sitting in the Rittenhouse Club in Philadelphia and listening to a radio address in which FDR asked, "I wonder what is being said by my rich friends in their overstuffed armchairs in their well-stocked clubs." "All four men recoiled," Roosevelt said, "and one of them, finding his voice, exclaimed, 'My God, do you suppose that blankety blank could have overheard us?' "

Finally, it should be noted that FDR himself once categorically denied his ever having been disappointed over Porcellian. While himself a student at Harvard, his son James once asked his father why, if he had himself been so upset at failing to make the club, he urged his sons to join the Fly. Didn't that imply that the Fly was only second-best? The whole Porcellian story was "a damned canard," FDR answered—though his son is not sure now whether this might not have been a "rationalization."

Sources: Walter Trohan, *Political Animals,* page 9; Hassett, pages 119–120; Alfred B. Rollins, Jr., *Franklin D. Roosevelt and the Age of Action,* page 192; interview with James Roosevelt.

The *Crimson* would provide the vehicle. It was at the center of things, serving as a sort of unofficial bulletin board for the university. Students and faculty alike read it faithfully over breakfast, and even professional newspapermen stationed in Boston scanned its columns in search of items of interest to the wider world. To be its editor was to control the flow of all that information; to compose its daily editorials was to serve as spokesman for the entire Harvard community.

Nothing during his Harvard years meant as much to him as the newspaper and his role in it.[13] As a sophomore he was already spending six hours a day at its grimy, ink-spattered headquarters on Massachusetts Avenue and he was rewarded that spring with election as secretary. A comic poster printed to announce the election of new *Crimson* officers listed him as "Frank, the Fairest of the Roosevelts." The following autumn he was made one of two assistant managing editors, in charge of the paper two nights a week, and in January 1903 he beat out his rival to become managing editor. Election as "president" (editor-in-chief) the next year was virtually automatic. He could have been graduated at the end of 1903; instead he enrolled in graduate school, ostensibly in order to win a master of arts in history and economics, actually so that he might continue as editor-in-chief of the *Crimson.*

His colleagues' memories of him at the newspaper were mixed. He was "a very good companion . . . with a ready laugh and a keen sense of humor," one remembered, but not outstanding—"many of the other men on the board . . . showed greater ability." W. Russell Bowie, his managing editor (and successor as president), recalled that he "liked people . . . and made them instinctively like him. Moreover, in his geniality there was a kind of frictionless command."

This was especially evident in his relation with the printers, two paid Scottish professionals named Mac and Ed who were often impatient with the students' amateurism and missed deadlines, but who responded to Franklin's occasional requests to remake the forms to make room for a late-breaking story "with alacrity and complete approbation." Such familiar ease with the paper's employees was never confused with equality; the same feeling had characterized Mr. James's relations with the men and women who worked for him; his concern for their welfare and sympathy with their problems was warm and genuine but always distanced.

13. In later years, FDR enjoyed telling the reporters assigned to cover him that he understood their problems because he, too, had been a newspaperman.

Certainly neither Franklin's classmates nor the members of his staff were ever confused. "I think it is doubtful whether you would consider his association with others in college as democratic and widespread," Tom Beal gently recalled. Walter E. Sachs, a *Crimson* editor was more direct: "He was rather a snob. . . . As far as I know, he was not then interested in the working man—that came later. . . . He did not have the 'common touch' at all in those days—seemed ill at ease with people outside of his group."

Franklin's quarrel with the club system was purely personal—he had simply been denied his rightful place in its midst—and he was too closely allied with the young men of the Gold Coast to wish to challenge their authority. The Harvard Union was opened in 1901, an enormous, splendidly appointed complex of paneled offices and game rooms, a library and dining hall, which was intended to serve as an inclusive, all-campus club, a place where Gold Coast clubmen and their less exalted classmates from the Yard might find common ground. Franklin attended the opening ceremonies, which he found "most impressive," and he was later appointed the Union librarian, but he spent little time there, and when plans were announced to move the *Crimson* offices to a new suite of rooms in its basement, he was against it. The move would damage the exclusive "esprit de corps" that had developed in the grimy old quarters, he said, and he feared that the traditional punch nights might be barred from university property. This last was especially important to him since he had taken it upon himself to mix and serve the sticky-sweet punch for these convivial evenings, thereby overseeing both the flow of drinks and the conversation that went with it.[14]

A junior member of the staff suggested to him that the newspaper abandon its traditional practice of publishing lists of the men who had made the clubs in the precise order of their election, on the grounds that such publication was inherently undemocratic. The lists conferred aristocratic status on certain students, he pointed out, dictating even the seating arrangements in Boston dining rooms, and they further humiliated those who had failed to measure up. Though Franklin

14. He continued this practice into the White House. Each evening before dinner, during what he liked to call "the children's hour," FDR would invite a few associates to join him for cocktails, which he ceremoniously mixed himself while telling stories. "He seemed to experiment on each occasion with a different percentage of vermouth, gin and fruit juice," the speech writer Samuel Rosenman remembered, and the results were often sweet and slapdash like the *Crimson* punch, and sometimes distinctly alarming—gin and grenadine, for example. Few guests complained.

Source: Working with Roosevelt, page 150.

himself had been one of these, he refused to consider stopping the practice; publication of the lists was discontinued the year after he left Cambridge.

His editorials were entirely conventional. He echoed Endicott Peabody's humorless fervor over football, time and again exhorting the teams to play harder, and urging those on the sidelines to ever-greater enthusiasm. At one game against Brown, Franklin himself led the cheers, though he "felt like a D. . . . F. . . . ," he told his mother, "waiving my arms & legs before several thousand amused spectators! It is a dirty job," he continued without irony, "one gets chiefly ridicule —but some poor devil has to suffer & one can't refuse." (His mother answered that while she was glad "you sacrificed yourself and did it," she wished him to remember in the future that "in cheering you were *waving* your arms, not '*waiving.*' ")

Franklin was especially hard on the freshman team, whose loss to Andover, 51–0, he called "a wretched showing" for which "the whole Freshman Class" was to blame. But it was his excoriation of the varsity team itself—now managed by Lathrop Brown—that got him briefly into trouble. In November, Harvard had to come from behind to beat the fast but far lighter Carlisle Indians, 12–11. The team might consider itself satisfied with such narrow victories, Franklin wrote, but "the undergraduates watching the game were not so well satisfied as the eleven. They have grown somewhat weary of the slow, listless play of certain men in the line, who seem to think that their weight is a sufficient certificate of admission to membership on a university team. They are weary of a spirit that will not awake till the team is in a desperate crisis, and goes to sleep again when the crisis is fancied to be past. They are weary and angry—why?—because they know there is no reason why the team should not be powerful, aggressive, and withal, successful, if it wills to be. . . . How long must the University wait?"

Franklin's tone evidently annoyed a good many of his readers, although he assured his mother "at least half the college think it was quite called for. *Something* of the kind was indeed necessary." Henry James II, then a third-year law student, wrote in to protest Franklin's "editorial sarcasms," which bordered on personal attacks; if people were so grim about amateur athletics, James said, "the fun of the game will be spoilt for all."

Franklin was not openly repentant. "I am glad to say the effect has been just what was wanted," he told Sara, "it has stirred up the team by making them angry and they are playing all the harder for it." But a few weeks later he did make a point of paying tribute to those students about to be awarded academic prizes. A great university, he said, should strive to be "all things to all men," to reward "mental training" as well as athletic prowess or social distinction, and "of late years, the prominence of the unacademic side has perhaps been unduly emphasized."

He did confront the university administration on two fronts: the need for wider boardwalks to cross the Yard—the narrow planks then laid across the mud, he said, were "licensed highways to the Stillman Infirmary"—and for better protection against fire in Harvard dormitories. All that stood between the university and a major disaster, Franklin wrote, were "flimsy wooden staircases" and a single knotted rope for each suite "of such character that more than one person would find great difficulty in reaching the ground without a broken neck." Two weeks later, 602 people were burned alive or crushed to death in the Iroquois Theater fire in Chicago, and one *Crimson* reader, writing in to support the editor's call for greater safety, compared the Harvard corporation's apparent obliviousness to danger to the laxness of the Chicago authorities who had permitted locked exits and overcrowding to compound that tragedy. Franklin—who had himself so recently been accused of being too personal in print—swiftly disassociated himself from this letter: "In its sarcasm," he noted loftily, "the communication . . . seems to us in rather bad taste." Nonetheless, he continued to urge change, and in the spring new safeguards were finally installed.

His *Crimson* editorials also reveal his continuing impatience with academic abstraction, his growing interest in practicality and power. Even his courses in history and economics had come to seem irrelevant. The picture of America they presented was removed, bloodless, misleading—a perennially tidy place where checks always offset balances, and the precise intentions of the founders of the republic could clearly be discerned. Franklin already knew that the real world was infinitely more harsh, intricate, and challenging than that. Even at Groton and Harvard his defeats had shown him that things were rarely as simple and straightforward as they seemed, as his mother had said they were.

In order to succeed in later life, he knew he needed "actual experience." He had joined the Harvard Political Club, which invited outside lecturers to speak on political issues, but even that was not enough. He also wanted a "practical idea of the workings of the political system—

of the machinery of primary, caucus, convention, election and legislature," and "with such a large city as Boston close at hand," he said, he saw no good reason why he could not get it: "It would be easy to send out parties, under the guidance of some experienced man, which in one day could learn more than through the means of lectures." No such safaris into Boston's political wilderness were mounted from Cambridge in Franklin's time.

He had to content himself with the political lessons that might be learned on the campus itself. In December of 1903, he ran against five opponents for class marshal. The contest had been rigged in advance; only the three top men would win, and the clubs had quietly agreed on their own slate. Franklin was not on it. He used his newspaper to try to alter the odds. "There is a higher duty than to vote for one's personal friends," he wrote the day before the vote was to be taken, "and that is to secure for the whole class, leaders who really deserve the positions." But he knew he would lose—"I don't stand the least show" of winning, he told his mother that same day—and he was right. He came in fourth.

But he persisted, campaigning hard for still another office a few days later, chairman of the 1904 class committee. This time he won easily, capturing 168 out of 253 votes cast. This was the first electoral victory of his life.

As always, Sara rejoiced in Franklin's triumphs, large and small, faithfully recording each new club he had joined at Harvard, listing each victory of his rowing crew, saving every complimentary clipping. But she was never startled by them. "His father and I always expected a great deal of Franklin," she once said. "We thought he ought to take prizes, and we were pleased but not surprised when he did. After all, he had many advantages that other boys did not have."

His failures were not noted. Like her father, she did her best always to overlook unpleasantness, to act as if nothing untoward had happened. It was a trait which would reappear in her son as well. "If something was unpleasant," Eleanor Roosevelt once said, "and he didn't want to know about it he just ignored it. . . . I think he always thought that if you ignored a thing long enough, it would settle itself." As a result, a certain selective candor always characterized relations between mother and son.

Sara's life at Springwood was slow, uneventful, lonely. She remained relatively young and vigorous, but was expected always to appear elderly and sedate. When a widowed friend came to stay with her, she did not even dare walk home from St. James but had to "do the 'old lady act,' " she told Franklin, and ride, limiting herself to "a dignified stroll" on the estate later in the day. She did her best to keep occupied, overseeing the daily work of the farm, sponsoring a cooking class for local girls, visiting the Gaulladet Home for aged and infirm deaf-mutes, where conversation was necessarily limited to hastily penciled notes. An inmate once greeted her with one that read "I notice you have grown fat," to her great amusement. But her truncated life was truly whole again only when she could share it with her son.

Franklin worked hard to keep her informed about his busy college life, but she always wanted to hear more. "Remember," she ended one letter, "it takes only 10 or 15 minutes to write a nice letter to your ever-loving Mother." He visited her often at Springwood, Fairhaven, and New York, and he did what he could from a distance to shoulder as many of her everyday burdens as she would permit, hiring a new captain for the *Half Moon II* and offering counsel when she had trouble with the servants.

Winter at Springwood had always been the most dispiriting season: a raw wind blew in off the Hudson; snow blanketed the lawns and sometimes cut the house off from the road; most of the Roosevelts' wealthy neighbors moved elsewhere until spring. Sara now found it "intolerable," and she resolved in the winter of 1902 to move to Boston and be close to Franklin. This was not a new idea, though widowhood made it seem more urgent. She and Mr. James had always planned to winter in Boston while Franklin was at Harvard, and their next-door Campobello neighbors, the Hartman Kuhns, had once offered to let them occupy their handsome house at 36 Commonwealth Avenue, since they themselves planned to spend the cold weather elsewhere. Now Mrs. Kuhn renewed the invitation, and Sara accepted, moving there in late March. Dora Forbes, then still a widow, came with her. (Mrs Kuhn's son, Hamilton, died suddenly not long after the Delano sisters arrived, and they quickly moved to an apartment at 333 Commonwealth Avenue so that their grieving friend could return to her own home.)

She stayed two months, enjoying the city where many old friends and family members lived and still more came to see her, attending concerts and lectures, visiting museums and galleries. But it was the proximity to Franklin she enjoyed the most. She once explained that it had been her aim simply "to be on hand" in Boston "should he want me," never to "interfere with his college life," and she no doubt meant it. But strain was inevitable. First at Groton, then at Harvard, Franklin had been able to maintain at least a measure of independence from her. His amiable torrent of letters assuring her he was doing well helped blunt her constant anxieties about him. Distance allowed him to take her ceaseless exhortations to dress warmly, down his castor oil, pay his bills on time, and be courteous to everyone with patient grace. He was too loving and dutiful actively to oppose her coming; he knew he was all she had.

At first he seemed delighted that she would be close by. "I am so anxious for you to get the Kuhn's house," he had written her when her plans were being shaped. "You must arrange it." But as the time of her arrival approached, he removed himself from the decision a little: "I am sorry I can't see to anything about the house, but I shall be otherwise engaged." Once she and Dora were in place, however, he came frequently to tea or to dine and sometimes to spend the night. She gave lunches and teas for his friends. Franklin became her frequent escort, taking her sleighing or to the theater or for long rides in the runabout he kept off campus.

We cannot know all that passed between them. Franklin's rejection by Porcellian took place while Sara was in Boston, which can only have made that unexpected setback still more humiliating. Then, too, Sara was accustomed to obedience. Conflicts between her schedule and his caused tensions that could have no satisfactory resolution. If he interrupted his frenetic routine to attend to his mother, he could not avoid resenting it, however unbothered he may have tried to seem. If he left her on her own too long, her injured air of resignation must have made him feel guilty.

Sara's first Boston winter lasted barely two months. The following year she returned for three, renting a second, more spacious flat at 184 Marlborough Street and hoping for the same kind of comforting closeness with her son. For his twenty-first birthday she gave him a portrait of herself by Prince Pierre Troubetzkoy. Franklin was "*much* surprised and is delighted," she said. "She was an indulgent mother," a family friend once wrote, "but would not let her son call his soul his own." Her emotional discretion was matched only by Franklin's, but even in her decorous journal for that winter there are scattered hints that her busy son, now secretary of the *Crimson,* chafed under such close and constant maternal attention. In February, she gave a dinner for visiting relatives to which her son did not come. "Franklin cannot leave the *Crimson,*" she noted. And the next month, when Sara and Franklin's godmother Nelly Blodgett together visited Mrs. Jack Gardner and were given a tour of her palace, Fenway Court—"no description gives an idea of its beauty," Sara said—he did not accompany them, nor did he attend a dinner for some of her friends that evening. "I was *very* sorry Franklin did not dine at home," she wrote.

Sometime toward the end of her Boston stay, Franklin tentatively broached the idea of his taking a month's trip abroad during the coming summer with his friend and classmate Charles B. Bradley. This would be his first vacation apart from his mother, and she was clearly not pleased. He gently persisted, however, and their discussions continued after she returned to Hyde Park in mid-April.

"I really want you to tell me what you would want me to do," he wrote to her. "I have told you what I feel about it: that it would in all probability be good for me, and a delightful experience; but that I don't want to be away from you for four weeks in the summer; also that I don't want to go unless you could make up your mind not to care at all. I feel that it would be a very thoroughly selfish proceeding on my part."

"I am perfectly willing for you to go," she finally told him, "as it is only for a month and with a nice fellow. I do not think I should feel the same if it were for longer, or if it were with several fellows. Of course, dearest Franklin, I shall miss you but I am not silly and I have no intention of 'tying you to my apron strings.' . . . You are a dear boy to insist on leaving it entirely to me."

But even as she professed at least limited enthusiasm for his independence, she was unable to resist undercutting it. His desire to go abroad without her, she told him, reminded her of the time long before when he had begged for "freedom" at Springwood and had been granted a day of it. That had been harmless enough; so would this be. He had then been eight; he was now twenty-one. Nonetheless, she was still in charge. She had no doubt that he would be "perfectly happy and good" while overseas, just as he had been when a small boy. "I trust you will have a splendid time and be glad to get home as I know you will."

But when the time came for him to sail, she found the parting unexpectedly hard. She saw him safely aboard the White Star liner *Celtic;* then, as the warning whistle blew, signaling all guests to go ashore, she burst into tears. "I *meant* to be very brave," she admitted to him later, "but after all I played baby at the last. . . . It is . . . the thought of the ocean between me and my *all* that rather appalls me." She left the ship nonetheless, and boarded the Fall River Line steamer *Priscilla* for Fairhaven, her first stop on the way to Campobello. There she "watched till the *Celtic* came along and passed in front of me and saw so well that if I only had a strong glass I could have distinguished you, if you were on deck, I wondered if you were looking at me! I watched your great steamer going further and further from me with such a sinking of my heart . . ."

Franklin, too, had been upset. He scrawled his mother a note immediately, in time for the pilot to take it with him when he was dropped at Sandy Hook. He had in fact stood out on the deck and watched the *Priscilla* as it moved along behind the *Celtic.* "I saw a figure in front of the pilot house that I fancied was you as it waved," he said. Both Sara and her sister Kassie had given the young travelers baskets of fruits for the voyage. Aunt Kassie's was delicious, Franklin told his mother, and he and Charley would enjoy it all the way across the ocean; but "*your* basket I am going to eat *all alone* & give none of it to C.B.B.!" She was not to worry about him. "I always land on my feet—but wish so much you were with me."

He was more than dutiful while abroad, sending home a detailed day-by-day journal of the crossing as soon as he landed in England, followed by a series of breathless accounts of nearly everything he did ashore. But his delight in freedom was impossible to mask.

The ocean voyage was blissful—"delightful bath—enormous breakfast—usual routine of gourmandising . . . exciting games of shuffleboard, quoits & push golf." And lest his mother think he was being too frivolous, he said he had also "accomplished a good deal on this trip," having read a lot, worked over his plans for *Crimson* editorials for the coming year, and held "interesting talks with Arthur Gordon [a new shipboard acquaintance from Savannah, Georgia] on negro, political, educational & other topics."

Charley Bradley had fallen ill with what the ship's doctor diagnosed as malaria aboard the *Celtic,* and he was urged to go to Scotland for a week to recuperate. Franklin was truly on his own in London at first. He was not even momentarily concerned. He got himself a nice room, took a nap, then "had a bath & dined at Claridge's. Most excellent meal—with a pint of burgundy and a good 'segar.' " He ordered clothes on Savile Row: "1 dress suit, 1 dinner-coat suit, 1 winter suit, two summer suits & 1 frock coat & trousers" at one shop; riding breeches at another; riding boots and "patent leather button shoes" at a third. He called upon old family friends. Charley returned looking fit from Scotland. Two other Harvard friends materialized, Ned Bell and George Williamson, and "we had a most heavenly 21st birthday of Ned's at the Cafe Royal—just the four of us—[with] goldfish on the table—music, etc.—all in a perfect little private dining room."

And he spent nearly a week at Easton Hall near Grantham in Lincolnshire, the seat of his parents' old friend Sir Hugh Arthur Henry, Lord Cholmeley. There he savored the sort of country life his father and Rosy had worked so hard to recreate at Hyde Park. It was "a Dream of Nirvana," he told his mother, "almost too good to be true," and "as the situation [of the house] much resembles ours, I am taking notes and measurements of everything." He played billiards with Sir Hugh and sipped port "of about A.D. 1800 that made me almost weep for joy," and he played tennis and bridge with his host's three daughters, all of whom were roughly his age and had been his playmates during a much earlier visit to the manor. He reported to his mother how they had changed: "May is rather *better* but it is not saying a great deal, though she is very nice. Winnie is I think the nicest & quite stately & Aline is really quite pretty & less large than the others."

Aline took him fishing for trout on a private stream that wound through the grounds and landed four fish for him: "It seemed quite wonderful to be getting excellent sport within a couple of hundred feet of the house—and what a house!" She and her father also drove with him to Belvoir Castle, the still more grandiose home of the Dukes of Rutland, and after touring the "entire 'seeable' part of the house" he "met the Old Duke on horseback in a high hat, accompanied by his chaplain. The Duke is 87 or so & very old in looks—but it is wonderful that he can ride—just as my Great Grandfather R. did."

And with Aline and Sir Hugh again he attended a garden party at a third country house, where he reported a considerable social triumph. "As I knew the uncivilized English custom of never introducing people I had about three fits when I arrived and got separated from Aline & her Father—but I walked up to the best looking dame in the bunch & said 'Howdy?' Things at once went like oil & I was soon having flirtations with three of the Nobility at the same time. I had a walk with the hostess' niece over the entire house which was really perfect in every way—I mean the house—although the walk wasn't bad—I will have to wait to tell you about it in person—again I mean the house. Then I inspected the garden with another 'chawmer' & ended up by jollying the hostess herself all by her lonesome for ten minutes while a uniformed Lord stood by and never got in anything except an occasional 'aw' or an 'I sy.' "

This wisecracking teasing tone, with its apparently carefree talk of "flirtations," was characteristic of the way Franklin reported to his mother on all his friendships with young women. Everything was casual, all in fun, an amusing game—and one at which he claimed to be an inept player. In later years, the only story she remembered his having told her about his skills as a suitor was that he had once taken a girl for a ride on a dog cart and lost control of the horse; the girl had fainted twice from fright before he could get it to stop.

She was not to worry. He was still devoted only to her, and his evidently encyclopedic chronicle of all that he was doing was meant to assure her that he harbored no secrets that might threaten the single-mindedness of that devotion. But in fact, he was telling her only what he knew she wanted to hear.

He kept a sporadic Line-A-Day diary during his college years, never detailed and with long blank stretches between clumps of faithful entries. It is an imperfect record, but includes the only hint we have of the parts of his life he determinedly kept from Sara. In it, for example, he recorded having gone fishing a second time with Aline Cholmeley at Easton Hall, further downstream this time and perhaps out of sight of the house. "Not much luck," he noted in his diary, "for did not attend strictly to fishing." The next morning he left for London to rejoin Charley Bradley and move on to the Continent, but not before having a long morning "walk with Aline." Neither the reason for failing to catch more trout nor the next day's farewell stroll was reported to Campobello.

This pattern of concealing his genuine feelings while seeming faithfully to be revealing all had already been firmly established at Groton. The first letter in which he even hinted at an interest in the opposite sex was written home from there at age sixteen on December 4, 1898. It set the tone for all that followed:

"I have not yet had an answer from Laura [Delano, a cousin] about the Orange dance, but I suppose she can do it. I wish you would think up some decent partner for me for the N.Y. dance, to which I suppose I will be invited, so that I can get somebody early, and not get palmed off on some ice-cart like the Hoyt girl!! Who do you think it would be nice to have at Hyde Park with the crowd? You had better send me a list."

Sara complied two days later: "About the dancing class, I send a short list of girls either one of whom you may be pleased to dance with, and you ought to write at once—

Mary Newbold
May Soley
Muriel [Delano Robbins]
Helen [Roosevelt]

As you know very few girls you ought to make haste."

Of the girls his mother thought suitable, two were cousins; Helen Roosevelt was his half niece; Mary Newbold was his next-door neighbor and childhood playmate.

It was true, of course, that Franklin knew "very few girls" at sixteen; he had not even known many boys until he entered Groton. But throughout his final two years at school his mother showed little inclination to widen his circle of acquaintances. She accepted or rejected all invitations on his behalf, drew up the guest lists for his infrequent house parties. He left everything to her: "Don't you think we had better ask up one or two girls on the 2nd? . . . I don't know any so trust you entirely"; "Please let me know if I am to accept the Soley invite"; "More shindies to attend to! The enclosed [invitation] came last night and what is to be done about it? . . . I wish you could either decline or accept it as you think best." And he referred in especially dismissive terms to those few girls whose names his mother had not provided; they were all "ice-carts" or "pills" or "elephantine." From the first, he seems to have known that any sign of romantic interest on his part would be seen by Sara as a betrayal of their exclusive devotion to one another.

Franklin's air of weary indifference as to which girls he danced or dined with and his willingness to have his mother make all the arrangements may have been unfeigned at first. Like his physical and social development, his sexual growth was probably slower than that of most boys. That fact may have formed part of the difficulty he encountered among his peers at Groton. Since he could not at first genuinely share in their adolescent obsession with the girls they glimpsed only during their brief holidays from boarding school, he was forced to simulate it, thereby perhaps adding further to his reputation for "insincerity."

He did not remain indifferent for long, however, as his Harvard diary makes clear, although the tone of his letters home remained the same. In June of 1901, after his six months of deep mourning had ended, Sara invited Franklin to bring two classmates home for a quiet country weekend. Franklin asked whether she might possibly also ask three girls to come as well: Alice Draper, perhaps—she was a sister of a Groton classmate and the daughter of Sara's friend Mrs. William Draper, whose father had founded the *New York Sun*—and Cousin Muriel Robbins and a third girl of his mother's choosing. She was not sure she thought even this was wise, Sara answered. Alice was still in mourning for a relative, and in any case "you will have a very good time, girls or no girls . . . Edmund [Rogers] has boys alone and prefers it and I daresay you boys will also." Franklin was then nineteen.

As late as October of the following year, he was still writing home to ask, "What do you think of my taking M.D.R. [Muriel Delano Robbins], Helen [Roosevelt] & Mary Newbold to see the Harvard-West Point game at West Point Saturday afternoon? . . . If you approve make arrangements as to trains."

The list of girls who bore Sara's imprimatur grew a little longer with the years—longer but no broader—until it also included Frances Pell, Jean Reid (the daughter of Mr. James's old friend Whitelaw Reid, editor of the *New York Tribune*), and two more cousins—Alice Roosevelt, the President's daughter, and Eleanor Roosevelt, the daughter of Franklin's late godfather, Elliott Roosevelt, a tall shy girl for whom Sara felt rather sorry.

Over the years, several members of the Oyster Bay branch of the Roosevelt family were asked what sort of suitor Franklin had been in his Harvard days. Corinne Robinson Alsop, Cousin Theodore's niece, recalled that she and her friends had privately called him "the feather duster" and "the handkerchief box young man" because he so resembled the slender, prettified swains that then adorned presentation boxes of ladies' handkerchiefs; he was altogether too good-looking, too chatty, too eager to please. Alice Roosevelt was more brutal. "He was the kind of boy whom you invited to the dance but not the dinner," she said, "a good little mother's boy whose friends were dull, who belonged to the minor clubs and who was never at the really gay parties."

Their memories may have been colored by time and envy. "We used to say 'poor Franklin,' " Alice Roosevelt once admitted. "The joke was on us." When his engagement was announced, at least one young Boston woman is known to have taken to her bed for several days out of sorrow and disappointment, and Franklin's diary, spotty as it is, shows that he did not limit his attentions to those girls on his mother's lists. It also offers vivid proof of his highly developed ability to hide his feelings even from those who thought themselves closest to him. Lathrop Brown, who remained his roommate throughout his Harvard career, once wrote with apparent confidence that until Franklin became engaged, he "had had no serious affair with any girl, which was remarkable in view of his exuberance."

It would indeed have been remarkable had it been true. There were suggestions that he had been interested for a time in a Boston girl named Dorothy Quincy. Her name appears often in his diary—though never in his letters home—as his guest at football games and suppers and theater parties. On December 12, 1902, for example, he escorted her first to dinner and then to a dance where "everything was glorious. Got back at 6 A.M. Didn't go to bed." Dorothy Quincy had been lovely, Brown remembered many years later, but Franklin had never been serious about her, "saw her no more than half a dozen girls who went to the same dances."

FDR's sons Elliott and James have both written that during his college years their father courted Frances Dana, granddaughter of both Charles Henry Dana and Henry Wadsworth Longfellow. She, too, was lovely, but, according to the story, her Roman Catholicism made Sara discourage even the thought of marriage. If this tale is true, however, the romance must have been relatively brief, for Frances Dana's name appears nowhere in his diary.

That of Alice Sohier does, frequently. She was the youngest of two daughters of a fine old North Shore family. Her mother was an Alden, a member of a New England clan still older than the Delanos, and her father was Colonel William D. Sohier, former Republican state legislator and commissioner of roads, an enthusiastic yachtsman with a townhouse in Boston, an octagonal summer house near Manchester, New Hampshire, another summer place at Northeast Harbor, Maine, and an estate in Beverly, just up the shore from the vacation home of Franklin's friend and classmate, Tom Beal.

Alice Sohier was not yet sixteen when Franklin first met her during his freshman year. The story in the Sohier family has it that one day early that autumn, Alice, her older sister, Eleanor, and their mother returned together to their Boston home from a shopping trip to find Franklin Roosevelt asleep on the sitting-room sofa. He and two other freshmen—one of whom knew the Sohiers well—had sought sanctuary there to avoid the traditional hazing from roving bands of sophomores.

The girl Franklin saw when he awoke was tall, slender, delicate and astonishingly beautiful—"of all the debutantes [of her] year," FDR wrote many years later, "she was the loveliest." He soon began to call at the Sohier home. Mr. and Mrs. Sohier liked him. So did Alice, perhaps initially flattered by the eager attentions of a Harvard man nearly three years older than herself. He was handsome, high-spirited, well connected and bursting with plans. He was considering a career in politics, he once confided to the family; in fact, he thought he might one day be President. "Who *else* thinks so?" an older cousin asked, and all the Sohiers laughed.

Franklin did not start to keep his Line-A-Day diary until January, 1901, just a few weeks after his father's death, and there are understandably few entries in it during the quiet winter and spring of formal mourning that followed. But he stayed with the Sohiers at their Manchester home in June, his first real social engagement after his six-month period of mourning had ended. Again, there are long stretches of blank pages in his journal for the rest of 1901, so that it is impossible to know how often he and Alice were together. But by the beginning of the following year they were seeing one another nearly every weekend. The entries tumble along: "To see Alice Sohier"; "dance with Alice Sohier"; "A.S. for supper"; "To Sohiers in evening."

At some point their friendship developed into something more serious. Franklin was sometimes more ardent than Alice liked. "In a day and age when well brought-up young men were expected to keep their hands off the persons of young ladies from respectable families," she confided to a relative half a century later, "Franklin had to be slapped—*hard.*" At least once, she recalled, he had ridden back to Boston from Beverly on the train with the bright red mark of her hand across his cheek. But she continued to enjoy his company and some time during the spring of 1902 they evidently at least discussed marriage. Franklin was then just twenty, Alice only seventeen, but he already had firm views about the sort of family he wanted. As one who had sometimes felt isolated as an only child, he told Alice, he hoped to have a lot of children—at least six.

In early July, after school had ended for the summer, Franklin set out from Boston aboard the *Half-Moon* on a two-week cruise to Campobello. Two classmates accompanied him, Lathrop Brown and Amon Hollingsworth. Their first stop was Beverly. They anchored in front of the Beal home on the seventh. The Sohiers brought Alice over to dinner, and the next day the young people played tennis before Franklin took them for "a good long sail" to Marblehead and back. Alice shared his love for the sea; she had been taught to sail by the yachtsman Cornelius Vanderbilt III. That evening Franklin was the Sohiers' dinner guest, and afterward he had a serious talk with Alice. Later, jotting down his usual skeletal account of his day before going to bed, he added a line in a private code: "AND SPEND EVENING ON LAWN. ALICE CONFIDES IN HER DR." Whatever Alice said to him as they sat outside that warm evening on the Beverly shore was startling enough for Franklin to want to conceal it from anyone who might happen to come upon his diary, so unnerving that the next day he felt compelled to add a second coded message: "WORRIED OVER ALICE ALL NIGHT."

No one will ever know precisely what Alice had told him, but the evidence at least suggests that it had to do with her own health and the likelihood of their marriage. She had been somewhat frail since birth, subject to a whole series of childhood ailments which doctors had been powerless to halt. "In those days," she remembered much later, "all they could do was give you either whiskey or brandy and hope for the best." Her internal organs were all abnormally small for her frame, or so her physician finally told her family, and the notion of bearing Franklin several children had alarmed her. It seems likely that she had finally confessed her worries to her doctor, and he had confirmed her fears: giving birth would be risky. (Many years later, Alice would tell a confidante that she had finally decided not to marry Franklin Roosevelt because "I did not wish to be a cow.")[15]

Franklin sailed north the next morning, but he may have continued to see her without his mother's knowledge: twice, he and Tom Beal undertook cruises south from Campobello, stopping in the vicinity of Northeast Harbor, where Alice spent summers with her family.

That winter, Alice's older sister, Eleanor, was to make her debut. She was a lovely girl, too, but not so dramatically beautiful as her sister, and their father decided that Alice should therefore be sent on a European tour during the Boston season so as not to outshine Eleanor. On October 7, Franklin saw her off aboard the *Commonwealth,* the Fall River boat that took her from Boston to New York on the first leg of her voyage. Alice was presented at the court of St. James's while she was abroad, traveled on the continent, and saw the pyramids of Egypt

15. Another coded message in Franklin's diary remains opaque. On February 14, 1903, he noted that "COMMONWEALTH SAILS." The *Commonwealth* was a packet that sailed to New York, connecting with ships bound for Europe. Who was on it this time and why Franklin felt called upon to keep it secret is unknown.

before returning home to make her own debut. By then she had attracted a great many other suitors, and Franklin himself had secretly become engaged. But they evidently remained friends, for he did find time to serve as an usher at her coming-out dance at Beverly in January of 1904.

"Once upon a time when I was in Cambridge," FDR wrote in 1928, "I had serious thoughts of marrying a Boston girl and settling down in the Back Bay to spend the rest of my days. Such was the influence of four years of that . . . [conservative Harvard] kind of association. . . . By the Grace of God I took a trip at that time, meeting numbers of real Americans, i.e. those from the west and south. I was saved, but it was an awfully narrow escape." He was half joking, of course, but it is still curious that he should have so altered what really happened. For it was Alice Sohier, not he, who took the trip that seems to have marked the end of their romance; she, not he, who backed away from marriage.[16]

As the summer of 1903 dragged on, Franklin's absence overseas continued to haunt Sara at Campobello. Without him, the island seemed populated by ghosts. "Not a day passes that we are not thinking of the great changes, my dear one, Mr. Pell and Hamilton Kuhn, all gone!" Even sailing she now found "mere drifting." Franklin's letters provided some solace: "So dear of him to write so constantly and fully of all he does!" Six postcards arrived from him in a single day, mountain views mailed as he and Charley Bradley meandered through the Swiss Alps before starting home.

16. Characteristically, Franklin avoided mentioning Alice Sohier to his mother as long as their romance continued. But once it had ended and he and Alice were merely friends again, he wrote of her freely. In October of 1903 he told his mother that Alice had suffered a severe bout with appendicitis and very nearly died, and in March of the following year he reported that she had been immobilized by some sort of hip ailment that baffled her doctors. "Poor Alice Sohier," Sara wrote when told of the appendicitis attack. "She certainly gets more than her share of illness."

Alice married Herbert Bramwell Shaw, an insurance executive, in 1910. They had just two children, five years apart, and were divorced in 1925. She remained a Republican all her life and deplored the New Deal with special vehemence, professing not to be surprised that FDR was "so careless with the country's money" since he had always overspent his allowance when she had known him. According to the granddaughter who became her confidante in her last years, she was always glad she had never become "the President's lady." She died in 1972 at eighty-six, having made sure that all her letters from Franklin Roosevelt were burned.

She and Eleanor Roosevelt met just once, at a Harvard-Yale game some time after the Roosevelts' marriage. Sara introduced them to one another, explaining that Alice had once been a good friend of Franklin's. "Yes," Eleanor said to her mother-in-law as she shook hands with Alice, "I have heard all about her."

Sources: Interviews with Emily and Bramwell Shaw, Alice Sohier's granddaughter and son.

He set sail from Liverpool on August 19. Sara could not help worrying that "the tremendous North West wind we have had all night" would slow his progress, and she was distressed, too, that she would not be on hand to greet him in New York. "It is so lovely to see a home face on the dock," she told him. "I never forget how I felt the first time I returned with you and Papa and did *not* see my father on the dock."

Franklin returned to her on August 26. "A perfect day," she wrote, ". . . such happiness to be together again. . . . Now that Franklin is back the Island is changed to me."

Mother and son returned to Hyde Park together. Franklin had his tonsils removed before going back to Harvard, bearing it "with his usual stoicism and cheerfulness," she noted. And, "Later I took him for a drive & he was able to enjoy eating ice cream." They discussed his future. She had initially hoped that he would enter Harvard Law School, as his father had before him; it was the finest possible preparation for the sort of life Mr. James had led, and Rosy feared that if Franklin did not begin his law studies now he might lose interest in the profession altogether. But the *Crimson* came first for Franklin; nothing was going to interfere with his running it, and he did not think serious study of the law would be possible with all his "outside interests." And so when he got back to Cambridge and after "a Great Fight in my mind," he enrolled for graduate courses in history and political economy, though "I do not in the least expect to get a degree." Sara acquiesced.

He came home for a house party in October and again to cast his first vote in November. Sara proudly drove with him to the town hall, where, since this was an off-year election in which the fortunes of Cousin Theodore were not affected, he voted Democratic. "Hooray for the Dimocrats of Hoide Park!" he crowed when told of their local triumph a few days later.

Whenever Franklin left her, Sara missed him "dreadfully," but his absence that November was made still more difficult when the blocks of granite she had ordered for the tomb Mr. James had designed for himself and his first wife finally arrived from Scotland. She drove up to the churchyard and watched from her carriage with Rosy while her husband's casket was laid to rest at last and workmen began installing the stone. "I stayed at St. James till the work was finished," she wrote. "Then came home and did not go out again. It brings so vividly to mind the sad earthly part of it." Only the final carving and polishing remained.

There were other sad reminders of death and of the old days at Springwood that autumn. Miss Alice Clay, the "perfect lady" from England whom Mr. James had imported to tutor his son in 1893, had stayed on to work for another family after Franklin outgrew her. She had now fallen ill and been hospitalized for what the doctors called "anemia and neurasthenia." Sara took her home to care for. She would remain for several months, wasting away despite the hours Sara spent at her bedside and the doctors and trained nurses she arranged to have on hand.

Thoughts of Franklin and the future kept her spirits up. She was determined that this would be the last year they would be so far apart. The next autumn she planned for him to be in New York, not Cambridge, attending Columbia Law School, which, she assured him, "now stands very high." There, she could personally help shape his career—"I still have a few friends of your dear father's who could take an interest"—and Rosy could see that he got "to be known among the best men." And it would bring him close to Springwood: "I merely wish you would think seriously of it," she told him, "and to realize how much it will be for you and for me, for you to be near your own home, and not too much out of reach."

Meanwhile, she looked forward eagerly to Thanksgiving, which she and Franklin were to spend together at the Delano homestead at Fairhaven. There, with him at her side and surrounded by her brothers and sisters and their families, her life would seem complete again.

She had no way of knowing that the little diary that Franklin kept in his luggage now contained another coded secret that threatened to alter the unique intimacy between her and her son forever.

CHAPTER 7

E IS AN ANGEL

After the silence of Springwood without Franklin, the cheerful bustle of the traditional Delano Thanksgiving at Fairhaven must have seemed doubly comforting to Sara. She had come up from New York aboard the train with Annie and Fred Hitch, and with Warren and his wife, Jennie, who managed the Homestead for the family, and their four girls. Franklin had boarded the train en route. Fred and his wife, Tilly, came all the way from Chicago. Only Dora Forbes and the Colliers were absent, but Kassie's son, Warren Robbins, made it to the gathering from Groton.

Thanksgiving morning was cold and clear. The sun shone brightly on the harbor and on the white clapboarded houses as the Delanos trooped together once again to church; and it warmed them afterward when they all stopped for a moment to lay armfuls of flowers at the family tomb in Riverside Cemetery.

They did their best to recreate old times at dinner, prepared by the elderly retainers who looked after the house throughout the year and presided over by Warren, his neatly trimmed beard silver now as he carved the turkey with as much of his father's old flourish as he could muster. Then he rose to propose the annual toast:

> Here's to the past!
> And to those who have peopled it!
> May we e'er make the best of it!

Here's to the future!
To our hopes! Our ambitions!
To our Sons; and our Daughters!
And may our traditions
In their hearts ever dwell;
And continue in those of their children—as well!"

After dinner, the Delanos gathered around the piano in the parlor as they had so many times before and sang old favorites, Sara's confident soprano and Franklin's rich tenor clearly audible above the rest.

Sometime later that day, Franklin took his mother aside—perhaps outside in the walled garden, fragrant with the tang of apples that had fallen from the old trees beneath which Sara had played in her grandfather's time—and told her his astonishing secret. It fell upon her like the blows of a hammer.

He had fallen in love with his cousin Eleanor Roosevelt.

He had asked her to marry him.

She had said yes.

No one now can know all they said to one another that evening. Sara noted in her journal only that Franklin had given her "quite a startling announcement." She and her son were both reticent, both strong-willed; neither ever wished to wound the other. Perhaps at first she thought—or hoped—that this sudden infatuation was just another evidence of her son's boyish impetuousness. Like his eight-year-old's wish for "freedom," like his more recent desire to travel abroad on his own, it was something he was sure to get over. In any case, at twenty-one, Franklin was far too young to marry. Her own father had been thirty-three when he married—already "a man who had made a name and a place for himself," she later remembered having told Franklin, one "who [had] something to offer a woman." And Franklin's own father had been fifty-six when she had married him. Cousin Eleanor was a lovely girl, but she was only nineteen. Sara exacted the promise that the engagement would remain a secret for at least a year. That would give Franklin and Eleanor plenty of time to think things over. In the meantime, no one must be told. Mother and son returned to the family as if nothing had happened.

But whether or not Sara expressed it openly at Fairhaven, the prospect of marriage for her son meant that she was to be left alone again, this time for good. Franklin and Eleanor had often been together over the past year, but there had been no hint of a romance; at least none that she had detected. She had thought Franklin was telling her all that he was doing, but clearly he had told her nothing that truly mattered. She had been patronized.

On December first, Franklin took Eleanor to see his mother at the Roosevelt apartment in the Renaissance Hotel, and Sara had what she described only as "a long talk with the dear child." Both Franklin and Eleanor sensed her fear and resentment, and sought as best they could to reassure her.

Franklin wrote to her from his office at the *Crimson* as soon as he got back to Cambridge.

"Dearest Mama—I know what pain I must have caused you and you know I wouldn't do it if I really could have helped it—*mais tu sais, me voila!* That's all that could be said—I know my mind, have known it for a long time, and know that I could never think otherwise: Result: I am the happiest man just now in the world; likewise the luckiest—And for you, dear Mummy, you know that nothing can ever change what we have always been & always will be to each other—only now you have two children to love & to love you—and Eleanor as you know will always be a daughter to you in every true way."

Eleanor wrote, too, addressing her letter to "Dear Cousin Sally." "It is impossible for me to tell you how I feel toward Franklin," she said. "I can only say that my one great wish is always to prove worthy of him." Sara had been very good to her, she wrote. "I know just how you feel & how hard it must be, but I do want you to learn to love me a little."

Eleanor Roosevelt was never certain of anyone's love. In her voluminous autobiographical writings she sought the reasons for her insecurity in the half-remembered events of her parched childhood. She puzzled over their meaning, turned them over and over, altered details, rearranged their sequence, as if by doing so—like a player at solitaire who may find at any moment that she has dealt herself a winning hand—everything would suddenly fall into place.

But it never did for her. "She knew she had a ghastly childhood," her younger cousin Corinne Robinson Alsop once wrote, "but she didn't realize how ghastly it was." What seems certain is that her early years were nearly as empty of approval and constancy as Franklin's were surfeited with them. Like Sara Delano Roosevelt, she worshipped her father. "He was the center of my world," she said. But unlike

Warren Delano, Elliott Roosevelt was a frail and unsteady object of veneration.

He had seemed at first far more promising than his older brother, Theodore, who was known as "Teedie" and "Thee" as a boy—small, spindly, at once hyperkinetic and bookish, with a voice that squeaked when he was not wheezing with asthma. Elliott was taller, better-looking, more athletic, good-humored, gregarious, and, according to one childhood friend, "entirely lacking in Theodore's egotism." And he was celebrated within the family for his tenderness and generosity: he went out walking one wintry New York morning while still a small boy wearing a new coat and returned without it; asked what had happened, he said that he had given it to a poor boy who had seemed cold.

But there was within him almost from the first a sad conviction that he would never be able to hold his own in the loving but relentless competition that characterized life among the Oyster Bay Roosevelts. Theodore swiftly outdistanced him, and by the age of fifteen, Elliott had completely subordinated himself to his older brother. "Oh father," he wrote that year, "will you ever think *me* a 'noble boy'? You are right about [Teedie] he is one and no mistake, a boy I would give a good deal to be like."

But he was not like him, could not make himself be like him. He entered St. Paul's School at sixteen, where he did poorly and left in the middle of the term after suffering a series of blinding headaches and mysterious seizures which no amount of "anti-nervous" medication seemed able to forestall. The best diagnosis doctors could offer was periodic "congestion of the brain." Like Theodore's sieges of asthma, which eased significantly as soon as he left home for Harvard and was no longer in daily contact with his fond but demanding father, Elliott's attacks may have been in part an unconscious avenue of escape from competitive pressures he could not otherwise withstand. In any case, they ruled out college and the unavoidable comparisons with Theodore it would have ensured. His health and sense of well-being seemed always to flourish the further he went from home and responsibility, and he spent nearly a year out west, happily hunting and ranching on his own. Theodore joined him there one summer, and Elliott wrote and illustrated an entertaining account of their adventures together in which he referred to himself in the third person throughout as "Nell" and "she," as if by being the first to point out what his brother and father evidently considered his feminine weakness the charge could be defused.

He was closer to his mother, whom he called "beloved Motherling," than to his father, but when Theodore Roosevelt, Sr., fell fatally ill with cancer of the bowel in 1878, it was Elliott who nursed him for weeks, showing a devotion, his sister Corinne remembered, "so tender that it was more like a woman"; and his failure to keep his father alive may have added further to his seventeen-year-old's sense of his own inadequacy.

In any case, two years later in the autumn of 1880, with Theodore soon to run for the New York Assembly and already acting as head of the family, Elliott set out upon a leisurely trip around the world, to be interrupted by several months of big-game hunting in India. Sara and Mr. James, then embarking on their honeymoon, were his fellow passengers aboard the *Germanic* on the first leg of his journey; they found him such good company that they urged him to make their London rooms his own during his stay there, and later, when Franklin was born, they asked him to be their boy's godfather.

Elliott was gracious and dashing, solicitous and genial, but incapable of sustained effort; even the editing of his own letters from India into a book intended to match Theodore's *Hunting Trips of a Ranch Man* would prove too much for him. He claimed never to be jealous of his brother's successes; he loved Theodore far too much for that, he said; knew that his brother was a "far better man than he." Yet the very effusiveness of his tributes to Theodore seems suspect, a mask for a wealth of unacknowledged envy for the older brother who seemed always able to do everything better than he could. "My darling old brother," he wrote from India. "I would like to do *anything* under you, Thee—for you are the sort of man to lead at any kind of a hard time or place, and I do feel such entire trust and confidence in your ability and pluck that at anything from a 'bowery reform' politically to a boat race I should like to put my strength to help yours and follow you—and I will, too, Teddy."

He seemed to feel vaguely guilty at indulging himself in India, while his brother and sisters were settling down. He really ought to get a job when he got home, he wrote to his new brother-in-law, Corinne's husband, Douglas Robinson. "Are there no broad acres covered with pine timber land set with gold and silver and coal near you . . . which I might reclaim and make a fortune, Marry too, and altogether not stand without the pale as I do? . . . I cannot bear to think of living in New York as an idle man." But he also knew he lacked the quality he called Theodore's "foolish grit," and he confessed to Bamie that he was simply unable to adopt as his own "our way"—the Roosevelt way—that meant "life for an end." And he had begun to drink.

His failings were still kept largely within the family, however, and when he returned to New York and entered Douglas Robinson's real estate business he was thought a glamorous catch. So was Anna Hall, just eighteen in the winter of 1881–82 and, in Elliott's words, "a tall slender fair-haired little beauty—just out and a great belle."

Friends brought them together, they fell almost instantly in love, and at Algonac during a Memorial Day house party arranged for them by their friend Laura Delano (just weeks before she burned to death), they agreed to marry. The wedding was set for December first. Their courtship provided vivid evidence that opposites attract. Anna was the eldest of six children of Valentine G. Hall, Jr., a rich and reclusive country gentleman who had never felt the need to work and who brought up his family in a big secluded house called Oak Terrace at Tivoli, up the Hudson from Hyde Park. He was puritanical and pious —a live-in clergyman was in constant attendance, his granddaughter Eleanor Roosevelt once wrote, "in order that he might have someone with whom to talk on equal terms"—and he at once tyrannized and indulged his wife, Mary Livingston Ludlow, a member of two of the oldest and most powerful River families. She was pampered with fine clothes and jewelry but not allowed ever to shop on her own, not taught even how to write a check, so that when her husband died in 1880, leaving her with six children under seventeen, she was at first very nearly helpless. As the eldest, Anna did her best to help, but all four of the youngest children were scarred by their fatherless upbringing. The two boys, Edward and Valentine, would eventually retreat into a more or less permanent alcoholic haze.

Accustomed to the cheerless Hall household, in which self-denial was the highest virtue and pleasure was dismissed as frivolity, Anna was especially drawn to Elliott's gaiety and high spirits. She was often bored. "I am just pining for excitement," she once told him, and he did his best to provide it. He gave her a spectacular necklace fashioned from the claws of a tiger he had shot in India, played tennis with her on the Tivoli courts, took her for "jolly drives" along the nearby Woods Road, and let her watch him play polo at the Meadow Brook Club on Long Island.

Elliott, in turn, saw in Anna's earnestness and reserve something of the stability and substance he knew he lacked on his own, and he worked hard to match it. He took her with him on his regular inspections of the charities established by his late father—the New York Orthopaedic Hospital and the Newsboys Lodging House—and he offered to read aloud with her "some of my favorite chapters and verses in the little Testament" that he said he found "a comforting and joyous though silent companion," and carried with him wherever he went.

Their love letters were heady and joyous for the most part—Elliott thought Anna "my Queen, my *Heaven,* so holy, sacred & near God are you"—but here and there were hints of the trouble to come. Each was jealous of the other. Anna worried that "the demon distrust" had an unshakable grip on her; "I have such wretched feelings that I trust nothing and no one." She worried, too, that she had told him too much about herself, "not *heard* enough" about him. And Elliott already suffered from unnerving spells of suspicion and despair. Make up your mind that "you *will* be happy," Anna told him after receiving one discouraged letter. "Say to yourself that *you know* I am true and that you will trust people. It should make you feel so, so much happier." Elliott vowed to banish all distrust: "I shall be pure in heart, noble in honor and strong in love." But at least once, while visiting Anna at Tivoli, he had some kind of seizure and had to be helped home on the train.

Elliott's family was delighted with the match. Anna would provide the motivation Elliott needed to make something of himself, Theodore told Corinne; she would give "the dear old boy . . . something to work for." The wedding itself at Calvary Episcopal Church, just around the corner from the old Theodore Roosevelt home on East Twentieth Street, on December 1, 1883, was "a Noted Hymeneal Event," according to one newspaper and "one of the brilliant social events of the season" in the columns of another. Theodore was Elliott's best man. Sara and Mr. James were among the guests that crowded into the church; their unaccustomed absence had frightened two-year-old Franklin, left behind for the day at Algonac.

The newlyweds were among the most popular young couples in the same fashionable set in which their friends the Rosy Roosevelts were so prominent. Anna helped establish a series of dances at Sherry's restaurant, organized because even Mrs. Astor's Patriarchs' balls were thought insufficiently exclusive by her and her friends. At Newport and Meadow Brook and at the annual meet of the New York Coaching

Club in Central Park, Anna was singled out for her beauty and the grace of her carriage—this last the legacy of her late father who had insisted that she take long walks daily at Tivoli with a stick across the small of her back, held in place by the crook of her elbows.

Eleanor Roosevelt would one day write that her mother had been the most beautiful woman she had ever seen. A woman friend noted that Anna "never entered a room as others did—she seemed almost to float forward." Robert Browning himself was so struck by her that he begged to be allowed just to read aloud to her while she had her portrait painted one summer when she and Elliott were in Switzerland. Corinne Robinson Alsop also remembered the unique impact of Anna's beauty. She was taken to the Elliott Roosevelts' for a Christmas party as a very small child. The door flew open at her mother's knock, she recalled, and "Uncle Ellie bounded down the stairs" and picked her up in his arms; his genuine affection seemed palpable. But he was entirely forgotten a moment later for "behind him on the stairs I saw Aunt Anna, dressed in some blue-grey shimmery material. She seemed so beautiful that the vision stayed with me all my childhood, and while I was entranced by fairy tales, all the fairy godmothers were dressed as Aunt Anna was dressed."

Anna Hall Roosevelt lived for that kind of admiration. Her "love of the approbation of those dear to her was remarkable," one friend wrote after her death; she had been "made for an atmosphere of approval." She got plenty of it at first from her admiring husband, "the most lovable Roosevelt I ever knew," according to a friend who had known a good many of them.

In February of 1884, tragedy interrupted what must have seemed an idyll to their friends when, on a single harrowing day, first Elliott's mother and then Theodore's young wife, Alice Lee, died in the Roosevelt home on West Fifty-seventh street. "There is a curse on this house," a distraught Elliott told his sister, Corinne, when she arrived. "Mother is dying and Alice is dying too." Alice Roosevelt had succumbed to Bright's disease just two days after giving birth to "Baby Alice," the child that the unfailingly generous Bamie would raise until her brother remarried in 1886. And so, when Anna found herself pregnant that spring and often felt unwell, both she and Elliott were especially anxious.

The safe healthy birth of Anna Eleanor Roosevelt on October 11, 1884, came as a great relief. To her father, Eleanor Roosevelt wrote, "I was a miracle from heaven." His brother, Theodore, was her delighted godfather. But to the mother for whom she was named she seems to have been something of a disappointment, even an embarrassment, almost from birth. Anna Hall and all her sisters had been taught that beauty and grace, charm and rectitude were the qualities that mattered most in women. Eleanor did not measure up. She was plain and grave, even as an infant. "Very solemn," she herself recalled, "entirely lacking in the spontaneous joy and mirth of youth." During two of her early years she was made to wear an ugly, uncomfortable steel brace to forestall curvature of the spine.

Something else may already have been at work within Anna as well, something that would prevent her from developing for her daughter the same warm maternal feeling that she would later display toward her sons. Her marriage was already troubled. Despite his promises, Elliott seemed unable really to settle down; he was already spending a good deal of time away from home; ignored his business in favor of hunting, yachting, drinking; and when he was with her had begun privately to veer between depression and elation, exuberance and self-loathing. Anna loved her husband, but nothing she could think to do seemed to steady him. Perhaps Eleanor, who greatly resembled her father, came to seem to her a symbol of that growing difficulty and of the feelings of dread and helplessness it had begun to engender. Perhaps, too, the demands of caring for a genuine infant initially seemed more than she could bear when her husband was himself behaving more and more like a child.

Sometime during 1886, her parents took Eleanor with them on a weekend visit to Springwood. Significantly perhaps, the point of the trip was for her father to see his godson, Franklin, then four years old, not for the James Roosevelts to see his daughter. This was the first meeting between the children, though neither could remember it in later years. Franklin was a dutiful host, tirelessly carrying his unsmiling two-year-old guest back and forth across the nursery floor on his back. Later, Eleanor came down for tea but was too timid to venture further than the parlor door, standing there in a starched white frock, her finger in her mouth, until her exasperated mother called out, "Come in Granny," explaining to Sara and Mr. James that she called her daughter that because Eleanor was "such a funny child, so old-fashioned." When Eleanor was old enough to understand this explanation, which her mother freely offered whenever strangers were present, it made her want to "sink through the floor in shame."

She would continue to suck her fingers well into her childhood, and she chewed her fingernails later, stopping only when she reread a letter from her father in which he had urged that she "take good care of those cunning wee hands that Father so loves to be petted by." She would have done almost anything to please her father. All her earliest memories centered around him. She remembered dressing up and dancing for him when very small, solemnly whirling and pirouetting in the dining room until he signaled an end to the performance by sweeping her high into the air while the guests applauded, then kissing her good night.

"With my father I was perfectly happy," she said. "He would take me into his dressing room in the morning, or when he was dressing for dinner, and let me watch each thing he did." The qualities in Eleanor that bewildered and irritated her mother seemed to make Elliott identify with her all the more closely. He had himself been a disappointment to his family and to himself. Even his pet name for her seemed to echo his sense of inadequacy. He had disparaged himself as "Nell" when he was a boy; he now called his daughter "Little Nell," only in part after the heroine of *The Old Curiosity Shop.* And he evidently found her premature solemnity engaging rather than odd, asking her to pose especially sternly for a photographer, one small admonitory finger raised, and then having a portrait painted from the photograph which he liked to call "Little Nell Scolding Elliott."

She was not alone in scolding him; Anna was increasingly troubled by Elliott's behavior. The Elliott Roosevelts were still among the city's most sought-after couples, giving or attending dinners or dances or theater parties nearly every evening of the week. A French nurse, her name now lost, cared for Eleanor, watching her so closely that the little girl was fluent in French before she could speak English.

But Elliott had grown increasingly erratic, by turns edgy and ebullient at home, more and more involved with his hard-drinking, hard-riding friends at Meadow Brook. In the spring of 1887, he suddenly resigned from his brother-in-law's firm, explaining that he was no longer up to the work. Something was seriously wrong, and Anna suggested that rather than face another idle, purposeless summer on Long Island they travel together to the Continent, taking her sister Elizabeth, known as "Tissie," and Eleanor with them. Three months of relaxation away from the anxieties and temptations of New York should help restore her husband's equilibrium.

One of Franklin Roosevelt's first memories had been the air of calm and confidence with which his parents had surrounded him at three when they thought the *Germania* was going down. One of Eleanor

Roosevelt's earliest memories, too, had been of a near-disaster at sea, but its meaning and impact were entirely different.

One day out of port at about five in the afternoon and blanketed in fog, their ship, the *Britannic,* was struck by another steamship, the *Celtic,* her prow plunging ten feet into the *Britannic*'s steel side and ripping away some twenty feet of thick plating that sheared its way across the crowded steerage deck. A twelve-year-old girl was decapitated, her father dismembered. Other passengers were crushed under great heaps of fallen superstructure, smashed lifeboats, and tackle. A child's leg lay on the deck, the body to which it had been attached evidently driven overboard. Injured men and women screamed. Water poured through the torn hull. Panicky stokers seized and launched one lifeboat; four more boats were lowered, filled with women and children, the captain standing by with a loaded pistol to make certain that no men tried to crowd them out.

Elliott ushered Anna and her maid into one of them, then jumped in beside them at the last moment, ordered to do so by an officer because there were too few crewmen aboard to man the oars. He was the only man among the cabin passengers to leave the *Britannic.*[1]

Eleanor did not consciously remember any of these details. "I remember only that there was wild confusion," she wrote. "My father stood in a boat below me, and I was dangling over the side to be dropped into his arms. I was terrified and shrieking and clung to those who were to drop me." Her father shouted encouragement, struggling to stay on his feet in the crowded boat. The crewmen managed finally to pry her fingers loose, and she fell screaming through the air to safety.

1. The *Britannic* did not sink, the crew having managed to staunch the inrushing water with lashed-together mattresses, and she eventually managed to limp back to New York, alongside the *Celtic* and escorted by three other liners. Most of her cabin passengers had remained aboard and, once safely ashore, one of them, the California railroad millionaire, Collis P. Huntington, made a point of scornfully mentioning Elliott Roosevelt's apparently premature flight to safety to the newspapers. Only Elliott and John Paton, a prominent Wall Street banker, had accompanied the women across to the *Celtic,* he told the *World.* Two days later, Paton wrote in to correct Huntington's story. *He* had not left the *Britannic* to rejoin his wife and daughter until the crisis had passed, he said. Elliott never bothered to write in his own defense. But Cecil H. Alleyne, a fellow passenger and a friend of Elliott's, wrote to him from the Knickerbocker Club to express his indignation at Huntington's unjustified attack: "I feel excessively annoyed at the manner in which your name has been brought up. No one who saw the cool, collected and generous manner in which you helped the 3rd officer's boat with women and children can help feeling distressed at the sneer implied in Mr. Huntington's report. Mr. Mencken, the 3rd officer who *ordered* you into the boat . . . told me that had you not obeyed his command to come aboard and take an oar he would have had to put off for what at the time might have been a 350 mile row with one oar short. . . . No one could have behaved with more coolness and bravery."

Sources: The *New York World,* May 23 and 24, 1887; Roosevelt Family Papers Donated by the Children, FDRL.

The Roosevelts were taken aboard the *Celtic* and returned to New York, where they immediately booked passage to Europe on another ship.

But the traumatized little girl now wept and shook at even the thought of going to sea again. Her parents, still preoccupied with getting abroad for the sake of Elliott's health, were baffled and irritated by her obvious terror. No admonitions to be brave seemed to help.

Her great-aunt and -uncle, Mr. and Mrs. James King Gracie, volunteered to care for Eleanor at their summer home at Oyster Bay while Anna and Elliott went overseas; the Roosevelts planned to return in August.

Aunt Gracie reported to Corinne on her trip home from New York with her small grand-niece: "She was so little and gentle & had such a narrow escape out of the great ocean that it made her seem doubly helpless & pathetic. . . . She asked two or three times . . . where her 'dear Mamma was, & where her Papa was, & where is Aunt Tissie?' I told her they have gone to Europe. She said 'where is baby's home now?' I said 'baby's home is Gracewood with Uncle Bunkle and Aunt Gracie' which seemed to satisfy the sweet little darling. But as we came near the Bay driving . . . she said to her uncle in an anxious alarmed way 'Baby does not want to go into the water. Not in a boat!."

Her parents stayed abroad for six months, not three, an unimaginably long span for a child still less than three years old. Anna worried about her—"I do so long for her," she wrote home—but Elliott's recovery came first. She knew it had been "wiser to leave her." Eleanor collected eggs for breakfast at Oyster Bay, played quietly by herself on the big empty grounds of the Gracie estate, listened to stories of Brer Rabbit her Aunt Gracie had learned as a girl in Georgia. She seemed content enough, if awfully quiet, but inside herself Eleanor was sure she was being punished. If she had been brave, as her father had asked her to be, she would be with him and with her mother; because she had not been, she had been abandoned. It was the first of a long series of separations from her parents, each of which she saw as abandonment or exile.

"Fear has always seemed to me the worst stumbling block which anyone has to face," she would write many years later. "It is the great crippler. Looking back it strikes me that my childhood and my early youth were one long battle against fear." That battle continued unabated all her life. She never entirely conquered her terror of the sea, but nothing else was ever allowed to frighten her if she could help it.

It was her future husband who would declare that "the only thing we have to fear is fear itself—nameless, unreasoning, unjustified terror." But it was Eleanor who knew it first and most unmistakably.

Her parents finally returned to her in the autumn of 1887, rented a cottage at Hempstead, just a few miles from Meadow Brook, and began to build themselves a splendid new summer house. Although Elliott generally felt better after his half-year abroad and was welcomed into his Uncle Gracie's realty firm, he was already eager to get back among his sporting companions. Soon he was riding as recklessly as ever, breaking first an arm and then his collarbone in pursuit of foxes and, after recovering from both falls, organizing and leading a midnight hunt, hurtling walls and ditches in the dark. He was always ready for risks, liked to live at the edge, as if determined to prove his bravery to others and to himself.[2]

Theodore, who was himself no stranger to risk-taking, worried about him, wondering if a warning against "imprudence" would help or only make matters worse. "I do hate his Hempstead life," he told Bamie. "I don't know whether he could get along without the excitement now, but it is very unhealthy and it leads to nothing."

His Hempstead life delighted Eleanor. The year she spent with her parents there may have been the most contented of her childhood. She was "as happy as the day is long," Elliott noted. "Baby Eleanor goes up to look after [the new house] every day and calls it hers." Her father was often home (though when he was not, Anna wrote, Eleanor could be "fiendish"). There were puppies and kittens with which to tumble on the lawn, and her Cousin Alice often came to play. In October of 1888, "the funny little tot had a happy [fourth] birthday," her father

2. His motivation may have been still more self-destructive. Elliott once wrote a curious and melodramatic short story called "Was Miss Vedder an Adventuress?" Its date is unknown, and he does not seem ever to have tried to have it published. The protagonist is a beautiful unmarried woman nearing forty who has fallen on hard times. When an old and dogged suitor proposes marriage as a solution to her problems, she turns him away. "My life has been a gamble," she explains. "I lived for pleasure only. I have never done anything I disliked when I could possibly avoid it. . . . I knew the end had to come some time, but I never thought of it. I hoped against hope that something would turn up to pull me through. It was the hope of a gambler." With that, she retires to her hotel room, lights candles on her dresser, and gazes at herself in the mirror while holding a pistol to her heart. Before she pulls the trigger, she muses aloud, "What a frivolous, useless thing you were. Still, you never did anyone any harm but yourself and now there will be no one to regret you."

For Miss Vedder, death was preferable to responsibility. The problem for Elliott was that he had been unable to avoid responsibility and its terrors; there were plenty of people to regret him.

Source: Elliott Roosevelt Papers, FDRL.

assured Bamie, "and ended by telling me when saying goodnight (after Anna heard her say her prayers) that she loved everybody and everybody loved her. Was it not cunning?" It was also uncharacteristic; she would rarely feel that way again.

They moved into their new home in the late spring of 1889. Shortly thereafter, Elliott shattered his ankle practicing somersaults for a society circus. The ankle set badly, had to be broken and reset. "I remember the day very well," Eleanor wrote, "for we were alone in his room when he told me about it. Little as I was, I sensed that this was a terrible ordeal, and when he went hobbling out on crutches to the waiting doctors, I was dissolved in tears."

Weeks of agony followed, weeks when Elliott grew to rely still more heavily on alcohol and drugs. The pain eventually abated; the twin addictions it had encouraged never did.

Anna was now pregnant again, and as the birth of her second child drew near, Eleanor was sent away, this time to stay with her Grandmother Hall at Tivoli. In her autobiography, Eleanor made a curious but perhaps revealing error. After recounting what she could remember of her frightening experience at sea and of her long lonely stay with the Gracies while her parents were abroad, she writes, "One little brother must have been born about this time, Elliott Roosevelt, Jr., but of his arrival I have no recollection whatsoever." Actually, two years had intervened between these events; Elliott, Jr., was born in the autumn of 1889. But the fact that she later believed his birth had coincided so closely with what she saw as her parents' abandonment of her may have meant that her brother's arrival, too, when it eventually came, had seemed to her child's mind still another punishment. Her parents would not have *needed* another child if she had been all that they had hoped she would be.

The first of her letters to have survived, dictated from Tivoli to her mother's sister, Edith, known to Eleanor as Aunt Pussie, treats the baby's birth with obvious ambivalence:

"Dear Father, I hope you are well and Mother too. I hope little brother doesn't cry but if he does tell the nurse to give him a tap tap tap. . . . I love you very much and Mother and Brother, too, if he has blue eyes. Your precious little Eleanor."

Her father was delighted with his son—"simply adores him," Anna noted—but his dependence on liquor and narcotics was steadily worsening. He again gave up business, and sometimes became so "excited," Anna noted, that he was "unnatural," yet could not abide inactivity.

He tried to resume his riding, fell from his horse, and was kicked in the head; he began to talk openly of suicide and finally fled to the south in search of a cure. Eleanor was again greatly disturbed at his absence, desperate to have him back. "Eleanor lunched with us yesterday," her Aunt Tissie wrote Elliott. "She rushes to the stairs every time the bell rang to see if it was her Papa. 'I shall be so glad to see my *dear* father,' she kept saying."

Anna did her best to hold her family together while encouraging Elliott toward self-control. It was painful for her to be apart from him. She and the children would help him wage "that old hard fight," she assured him, "but Nell, it must be an entire conquest. A partial one is *no good*. . . . We can't do without you. . . . I do love you so and want you to be my darling strong boy," she said. "I think I would be the happiest woman living if you would ever be well and give up all wines and medicines. Do, dear, throw your horrid cocktails away."

But he could not do it. He returned to her little better than when he left, and plunged immediately back into the old reckless life. Theodore now noticed that ordinary conversation with Elliott was no longer possible; his brother would begin a story, forget what he had been trying to say, lapse into bewilderment and despair. And he wandered the house at night, unable to sleep; he vanished for days at a time and pursued other women. One of them, a pretty housemaid named Katy Mann, he secretly brought to his own bedroom; she became pregnant. In July of 1890, Anna determined that the whole family should go abroad to see if a year or more spent quietly in the health resorts of Germany, Switzerland, and Italy might bring Elliott to his senses and save their marriage.

The trip went well enough at first. Elliott tried hard not to drink; Anna watched him closely, and European friends also helped keep him sober. In Berlin, when the Roosevelts went backstage at Buffalo Bill's Wild West with Count Sierstoff, an old hunting companion of Elliott's, the showman poured Elliott a glass of whiskey with which to drink his health. Sierstoff took it from Elliott's hand, explaining that his doctors forbade it.

For five-year-old Eleanor, the tour was unalloyed joy: despite the terrors of the Atlantic crossing, she was with her father every day. All her life she would treasure her few oddly selective memories of their travels together. At Venice, her father had insisted on poling his own gondola along a canal, she remembered, "singing with the other boatmen, to my intense joy." And when she begged for her own glass of the frothy, delicious-looking drink being enjoyed at the other tables at a German outdoor cafe, he ordered one for her, insisting that "if you have it you have to drink the whole glass." She did, hating the bitter taste. She was "disillusioned and disappointed," she wrote, but by the beer (which she never learned to like), not by her father, never by her father.

Only her timidity seemed to annoy him, and because it did, she did her best to disguise it from him. Riding a donkey in the mountains above Sorrento and faced with an especially steep downhill slope, she was unable to keep from turning pale while her father was watching. Forty years later, she said, she could "remember still the tone of disapproval in his voice, though his words of reproof have long since faded away."

Those words—or their cruel gist—later came back to her. In an article written in 1939 she described the scene as if it had happened to someone else: " 'You are not afraid are you?' The tone was incredulous, astonished, and the man looked down from his horse to the child on her small donkey. The eyes were kind, but she sat shivering and hung back, looking at the steep descent. A steely look came into the man's eyes and in a cold voice he said: 'You may go back if you wish, but I did not know you were a coward.' "

Though Eleanor could not know it, her father's uncharacteristic harshness toward her on the hillside above Sorrento was a symptom of the personal agony through which he and her mother were now passing. For several weeks, he had been without the comforting obliviousness alcohol always induced in him. There were "awful attacks of depression every day," Anna told Bamie; some were dispelled in moments; others could only be overcome by hours of rapid walking on his painful, poorly knit ankle. Anna offered encouragement but also maintained a strict and distrustful vigilance. She had become more keeper than wife. At Salzburg in early October, the Roosevelts spent several days in the country home of another old hunting friend, Count Arco. Elliott was "an angel up to Wednesday night," Anna reported to Bamie, and since she was exhausted and did not feel well, she had taken to her bed that evening. "Then I *think* he drank champagne for dinner, though he denies it. Think of my position. I could not leave my bed. He got through without excess but I feel quite sure he took something . . . that night, too, but nothing to be noticed." Though still ill, Anna stayed by his side all the next day. By Sunday, she continued, Elliott was terribly "restless . . . and I knew if it were possible he would get something." He slipped out of his room and down the stairs. Anna heard him, and "I immediately followed. Tried the drawing room, sitting room, and finally the smoking room. There he was with the brandy and water. Nothing was left out at Arco's, the head butler having the keys. [Elliott] had ordered it and was setting down the first glass. I was furious. Said so. It affected him at once . . . I don't think the [other guests] could have noticed." Neither, of course, did Eleanor.

Elliott managed to keep from taking another drink for the next few days, and Anna, grasping at the slimmest suggestion of his improvement, saw in this proof of "how much better he is. But Bamie," she continued, "I have never been so worried about him as for the past week." Elliott had fallen into a "melancholy from which nothing rouses him." He could not sleep at all, "believes himself everlastingly lost . . . irrevocably disgraced . . . [believes also that] as long as he stays with us he injures the children and myself. . . . I stayed awake three nights fearing his mind would give way. . . . He also believes there is something dreadful awaiting us in the near future."

By midwinter of 1891 it was clear that Elliott could not be restored to health on his own. He entered an Austrian sanitarium. Anna, now pregnant again and with two children to care for, sent for Bamie to come and help her. In April, for reasons still unclear, the Roosevelts suddenly left Austria and rented a small house at Neuilly on the outskirts of Paris, where they would await the baby's arrival.

Eleanor was again an inconvenience. Not yet seven, she was sent off to a convent school to be "out of the way." There, too, she felt herself an intruder. The other girls spent hours decorating their shrine to the Madonna. Eleanor, a Protestant, was not allowed near it. Instead, she remembered, she was "always kept on the outside and wandered by myself in the walled-in garden." There, one day in late June, she would learn that she now had a second baby brother, named Hall.

Years later, recalling her loneliness and fear at the convent, she still thought her misery must somehow have been her own fault. The problem had been "her own inordinate desire for affection and praise," she concluded, perhaps brought on by the fact that her mother had made her "keenly conscious of my own shortcomings." In fact, of course, her desire for praise and affection, for the normal outward signs of parental approval, was the inevitable result of having had so little of either. Nonetheless, still blaming herself, she explained that she then "fell prey to temptation." Another little girl had swallowed a coin, frightening the sisters but riveting the attention of the other girls. "She was the center of everyone's interest," Eleanor wrote. "I longed to be in her place." But more important, the other girl had been sent home to recuperate, and that, above all, was what Eleanor wanted most for herself.

She told one of the sisters that she, too, had swallowed a coin. She was not believed. She insisted that she was telling the truth. The sisters demanded she confess. Trapped, she fell silent. Her mother was summoned, told her daughter was a liar and incorrigible, and asked to take her away from the school.

"The drive home was one of utter misery," Eleanor remembered, her mother steadily berating her as they rode together in the carriage, and continuing her denunciation even after they reached their house. "I could bear swift punishment of any kind far better than long scoldings," she recalled. Scoldings put into words her darkest secret fears about her own worth; she was now officially a liar as well as a coward.

She found her father at home when she got there and gratefully remembered that he had been the only person in the household who "did not treat me as a criminal." In a brief tactful passage that constitutes the closest she ever came to criticizing her father in print, Eleanor added that while she was away at the convent, he had given "my mother and his sister a great deal of anxiety."

In fact, he had been making their lives what Theodore called "a brooding nightmare." Paris had proved too tempting for Elliott to resist. He disappeared into the city for days at a time, took a mistress —a married American expatriate with two children, Mrs. Florence Bagley Sherman of Detroit—again talked of suicide, and when, back in New York, Katy Mann, the domestic who had now borne his illegitimate son, went to the family lawyers and threatened to expose him if the child was not adequately provided for, he was unable even to tell Anna whether or not the baby could be his.

His brother, now one of three public service commissioners in Washington, was outraged. The scandal could damage his career, but far worse was the knowledge that his own brother had now shown himself to be "a maniac morally as well as mentally," "a flagrant man-swine" who had betrayed his wife and family. For Anna to go on living with him would be "little short of criminal. She ought not to have any more children, and those she has should be brought up away from him." The family would pay to silence Katy Mann—the story never did reach the newspapers—but Elliott must be locked up in an asylum for "a term of years." If he did not go voluntarily, Theodore and Bamie would go to court in New York to have him declared mentally incompetent.

Elliott struck back. He would divorce his wife if she dared leave his side, he said, and would cut the children from his will. Finally in early June his "violence" caused Anna, then nearly nine months pregnant, to suffer what Bamie called an "hysterical attack." Bamie had him seized—"kidnapped," Elliott complained—and placed in the Chateau Suresne, a nearby asylum. But he did not stay there long. When Hall Roosevelt was born on June 28, Elliott was back at his wife's bedside. Theodore thought Anna's having sent for her husband markedly "foolish" and despaired at the legacy the new baby had inherited from his father, but perhaps Anna had hoped that being present at the birth of their third child might finally remind Elliott of how close they once had been, of how close they could be again if only he would reform.

If so, she was mistaken. He could no longer control himself, moaned that he was losing his mind, fended off the invisible demons of delirium tremens. This was the father to whom Eleanor returned from the convent. Yet all she remembered of this grisly time was that he had been momentarily kinder to her than her harassed, drained, preoccupied mother had been.

Anna and her children and Bamie returned to New York in August. Elliott remained behind, back in the Chateau Suresne. The Elliott Roosevelts would never again live together as a family.

Theodore and Bamie did go to court later that summer. Several New York dailies ran front-page stories headed ELLIOTT ROOSEVELT INSANE. Theodore's affidavit charged that his brother's unfortunate madness had been "produced or aggravated, to what extent could not be definitely told, by excessive alcoholism." Elliott denied the charge in a letter written from the asylum to the *New York Herald*. He was neither insane nor an alcoholic, he claimed, merely suffering from the effect upon his nervous system of too many riding mishaps. His brother and sister did not back down, however, and in January of 1892, Theodore traveled to Paris to confront him. The suit would be dropped and Anna would not seek a divorce provided Elliott returned to the United States at the end of his six months in the Chateau Suresne, underwent a five-week "cure" at a sanitarium for wealthy alcoholics run by a Dr. Keeley at Dwight, Illinois, then agreed to spend two full years of probation on his own and away from his wife and children. Elliott surrendered, Theodore wrote Bamie, "was utterly broken, submissive and repentant . . . and said he would do all in his power to prove himself really reformed. He was in a mood that was terribly touching. How long it will last of course no one can say."

It did not last long. Elliott made it through the Keeley cure because it was "Anna's wish," but then tried to renegotiate his probation so that he might be able to demonstrate his new-found steadiness "*in my family* with the aid and strengthening influence of Home." He was alternately repentant and angry now, and uniformly self-pitying. It was "wicked and foolish" to force him to endure this trial on his own, he said, but "the spirit in which I do what Anna demands is one of entire unselfishness and self-abnegation." His wife's resolution wavered momentarily, then held firm. Elliott could not come home; she missed him terribly, but neither she nor the children could endure another reconciliation that did not take.

Stung, Elliott now accused her of having a lover, charged that Hall had not been his child. Anna wearily forwarded his letter to Bamie—as she now routinely did with all her correspondence with her husband—along with a despairing note of her own: "His letter is certainly that of a madman. First he brings the most abominable charges against me. Then says I am a noble woman & he trusts me entirely. . . . I would like to write and tell him that he had to take back what he said in writing, or if he really thought it, to write and say with whom, when and where, so I could disprove his statements. . . . And yet his letter is so hopelessly sad . . . and yet I feel I ought not on his account pass this over again, nor on the child's."

Elliott settled in the small Virginia town of Abingdon, where he was to manage Douglas Robinson's sprawling mountain properties, and where no one had ever seen anyone quite like him. He took rooms first above a store and then in the home of a judge's elderly widow, who found him delightful. "He was the life of every party," a local newspaperman wrote many years later, without apparent irony and after interviewing elderly residents of the town. "The girls and young ladies were in the height of their glory when invited to drive with him behind his fast-stepping trotters." He kept a pack of hunting dogs and a stable of horses, organized winter coasting parties and after-dinner singalongs, and did trick riding, too, specializing in gallops across the railroad trestle west of town just ahead of oncoming trains. His responsibilities included the coalfields at Coeburn, sixty miles away across the mountains, and he was warmly remembered by the hill people at whose cabins he stopped along the way. He was fond of cold buttermilk, they recalled, and if he helped himself to some while they were not at home, he always left a shiny five-dollar gold piece on the kitchen table. Even the miners who worked for him liked him.[3]

Just as he had functioned best as a boy the farther he got from his father and older brother, so he was now doing better without responsibility for his wife and family. But he was embittered by his exile, and was drinking again whenever he was alone. One evening, drunk and naked, he knocked over a lamp and burned himself badly. Abingdon friends wrote to Theodore, suggesting he come down and try to "influence" his brother, but he refused. "It was absolutely useless," he said.

For several weeks that summer, Anna took her children to Bar Harbor, Maine, where as always her beauty attracted the attention of a number of men. She attended a "beauty dinner" at the cottage of the Turkish ambassador and was universally thought the most striking of all the guests. But she remained married, did not wish ever to overstep the bounds of propriety or do anything to encourage gossip. She consulted Bamie as to what she could and could not do. Might she, for example, go riding or rowing with a man—provided she never went again? It was "an awful temptation," she wrote, "when one feels desperately lonely and wildly furious with the world at large, not to make up one's mind to pay no attention to criticism as long as one does no wrong and to try to get some fun out of the few years of our youth. I hate everything and everyone and so am most of the time so miserable that I feel anything one could do would be a comfort to forget for one moment."

In the evenings at Bar Harbor, Eleanor sometimes lay in bed, pretending to be asleep, and listened to her mother and her aunts and uncles murmur anxiously about Elliott. "Something was wrong with my father," she concluded, "but from my point of view nothing could be wrong with him." Nor would anyone tell her exactly why it was that he was not with them. "If people only realized what a war goes on in a child's mind and heart in a situation of this kind," she wrote many years later, "I think they would try to explain more than they do to children."

But if she was unsure of the causes of the war, she had not a

3. When one old woman with whom he had often stayed was told some years later that Elliott's brother, Theodore, was now President, she replied that for that reason alone he deserved the job.

Source: Richmond Times Dispatch, February 24, 1935.

moment's doubt as to whose side she was on. Back in New York that autumn, Eleanor remained fearful, withdrawn, lonely. When she was taken to parties she burst into tears at being among "strange children." And, although Anna tried hard to provide reassurance she seemed as powerless to help Eleanor as she had been to aid Elliott. Even when she set aside what she called "mother's hour" each evening from six to seven to read to Eleanor and her brothers, the little girl felt "a curious barrier between myself and those three." Elliott, she remembered, was always angelic, "so good he never had to be reproved," and little Hall was content just to rest quietly on his mother's lap. Eleanor sat apart from the others on a footstool, gazing up into her mother's face, quiet, unsmiling, reproachful.

How much the barrier between them was of her own making, it is impossible now to judge. She did not understand what had gone wrong between her parents. Nor had she any idea of how hard her mother had struggled to keep the family together. All she knew was that her mother had now sent her father away. That knowledge bred a terrible anger, an anger apparently so frightening that she dared not express it openly. The result then (and throughout her life, whenever someone had angered or disappointed her) was aggrieved silence.[4]

Her anxious distracted mother knew something was seriously wrong between them and tried to give Eleanor special attention. It was she, not her younger brothers, who was allowed to sleep in her mother's bedroom. Anna made a point of reading aloud to her daily, and often kept Eleanor with her after mother's hour while the nurse put the boys to bed, but with her acute child's sensitivity the little girl sensed always that in doing these things for her, her mother was making "a great effort," and was all the more alienated. Her mother,

4. Mrs. Sherman, Elliott's mistress in Paris, had thought Theodore and Anna cruel to force him to leave France and undergo the Keeley cure. "How could they treat so noble and generous a man as they have," she wrote in her diary the day he left Paris for Illinois. "He is more noble a figure in my eyes than either his wife or brother. She is more to be despised, in her virtuous pride, her absolute selfish position than the most miserable woman I know, but she is the result of our unintelligent, petty, conventional social life. . . . If she were only large-souled enough to appreciate him." A year later, on the anniversary of his departure from her and only a few weeks after Anna died, she added a note in the margin: "I am sorry if these words seem cruel now, but death cannot alter the truth. January 28, 1893."

Some years later she sent this and three other brief entries from her diary having to do with Elliott to his sympathetic sister Corinne. Still later, Corinne evidently sent them on to Eleanor, who kept them carefully all her life in a little scrapbook labeled "For Anna's Children," which had been compiled by Grandmother Hall or one of Eleanor's aunts and was otherwise filled with affectionate tributes to her mother. Mrs. Sherman's views of Anna more accurately mirrored Eleanor's own.

Source: Anna Hall Roosevelt Papers, FDRL.

she once wrote with cold precision, was both "kindly and indifferent."

Only once in all her writings did Eleanor Roosevelt recall an instance in which she displayed her rage at her mother in front of others, and then she did it so indirectly that neither she nor her mother was sure just what had happened. When the little family first returned from Europe, Eleanor's Great-Aunt Maggie Ludlow, whose house stood next door to Oak Terrace at Tivoli, was horrified to learn that in their desperate flights in search of a cure for Elliott's afflictions, her grand-niece's parents had ignored the child's education. At seven, Eleanor could neither read nor write well, nor could she cook or sew. Mrs. Ludlow, who was "very handsome, very sure of herself," Eleanor recalled, rebuked Anna for what she said was her irresponsibility and directed her own companion, an Alsatian seamstress named Madeleine, to move in and make up for lost time.

The next fall, Anna herself sought a more systematic solution to the problem. She moved into a new house at Sixty-first and Madison, transformed a room on its top floor into a schoolroom, hired Frederic Roser, a fashionable schoolmaster, and his female assistant, and invited the daughters of seven friends to share Eleanor's lessons. Anna came to the class the first day and seated herself in the back of the room. So did the mothers of several of the other girls. Eleanor was asked to stand and spell a series of words no more complex than "horse," words she already knew perfectly well. She suddenly seemed unable to spell even the simplest of them. She stammered, started over, lapsed into silence, and was asked finally to resume her seat. "I was always disgracing my mother," Eleanor remembered later. "She took me aside afterwards and told me seriously that she wondered what would happen if I did not mend my ways!" Eleanor blamed her own otherwise inexplicable failure on her shyness, and perhaps that was all it had been. But no more dramatic tableau could have been staged to point up publicly what she saw as her mother's neglect of her.

Eleanor Roosevelt's autobiography does include one revealing instance of closeness with her mother during their brief time together. In New York that winter Anna suffered from shattering headaches, so painful and so unrelenting that she spent hours in bed with the curtains drawn until they passed. Eleanor would sit with her silently in the dark, stroking her head. "People have since told me that I have good hands for rubbing," she wrote, "and perhaps even as a child there was something soothing in my touch, for she was willing to let me sit there for hours on end. The feeling that I was useful was perhaps the greatest joy I experienced."

That would be true all her life. To be useful was to feel that she belonged to somebody; if she could not be loved, she could be needed.

In October of 1892, just six weeks after moving into her new home, Anna underwent surgery for some unknown malady. Yet again, Eleanor was sent away during a family crisis, first to the Gracies' (where she celebrated her eighth birthday), and then to Oak Terrace.

Elliott begged to be allowed to visit Anna. His mother-in-law refused to permit it. Corinne, who had been the most sympathetic of his siblings and was therefore the one he now trusted most, was designated to tell him why. When Anna went under the ether, Corinne explained, she had cried out that she no longer had the desire to live; life with Elliott had become unbearable. Elliott wrote back directly to Mrs. Hall: "Did she say she wanted to die, that I had made her so utterly miserable that she did not care to live any more? And did you say that was what your poor child had been suffering in silence all these past killing months? . . . I have no excuse to offer. I am certainly not crazy. I have tried to do right. . . . Know, Mrs. Hall, that for all the suffering I have caused I have suffered ten-fold more myself. For it was *I* who sinned and *I* know it, and I had none of the Divine comfort of being able to *grant forgiveness.*"

Anna seemed to rally after the operation, then contracted diphtheria. Again Elliott pleaded to be permitted to come: "I ought to be with her unless my presence is *actually distasteful* to her." It was. Anna had her mother wire back, "Do not come." By now Elliott was consumed only with his own plight. His wife's illness was forgotten. "Oh, Mrs. Hall," he wrote, "I have been so much alone. . . . My nature is really starved for love." He could not understand why Anna said she *feared* him. "Before God, I say it, I am honestly worthy of her trust and love —for even in my drinking I never did a *dishonorable* thing, nor *one cruel act* towards my wife and children."

But most of his married life had been a cruel act, even if he had been genuinely helpless to make it otherwise, and Mrs. Hall did not relent. Anna died on December seventh without seeing her husband again. He hurried north as soon as he got the news and wept at the sight of his wife in her coffin, still lovely in a pale pink wrapper, white lace gathered at her wrists and throat.[5] She had left the children in the care of her mother in her will, but both the Halls and Roosevelts now worried that Elliott might sue for his children in court or even resort to kidnapping. Theodore's second wife, Edith Carow, suggested that a good nurse be hired right away for Elliott, Jr., and for Hall, so that if Elliott insisted "on taking the little boys to Virginia . . . at this age they cannot come to much harm. . . . I cannot help feeling he would tire of them in a short time." Eleanor presented a more delicate problem. She was old enough to be permanently affected by being around the women "of very doubtful character" with whom Edith believed Elliott continued to surround himself. She should be sent off immediately to boarding school: "I do really think if anything . . . can be done for Eleanor it will be by a good school. I do not feel she has much chance, poor little soul."

Neither family need have worried. Elliott was no longer able to be consistent even in his grief or his yearning for his children. At a ghastly Christmas dinner at Eleanor's Aunt Tissie's he appalled the other guests by breaking into jubilant song. He had been "gay as a butterfly," Bamie told Theodore, "drinking and singing all the comic songs." He did not contest his wife's will.

"I can remember standing by a window when Cousin Susy [Parish] told me that my mother was dead," Eleanor wrote. "She was very sweet to me, and I must have known that something terrible had happened." She "must have known," yet her initial reaction was not of her own loss but of "the one fact [that] wiped out everything else—my father was back and I would see him very soon." Her thoughts were all of him, of how her mother's death would affect him, and of how she would now be able to comfort him in his sorrow. It had been "a tragedy of utter defeat for him. No hope now of ever wiping out the sorrowful years he had brought upon my mother—and she had left her mother as guardian for her children. . . . He had no wife, no children, no hope!"

The new house was sold, Eleanor, her brothers, and their belongings were moved to Grandmother Hall's narrow brownstone on West Thirty-seventh Street. "After we were installed my father came to see

5. She was just twenty-nine. Her death was only a slight disturbance on the surface of the New York society in which she had played so prominent a part. A society columnist noted: "It had been thought that the sad death of young Mrs. Elliott Roosevelt who, had she lived, would have been one of the patronesses, would have greatly dimmed the brilliance of the [ball at Sherry's], but New York is a large town and 'we are soon forgot,' so that the absence of the few who stayed away was hardly noticed."

Source: Anna Hall Roosevelt Papers, FDRL.

me," Eleanor wrote, "and I remember going down into the high ceilinged dim library. . . . He sat in a big chair. He was dressed all in black, looking very sad. He held out his arms and gathered me to him. In a little while he began to talk, to explain to me that my mother was gone, that she had been all the world to him, and now he had only my brothers and myself, that my brothers were very young, and that he and I must keep close together. Some day I would make a home for him again; we would travel together and do many things which he painted as interesting and pleasant, to be looked forward to in the future together.

"Somehow it was always he and I. I did not understand whether my brothers were to be our children or whether he felt that they would be at school and college and later independent.

"There started that day a feeling which never left me—that he and I were very close together, and some day, would have a life of our own together. He told me to write to him often, not to give any trouble, to study hard, to grow up into a woman he could be proud of.

"When he left, I was all alone to keep our secret of mutual understanding and to adjust myself to my new existence."

Later, she would add that she had made herself "as the years went on into a fairly good copy of the picture he had painted," so that she might be ready when "the wonderful day came" when she and her father would "fare forth together." But of course that day never came.

He wrote to her regularly from Virginia at first, long emotional letters addressed to "Father's Own Little Nell" and filled with exhortations to study hard and learn the discipline he so conspicuously lacked so that "Then! Oh, my pretty companionable Little Daughter, you will come to Father and what games we will have together to be sure." He told her of his horses, of his six dogs—"Fox terriers Mr. Belmont gave me (to comfort me in my loneliness)"—and of the other little girls he now saw regularly while Eleanor could not see him at all. She must not be jealous of them, he said, for "No other little girl can ever take your place in my heart."

On Easter Sunday in 1893, he told her he had "*thought of you all day long,*" then went on, with a cruelty no less searing for being unconscious, to talk of "Little Miriam . . . who every night comes into my room and I do so often wish it were . . . you." The fields, he continued, "are covered with a soft mat of thick blue grass and painted by the most lovely blue and white violets. . . . They smell so sweet.

Just like your sweet little self when I pick you up and bury my face in those soft baby cheeks." Eleanor kept his letters all her life.

Later that spring, both of Eleanor's brothers came down with scarlet fever. Eleanor was immediately sent out of harm's way to stay with the Ludlows at their summer home in Newport. Hall recovered. Elliott, Jr., developed diphtheria and did not. Their father raced north again, this time to find his eldest son dying. He wired Eleanor that "dear little Ellie" would not live. She wrote back, trying at age eight to offer grown-up solace to her father: "We must remember that Ellie is going to be safe in heaven and to be with Mother who is waiting there and our Lord wants Ellie with him now, we must be happy and do God's will and we must cheer others who feel it too."

"My little brother Ellie was simply too good for this world," Eleanor wrote many years later; the unspoken corollary of that belief was that she herself was not so good. Perhaps she saw in her brother's early death still another instance of her own failings; as her dead mother's surrogate she should somehow have been able to prevent it. She would later almost desperately seek to serve as a mother to Hall, to make him feel "as if he belonged to somebody," she said.

Elliott's unreliability now increased. He wrote less often and when he did, seemed to take unconscious pleasure in describing the fun he had with other children. He rode each morning with six of them, he told Eleanor, "over these broad fields for one or two hours; we . . . never fail to return without roses in the cheeks of those I now call my children. Do you continue to ride? Learn the right way so that I will not have to teach you all over again." He also arranged to have the two children of Mrs. Sherman write letters to Eleanor, carefully explaining that their mother had been his "good friend" in Paris in what seems clearly to have been a way of getting back at his unforgiving mother-in-law. And he repeatedly failed to visit when he had promised to do so. Eleanor never let her faith in him weaken. Between visits she memorized verse with which she hoped to please him, learning all of "Hiawatha" because he once said he liked it. Gifts sometimes arrived from him—a puppy, a kitten, a pony the week her brother died. Small tokens for the most part, but enough so that later she would write that her father "had loved to give and tried always to find just the thing which would rejoice the heart of the one receiving his gift. You always felt surrounded by his thought and love."

She was as eager to see him as she had been when she was an infant. But when he did turn up things did not always go well, though

Eleanor did her best every time to be worthy of his time and interest. She was sure he thought her a coward—he had told her so—knew that she must never again betray her fear as she had after the long-ago disaster at sea; otherwise he might not come back at all. He arrived to take her driving one afternoon, and as he urged his favorite hunter, Mohawk, up Madison Avenue, the horse was startled by a streetcar, reared, and plunged. Her father lost his silk hat getting him under control again, and while a policeman dusted off the hat and brought it to him, he turned to Eleanor and asked, "You weren't afraid, were you, Little Nell?" She swore she had not been. Later, in Central Park and impatient at finding himself at the tail end of a long line of slow-moving carriages, he laughed and told her, "If I were to say 'hoopla' to Mohawk he would try to jump them all." Eleanor smiled as if enchanted by the idea, but "inwardly I prayed that he would do nothing of the kind. In spite of my abject terror, these drives were the high point of my existence."

Another time, out for a walk with Eleanor and three of his cherished terriers, he was evidently overcome with the need for a drink. He stopped in front of the Knickerbocker Club, handed Eleanor the dogs' leashes and told her to wait with the doorman, then hurried inside. He did not return for six hours, or so Eleanor remembered, and when he did he emerged unconscious, helped into a passing cab by the porters. The doorman sent Eleanor home in another.

After that, even brief visits were discouraged by Grandmother Hall. That fall, Elliott began slipping in and out of New York without telling anyone, then moved there permanently, picking up his mail at the Knickerbocker Club but actually living in a rented uptown house under the name of Maxwell Eliot with only his valet and another mistress, a Mrs. Evans, for company.[6] Though Eleanor's father now lived less than three miles away, she saw him only rarely. He wrote confused letters and telegrams to his brother and sisters, alternately chiding them and asking forgiveness, then refusing to see them when they responded. He once took Mrs. Evans with him to the Boone and Crockett Club and had her sign the visitors' book as "Mrs. Maxwell

6. During the last months of his life, Elliott seems to have had two mistresses—Mrs. Evans in New York and his friend from Paris, Mrs. Sherman, who evidently spent the summer on the Massachusetts coast in part to be near him. Mrs. Sherman kept up a correspondence about Elliott with Corinne Robinson for some years. The Roosevelts would eventually provide a cash stipend for Mrs. Evans, its sum increased after *Mr.* Evans appeared in the family lawyer's office waving a loaded revolver.

Source: TR to Bamie, August 25, 1894; Theodore Roosevelt Collection, Houghton Library, Harvard.

Eliot"—an instance, his embarrassed brother told Bamie, of "the queer low cunning which runs through Elliott's most insane or foolish moments. A nice man, our brother."

Elliott was drinking from half a dozen bottles of alcohol each morning, according to Theodore: anisette and brandy, champagne and crème de menthe, anything that would blur his anxieties, ease the mysterious frenzy that now made it impossible for him to sit still for more than a few minutes at a time. In May he spent the night in a police lockup, having been too drunk to pay his cabman or tell him where he lived. In July he drove into a lamppost while drunk, was thrown from his carriage, and injured his head. "Poor fellow!" Theodore wrote. "If only he could have died instead of Anna!" There was nothing anyone could do, he said. "He can't be helped, and he must simply be let go his own gait."

On August 13, 1894, still suffering from the effects of his carriage accident and confused by delirium tremens, Eleanor's father tried to climb out an upper-story window of his house on 102nd Street, raced hysterically up and down the stairs, fell back into a final shuddering seizure, and lost consciousness.

He died the next day. Eleanor's aunts Maud and Pussie together told her he was dead. She said, "I did want to see father once more," and cried herself to sleep that night. But in her heart she refused to believe it. Her father had so often been away; surely he had not now left her forever. "I finally went to sleep," she remembered, "and began the next day living in my dream world as usual. . . . From that time on I . . . lived with him more closely, probably, than I had when he was alive."

A few years later, Eleanor wrote a composition in a little notebook given to her by her Aunt Pussie. It shows how powerful the pull of her father's memory was for her; how deep the sense of betrayal it left:

> She had waited so long, so long. One night she awoke. Someone was whispering in her ear. Suddenly the room seemed to be filled by millions of shadowy forms who whispered to her, "He has broken his word. He has broken his word." She could stand it no longer & she cried out in the dark "Oh my father come" & a voice answered "I am here" & he stood beside her & his cool hand lay on her hot head. She clasped it in both of hers & sighed contentedly. "Oh I knew you must come" but he answered, "I have kept my word I have come back I must go away again," & the

child cried out "Oh! take me with you I have waited so long & it has been so hard I cannot stay alone." He bent down and kissed her & she fell asleep. The next morning the people who had never understood came in & looked pityingly at her lying cold & dead & they said "poor child to die so young (how sad)" & a few tears were shed & then she like all those who have ceased to move in this earthly sphere sank into oblivion.[7]

Through all his sad wanderings, Elliott Roosevelt had carried with him the small leather-bound Bible from which he had once read to Anna Hall. His daughter inherited it, and kept it always at her bedside. Sometime during the final months of her own long life, seventy-seven years old and staying at Val-Kill, the little house she and two friends had built for themselves a mile or so east of Springwood, she showed the battered testament to a young friend who was both a bibliophile and an Episcopal priest and asked him how it might be repaired. The binding had split; the pages had torn loose from the spine. He told her where to go to have the work done, but she did not seem satisfied. Something else was troubling her. She didn't know whether he was aware of it, she said suddenly, but her father had died in circumstances which, in strict religious terms, might not be thought morally correct. "Do you think it's possible," she asked, "that because of that I won't see him? Do you think it could be a bar to his being in heaven?"

The young priest did his best to reassure her. "*I* couldn't keep him out for that," he said, "and God must be much more generous than I am or none of us stands a chance there."

She smiled. She would be reunited with her father at last.[8]

7. A second essay recreates the moment when her father told her she could not come to live with him after her mother died: "A child stood at a window watching a man walking down the street, the little face was white and set & the big tears stood in the brown eyes but the mouth smiled till the man was out of sight. . . . Her father [was] the only person in the world she loved. Others called her hard & cold but to him she was everything lavishing on him all the quiet love which the others could not understand. . . . He never knew what that smile cost . . . a time came when there were no more letters & a grown up person told the child that her Father was dead, but the child did not cry. Dead people did not come back & her Father had promised to come & she could not bear to hear him spoken of as dead but at last she grew accustomed to it, they were making a mistake but what was the difference? The years went by & she still believed, but doubts came sometimes now."

Source: Lash, *Eleanor and Franklin,* page 729.

8. She never tired of talking about her father; never gave up trying to persuade friends and family of his virtues or making small gestures in his memory. In 1930, she wrote to thank her Aunt Corinne for having given a bed in her father's name to an old soldiers' home: "I always do some little thing on his birthday which I think he would have liked to do. I remember so many things he did when I was little, not only for me and they were always a little different from the way other people did them!" Three years later, she published *Hunting Big Game in the Eighties,* a collection of Elliott's letters "Edited by his Daughter Anna Eleanor Roosevelt," in part so that his grandchildren could get some firsthand sense of his charm and vivacity. *This Is My Story,* the

The confused legacy of her parents marked Eleanor Roosevelt's whole life. Her anger at her preoccupied mother was barely contained, and Anna Roosevelt's early death had barred forever the sort of reconciliation between them that might have come about had Eleanor ever understood her father's weaknesses, or seen that her mother's devotion to her husband had been very nearly as powerful as her own; Anna, too, had been desperate to hold fast. But as it was, Eleanor remembered most her mother's severity and distance and that, in turn, equipped her poorly for being a nurturing mother to her own children.[9]

The impact of her father's memory was still more complicated. Her idolization of him—her wish to have even her grandchildren think of him only as a "kind and loving and charming personality"—was both a source of great strength and of dangerous weakness. It left her determined always to embody those qualities he urged most strongly upon her—"unselfishness, generosity, loving tenderness, and cheerfulness." But there was in her, too, however deeply buried, great anger at the man who broke so many promises, failed to come for her, finally abandoned her through death. That anger helped distort her perception of people, made her tend to exaggerate their virtues at first, and to be inordinately disappointed later when, inevitably, they failed to act as she had dreamed they would.

From the sad lives of both her parents she learned, too, that no one's

---

first volume of her autobiography, published four years later, is dedicated "to the memory of my Father who fired a child's imagination."

After her mother died, Elliott had presented a big pulpit Bible to the Abingdon Episcopal Church in her memory; when it was destroyed in a fire, Eleanor replaced it with another, inscribed by her to both her parents.

In a letter to Corinne from India in 1881, Elliott had written a rhapsodic description of the Taj Mahal by moonlight: "The huge white dome in the quiet soft shadows is . . . breathlessly beautiful [in] the intense quiet of an eastern night. The stars and moon casting it seems all their light on this huge pearl of purity surrounded by the black shadows of the river. . . . I have no words for it all." And he had later promised Eleanor that he would one day take her to see it. She visited India on her own in 1952 and insisted on taking time out from her usual frenzied schedule to realize at least part of that old dream, sitting alone in the moonlight on the same carved marble bench on which her young father had sat seventy years before. She had prepared herself to be disappointed, a friend recalled, but she was not. The Taj Mahal was all Elliott Roosevelt had said it was.

Sources: Roosevelt Family Papers Donated by the Children, FDRL; *Richmond Times Dispatch,* February 25, 1935; A. David Gurewitsch, *Eleanor Roosevelt: Her Day,* page 96.

9. The memories of Anna Roosevelt, Eleanor's daughter, seem an eerily faithful replication of her mother's memories of Anna Hall. "She [Eleanor] felt a tremendous sense of duty to us," Anna said. "It was part of that duty to read to us and to hear our prayers before we went to bed, but she did not understand or satisfy the need of a child for primary closeness to a parent." Eleanor herself more or less agreed: "I was certainly not an ideal mother. It did not come naturally to me to understand little children or to enjoy them. Playing with children was difficult for me because play had not been an important part of my own childhood."

Source: Both quoted in Lash, *Eleanor and Franklin,* page 198.

love for her was likely to last, that those upon whom she counted most would let her down.

Eleanor spent the next five years with her Grandmother Hall, who always seemed to her "a very old lady" though she was not, at least in years. She had aged prematurely from having coped alone for so long with the temperament and eccentricities of her troubled children: not just poor Anna, but Pussie, who experienced a series of tempestuous but unsuccessful love affairs, and Eddie and Vallie, who each tried business and marriage, eventually failed at both, and returned home to live and drink. Grandmother Hall spent most of each day in her room, coming downstairs only to greet her infrequent visitors, and to conduct prayer services morning and evening "to which . . . every servant and even the coachman was expected to come." She seemed "exhausted," Corinne Robinson Alsop wrote, and "when she had to take [in] two forlorn little [grand] children, she was incapable of giving them anything but a meagre, weary, left-over love."

That severely qualified love usually took the form of discipline. Blaming herself for having failed to control her own offspring, she was now determined to maintain a firm hold on her grandchildren. "We were brought up on the principle that 'no' was easier to say than 'yes,' " Eleanor remembered, and that sense of austere decorum pervaded the house on West Thirty-seventh Street. Young Corinne Robinson was fond of Eleanor, but never wanted to visit her there—had to be "sent" by her mother, she said—because it was so grim. A single flickering gas jet lit the narrow front hall. There was a dimly lit drawing room, formal and uninviting, and a second still darker parlor, and beyond that "a frigid looking dining room where we had our supper in solemn silence as we were all affected by the unbroken gloom. There was no place to play games."

Eleanor continued to attend Roser classes, held now not in her own home but in that of one of her seven classmates. The curriculum was haphazard. "Bits of poetry, dabs of Greek and Roman history, a very superficial variety of English," Corinne remembered, "and nothing else." And when Mr. Roser himself took the class, the teaching was farcical. He wore always a Prince Albert coat, pulled importantly at his side-whiskers while murmuring, "Young ladies, young ladies," and was utterly without humor. "There is a distinction between reasonable and unreasonable merriment," he often said when one of the girls could not contain her laughter, and the distinction seemed to be that the former did not exist. Eleanor was a sober, diligent student, nonetheless, especially fond of poetry and of writing short stories whose heroes and heroines were often lonely children who "yearned most for love."

She also studied French and each week endured the fashionable Dodsworth dancing classes. Corinne remembered them, too. The girls left their coats and little fur-lined shoes downstairs, changed into dancing shoes, then climbed the stairs to the studio itself, where they curtseyed to Mrs. Dodsworth, "whose hair had the stiffest ondulé, whose voice had the most liquid modulation, and whose person was sheathed in a dress covered with spangles or embroidered with pearls. . . . She sat at a painted Louis XIV desk with a register to mark our attendance which she did with a fine pen, holding her little finger slightly extended while she wrote." It was Mr. Dodsworth who gravely explained the mysteries of the waltz and gavotte, two-step and polka to the children. He was, Corinne wrote, "the impersonation of elegance and etiquette coupled with a stinging sarcasm and discipline."

The Dodsworth classes were special agony for Eleanor. She was tall for her age, shy and thin and awkward, and she was dressed oddly. "My grandmother believed in keeping me young," she once explained, and insisted that she wear "dresses that were above my knees when most of the girls my size had them halfway down their legs." The other girls would have laughed aloud had they not thought her so sad.

She preferred the summers she spent at Oak Terrace. Like Franklin, Eleanor continued to spend much of her childhood without the companionship of children her own age. A school friend who lived just five miles from Oak Terrace was allowed to visit her for just one day each summer, and Eleanor was permitted to repay the visit, also for a single day. Unlike Franklin, she had precious little compensatory attention or approval from the adults close to her, though her uncle Vallie did show her how to jump her pony and she sometimes rowed to town before breakfast with her Aunt Pussie to pick up the mail.

Her only companion most of the summer was Hall, six years younger, for whom she tried to be more mother than sister, calling him "the kid" and writing to him regularly whenever they were apart. They climbed together around the third-floor gutters of the big house and got caught, watched the laundress wash and iron their aunts' voluminous petticoats, trapped tadpoles in the pond. But most of the time Eleanor read, sitting beneath the big trees on the lawn or in the attic or in a corner of the library, where she tried not to look too long at the turbulent Doré illustrations that both fascinated and frightened her in her grandfather's massive Bible. She enjoyed the quiet at Tivoli especially, because it allowed her to live without interruption in her dream world "in which I was the heroine and my father the hero." That dream sustained her day and night; she retreated into it contentedly whenever she was out walking, she remembered, "or when anyone bored me."

Yet Tivoli may also have been the scene of a still darker passage in her stunted childhood. Madeleine, the French-speaking companion her Great-Aunt Maggie had assigned to her in 1891, remained with her daily for nearly seven years, while caring for Hall—whom she much preferred—as well. Eleanor never liked her, was in fact "desperately afraid of her" all that time, though she could never in later years remember precisely why. She did recall that Madeleine was a demanding teacher. When Eleanor's darning did not suit her, she would take scissors and snip it all out, leaving her pupil a big round hole to fill in all over again. And she was rigid about the rules Grandmother Hall laid down: no reading in bed before breakfast; no novels on Sundays; to bed precisely on time each evening. When, as often happened, Eleanor slid down the steep mossy roof of the ice house and smeared her white drawers with green, she always "told my grandmother before I went to Madeleine, knowing that both of them would scold me, but that my grandmother would scold me less severely." She also recalled that Madeleine "did not like to be disturbed in the evenings, and yet she had to do my hair when I came to bed, and if I was a few minutes late I not only got a scolding, but my hair was unmercifully pulled."

Still, Eleanor sensed that had not been all of it. "Madeleine caused me many tears," her former charge wrote, in what seems to have been genuine bewilderment over the reasons for them, but "I have no recollection of why she really frightened me." It was a mystery best forgotten, she concluded. "How silly it all seems today, and how hard to understand the workings of a child's mind!" But if she remembered Madeleine's petty cruelties, what else was it that had been so terrible that her conscious mind could not later summon it up? Had there been more physical abuse than mere hair-pulling? Might there have been an element of molestation in it, something that might help account for her later deep ambivalence about sex? No one will ever know. But whatever it was, it impelled her finally, at thirteen and on the edge of adolescence, to tell her grandmother about it as they walked together in the woods. She could not stop her own sobbing as she "confessed" it, she remembered, and whatever it was, it compelled her grandmother instantly to send Madeleine back to Mrs. Ludlow and replace her with one of her own maids.

Contact with her father's ebullient clamorous family was sharply curtailed, Grandmother Hall, who had always been a little scornful of the Roosevelts for being "in trade," perhaps also believing that Elliott's brother and sisters had somehow been partly to blame for her daughter's tragedy.[10] Even visits with Eleanor's gentle, fond Auntie Gracie were forbidden. She did manage at least one visit to her Uncle Ted's boisterous clan at Sagamore Hill. The contrast with her own isolated life could not have been more dramatic. There were as many as sixteen cousins on hand. Uncle Ted greeted her with almost frightening enthusiasm. "Eleanor, my darling Eleanor," he shouted, hugging her to him with such vigor, his wife noted, "that he tore all the gathers out of Eleanor's frock and both buttonholes out of her petticoat."

During the next day and a half, she tried her best to keep up with the others as Uncle Ted led them on obstacle races or pellmell down the same steep dune that had so impressed Franklin on his boyhood visits, "desperately afraid," she remembered, but resolutely not showing it.

Alice Roosevelt was her closest cousin in age but not in temperament. She, too, had in a sense lost her parents—her mother just hours after her birth, her father when he remarried and had five more children. Her resentment of her stepmother was deep (and reciprocated), and she responded to what she saw as her father's abandonment entirely differently from the way Eleanor had reacted to her own loss. Alice became boisterous, self-dramatizing, a leader in boys' games—she took special pride in such unladylike feats as placing both feet behind her head—and apt at any moment to lash out in caustic anger. Both girls were frightened of swimming and slow to learn. Each left a record of the same sunny afternoon on the Oyster Bay waterfront as Theodore sought to get them both accustomed to the water. Alice stood weeping on the dock, she remembered. "I can see my father shouting to me from the water, 'Dive, Alicy, dive.' " Although she wanted to please him, he seemed "a sea monster to her" then, she said,

10. This evidently suited Uncle Ted's wife, Edith. "Anna's children are with Mrs. Hall, still at Tivoli," she wrote shortly after Elliott's death. "I believe they are very well, but as you know I never wished Alice to associate with Eleanor so shall not try to keep up any friendship between them."

Source: Quoted in Lash, *Love, Eleanor,* page 25.

"flailing away in the water, peering nearsightedly at me without glasses and with his moustache glistening wet." She finally jumped in, but before she did "I cried. I snarled. I hated."

Eleanor, whose own fear of the water had been born when the *Britannic* seemed doomed, and was far greater than Alice's, did not even protest. "She was always so fine about that sort of thing," Alice said. She dove in to satisfy her uncle and sank right to the bottom. When she finally came up gasping, another cousin playfully pushed her under again. She had been "very much frightened," she wrote later, and "never again would I go out of my depth." But no one was allowed to know it; no one must ever see that "I was a good deal of a physical coward."[11]

"Poor little soul, she is very plain," her Aunt Edith wrote to Bamie after this visit. "Her mouth and teeth seem to have no future. But the ugly duckling may turn out to be a swan." Even that qualified optimism seemed unjustified that December, when Eleanor was permitted to attend her Aunt Corinne's Christmas party. This annual event was always "more pain than pleasure" to Eleanor because "the others all knew each other very well and saw each other often." There was coasting (which she only rarely dared attempt) and skating (at which she was poor), and the climax was a formal dance to which she again had to wear a short little girl's dress while all her contemporaries came dressed as young ladies. Miserable on the sidelines, struggling to stretch her dress as far down over her knees as she could, she watched as Alice in her long gown danced with her handsome sixteen-year-old cousin, Franklin Roosevelt of Hyde Park. When the music ended,

11. She did not dare even try to swim after that until 1922, when she was herself a mother, her husband's illness had curtailed his own swimming, and she wanted to be able to watch over her own children in safety as they swam. Diving took much longer—until the summer of 1939, in fact, when she was fifty-five years old and took lessons from Dorothy Dow, a junior member of her White House staff. "Finally she could dive," Dow wrote that summer, "not only from the side of the pool but from the diving board as well. She was anxious to perform for the President, as he said he didn't believe she could do it. One day he drove over from the Big House [Springwood] to Val-Kill [Eleanor's own nearby cottage], and sat at the edge of the pool. I sat down on the grass beside him, and he said, 'I understand that you are the one who taught her all this.' I acknowledged the fact. So, Mrs. R. walked out on the board, got all set in the proper form and went in flat as could be. She could have been heard down at Poughkeepsie! I thought the President would explode laughing, and his hand came down on my shoulder so hard I almost fell over. Mrs. R. came up red in the face, with a really grim expression, said nothing, walked out on the board again, and did a perfect dive. We all gave her a big hand, and she was pretty proud of her accomplishment—which she certainly should have been." She never learned to like diving, but after that summer, whenever it was warm enough, she made a point of plunging into her pool once a day because, she said, "it is good for my character."

Sources: Ruth K. McClure (editor), *Eleanor Roosevelt, An Eager Spirit: The Letters of Dorothy Dow 1933–1945*, page 104; Lash, *Eleanor Roosevelt: The Years Alone*, page 173.

Alice whispered in his ear. He looked toward Eleanor, squared his shoulders, and came toward her. Would she care to dance with him? She never forgot his gallantry.

At fifteen, Eleanor was again sent away, this time to finishing school in England. But this exile was different from the others. The three years she would spend at Allenswood, not far from London, were "the happiest of my life."

We cannot be sure precisely why she was suddenly sent abroad. In *This Is My Story*, Eleanor would write that her grandfather had felt that the Hall household now had "too much gaiety for a girl of fifteen," her tactful way of saying that the unpredictability of Uncle Vallie's behavior now that he was drinking steadily, and the emotional turmoil that inevitably accompanied each of her Aunt Pussie's failed romances, had been thought bad for her. Then, too, toward the end of her life, Eleanor's mother had told friends that she greatly regretted her own lack of "systematic knowledge" and hoped to do better by her children. Perhaps her grandmother's exhaustion played a part in the decision as well. By sending one of her two grandchildren into someone else's care, her own burdens would be eased at least a little.

Allenswood was chosen because Bamie Roosevelt—Eleanor's beloved "Auntie Bye"—had attended its predecessor school in France. Its headmistress, Mademoiselle Marie Souvestre, would become one of the most important persons in Eleanor's life; only her father—or, rather, her child's memory of her father—had more impact upon her.

A former pupil remembered her first sight of Mademoiselle Souvestre some twenty years before Eleanor entered her school. Her face was "rather broad," she wrote, "a low forehead, dark hair with a thread or two of grey in it, parted in the middle, gently waving on the temples and gathered up into a bunch of curls at the back of her head. A curious kind of hairdressing which I have never seen except in pictures or statues. The features were regular, clearly cut . . . nose, lips and chin fine and firm. The eyes were grey, sometimes clear and translucid, sometimes dark, impenetrable, burning." She was now seventy, stout and short, her head seemingly too large for her body. But her hair was still drawn back in the classic manner (though it had turned entirely white), and her gray eyes were still keenly interested in everything that went on around her. They "looked through you," Eleanor remembered; "she always knew more than she was told."

She looked kindly from the first upon the tall, slender, diffident American girl who arrived at Allenswood in September of 1899 in the company of her Aunt Tissie—her mother's sister, now Mrs. Stanley Mortimer—and bringing with her all of her letters from her father in a bundle tied with ribbon. Mademoiselle Souvestre may have been predisposed to like her; she had been fond of Aunt Bamie, had known both of Eleanor's dead parents, and had lost her own father at an early age. And she must have been delighted to have a new student whose French was so effortless; all conversations and all classes at Allenswood were conducted in that language.

But it was more than that. Although Eleanor was not aware of it, her grandmother and one or two of her aunts had written to Mademoiselle Souvestre before she arrived, telling her of the child's troubled past and expressing their worries for the future. She was a good girl, they said, but fearful and sadly unattractive, sometimes untruthful—or, rather, afraid sometimes to tell the truth—easily swayed by others, subject to headaches and sleeplessness.

The headmistress absorbed all this, but sensed as well the reserves of strength within her new pupil, strengths which her relatives had overlooked in their remote solicitude and which she would now work hard to bring out. There were some thirty-five girls at Allenswood; the newcomer was assigned the place of honor across from Mademoiselle Souvestre at the dining table.

To sit there, an earlier student remembered, "was an education in itself." Mademoiselle Souvestre was witty, her speech darting "here and there with the agility and grace of a hummingbird . . . No one was safe, and if one laughed with her, one was liable the next minute to be pierced oneself with a shaft of irony. . . . But her talk was not all epigrams. One felt it informed by that infection of ardour, that enlivening zest, which were the secrets of her success as a schoolmistress. There was nothing in which she could not infuse them. . . . The dullest of her girls was stirred into some sort of life in her presence, to the intelligent she communicated a Promethean fire which warmed and coloured their whole lives."

But her interest in Eleanor went well beyond intellectual stimulation; that she provided to all her girls receptive enough to benefit by it. Toward Eleanor she seems to have felt from the first a special sense of affection and responsibility—she herself characterized her feelings toward her as "maternal"—and in time she quietly saw to it that the girl's outdated clothes were replaced by modish ones from Paris, and even did her best to inculcate in her some of her own Gallic sense of irony and amusement.[12]

This marked the first time since her infancy that any adult had been truly interested in Eleanor for herself. Her father's early and uncritical affection and encouragement had given her a sense of her own worth that everything that happened to her since had seemed calculated to extinguish; Mademoiselle Souvestre rekindled it. The results could be seen almost instantly.

Eleanor's life at Allenswood was in its way as Spartan and regimented as Franklin's had been at Groton. All the girls wore uniforms—straw hats, striped school ties, shirtwaists, and long skirts; each girl was permitted just three ten-minute baths a week; even bureau drawers were opened and inspected for neatness; the heat in the old buildings was so weak, Eleanor remembered, that "one had positively to sit on the radiator to feel any warmth," and many of the girls developed chilblains.

She did not. In fact she could not remember ever having been ill at Allenswood, even for a day. She slept soundly, had no more headaches. Everything about life at the school seemed to please her. At Allenswood, she wrote later, "I felt that I was starting a new life, free from all my former sins and traditions . . . this was the first time in all my life that all my fears left me. If I lived up to the rules and told the truth, there was nothing to fear."

Among the Halls and the fashionable young people she had known in New York, where a premium was always placed on looks and vivacity and convention, she had felt inadequate, lost. But at Allenswood, where friendship, loyalty, and intellect took precedence, she shone. Her three years there would teach her that there were ways in which she could be a success.

She did well even at sports, and made the first field hockey team, "one of the proudest moments of my life."[13] Unlike Endicott Peabody,

12. In this last effort she knew she had not entirely succeeded. After Eleanor left Allenswood, Mademoiselle Souvestre often spoke of her with her younger cousin, Corinne Robinson. "*Chère Tottie,*" she would say with obvious affection (using the pet name used by Eleanor's aunts), and then, shrugging helplessly, "*mais pas gaie, pas gaie.*"

A friend who knew Eleanor Roosevelt intimately during her last years recalled that "she enjoyed humor and loved to laugh. But she never made a joke—at least as far as I know."

Source: Corinne Robinson Alsop's unpublished memoir, Alsop papers, Houghton Library, Harvard; interview with Edna Gurewitsch.

13. Characteristically, after reporting this triumph in her autobiography, she sought to minimize it: "I realize now it would have been better to have devoted the time which I gave to hockey to learning to play tennis, which would have been far more useful to me later on."

Source: This Is My Story, page 59.

however, Mademoiselle Souvestre thought sports "more or less useless." It was the intellectual and moral development of her girls that interested her. They were to be trained to think and act on their own, while maintaining at the same time "their grace, their freshness of sentiment, and elegance which are the charm and smile of life."

There were other teachers at Allenswood, but, just as at Groton, the school centered around its founder; only Mademoiselle Souvestre really mattered. She taught history and literature and French in her library, filled always with flowers, its walls lined with books and with nudes by such artist friends as Rodin and Puvis de Chavannes which startled some of the new students at first. The girls sat on small chairs on either side of the fireplace in front of which the small determined figure of the headmistress strode back and forth, punctuating her torrent of facts and opinions and asides with a pointer, and pausing now and again to hurl a challenging question at her listeners. She made them question every assumption they had brought to their lessons, refused to allow them to parrot back to her her own opinions—"Why was your mind given you but to think things out for yourself?"—and when she found a girl's essay insufficiently thought through, she did not hesitate to tear it in half in front of her classmates.

Her opinions were clear, crisp, and unconventional, the radical legacy of her late father, the novelist and philosopher Emile Souvestre, to whom she had been deeply attached. She favored trade unions, believed Dreyfus innocent, and, although most of her pupils were English, sided with the Boers in the South African war; during that conflict, English girls were free to celebrate British victories in the gymnasium, but while they did so she gathered around her in the library the rest of the students—American, Dutch, Swedish, Russian, Latin American—and lectured them on the rights of small nations to follow their own independent paths.[14]

Such opinions disturbed some of her students but fascinated Eleanor, in whose home such things had rarely been discussed. Only

14. Her private life had been unconventional as well. She had founded Les Ruches, her first school outside Paris, in partnership with another woman, who was also evidently her lover, and it had closed its doors shortly after Bamie left it when the two women quarreled bitterly. An agitated and highly colored account of life at Les Ruches and of the school's disintegration may be found in a novel called *Olivia*, published in 1949 under a pseudonymn by Dorothy Strachey-Bussy, the biographer Lytton Strachey's sister, who had been a pupil in the French school and later taught Eleanor English at Allenswood. There is no evidence that Eleanor knew of her teacher's sexual preference. This should not be surprising. It was a determinedly reticent age, and Mademoiselle Souvestre was an old and imperious lady when she and Eleanor knew one another.

Mademoiselle Souvestre's blunt atheism bothered her. Accustomed to the grave, unexamined pieties of "my dear, religious grandmother," she found her teacher's sweeping scorn for every form of worship somewhat alarming. Mademoiselle Souvestre, she wrote, "could not comprehend a God who would think of bothering about such insignificant things as human beings, and . . . religion which preached reward for good behavior and punishment for bad she considered food for small minds." Exposure to such heresies "did me no harm," Eleanor would conclude many years later. "Mlle Souvestre shocked me into thinking, which was beneficial." But she did not adopt her teacher's doctrines as her own.[15]

She remembered most fondly the many evenings she spent in the library listening eagerly as Mademoiselle Souvestre read poetry aloud. Another rapt pupil recalled the extraordinary power of her reading: "She read simply and rapidly, without any of the actor's arts and affectations, with no swelling voice, with no gestures beyond the occasional lifting of her hand in which she held a long ivory paper cutter. But the gravity of her bearing and her voice transported me." It transported Eleanor, too, and if the poems were those the headmistress especially liked, she remembered, "she read them over two or three times, and then demanded that we recite them to her in turn." Eleanor, who had long before delighted her father by reciting his favorite verses to him, was especially good at this and found such evenings "exhilarating."[16]

During Easter vacation in 1901, Mademoiselle Souvestre took Eleanor with her to Florence. For Eleanor, accustomed as she said only to "regular trips from New York to Tivoli and back," travel with her teacher was "a revelation." Mademoiselle Souvestre sometimes changed her itinerary at the last possible moment—something Eleanor's grandmother would never have dreamed of doing. She always ate local food and drank native wines (diluted with water for Eleanor) and stayed in modest hotels and pensiones unused to foreigners. And she shrewdly encouraged her young, still-timorous charge to accept responsibility for herself, to explore life on her own. All the packing and

15. When Eleanor attended a Christmas midnight mass with Mademoiselle Souvestre at St. Peter's in Rome in 1902, and the schoolmistress obviously enjoyed the music and candlelight, Eleanor was greatly cheered. It was proof, she wrote much later, that "Mlle Souvestre was not an atheist at heart."

Source: This Is My Story, page 94.

16. Until the end of her own life, Eleanor Roosevelt loved to read or recite poetry to friends and family in the evenings.

unpacking was left to Eleanor; she was expected to see to tickets and travel arrangements. When they reached Florence, Mademoiselle Souvestre told her, "My dear, I should be exhausted if I walked the streets with you, but the only way to know a city is . . . to walk the streets. Florence is worth it. Take your *Baedeker* and go and see it . . . and we shall discuss what you have seen." Eleanor did as she was told, even steeling herself to ask directions when she found herself lost in the twisting old streets. "I spent hours in churches," she remembered. "In the galleries I sat before certain pictures and barely glanced at others. I can still see Botticelli's 'Spring,' with its riot of gay figures and flowers. I loved the little Della Robia babies that decorated both the outside and inside of so many buildings; the statues in the square; the old Ponte Vecchio lined with its funny little shops, where I prowled looking for gold and silver work."[17]

Each evening, back at their hotel, Eleanor would describe to Mademoiselle Souvestre all that she had experienced, prompting her teacher to respond with rapid-fire discourses on art. Eleanor left no record of these, but another pupil vividly conveyed the rush of her remarks after her own initial visit to a museum. Everything was ostensibly said more "to herself . . . than to me," the former student wrote. "What was the common factor that made each of these pictures a work of art? Could I tell her that? And how, with such material substances as canvas, oil, pigments, were such immaterial effects produced? The plastic arts! Had I ever thought how different they were from the other arts, from literature, the art of words? From music, the purest—or was it the impurest—of them all? . . . And so on, seeds flung at random into the air, some to take roots, some, alas, to be lost forever."

Eleanor wrestled earnestly with these questions and remembered always the impact upon her of great art experienced for the first time. But more than that, she retained the memory of her first taste of freedom, her first evidence that she could be effective and capable in the real world. "Though I lost some of my self-confidence and ability to look after myself in the early days of my marriage," she wrote, much

17. Evidently embarrassed by this evidence of an adolescent's understandable delight in her own independence and pleasure in being able to acquire beautiful things, Eleanor added an explanation when writing her autobiography: "As usual, gifts were on my mind; for when I did go home . . . I wanted to take some thing from my travels to everyone." A lengthy gift list survives from her Allenswood days, including the names of friends, family members, teachers, even Madeleine, the Alsatian nurse she had found so threatening. Already at sixteen, she was only able to enjoy herself if persuaded that by doing so she was benefiting others.

Sources: This Is My Story, page 87; Lash, *Eleanor and Franklin,* page 85.

later "when it was needed again later on it came back to me more easily because of these trips with Mlle Souvestre."

She held tight to those memories that summer when she returned to America for the first time in two years. The voyage home provided an abrupt reminder of the bitter reality of life with her own family. Aunt Pussie acted as her chaperone. She was as usual swept up in a new romance, this time with a young Englishman whom she had just met in London and now had had to leave behind. She took to her berth the moment she and Eleanor went aboard their ship, cried day and night, and said she was tempted to jump overboard in her grief. Her niece, with whom she shared the cabin, believed her and spent most of the stormy crossing anxiously watching to make sure she did not make good her threat.

Not long after they landed in New York, Eleanor and Pussie visited relatives at Northeast Harbor, Maine, where one day Eleanor evidently said something that enraged her excitable aunt. In her fury, Pussie told Eleanor she was far too plain ever to have "the beaux that the rest of the women in the family had had." And when that failed to wound the seventeen-year-old deeply enough—or at least when it did not visibly shake her usual outward stoicism—she lashed her further with lurid details of just what it was that had been wrong with her dead father, just how his noisy disintegration had brought shame to every member of the family.

Eleanor begged to be allowed to go back to Allenswood for one more term. Mademoiselle Souvestre urged it, too. "I am sure another year of a regular and studious life will be in every respect mentally and physically beneficial," she wrote to Grandmother Hall. "Her health, though excellent, is perhaps not yet settled enough to make it desirable for her to face all the irregularities of a society life." Mrs. Hall wearily agreed—her own children's irregularities may have been all she wanted to contend with that year—provided Eleanor could find someone else going to England who would be willing to escort her. It was a measure of her granddaughter's new determination that she went on her own to a New York employment agency and hired a "deaconess" to accompany her on the voyage, an elderly churchwoman who looked respectable enough to reassure the family.

She returned to Allenswood for her final term in triumph. Mademoiselle Souvestre was "very glad to see me," she noted. Her success with her headmistress and with her other teachers was not entirely surprising—like Franklin, she had sought almost desperately to please adults all her young life—but she was just as popular among her schoolmates. Young Corinne Robinson, who entered Allenswood during Eleanor's last year, remembered that while everyone knew that her older cousin was Mademoiselle Souvestre's "supreme favorite," she had somehow "made no enemies through this favoritism." Eleanor was "everything" to Allenswood, she said, "the most important person at the school." Other former students also remembered that she was somehow set apart—"so much more intelligent than all the others," one wrote. Another thought her "much more grown up than we were," and remembered that at Allenswood Eleanor already had "a serious view of life, and once confided to me that all she wished for was to do something useful: that was her main object."

Mademoiselle Souvestre made her a sort of unofficial member of the staff, assigned to help slow learners keep up with their classmates and to make newcomers feel at home. Younger girls especially admired her. "Saturdays," Corinne remembered, "we were allowed a sortie into Putney which had stores. Young girls have crushes, and you bought violets or a book and left them in the room of the girl you were idolizing." Eleanor's room was filled with violets every weekend.[18]

Her teacher took her traveling again that year, to Rome at Christmas, to France, Belgium, and Germany at Easter, and seems to have urged her to stay on still longer at Allenswood, even to think of making a career of teaching. Eleanor had an insatiable appetite for knowledge, and an instinctive talent and enthusiasm for imparting it to others. "I have not found [her] easily influenced in anything that was not perfectly straightforward and honest," she had told Grandmother Hall early in Eleanor's time at Allenswood, "but I often found that she influenced others in the right direction. She is full of sympathy for all those who live with her. . . . As a pupil she is very satisfactory, but even that is of small account when you compare it with the perfect quality of her soul." For her to expend that energy and sympathy and talent

18. During her first term, Eleanor herself had evidently developed such a crush, on a brilliant but tempestuous girl whom she called only "Jane" in her autobiography. Jane's vivid beauty and uncontrollable tantrums must have been reminiscent of Aunt Pussie. She and Eleanor studied history together with Mademoiselle Souvestre. "There were perhaps eight other girls in our class," Eleanor remembered, "but as far as I was concerned there was no one but Jane." She was thought a good influence on Jane, Eleanor wrote, "because I was quiet and docile," but there was just so much she could do, and when her friend hurled an inkstand at the German teacher, Mademoiselle Souvestre expelled her. Eleanor was "heartbroken," she remembered, but even her tears could not persuade the headmistress to change her mind; Jane left the school. She and Eleanor continued to correspond for several years, Eleanor wrote. Jane's "glamour," she said, was unforgettable.

Source: This Is My Story, pages 62–63.

for leadership on making a place for herself in conventional New York society seemed to Mademoiselle Souvestre a terrible waste.

Eleanor agreed in principle. Even before she had come to the school she had written an essay entitled "Loyalty and Friendship," which had shown how little sympathy she had for the social whirl in which her aunts spun with such enthusiasm. There were few real friendships among women, she had written, because women were not taught to value the quality of loyalty that alone makes true friendship possible. "A woman will kiss her best friend one moment," she wrote, "then when she is gone will sit down with another best friend & pick the other's character to pieces.

"It may seem strange," she had continued, "but no matter how plain a woman may be if truth & loyalty are stamped upon her face all will be attracted to her & she will do good to all who come near her & those who know her will always love her for they will feel her loyal spirit, & have confidence in her while another woman will never have anybody's confidence, simply because those around her feel her lack of loyalty & by not having this great virtue she will lose one of the greatest gifts that God has given man, the power of friendship."

Eleanor had demonstrated that power at Allenswood, had managed to become the loyal, trusted friend of students and teachers alike; and she would never entirely abandon her dream of becoming a teacher in the tradition of the extraordinary woman who had changed her life.[19]

But her immovable sense of duty would finally not permit her to go against the wishes of her family. "To my Grandmother," she recalled, "the age of eighteen was the time that you 'came out'; not to do so was 'unthinkable.' " She had to go home; it was time to enter the adult world.

And, although she did not mention it in her autobiography, another impulse worked against her staying on in England. In her absence, her young brother Hall had increasingly come under the care of her erratic Aunt Pussie. Eleanor worried about the effect Pussie might have on him; worried, too, perhaps that he might not forgive his sister if she did not return to him before too long. Better than most

19. Like her memories of her father, her recollections of Mademoiselle Souvestre were uniformly admiring. That her teacher had shown genuine affection for her was all Eleanor needed to know to love her without qualification. Corinne Robinson Alsop and others, though also admiring, were more objective. The headmistress could be brutally impatient with slower students, prized emotion and moral fervor above rational analysis, and sulked and slammed doors when her tiny, worshipful assistant, Mademoiselle Samai, failed to answer her summons swiftly enough.

Source: Lash, *Love, Eleanor,* pages 29–30.

people, she knew the bitterness abandonment bred. She and Hall were all that was left of their little family. They belonged to one another. Neither could afford to lose the other.

In later years, Eleanor was not entirely uncritical of what she had learned at Allenswood. It had failed to fill all the gaps left by her early schooling under the fashionable Mr. Roser; there were whole fields of inquiry in which she would never receive a solid grounding and had to depend on what she called "the quickness of my mind to pick the minds of other people and use their knowledge as my own." But the time she spent with Mademoiselle Souvestre had forever changed her, she wrote. "Whatever I have become since had its seeds in those three years of contact with a liberal mind and strong personality."

Her teacher felt just as strongly about her. Eleanor Roosevelt had "the warmest heart I ever encountered," she told Grandmother Hall; and when Eleanor returned to America in the summer of 1902, Mademoiselle Souvestre wrote to say that "I miss you every day of my life."

Eleanor spent most of her seventeenth summer at Tivoli, where things had gone from bad to worse in her absence. Pussie was away most of the time, living in New York, and her grandmother spent still more time closed up in her bedroom. The reason was Vallie, whose drinking now sometimes caused him to become violent, raging through the house in search of someone to strike. A full-time keeper was employed to keep him sober, but whenever he could elude him, he liked to crouch in an upstairs window and fire his shotgun at anyone who happened to be on the lawn. The neighbors no longer called; Eleanor and eleven-year-old Hall learned to stay close to the trunks of the big sheltering shade trees whenever they ventured outside. Eddie was married now, but he too sometimes came home to carouse with his older brother. Grandmother Hall was helpless to stop them. She did permit Eleanor to invite one of her Allenswood friends home for a weekend, but the strain of worrying over what her uncles might do proved unbearable. She never again dared ask a girl friend to visit her in the country. "It was not," she noted, "very good preparation for being a gay and joyous debutante."[20]

20. I was fortunate enough to visit Oak Terrace with members of the Roosevelt family on the occasion of Eleanor Roosevelt's centennial in October of 1984. It is a derelict house now, owned but only sporadically occupied by an Estonian religious sect whose members do their best on weekends to keep it from further delapidation. Despite their earnest efforts, a porch recently fell off; plywood covers the windows of Eleanor's third floor room, its rotten floor too weak to support visitors; and a tangle of trees and bushes behind the house hides the river and covers the

There was at least one bright moment that summer. While she was sitting in a railroad coach one morning on her way back to Tivoli from a visit to New York, her Cousin Franklin stopped to speak to her. They had not seen one another since they had danced together at her Aunt Corinne's Christmas party three years earlier. They talked for a while, Franklin swaying above her in the aisle—he was soon to begin his third year at Harvard—then he escorted her into the next car, where she was invited to sit with him and his mother. Sara Delano Roosevelt was very beautiful and very imposing, Eleanor remembered, nearly as tall as she, and swathed in black veils that hung from her hat to the floor. They chatted pleasantly until they reached Hyde Park and Franklin helped his mother from the train. Eleanor continued on to Tivoli.

That autumn, Eleanor and her grandmother escorted Hall to Groton, where he would spend the next six years. Grandmother Hall would never again bother to visit him there. "Somehow or other," Eleanor wrote, "the real responsibility for this younger brother was slipping from her hands into mine." She would write and visit him faithfully throughout his school career, as that was "what all good parents were expected to do."

Just as Anna Hall had been the mainstay of her turbulent family in the brief period between her father's death and her own marriage to Elliott Roosevelt, her daughter, not yet eighteen, was now becoming the stable, strong one upon whom the weak relied. She moved to the city for the winter of her debut, sharing the dark house on Thirty-seventh Street with Pussie, fourteen years her senior but still unmarried and engaged in simultaneous romances that frequently drove her to stop eating, threaten suicide, and take to her bedroom for days at a time. It was again left to Eleanor patiently to persuade her that life was worth living. Vallie and Eddie visited sometimes, too, invariably intent on what Eleanor called a "spree," and she found it necessary to have triple locks installed on the inside of her bedroom door to bar nocturnal visits from her restless, drunken uncles. But she also often went out to find them when they did not return at night—escorted through the dark streets by her maid—and she was sometimes able to persuade one or both to come home to sleep it off.

lawn that once rolled smoothly down to the water's edge. After Grandmother Hall died in 1919, Vallie lived on here alone until his own death in 1934, taking shots from time to time at the neighbor's children, who liked to see how close to the house they could creep, and filling his days breaking up gravel for the twisting, ungraded forest drive that still leads in from the road. Eleanor dutifully looked in on him until the end.

The effort took its toll. She visited her Aunt Corinne one weekend, "burst into tears, and said, 'Auntie, I have no real home,' in such a pathetic way," Corinne wrote, "that my heart simply ached for her." Nonetheless, Eleanor remembered, "a certain kind of strength and determination which underlay my timidity began to make itself felt that year." For the rest of her life she would be expected to make the arrangements so that others might live their lives more serenely. She was rarely unequal to the task.

"This period," she also wrote, "was my first real contact with anyone who had completely lost the power of self-control." All her life the actions of anyone who seemed unable to control himself made her withdraw. Her face froze in their presence, so did her emotions. The ghastly memory of Vallie's lurching rages haunted her, and that haunting would later be intensified when her brother, Hall, whom she had worked so hard to make feel as if he belonged to somebody, showed signs of the alcoholism that eventually killed him. But Vallie's excesses had not been her "first real contact" with such things. They must have stirred memories of her own father's dark side as well, however deeply buried—the half-heard nighttime quarrels between him and her mother; the cloying reek of liquor that clung to him even during their treasured visits together; the sight of him being carried senseless from his club while she followed along as best she could at nine, holding his three terriers on their leashes.[21]

"Something locked me up," she once told a close friend; something made spontaneity, emotional abandon, physical contact, difficult for her all her life. She had every reason to fear what lack of control could do to other people. But she must also have feared on some far deeper, still more frightening level, that the potential for such behavior lived within her as well. She had always to make sure she did not let anyone know of its existence, must keep herself secured against it. There developed within her, she wrote, an "exaggerated idea of the necessity of keeping all one's desires under complete subjugation."

Eleanor was eighteen in October, and was to make her debut with many other girls at the big Assembly Ball at the Waldorf in December. It was a frightening event for "ninety-nine per cent of us," one of her

21. Having to care for troubled people was a burden she bore patiently but constantly throughout her life. In the early autumn of 1962, already exhausted by the disease that would soon kill her, she told a friend of a nightmare from which she had just awakened in which her brother, Hall, and her turbulent son, Elliott, were "piled upon her" until it seemed she could not breathe.

Source: Lash, *A World of Love: Eleanor Roosevelt and Her Friends, 1943–1962,* page 553.

peers remembered. "No, I would make that ninety-nine-point-nine per cent." But Eleanor's fears were increased by her own conviction that she would never be able to measure up to what a Hall or a Roosevelt woman was supposed to be. Her own mother and aunts had been the most beautiful debutantes in New York in each of their seasons; four other Roosevelt girls, among them the glittering Alice (whose own White House debut had so delighted Franklin), were to attend.

Eleanor was well dressed for the evening, she remembered—her Aunt Tissie had ordered a gown made for her in Paris—"but there was absolutely nothing about me to attract anybody's attention." She was too tall, she thought, too serious; she danced badly, had lost touch with her few old friends among the girls, and knew only two eligible men, both much older than she: W. Forbes-Morgan, a perennial suitor of Pussie's, and Robert Ferguson, an Englishman and former Rough Rider who was an admirer of her Auntie Bye. "I do not think I quite realized beforehand what utter agony it was going to be or I would never have had the courage to go," she wrote. "Bob Ferguson introduced a number of his friends, Nick Biddle, Duncan Harris and Pendleton Rogers. But by no stretch of the imagination could I fool myself into thinking I was a popular debutante."

In this her distorted sense of her own unattractiveness warped the record. Many years later, Duncan Harris, one of the young men she met that evening and who dined and danced with her often that winter, read the above passage in her autobiography and wrote her a note from the Union Club to set the record straight: "I hasten to tell you that you are far too modest about your appeal to the gilded youth of 1902. Bob Ferguson, Nick Biddle and I were not doing heavy duty at parties, and I remember well that when we asked you to dance it was because we wanted to, and, contrary to your story, the spirit of competition was distinctly present." By any objective standard, Eleanor was in fact a successful debutante, invited to the all-important Astor Ball and to the small exclusive dinners and theater parties that were the true tests of popularity. Yet she never believed it. Her mother's ghost and her Aunt Pussie's vivid presence presented a contrast with her own looks and charm she could never imagine matching; because she was such a disappointment to herself, she was certain she had disappointed others.

She did not disappoint her Cousin Franklin. She intrigued him. He had always liked her, telling his mother, after he had danced and talked with her at the Robinsons' Christmas dance when Eleanor was just fourteen, that she "has a very good mind," and suggesting that same season that she be invited to a Springwood house party that did not finally come off. And her three years at Allenswood had made her still more appealing. She was tall but womanly now, rather than rail-thin, with her hair piled on top her head; an "interesting talker," according to one of her frequent dance partners, "always gracious and pleasant" and more substantive somehow than most of her fellow debutantes. Shrewd hostesses seated her next to older guests because she could be counted on make grown-up conversation, a practice she disliked but could do nothing about.

Her name first appeared in Franklin's Line-A-Day diary on November 17, 1902—just five weeks after he saw Alice Sohier off to Europe. He attended the New York Horse Show at Madison Square Garden that evening, and sat in Rosy's private box. Eleanor was there, too, as the guest of her friend Helen Roosevelt Roosevelt and her new fiancé, Teddy Robinson, Aunt Corinne's son; and after the show, Rosy took Eleanor and Franklin, Helen, and Mary Newbold to dinner at Sherry's. Two weeks later, Franklin lunched with Eleanor and Helen in New York, and two weeks after that, out shopping with his mother just two days before Christmas, he managed to get Sara and her last-minute packages back to the Renaissance Hotel by three-thirty so that he could get away for tea with Eleanor.

They were together again for New Year's—at the White House in Washington, where they stood with the family and watched TR greet thousands of well-wishers. They dined with him in the state dining room, then attended the theater, where, Franklin noted happily, he "sat near Eleanor. Very interesting day."

When Rosy gave a dinner for Franklin to mark his twenty-first birthday on January 30, 1903—"very jolly!" the guest of honor noted —Eleanor was one of those who raised her glass with Sara to drink "the dear boy's health."

Sara took her second apartment in Boston to be near Franklin that winter, so that he found it difficult to find excuses to leave Harvard for weekends in New York. He may have written to Eleanor over the next few months, and she may have written back, but no such early letters between them survive.[22] Eleanor once described the special strictures under which even casual correspondence between single men and

22. Any account of the Roosevelt courtship is necessarily one-sided. Franklin carefully hoarded Eleanor's love letters to him. She kept his, too, for many years but eventually destroyed them all, probably in 1936 when she was at work on the first volume of her autobiography, *This Is My Story*. What he wrote to her, then, must now be reconstructed from her responses to it.

women then had to be undertaken: "It was understood that no girl was interested in a man or showed any liking for him until he had made all the advances. You knew a man very well before you wrote or received a letter from him . . . and to have signed one in any other way than 'very sincerely yours' would have been not only a breach of good manners but an admission of feeling which was entirely inadmissible."

Still, they managed to keep in touch, and Eleanor came to Springwood for a four-day house party in late June, one of a party of six and accompanied by her maid. It was a relatively quiet visit. A steady rain kept everyone inside most of the time; they played blindman's buff, dined at the Rogerses' chateau, and took one long walk in the dripping woods. Three weeks later, she was back again with five other cousins. The weather was better. There was a hayride along the Albany Road for the group Sara called "my six young people," and a long stroll along the cliffs overlooking the Hudson.

They all spent the hot afternoon of July 7 lying on the lawn, talking quietly beneath the trees. Later, Franklin took his guests and Sara for a dinner cruise on the *Half Moon,* gliding home on the broad, dark river and gazing up at the lights of the great estates perched on the cliffs above them. Franklin was "at his best" aboard his boat, Young Corinne Robinson remembered—"handsome at the tiller, a splendid sailor and completely confident." He was evidently especially eager to make a good impression that evening, for back in his boyhood room after the others had gone to bed he noted in his diary that the whole day had been "great fun." Then he added a new message in the private code he knew his mother could not decipher: "E IS AN ANGEL."

He was in love. We do not know how Eleanor felt about him then, but Franklin was soon to leave on his trip to Europe with his Harvard friend Charley Bradley, and before he put Eleanor aboard the train back to New York he invited her to visit him and his mother at Campobello just as soon as he got back. She agreed to come.

Whenever FDR was introduced to a newly engaged couple during the presidential years, he always made a point of congratulating the bride as well as the groom. Grace Tully, his White House secretary, once asked him why. "He quickly explained," she wrote, "that he [had] felt the need for it at the time of his engagement. . . . With the mock sense of injury he sometimes affected, he said that when his engagement was announced, all the congratulations were showered on him for securing Eleanor as a wife. He felt, he said, that some people at least should have congratulated her for securing him as a husband."

His sense of injury may not have been wholly feigned. Perhaps the most frequently asked question about the Roosevelt courtship is just what it was that so handsome and engaging a man as Franklin Roosevelt saw in his tall, sober cousin. But that question was rarely asked when the Roosevelts were young. *Eleanor* was then the Roosevelt that mattered, the niece of the President of the United States. In its chatty coverage of the 1902 New York Horse Show at which Franklin and Eleanor had shared Rosy's box, *Town Topics* carefully noted her presence and ignored his. Franklin was an unimportant member of a comparatively obscure branch of the family. Nor was he the only young man interested in Eleanor; during their long and largely secret courtship, Eleanor had tactfully to discourage several would-be suitors.

She was not a beauty—a "belle," as Alice Sohier was, or her own late mother had been, or her own aunts were—but she was undeniably attractive. Because she was both tall and slender, she was inevitably described as "willowy"; was so described so often, in fact, that in the second summer of her courtship she would take part in a tableau with Franklin dressed *as* a willow tree. Her eyes were soft and blue, and he especially admired her long gleaming blond hair.[23] The prominent Roosevelt teeth which had so distressed her Aunt Edith (but which neither she nor any other member of the family ever troubled to have straightened) were less obvious when Eleanor was young than they would one day become. And there was about her always an air of serious intelligence, of genuine sympathy and interest, that encouraged both men and women to confide in her, to reveal what she herself once called their "heart's secrets."

Those qualities must have been a comfort to Franklin in the autumn of 1902. He began seeing Eleanor just weeks after he had stood on the Boston wharf and watched Alice Sohier set off for New York and the wider world beyond. Alice had proved more than a match for him. Volatile, independent, and vividly aware of her own beauty and desirability, she had eluded his charm, fended off his advances and finally refused his offer of marriage. "She had flocks of beaux," a member of her family remembered; "She was having too good a time to be very serious about marriage." For all her youth, she had been more self-assured at seventeen than he had been at twenty.

By contrast, the shyness and insecurity bred into Eleanor by her

23. Once during the presidential years, Frances Perkins noticed for the first time a portrait of a youthful Eleanor that hung above the door of his White House study. FDR saw her studying it. "The hair is just right, don't you think?" he asked. Then, fondly, "It looks just like her now."
Source: Quoted in Graff, Ginna, and Butterfield, *FDR,* page 191.

arid childhood must have held a special appeal for Franklin. Alice had not wished or needed to be cared for, and Franklin's mother had always sought to shelter him from unpleasantness of any kind. Eleanor now provided him with the opportunity to provide some shelter of his own. "He had always been so secure in every way," Eleanor once said of their early years together, ". . . and then he discovered that I was perfectly insecure." He took pleasure in the way his insouciant buoyancy helped calm her fears, and perhaps felt that Eleanor, unlike Alice, could be counted upon to remain constant.

And there was still another bond that may have drawn Franklin to her. Like him, she had spent much of her youth in the company of adults and away from other children, and the result, according to a close friend, was already a certain "aloofness from the careless ways of youth." Eleanor shared what Sara once called Franklin's "kind of a kinship with older people." She was able to fit with little effort into his world, in which Sara and her friends and relations still played such an important part.

She rejoined that world on September 28, 1903—just three days after Franklin returned to Sara from his European vacation—arriving at Campobello with her maid for a five-day stay. There were picnics and sailing expeditions—Franklin at the helm, Eleanor steeling herself against her old fear of the ocean and the seasickness that fear often intensified. Sara always accompanied them, along with a full complement of neighbors and their families and guests, and on Sunday morning the three Roosevelts attended services together in the little board-and-batten Anglican church at Welshpool. Franklin and Eleanor did manage to attend one event without Sara, a "young dinner" at the Pells', and on their last day together they took a carriage ride along the northern edge of the island and later read aloud to one another from Robert Louis Stevenson's *Christmas Sermon* before Sara and Franklin took Eleanor in the *Half Moon* to her train at Eastport, Maine.

Sara evidently noticed nothing out of the ordinary in the attention Franklin continued to pay to Eleanor. Perhaps her deep satisfaction at having her son back at her side again had blinded her to what was happening. And there was at least one other young woman on the island of whose feelings for Franklin she may then have been more wary: Evelyn Carter, a lovely and outgoing British girl, the daughter of the British governor of Barbados and a guest of Sara's next-door neighbor, Mrs. Hartman Kuhn, was clearly charmed by him. But Mrs. Kuhn was shrewder than Sara, noting privately how much her boy seemed to admire his quiet cousin.

Master Franklin on his tenth birthday, January 30, 1892.

Facing page: James Roosevelt Roosevelt, Jr., Franklin's troubled half-nephew, "Taddy," rocks alone in his room at Rosy's "Red House," next door to Springwood, in 1888. *Above:* Taddy restrains a family pet at his father's home near Bicester, England, the following summer; his sister, Helen, appears in the window and Franklin, visiting England with his parents, stands at the right.

Rosy at the reins in 1886. His wife, Helen Astor Roosevelt,is at his side. Their children, Taddy and Helen, sit behind them with their governess.

Franklin's parents in 1896, photographed by their son in the garden of the Villa Britannia at Bad Nauheim during the family's fourth trip to Germany in search of a cure for Mr. James' weakening heart.

Sara and Franklin, just home from his second year at Groton, on the Springwood veranda in June, 1898.

Franklin as captain of the Groton baseball team, surrounded by his players, 1899 (left), and silhouetted aboard the *Half Moon* off Campobello later that same year.

Mr. James on "Bobby," the new saddle horse with which Sara surprised [illegible]

Franklin and his father and some of the Roosevelt dogs at Springwood less than a month before the death of Mr. James in 1900.

Eleanor Roosevelt at four, and (facing page) her father, Elliott Roosevelt, with some of the terriers that consoled him during his exile at Abingdon, Virginia.

Alice Sohier (opposite) at seventeen, dressed for her presentation at court in London in the spring of 1903. It was only after Alice left Boston for her extended tour of Europe and the Near East that Franklin began to court his cousin, Eleanor (above, center), shown here later that same spring with two of the other young women whom Sara thought it safe for her son to see: his cousin, Muriel Robbins (left), and his half-niece, Helen Roosevelt. Two weeks after this picture was taken at Hyde Park in June, Franklin confided to his diary that Eleanor was "an angel." (*Photograph of Alice Sohier courtesy of Emily Shaw*)

The announcement of their engagement still nearly three months off, Franklin and Eleanor share a quiet moment on the porch of the Roosevelt home at Campobello in August of 1904.

Eleanor stopped at Springwood for one night in early September, on her way back to Tivoli from Groton, where she had left Hall for his second term. They took a long drive together through the Roosevelt and Rogers woods. She told Franklin that she was worried about her brother, whom she now called "the Cherub" or "the Kid," depending on her mood. He was not doing as well as he might, was uncommunicative about how well he was fitting in. Franklin, in whom this must have struck a responsive chord, promised to look in on him after getting back to Cambridge. He, too, was anxious—but about himself. He was determined to make a success of his editorship of the *Crimson*, he told Eleanor, and he was worried about the demands it would make and was unable to decide whether enrolling in graduate school or law school would allow him the most time for his newspaper duties.

Although he faced a hectic schedule upon his return to Cambridge—producing the first issue of the *Crimson* with only a skeleton staff, ushering at a football game, deciding finally in favor of graduate school, preparing remarks on journalism and the virtues of Cousin Theodore's "strenuous life" for the incoming freshmen—he did manage to get to Groton on his very first weekend and reported to Eleanor by letter that Hall was getting on well and seemed to have plenty of friends. Along with his note, he evidently included a souvenir of their time together at Campobello—perhaps something as simple as a shell or a sea-smoothed stone.

Eleanor responded gratefully from Rivoli on October 3 in the first of her letters to him that has survived. She was grateful for the "token from the sea," she said, though the requirements of courtship required that she be a little embarrassed at accepting it: "I think you should have sent [it] to someone else . . . don't you?" His good news about Hall had relieved her mind, especially since "I can't tell much from his letters."

Another note from Franklin told her of his decision to take graduate courses. He was evidently unsure that he had done the right thing, not convinced his studies would lead anywhere. Eleanor was pleased for him. "You know quite well you need not apologize for writing about yourself," she wrote. "I should think history and political economy would be most interesting and much the most useful for you in the future and *of course* you are going to get an A.M." She was already eager to see him again. He and his mother had invited her to come back to Hyde Park for the weekend of the sixteenth—along with the usual clutch of cousins, family friends, and Harvard classmates—to see the Harvard–West Point game at the Academy. Might he escort her back to Tivoli, she asked, and stay the night on his way to Cambridge on Sunday?

He was not able to arrange that, but the weekend went well anyway. Harvard won five to nothing, despite a steady rain that turned the field into a bog, and on the way back to Springwood, Franklin and Eleanor somehow managed to catch the train while his mother and the rest of the party missed it, and so were able to have the half-hour train ride home alone together—alone, that is, except for Eleanor's maid. Even this extended proximity apparently did not alarm Sara; she merely noted in her journal that "we all got home on different trains." Perhaps she was distracted by her continuing concern for Miss Clay, Franklin's former tutor, still in her charge and now suffering such pain that Sara did not dare leave her side for long.[24]

Sara was only the most formidable obstacle to closeness between Eleanor and Franklin. Eleanor herself once outlined a few of the constraints under which Franklin then had to press his suit. "You never allowed a man to give you a present except flowers or candy or possibly a book," she wrote. "To receive a piece of jewelry from a man to whom you were not engaged was a sign of being a fast woman, and the idea that you permit any man to kiss you before you were engaged to him never even crossed my mind." The couple could never truly be alone together. Eleanor's maid served as a chaperone whenever a relative was not available, even when Franklin took her for long drives in the Roosevelt carriage.

Despite it all, their friendship was developing into a genuine romance. Eleanor's letters were now signed "Your affectionate cousin," which in the decorous, infinitely shaded language in which courtship was then conducted was a sure sign of growing intimacy, and when she was invited to a house party at Ellerslie, the Rhinecliff estate of former Vice President Levi P. Morton, she accepted, because, she told Franklin, "I think I'll chance there being there someone I like." She knew he was coming, too. He had done his best to throw his mother off the track. "I don't remember whether I told you . . . that I have accepted the Mortons' invite," he wrote home with elaborate casualness. "Lyman [Delano] is going also." Sara was not told that Eleanor would be among the guests, though she did eventually find out and note the fact in her journal.

24. Miss Clay had evidently been misdiagnosed. She was in fact dying of cancer, and at her own request Sara finally sent her home to England to die.
Source: SDR Journal, FDRL.

Franklin evidently included a poem in one of his letters to Eleanor, perhaps one he had written himself. Eleanor thought it "splendid," but "what ideals you have to live up to! I like 'Fear nothing and be faithful unto death,' but I must say I wonder how many of 'we poor mortals' could live up to that."

On November 21—one week after the Morton house party, just a day after Sara and Rosy had watched workmen place Scottish granite above Mr. James's grave—Eleanor traveled to Boston at Franklin's invitation to attend the Harvard-Yale game. Aunt Kassie and her daughter, Muriel Robbins, came along as chaperones. Franklin met them at the train and they all spent the morning together, visiting an art exhibition at the Boston Public Library and wandering over the cobbled streets of Beacon Hill. That afternoon, Eleanor watched Franklin in his crimson sweater as he led the futile cheers at the stadium—Yale won, sixteen to nothing—and later he showed her and Muriel his cluttered room at Westmorly Court.

Eleanor, Muriel, Aunt Kassie, and their maids moved on to Groton that evening, where Eleanor now hoped to see for herself how Hall was faring. Franklin followed the next morning, and that evening described the day's events in his Line-A-Day diary. He had arrived "just in time for church," he noted, and with Eleanor at his side listened again to the deep familiar voice of the rector. "Lunch with Aunt K's party" followed. And then, changing to the same code in which he had first confessed his love for Eleanor, Franklin wrote: "AFTER LUNCH I HAVE A NEVER TO BE FORGOTTEN WALK TO THE RIVER WITH MY DARLING." During that walk they somehow contrived to be alone long enough for him to ask her to marry him, and for her to say yes.

No one knows exactly what they said to one another, but many years later, Eleanor confided to an intimate friend all that she remembered of it. Franklin had told her that "with your help" he would make something of himself one day, she said, and she remembered replying, "Why me? I am plain. I have little to bring you." The young couple quietly returned to the family. They ate "supper with all the relatives," Franklin noted, and then he added another coded message: "I AM TO GO TO NEW YORK NEXT SUNDAY."

But before he could keep that rendezvous he would travel to Thanksgiving at Fairhaven and tell his mother of his plans.

CHAPTER 8

KEEPING THE NAME IN THE FAMILY

What Franklin and Eleanor said to one another that autumn afternoon on the bank of the Nashua is perhaps less important than why they said it. For whatever Sara's complex motives were for seeking to discourage her son from marrying, she was undeniably right that he and Eleanor were very young to be considering such a step. Why were they in such a hurry?

Franklin's love for Eleanor was genuine; there can have been little conscious calculation in the feelings of the smitten young man who called her "an angel" and "my darling" in his diary and in a code only he could decipher. And he was accustomed to having whatever he wanted; from infancy on, few desires had been denied him for long.

Still, other factors may have added to his urgency that had less to do with love. Franklin was not the first Roosevelt who had hoped to link the Hyde Park and Oyster Bay branches of the family. His own father had once proposed marriage to Bamie; Bamie had once hoped to marry Rosy; Rosy's daughter, Helen, was now engaged to Teddy Robinson, Corinne Roosevelt's son. But in his case there was a further compelling incentive. His connection with Theodore Roosevelt had always been both a source of pride and frustration for him. At Groton and at Harvard he had been known always as a Roosevelt, but could never claim to be one of *the* Roosevelts. They came and went at will at the White House and at Sagamore Hill; he visited there, too, from time to time, but he had always to wait to be invited first. His sense of precisely how others regarded him was every bit as acute as his skill at pretending it did not matter; he must have known that most of his Oyster Bay relations were at least faintly scornful of him. He was an amiable enough guest, they thought, but "superficial," "without convictions," "terribly self-conscious." They made fun of his narrow shoulders and slight build. Franklin now stood six feet one and weighed 161½ pounds, Sara noted in her 1904 journal, "in silk pajamas and barefoot." They laughed at his overeagerness and called him "Miss Nancy" behind his back whenever he tried to play tennis; and he was thought entirely under the control of his mother.

By marrying Eleanor, whom TR himself had called "my favorite niece," Franklin hoped to gain the instant access to the presidential family that distant kinship had always denied him. His love for Eleanor was real, but her closeness to the immediate family of the man he admired most on earth must have been an important part of her dowry.

The same slowness to mature which helped make his cousins so underestimate him may have also added to his determination to marry soon in another way. Franklin had always lagged behind his contemporaries: his bigger, faster, more experienced schoolmates had routinely outplayed him at sports no matter how hard he tried, and when he had attempted to charm his way into the most exclusive circles among his schoolmates he had been rebuffed. These defeats bred in him anger and resentment—perhaps even a desire to get even—which he mostly managed to disguise. But they had bewildered him as well, and made him distrust taking further part in the sort of direct and open competition with his peers that might result in still more humiliation.

Alice Sohier's decision not to marry him may have had a similar impact. No contest was more open and direct than sexual competition; none held more potential for the kind of embarassment he hated most. Franklin's interest in girls had grown slowly, too, perhaps in part because of his closeness to his mother. Sexual desire itself may even at first have seemed to him—as it evidently did to her—a betrayal of her love and devotion. Sara's apparently sincere belief that Franklin had never been a "ladies' man" may have been in part proof of her inability to see things she did not wish to see—and of her son's skill at keeping hidden from her whole areas of his life. Certainly he loved the company of women—with whom he never felt the need to compete as he did with men—and he delighted in harmless flirtation, in teasing and flattery and dinner-table gossip, to the end of his life.

But if he did not compete with women, he knew he was expected to compete *for* them, and he may well have wished to run no more races he was not reasonably sure of winning. His early, over-eager courtship of Alice Sohier, now in Europe but soon to return and to be surrounded by suitors, had shown him that victory could be elusive, that in trying to win a girl of great beauty and vivacity he was likely to face a field of dangerous rivals. Now, by marrying his quiet cousin, he need never run again.

Finally, marriage meant increased distance from his mother. His earlier efforts to extricate himself from her incessant care—his voyage to Europe with his classmate rather than with her, his disinclination to stay at her side when she took an apartment in Boston, his determined secrecy—had pained her and may have distressed him. Marriage represented a legitimate way in which to justify to his mother (and to himself) the greater freedom he needed if he was to build an adult life of his own. That he had discussed it with Alice Sohier when just twenty shows how determined he was to get away. For all his solemn assurances to Sara that his marriage would alter nothing between them, that the addition of Eleanor to their family would only enrich his mother's life, he must have known that it would inevitably loosen the ties that bound them to one another. Certainly Sara knew it, and because she did, fought against it all the harder. And so, while for Franklin's classmates marriage meant an end to the freedom of bachelorhood, it would be for Franklin a declaration of at least partial independence.[1]

Eleanor herself once tried to explain her own eagerness to marry. "I had a great curiosity about life and a desire to participate in every experience that might be the lot of woman. There seemed to me to be a necessity for hurry; without rhyme or reason I felt the urge to be a part of the stream of life and so [Franklin's proposal] seemed an entirely natural thing, and I never even thought that we were rather young and inexperienced."

Eleanor found Franklin enormously attractive,[2] but his interest in

1. One member of the Sagamore Hill family has suggested to me an additional and eminently practical attraction Eleanor may have had for Franklin. Most of his inheritance from his father was controlled by his mother, who showed no sign of relinquishing it. Eleanor had an annual income of between $5,000 and $8,000, sums which, especially in those days, her relative told me, were much "better than a sharp stick in the eye." Still, Franklin might well have married a far wealthier woman, just as his half brother had; there were many of them in his circle. Eleanor's fortune was a comforting but not a crucial factor in his decision.

Sources: Davis, *FDR: The Beckoning of Destiny*, page 204; confidential interview.

2. In her autobiography, Eleanor wrote that when she told her grandmother of Franklin's

her also seemed inexplicable to her at first and she had been uncertain of his intentions. She found it hard to credit the intensity of his feeling for her and worried that she would inevitably prove a disappointment to him. But he had laid patient, peristent siege, and the very qualities in him that put off her cousins—his reliance on charm, his almost dandyish air, his genial gregariousness—may have helped pull her to him, for they echoed the charges her family had always leveled against her father. It seems clear that Franklin and Elliott Roosevelt had somehow merged on some level of her mind. Her love letters to Franklin were often signed "Little Nell," just as her letters to her father had been long before; and she often called him "boy, dear" and "boy, darling," the pet names Elliott's Aunt Ella Bulloch had used for him. As a small child she had been unable effectively to defend Elliott Roosevelt except in her dreams. Now, as a young woman, she could stand beside Franklin, could lavish on him all the "quiet love" she had once invested in her father. And by that devotion she would bring out all that was best in him; she would be useful, and hence dared hope that she might really be loved in return.

Marriage to Franklin also offered Eleanor the same bright hope of escape from unwanted competition that marriage to her seemed likely to provide for him. Shortly after she left Allenswood, Mademoiselle Souvestre had written to warn her against being drawn too deeply into the "turmoil" of society. "Give some of your energy, but not all, to worldly pleasures which are going to beckon to you," she wrote, "[but] bear in mind that there are more quiet and enjoyable joys than to be among the most sought-after women at a ball." She knew her favorite pupil well. Eleanor later wrote that her first New York season, "when my sole object in life was society," had nearly brought her to "a state of nervous collapse." She never fully overcame her fear of being found inadequate by society, but a secret engagement to Franklin would at least offer her the comforting private assurance that things for her were already settled, that over the coming year she need only *pretend* to compete.

With nothing much to do but dream of Franklin and fret over the

---

proposal, Mrs. Hall "asked me if I was sure I was really in love. I solemnly answered 'Yes,' and yet I know now that it was years later before I understood what being in love was or what loving really meant." Her qualifying remarks were written in 1936, with the full and bitter knowledge of all that had gone wrong between her and her husband in the intervening years. It seems clear from her many letters to her fiancé that the answer she gave to her grandmother in 1903 was not only solemn but heartfelt.

Source: This Is My Story, page 111.

demands made upon her by a society about which she did not frankly care, Eleanor found some new satisfaction in social work. Her relatives had always thought charity work worthwhile for a young woman, provided it was kept in its proper place. "You were kind to the poor," Eleanor wrote of the lessons they had taught her. "You did not neglect your philanthropic duties . . . you assisted the hospitals and did something for the needy." As a very small girl she had helped her father serve up Thanksgiving dinner to the newsboys in whom her grandfather had taken an interest, and her Aunt Gracie had escorted her through the wards of another favorite Roosevelt charity, the New York Orthopaedic Hospital, its wards filled with pitiable immobilized children. The Halls, too, had sometimes made gestures toward the unfortunate. Aunts Pussie and Maude had taken Eleanor with them to a Bowery mission to sing carols to the derelicts at Christmas. Uncle Vallie had once gone with her to Hell's Kitchen to trim a Christmas tree—though Eleanor later suspected that "some of his interest in good works was because a lady he thought very charming was also interested in them." And shortly after the death of Eleanor's mother, an anonymous friend had written to a New York newspaper to remind readers of Anna Hall's kindness; once, the writer said, he or she had personally seen Anna stop her coach on a city street to offer an aged and badly crippled woman a ride—even though the sufferer had been "an entire stranger."

Eleanor had something more substantial and consistent in mind. As a debutante, her name was automatically inscribed as an associate member of the Junior League. Most young society women left it at that. Eleanor became an active and enthusiastic volunteer. She had no practical grounding in social work, but neither did her young colleagues. "We were just a group of girls anxious to do something helpful in the city in which we lived," she once said of herself and her fellow volunteers. But she had the shining example of Mademoiselle Souvestre to remind her of the rewards of teaching, and she always found it easiest to define herself through what she could do for others.

She and Jean Reid, the daughter of Sara's friend Mrs. Whitelaw Reid, were assigned to the Rivington Street Settlement House two blocks south of Houston Street on the Lower East Side. Jean played the piano; Eleanor taught calisthenics and "fancy dancing" to a classroom filled with immigrant children, mostly Jewish and Italian. "The children interested me enormously," she wrote years later. "I still remember the glow of pride that ran through me when one of the little girls said her father wanted me to come home with her, as he wanted to give me something because she enjoyed her classes so much. I did not go, of course." At her own parents' insistence, Jean Reid drove to and from the settlement in the family carriage. Eleanor took public transportation, trying not to look frightened when drunks staggered out of the saloon on the corner where she waited for her streetcar. And she let little interfere with her duties; once when her class conflicted with preparations for a party to which her family was sure she should go, Eleanor went to Rivington Street instead, greatly annoying her Cousin Susie Parish, who thought her "obstinate."

Her classes were "the nicest part of the day," she told Franklin, and he was not to laugh at her about her work; if he had been living near her in New York, she might not have volunteered, she said, yet "one must do something, or not having the person who is all the world to me would be unendurable." But she was not really just marking time, for even when Franklin was in the city she met her classes. She allowed him to come down and escort her home one afternoon, and was embarrassed the next day when her girls crowded around her to ask if the smiling handsome young man who had come for her was her "feller"—an expression, she later said, "which meant nothing to me at the time."

Another afternoon, Franklin arrived at Rivington Street to find that one of the girls had suddenly fallen ill. He helped Eleanor take her home. Franklin himself had taught poor boys at the St. Andrews Boys Club in what he had proudly told his mother was "one of the poorest quarters of Boston," and he had at least once lectured on the birds of the Hudson Valley to slum children as a favor to his old Campobello friend Frances Pell. But nothing in his life had prepared him for what he experienced as he carried the ailing girl up the narrow tenement stairs that led to her parents' apartment—the long greasy unlit hallway, the sour trapped smells of cooking and bad plumbing, the incessant noise. Back on the street he could not get over what he had seen and smelled. "My God," he told Eleanor. "I didn't know anyone lived like that."[3]

It is interesting to speculate as to whether Eleanor would have been

3. Many years later, Eleanor would see Franklin's visits to Rivington Street as having been an important part of his preparation for public life. She had often deliberately arranged to have him pick her up there rather than at the Parishes', she told a friend over lunch at Val-Kill in 1961, because "I wanted him to see *how people lived.*" Then, leaning forward and smiling at the memory, "And it worked. He saw how people lived, and he *never* forgot."
Source: Interview with Mary D. Keyserling

so easily persuaded to marry Franklin had she begun her settlement work before he began to court her. (Later in her life, she would return enthusiastically to social work and to teaching, in part at least to rekindle some of the self-respect that her marriage ultimately failed to foster.) Still, Eleanor was just nineteen in the autumn of 1903, in love with her cousin, persuaded she could be of help to him, and infused with the then near-universal conviction that the duty of every young woman was to marry and have a family.

And in a curious way the closeness between Franklin and his mother—the sense of family unity that they conveyed whenever they were together—may have provided Eleanor with an additional impetus toward marriage. Her own family had been tumultuous, unreliable, only sporadically concerned about her. "Who did she have?" her cousin Corinne once asked, and then answered her own question: "Nobody." Grandmother Hall closed her New York town house that fall. Aunt Pussie moved in with Mrs. Ludlow on East Seventy-sixth Street. Mrs. Ludlow's daughter Susan Parish and her husband, Henry, took Eleanor into their adjoining home. Cousin Henry was tall and thin and soft-spoken, and he took enough interest in Eleanor to show her how to balance her checkbook and keep up with her bills. Cousin Susie was something else again, a big determined, infinitely proper woman—members of the family compared her to "a full-rigged ship"—who frowned on too much mail from Franklin and made it clear to her boarder from the first that she "might occasionally have guests for tea down in a little reception room," but she could not invite anyone casually for meals. Eleanor once wrote generously that her cousins had been "more than kind" to her while she lived in their house, but in fact in the fall and winter of 1903 she was as rootless as she had ever been, without a real home or anything like a real family of her own.

Sara Delano Roosevelt may have represented many things to the shy young woman who had fallen in love with her son, but among them must surely have been stability and strength. To a young woman whose own mother had been dutiful and distracted rather than loving, and then had died young, Sara's singular love for Franklin must have seemed something like a luxury, to be envied and perhaps even shared. Eleanor meant it when she told Sara in her first letter after the secret of her engagement had been broken that she hoped Sara would "learn to love me a little."[4]

4. Franklin's decision to tell his mother of his engagement at Thanksgiving may have been made on the spur of the moment, for he evidently told Eleanor at Groton he planned to tell Sara

Sara's love was not won easily. She had expressed her reservations about the engagement to Eleanor and Franklin during a long talk at the Hotel Renaissance on December first, and had exacted their promise to keep the secret for a year while remaining apart to test the depth of their commitment. Eleanor, whose instinct—like Franklin's—was whenever possible to try to please her elders, tried hard to understand Sara's complicated emotions. She did inform Grandmother Hall of her plans, and when her grandmother told her that her first priority was not to hurt Sara's feelings, she agreed. "I realize more and more how hard it is for her," she wrote to Franklin as soon as he got back to Cambridge, "& we must both try always to make her happy. She is coming to town today for a few days & says she will telephone & try to see me."

She did just that three days later and invited Eleanor to come shopping with her. She had a few more things she wanted to talk over. Eleanor reported them to Franklin in a long anxious letter that evening. He had been planning to spend the following weekend in New York, but Sara now insisted that he come for Saturday only, Eleanor wrote; he and Eleanor were to lunch and dine with her, and he was then to accompany Sara home to Springwood on Sunday morning. "Helen and Cousin Rosie have been asking when you were coming home," Eleanor wrote. "She [Sara] thinks they are sure to hear you are in New York & say you are loafing & never coming home & she also says if we all go to church together we are sure to be seen. She also thinks that you ought to go home on account of the place, & your interest in it. She asked me to write you & I tell you all this because I think it only fair. Of course it will be a terrible disappointment to me not to have you on Sunday as I have been looking forward to it & every moment with you is very precious as we have so little of each other, but I don't want you to stay if you feel it is your duty to go up & I shall understand, of course. . . . Whatever you do I shall know to be right but I don't quite think your Mother quite realizes what a very hard thing she was asking me to do for I am hungry for every moment of your time."

Sara had made a still more ominous suggestion during their talk.

he was coming to New York the following Sunday only to see George Marvin, a young English master at Groton who had become his friend. Characteristically, Eleanor had frowned upon that sort of subterfuge: "Please don't tell your mother you have come down to see Mr. Marvin on Sunday, because I never want her to feel that she has been deceived & if you have to tell her I would rather you said you were coming to see me for she need not know why. Don't be angry with me Franklin for saying this, & of course you must do as you think best."

She planned to take another house in Boston for three months that winter, Eleanor reported. "She said she hoped I would come & stay once or twice during that time but if she took the house she did not want you to be coming to New York. I can understand how she feels, but I'm afraid I can't promise not to want you more than twice in all that time." Eleanor would abide by his decision about that, too, she said, but, "Oh! boy dear, I want you so much. I'm worried & tired & cross & I don't know what I ought to do."

Sara wrote Franklin that same evening from the Renaissance, making no mention of her plan to rent a Boston house but reiterating the arguments she had asked Eleanor to make. She thought she and Eleanor had had "a nice talk," she said. "I have thought constantly of you & your hopes my dear boy, & I feel that in gaining Eleanor's love you are very fortunate for I have always felt that she is a *true* loyal nature & even though I have not known her very long really well, I feel very sure of her. Already I am getting over the strangeness of it & though I could have wished it were all to come a little later, it may be all for the best. Now I can't bear to disappoint you even a little, but you will judge & act as you think best. I think that next week when you will be with her all day & evening *Saturday*, it would be well for you to come home Sunday morning for the day. . . . Rosy and Helen will be there. They have both asked me *when* you w'd be home for a Sunday. Were you in town both days you could not fail to be talked about for *every* reason. . . . I shall come down next Friday & you will find me here Saturday morning. You will breakfast with me & I am asking Mrs. Parish & Eleanor to lunch here, & Eleanor will dine here, it is a quiet place & no one can talk."

Sara had plans for his Christmas holidays, too. She wanted him to accept "any nice dinners or parties you are asked to . . . in *New York*, keeping of course the 24th and 25th for Hyde Park. I know you will not want to, as Eleanor will be at Tivoli, but you must be patient & keep up your interest in home things & in making friends here [in New York] & please don't think I am unsympathetic & that I do not understand you for I do, & I know exactly what you really would prefer doing."

Armed with both versions of the talk between Eleanor and his mother, Franklin drafted a reply to Sara in which he displayed clear signs of the masterful tactician he would one day become. Since Sara had said nothing to *him* about her plans for renting a Boston apartment he saw no need to confront that issue until he could talk to her in person. Meanwhile, he played up every point in Sara's letter on which he and she could be made to seem to agree, and deflected or undercut rather than contradicted every argument she had made against his plan.

Dearest Mama,

Yours of Friday came yesterday & I have been thinking over what you say about next Sunday—I am so glad, dear Mummy, that you are getting over the strangeness of it all—I knew you would, and that you couldn't help feeling that not only I but you also are the luckiest & will always be the happiest people in gaining anyone like E. to love and be loved by.

I confess that I think it would be poor policy for me to go to Hyde Park next Sunday—although, as you know and don't have to be told, I always love & try to be there all I can—I have been home twice already this term & I feel certain that J.R.R. and Helen w'd be sure to smell a rat if I went back for *part of a day* just a week before the holidays, for they would know I had been in N.Y. a whole day. *Also,* if I am in N.Y. on Sunday *not a soul* need know I have been there at all as if we go to church at all we can go to any old one at about 100th St. & the rest of the day w'd be in the house where none c'd see us. Of course I suppose you have told no one you w'd see me Saturday. Now if you really can't see the way clear to my staying in N.Y., of course I will go to H.P. with you—but you know how I feel—and also I think that E. will be terribly disappointed, as I will, if we can't have one of our first Sundays together— It seems a little hard & unnecessary on us both & I shall see you all day Saturday which I shouldn't have done had the great event not happened.

Franklin did agree to "accept all invites for Xmas. . . . Indeed, I don't intend to give up things— It w'd not be right to you or E. . . . You can imagine how happy I am— It gives a stimulous to everything I do." But he hoped they could have a Christmas house party at Springwood, too; the usual crowd of friends and classmates and relatives—including Eleanor, of course.

As usual, Franklin had managed to seem reasonable, affectionate, good-humored, and solicitous of his mother's feelings, but he had not budged an inch, would be denied nothing. He would spend Saturday *and* Sunday with Eleanor, and he would see her over the holidays as well. Sara had been outmaneuvered. She still thought Franklin was making a mistake, she told him. "Of course you are sure to be seen in New York & the Parish servants will talk. . . . I am so glad to think of my precious son so perfectly happy. You *know* that I try not to think of myself. I know that in the future I shall be glad & I shall love Eleanor

& adopt her *fully* when the right time comes. Only have patience, dear Franklin, don't let this new happiness make you lose interest in work or home. I want so much to talk many things over with you & try to look ahead a little & plan." But she could not change his mind and dutifully began to draw up a guest list for the Christmas house party.

The next day was the third anniversary of the death of Mr. James. She and Franklin had spent the previous anniversary together at Springwood and in the afternoon had driven up to the cemetery with a wreath. December eighth fell mid-week in 1903, so that there had never been any possibility that Franklin could leave campus and his classes to be present on the sad day itself. But now, by refusing to come to Hyde Park until nearly two weeks after the anniversary in order to see Eleanor, he was leaving his mother alone with her memories. She wrote again to Franklin that evening, her resentment evident beneath the customarily serene surface of her note: "I have been up to the church with flowers & found Brother Rosy had been there with a huge bunch of roses & carnations on his way to his train. It looked so lovely, the big lower stone in place & all covered with snow, then my wreath & our flowers."

For Eleanor, at least, the struggle over the weekend had been worthwhile. "We have had two happy days together," she wrote Franklin after he had returned to Cambridge, "and you know how grateful I am for every moment which I have with you." She signed this letter, "Your devoted Little Nell."

"I am sorry to part with the old year," she wrote to Franklin on New Year's Eve; "it has been so good to me but the new is going to bring us both I hope still more perfect joy and love, if that is possible. Twelve is striking, so goodnight darling 'a Happy New Year to you—.' "

Franklin was running flat-out now, overseeing the *Crimson,* seeing Eleanor as often as he dared while not ignoring his mother, trying at least to pass his courses, and all the while keeping the great secret of his engagement even from his roommate. He fell asleep on the midnight train from New York to Boston, dozed in class, suffered constantly from the sinus trouble that always intensified when he was overworked and anxious. "It is dreadfully hard," he told his mother with his usual cheery bravado, "to be a student, a social whirler, a 'prominent and democratic fellow,' and a fiancé, all at the same time —but it is worthwhile."

But to Eleanor he evidently confessed that separation from her made him miserable, that he was drained and sometimes depressed. She worried about him. "I never knew such a busy person as you are," she told him. "Please try to get a little rest sometime." She was sympathetic when he lost his race for class marshal, and anxious that she herself was too happy; surely such bliss would arouse "the envy of the gods" and bring down disaster on them both. She heard a rumor that there was a diphtheria epidemic in Cambridge, and wrote pleading with him to be especially careful; diphtheria was "the disease I particularly dread having the people I care for exposed to"—the disease that had killed her mother and her oldest brother. Sara was worried, too, and Franklin assured both that it had all been a false alarm.

At some point that winter, perhaps during the Christmas holidays, Sara had told Franklin of her plan to rent a house in Boston to be near him. He had openly opposed it. The added strain of rationing still more of his time to make sure he was being sufficiently attentive to his mother would have been too much, and he would not even consider any scheme which would forbid him to see his fiancée for more than a week or two at a time. Remembering that the trip he and his mother had taken together to Europe the first summer after his father's death had been relatively without strain, he suggested as an alternative that they might consider a Caribbean cruise in March. Lathrop Brown could come, too. If he was to be cut off from Eleanor in any case, he might as well have the best possible time; the West Indies would be a much more congenial place to spend five frigid weeks in February and March than Cambridge.

Sara eagerly agreed. She would be traveling with her son again, and she may also have recalled her own voyage to China that had helped her forget Stanford White twenty-seven years before. Perhaps the memory of Eleanor would fade, too.[5]

5. The Caribbean voyage has always previously been described as entirely Sara's idea, but in part of an unpublished letter written to her son on April 21, 1934, she emphatically denied having initiated it. This letter represents her only firsthand account of her part in the Roosevelt courtship and marriage. She was moved to write, she told FDR, because of a new book, *The New Dealers,* a breezy insider's look at the Roosevelt administration by "The Unofficial Observer," a pseudonym for the journalist John Franklin Carter. Sara did not like its treatment of her: "The 'Unofficial Observer' seems *very* intimate with our family affairs & in the pages I read there were three falsehoods about me. I do wish I had been left out of the picture!

"*1st fib* (to use a mild term) that your Mother whisked you off to the West Indies to prevent your leaving Harvard to be married! Going to the W.I. was *your* idea, rather than for me to take a house in Boston.

"*2nd fib.* That 'I tried to defer your marriage'—the most I ever said was that you were both very young—18 and 21.

"*3rd fib.* That after your illness I wanted to 'take you to Hyde Park' to 'baby' you & make an invalid of you. All I did was to say that if the doctors thought best for you to have for some months a quiet life, I would keep Hyde Park open & live there for a time.

"Well, it makes no difference to me, tho' I felt badly *for a time* & slept badly, wondering *who* had told such tales. Now, I feel I would rather not *know.* Some people will resent it & it seems rather horrid. All the rest [of the book] seems interesting & I hope *true.*"

Meanwhile, on January 11, 1904, she again drove up to St. James Church alone and watched while the masons set the polished granite cap in place above Mr. James's grave. She had been too loving and dutiful a wife ever to consider going against her late husband's wishes in a matter so important as his burial: Mr. James lies next to his Rebecca, just as he had wished. But Sara did ask the stonecutters whether when the time came her casket might be slipped in above his and beneath the same side of the monument so that she, too, might be reunited with him. A drawing was made for her showing how this might easily be accomplished, and she filed it away against the future. "At last it is done," she wrote that evening, "and it is entirely as James would have had it done, but I have no more to do, only to think and *remember.*"

A week later, still another link with Mr. James was cut. Tip, the black Pomeranian that had been such a comfort to him in his last months, was killed by one of the many trains that sped along the river below Springwood each day. The big house echoed without him, she noted in her journal; the dog had been "with me all the time."

Perhaps to bolster her spirits, she went into the city and took Eleanor, Helen Roosevelt, and Muriel Robbins to the theater to see *Candida*—"the first play I have been to since my great sorrow. It seemed strange to be there. It is a clever little piece by Bernard Shaw."

Eleanor thought it much better than that. She had already seen it several times, evidently mesmerized by the character of the heroine, Candida, whose quiet but immovable devotion to her husband was the secret source of his strength. Her husband is "a first-rate clergyman," according to the playwright, a big hearty Christian socialist known for the eloquence and vigor of his preaching, and in the play's climactic scene Candida explains her little-understood role in her husband's life to a would-be lover, the penniless young poet Eugene Marchbanks. Her husband, she tells him, has been "spoiled from his cradle. We go once a fortnight to see his parents. You should come with us, Eugene, to see the pictures of the hero of that household. James as a baby! The most wonderful of all babies. James holding his first school prize . . . James as the captain of his eleven! James in his first frock coat! James under all sorts of glorious circumstances! You know how strong he is . . . how clever he is: how happy. . . . Ask James' mother and his three sisters what it costs to save James the trouble of doing anything but be strong and clever and happy. . . . Ask the tradesmen who want to worry James and spoil his beautiful sermons who it is that puts them off. When there is money to give he gives it: when there is money to refuse, I refuse it. I build a castle of comfort and indulgence and love for him, and stand sentinel always to keep little vulgar cares out. I make him master here, though he does not know it."

But her husband does know it, and "quite overcome," now acknowledges it to the world: "It's all true, every word. What I am you have made me with the labor of your hands and the love of your heart. You are my wife, my mother, my sisters: you are the sum of all loving care to me."

Both the tall diffident girl and the beautiful determined older woman whom she followed up the aisle of the theater at the end of the play that evening wanted to play Candida's role in Franklin's drama; each wished to be the sum of all loving care to him.

Franklin, Sara, and Lathrop were to sail on Saturday, February 6, aboard the *Prinzessin Victoria Luisa,* the same ship on which mother and son had cruised through the Scandinavian fiords two summers earlier. Eleanor and Franklin had hoped to spend a day or two together in New York before their long forced separation began, but at the last moment, Eleanor's Cousin Henry Parish fell ill and rushed out of town in search of fresh air; his wife went with him. "No one not even you dear can come to the house till they get back," Eleanor wrote Franklin in some desperation. "It is not proper for me to have you come to see me when I'm not chaperoned. I don't know what to do but perhaps you can think of something." Franklin could. He wrote his mother gently insisting that she invite Eleanor to Springwood for a day. "Nobody need know a thing about it and she wouldn't be any trouble as far as getting off is concerned—for I can pack all my things in half an hour." If she did not agree to invite Eleanor, he said, he would risk the scandal and go to New York himself on Friday to see her. Sara acquiesced, and Franklin and Eleanor had Thursday together at Hyde Park. Before they parted, Eleanor promised to be in Washington, visiting with Bamie, when Franklin and his mother reached there in March on their way home.

The cruise began badly two days later. Franklin was "tired and blue," Sara noted, "Lathrop Brown looks ill," and there were "too many passengers." The sea was rough as well, the air cold and dank. It took several days of sailing south before they began to feel better.

They stopped at St. Thomas, San Juan, and Barbados. It was Mardi Gras at Trinidad—the town of Port of Spain was "very gay," Sara noted—and in the evening she, Franklin, and Lathrop dined at the Queen's Park Hotel, and then the two young men attended a costume ball, dancing with the daughters of local officials while Sara looked on. Such dances were arranged at several ports "to entertain the passengers," Brown remembered, "and [to] give the people who lived in 'out of the way' places a chance to meet strangers and perhaps rich Americans." Among those with whom Franklin waltzed that evening was a beautiful Frenchwoman of perhaps thirty whose interest in the slim young Harvard senior with the celebrated name seemed unusually intense—or so Sara thought. Worse, Franklin seemed flattered by her attention, laughing even more heartily than usual as he whirled her around the floor. His mother may have hoped that their cruise would cool his interest in Eleanor, but not this way; the woman was clearly an adventuress. She chided Franklin. He was amused by her concern and enjoyed teasing her about it. Thirty-two years later, on his way to visit South America as President of the United States, FDR took the time to write a note to his mother suggesting that he might stop at Trinidad on the way home, "and perhaps I may meet the famous French lady!"[6]

The ship anchored off the Venezuelan coast on February 19, and the passengers went ashore. Sara enjoyed the precipitous train ride that took them over the steep hills to Caracas, but did not enjoy the "dirty hotel Venezuela" in which they spent the night. "Caracas is called *there* 'the Paris of South America,'" she noted, "but I failed to see the resemblance."[7] Entering the harbor at Santiago, Cuba, a week later,

6. Some years later a puzzled writer came across this opaque reference and wrote Lathrop Brown to ask him about it. "The 'Famous French Lady' is a character which has grown in the telling," Brown answered. "Many ladies of 30 can flatter youngsters of [22] and annoy the mothers of same. I think that here is a clear case of FDR being pleased by the lady's attention and equally pleased to find how annoyed his mother was about it. The whole affair was nothing as I remember. There are many idle hours on a cruise, and there was little enough to see and do on this particular one, except in Cuba." Then, with the discretion with which he responded to most questions about his roommate's Harvard years, Brown added a note: "I think I would omit any reference to the incident, lest it be misconstrued."

In most accounts, it has been assumed that the French lady was a fellow passenger aboard the Roosevelts' ship. But FDR's own reference to Trinidad in his letter to his mother suggests to me that he encountered her on that island—and that he left her there when the *Prinzessin Victoria Luisa* sailed on the next day. She may of course have been aboard, but had there been anything more to their relationship than a genial flirtation it seems unlikely that FDR would have continued for long to joke about it with his mother.

Sources: Lathrop Brown to Sidney Shalett, January 15, 1959, PPF 2094, FDRL; Roosevelt and Shalett, *Affectionately, FDR*, pages 30–31; SDR Journal, FDRL.

7. This visit—or FDR's colorful memory of it—inspired one of his favorite stories. He told it at the White House during a toast to the visiting president of Venezuela in January 1944. "When I was in college, in my senior year, I went down with my roommate on one of those —I am sorry to say *German*—cruises down through the West Indies. And we got down to

they sailed past Morro Castle and the rusting hulks of Spanish cruisers destroyed by U.S. Navy shells during the Spanish-American War, and eagerly went ashore to explore the battlefields of El Caney and San Juan, where Cousin Theodore had made himself a national hero just six years earlier; Franklin carefully photographed the ground over which his hero had led his celebrated charge.

Back aboard ship on February 29, and hurrying across the deck, Sara stumbled over an obstruction and fell forward onto her face. "I think I broke my nose," she wrote that evening, "the doctor says *not.*" But she spent three painful days in her berth, visited by the captain—"very kind and sympathetic about my horrid fall"—before getting up, her face still badly swollen "to go to lunch and pretend it is all right." The accident had shaken her badly, made her "too nervous and uncomfortable to enjoy anything" for days, even though "Dear F. tries to comfort me."

At Nassau on March 2 they were met by Evelyn Carter, the British governor's daughter, whom Franklin had first come to know at Campobello in August. Sara liked Miss Carter and thought her parents, Sir Gilbert and Lady Carter "very pleasant." Perhaps she quietly hoped that the young woman's obvious feeling for Franklin would demonstrate to him that he need be in no hurry to marry. They spent four

---

Caracas . . . and my roommate and I went up to the clerk of the hotel and said, 'What's doing tonight? We want to go to a cafe, someplace where they have dancing.' . . . I don't know what they would call it today, but probably a different name.

"And the clerk said, 'Oh, you can't do that. You have got to go to the opera.'

"My roommate and I said, 'We didn't come to Caracas to go to the opera.'

"He said, 'But you must. Everybody is going to the opera; they are giving *Pagliacci.*' Well, I had been to the opera with my mother several times. I said, 'I have never heard of *Pagliacci.*'

" 'But,' he said, 'the great artist is singing.'

"I said, 'I don't care.'

" 'But,' he said, 'it's Caruso.'

"I said, 'I never heard of him.'

"In New York nobody had ever heard of him, and yet at that time Caruso was considered the greatest tenor in all the world. He had sung at Caracas before, in Buenos Aires, in Rio and in Lima, I think. He was one of the great singers known to all South America.

"So, because there was nowhere else to go, we went to the opera. And he was perfectly marvelous.

"After we got back to New York, I talked to some of my musical friends about Caruso and *Pagliacci,* but they had never heard of him. Years later, Caruso was taken on by the Metropolitan Opera Company . . . and of course became the greatest tenor of all time. But I have always said that my roommate and I discovered Caruso."

FDR may in fact have attended the opera in Caracas, though his mother's journal makes no mention of it, but he did not hear Caruso, who was himself then at sea, on his way from New York to Monte Carlo; nor was the tenor unknown to New York music lovers, having just made his debut in their city.

Sources: Public Papers and Addresses, 1944–1945, pages 46–47; Stanley Jackson, *Caruso,* page 110.

days with the Carters, bathing in the brilliant blue water off Hog Island and later sitting beneath the palms, eating oranges and bananas and cracking open coconuts to drink the sweet milk. They played charades after dinner at Government House one evening, and the next morning boarded a glass-bottomed boat to watch shoals of brilliantly colored fish flicker over the bright coral. Franklin enjoyed himself in the Bahamas—he almost always enjoyed himself, wherever he was—and Evelyn Carter did her best to charm him. But he remained unmoved. "In the back of his mind," Lathrop Brown recalled many years later, "there was always Eleanor."

Eleanor herself was not so confident. Franklin's absence drove her dangerously close to despondency. Alone in her cousin's house she had been too sad even to write to her fiancé for two days. She felt exhausted and "cross with myself," she told him, and with Hall, who was doing poorly at school: "I don't really know how to make him more ambitious & it is really discouraging to have him so bad." But whatever her disappointment over Hall, her real anxieties centered on Franklin. Like her father, he had gone away, promising to return and always to love her. But could she believe him? Was he having such a good time in the West Indies that those promises would be forgotten? she asked in her first letter to him, adding "that's not *such* a very pleasing thought." As soon as he received the letter he telegraphed his reassurance.

The Roosevelts landed at Miami on March 6 and stopped in Palm Beach, where Sara noted the "crowds of overdressed vulgar people" that thronged the Royal Poinciana Hotel, and she and Franklin rode side by side in bicycle chairs to view the ostrich and alligator farms. Later, Sara added, "I watched Franklin in the surf and was glad when he came out."

They finally reached the Hotel Shoreham in Washington at a little after ten in the morning on March 10. A note was waiting for Franklin at the desk. It was from Eleanor: "Just a line to tell you how *more* than glad I am to have you here at last. I will he home as near twelve as possible, Honey, and I hope you will be able to get here. Auntie Bye, will, I think, be in about then also."

They could still not see one another alone. Bamie called Sara's room about noon, inviting her and her son for tea, not lunch. Too impatient to sit still till then, Franklin took his mother for a two-hour walk.

We know no details of Franklin and Eleanor's reunion that afternoon, but its outcome was clear. Years later, Eleanor would write proudly that despite the long sea voyage and his mother's hopes, "Franklin's feelings had not changed."

Sara did not surrender easily. The five-week cruise had not altered her son's determination; perhaps a still longer stay abroad would. Sometime during their brief stay in Washington, she took Franklin with her to see an old family friend, Joseph Choate, the venerable Republican lawyer and diplomat who was home for consultations from his post as ambassador to the Court of St. James's. Franklin's father had briefly served as secretary to Ambassador James Buchanan more than half a century earlier, she reminded Choate, and his half brother, Rosy, had been first secretary at London for several years. Wouldn't it be fitting if Franklin now joined him there for a time as his personal secretary? It would be such good experience for a young man interested in public life. The ambassador was courteous but unyielding: Franklin was too young, and, besides, he had already engaged a secretary.

Sara had emptied her arsenal. Franklin escorted her home to Hyde Park, then returned to Harvard. She wrote him the next night.

> Darling Franklin,
>
> I am feeling pretty blue. You are gone. The journey is over & I feel as if the time were not likely to come again when I shall take a trip with my dear boy, as we are not going abroad, but I must try to be unselfish & of course my dear child I *do* rejoice in your happiness, & shall not put any stones or straws even in the way of it. I shall go to town a week from Friday just to be with you when I can. I have put away your albums & loved fussing over them. . . . Oh, how still the house is, but it is home and full of memories dear to me. *Do* write. I am already longing to hear.
>
> Your loving,
> Mother

Sara missed Franklin terribly that spring. "I wish I could go into your room here and wake you this morning," she wrote from Springwood on the first of May. "It is like June and you would blink and call out, 'Shut the blinds!' " But she knew now that he would not ever be permanently there again, and that if she wished to remain close to him she must grow close to Eleanor as well. And Eleanor, who understood better than most the terrors abandonment inspired, sympathized with Sara's fears of a lonely future and sought to reassure her as best she could. "Don't let her feel that the last trip with you is over," she told

Franklin shortly after he returned from the West Indian cruise. "We three must take them together in the future, that is all, and though I know three will never be the same to her, still someday I hope that she will really love me and I would be very glad if I thought she was even the least bit reconciled to me now. I will try to see her whenever she comes in town."

The two women now seemed inseparable. Sara took "the dear child" with her to shop, to tea, to dine, to the theater and the opera, for long drives and short walks. "Always a pleasure to have the nieces," she noted one crowded weekend at Springwood, "and added joy to have Eleanor now." Sara traveled to Tivoli for luncheon one afternoon to meet Grandmother Hall. It went well, Eleanor reported to Franklin; "Vallie did not appear, much to my relief. [Sara] was very sweet. Grandma quite fell in love with her." Cousin Susie Parish felt the same; Sara had been "sweet" to her, too: "I don't think, Honey, your Mother could be anything else."

The Halls approved of Franklin, too. He visited Tivoli in May and made a point of admiring the fine books in Grandfather Hall's library. Even Vallie was "exemplary" while he was there, he told Sara. "I seem to have a good effect on him."

And Sara slowly drew Eleanor into the Delano circle. Its unquestioning family cohesiveness was a revelation to her. Among Sara's brothers and sisters, Eleanor wrote, "there was a sense of security which I had never known before. . . . They were a clan, and if misfortune befell one of them, the others rallied. . . . The Delanos might disapprove of one another, and if so, they were not slow to express their disapproval, but let someone outside so much as hint at criticism, and the clan was ready to tear him limb from limb!" To her pleased astonishment, they all welcomed Eleanor. Price Collier insisted on calling her by her first name, she told Franklin; "I really think it is about time you grew jealous!" And Mrs. Collier asked to be "called 'Aunt Kassie' the other day! I thought it was a little previous, however, & I have not done it yet, but I suppose I shall soon!" The prospect of meeting Aunt Dora, not due home from Paris until the fall, was somehow more daunting. "I'm afraid for fear she won't like me," she told Franklin. "Please say nice things about me to her, won't you?" Eleanor visited Algonac too, and found it "perfectly lovely. The house is fascinating & I would have liked to make Mr. Hitch tell me all about his things, but he had such a petrifying effect upon me that I hardly dared speak to him." "Mrs. Hitch was too sweet," however, and "the view is one of the finest on the river, I think. I wanted to stand and look at it all day." Her pleasure must have pleased Sara.

It was comforting to have Sara take such an interest in her and to have the Delanos so hospitable, but it was Franklin for whom she longed. "I wish you were here, dear, to kiss me goodnight," she had written him that winter, and by April she wrote that "I cannot even control my thoughts now. I find myself looking at a page and thinking of you." Every cold he developed was cause for alarm, every lapse between letters potential evidence that he was ill or losing interest. She lived for his letters. "The family think it so queer," she wrote from Tivoli, "that I should enjoy a cold drive of 8 mi. over atrocious roads every afternoon where there 'really is nothing to go for!' But I have good reasons." And she delighted in his triumphs and in the important part he said her support played in them. When he was elected permanent chairman of his class committee after losing his race for class marshal, she told him how pleased she was, "for I know how much it meant to you and I always want you to succeed. Dearest, if you only knew how happy it makes me to think that your love for me is making you try all the harder to do well, and oh! I hope that some day I will be more of a help to you."

Franklin and Eleanor managed to see quite a lot of one another that June. On the eighteenth, Helen Roosevelt married Teddy Robinson at Hyde Park. The older guests stayed with Sara at Springwood, the younger crowd at Rosy's. Franklin was an usher, Eleanor a bridesmaid, and they stood solemnly together in a formal group portrait of the wedding party. The tall hemlock hedge of Sara's rose garden served as the backdrop.

On the twenty-fourth, Franklin received his Harvard diploma at Cambridge. Eleanor sat with Sara in the audience in Sanders Theater. "F. in cap and gown sat on the stage," Sara noted proudly, "as he is a class officer." Only the absence of Mr. James lessened her pleasure and that of her son. The two women also attended a more informal traditional ceremony held outdoors behind Hollis Hall, a raucous mix of skits and gag gifts thought hilarious enough for the *Boston Globe* to cover in detail. Charlie Shea, for example, the best actor in the class, was given a big dry goods case out of which stepped a small black girl "to act as his leading lady." The captain of the baseball team was next "arrested for stealing bases by F. D. Roosevelt," the *Globe* reported, "who was given a New York policeman's helmet to start him on his political career as the successor of his uncle *(sic)*, Theodore Roosevelt." Everyone evidently thought that was funny, too.[8]

Eleanor planned to spend the month of August at Campobello, stopping on the way for a week at Islesboro, her Aunt Corinne's summer home in Dark Harbor, Maine. It was a busy place, with cousins and their friends coming and going. Other men sought Eleanor's company, and she had to find tactful ways to deflect their interest without betraying her secret. "I really think the family must think me a dreadful flirt," she told Franklin, "or an awfully poor one."

Franklin grew impatient. Why didn't she come to Campobello sooner and take the shortest route, he asked, changing trains at Millbridge, Maine, instead of going all the way through to Bangor? He could meet her at Millbridge. She didn't think that wise, she answered, for if her train was late and the connecting train left on time, she and Franklin might find themselves stranded with only her maid for an escort. "That is one of the drawbacks, dear, to not announcing our engagement though we did not think of it at the time."

Franklin remedied the problem his own way, sailing unannounced into Dark Harbor on the *Half Moon* with two Harvard friends, and staying several days. He wired Sara, who was expecting him at Campobello, that the coast was fogbound. Young Corinne Robinson, with whom Eleanor had been reading Browning sonnets when his yacht arrived, was pleased. "It was very nice to see him again," she noted in her diary, though "I cannot decide whether it filled E. with joy or not. I think he is very crazy about her, but she not about him. It is truly pathetic." In this instance, at least, Eleanor was evidently better able to conceal her feelings than Franklin was—or perhaps it was just that she took her pledge of secrecy more seriously than he did. In any case, Corinne and her mother both took Eleanor aside, she later told Franklin, and gravely warned her against injuring his feelings, "because they thought I did not realize how serious you might be, etc., and I led them on very wickedly and made believe I was much worried at the thought

8. Among the orations heard by the three Roosevelts that day was "The Millionaire in Politics," composed and delivered by one of Franklin's classmates, Fred Wayne Catlett. Of the nineteen millionaires then serving in the U.S. Senate, Catlett noted, all but three were self-made men: "This situation . . . is typical of the whole of political life,—that is, the man born rich generally shuns politics and scorns politics, while his energetic, ambitious but less aristocratic self-made brother dives with zest into the dirty but still alluring political pool." The problem was not that the very rich were running for office—they were, after all, bulwarks of "stability and conservatism so valuable in a republic," he reassured his Harvard listeners—but that the over zealous among them brought "illegitimate business methods" with them into the arena and bought their own elections. The remedy lay in reforming the voter, not the candidate, Catlett concluded; "we must give him a wholesale moral education to prevent his wholesale bribery."

you might really care for me in more than a friendly way! May I be forgiven for all my white lies."

The month at Campobello, once it finally began, went all too fast —"Oh! so quickly," Eleanor later wrote. She and Franklin walked and sailed and read aloud to one another, and did their best to have at least a little time alone together each day. Evelyn Carter was back on the island again; so was Frances Pell. But Franklin's interest in them was only polite. He played a good deal of golf while Eleanor and Sara went walking together, and he won both the Challenge Cup and the President's Cup, Sara noted, the latter "a very handsome silver one." And he and Eleanor took part in a series of tableaux at the club that raised eighty dollars for the island's tiny library. Franklin was "a very funny 'Douglas' [fir] in kilts, etc.," according to Sara. On August 29, Eleanor's last full day on the island, Sara and Mrs. Pell drove her and Franklin out to Eastern Head, a favorite picnic spot, and left them there to lunch alone beneath the pines and later to walk back to the cottage together along the shore road. The next day Sara and Franklin both escorted Eleanor to her train. "I wish you could have seen Franklin's face the night you left Campo," Mrs. Kuhn wrote Eleanor later. "He looked so tired and I felt everybody bored him. He could not stand Evelyn's chatter."

Franklin and his mother moved in October to a rented house at 200 Madison Avenue and he began his studies at Columbia Law School. They do not seem to have interested him much. He would fail two courses his first year, blaming circumstances rather than himself, just as he had at Groton. "It certainly shows the uncertainty of marks," he told Sara, "for I had expected much lower marks in some of the others and thought I had done as well on the two I failed as in those I passed with B." Part of the problem may have been the busy social life Rosy now arranged for him; as promised, Franklin's half brother introduced him to influential New York friends and helped get him elected to several of his clubs.

But Franklin's mind was largely occupied with seeing Eleanor and with the coming announcement of their engagement. On October 11, her twentieth birthday, he gave her as a secret gift her engagement ring, chosen at Tiffany's "after much inspection and deliberation." "I am longing to have my birthday present from you for good," she wrote to him from Tivoli, "and yet I love it so I know I shall find it hard to keep from wearing it! You could not have found a ring I would have liked better, even if you were not you! This sounds odd but is quite sensible."

The secret was becoming burdensome. Later that month Franklin and Eleanor were both guests at the Robinson home at Orange, New Jersey, where, young Corinne noted, "E. and F. are comic. They avoided each other like the black plague and told beautifully concocted lies and deceived us sweetly in every direction. I was so amused . . . of course suspecting something made it all the more sure. I would bet they are engaged." But when she asked Franklin about it as he took her for a drive in the runabout, he did his airy best to put her off. She was not fooled: "I had a splendid talk with F.R. and he enjoyed himself telling delicious stories (lies). I told him he had a very deceitful nature, which he has, I believe." Eleanor was no more communicative. Three days later, she and Corinne went driving. "We neither of us mentioned F.," Corinne noted in her journal, "but I think he was on both our minds."

The official announcement was finally to be made on December first, but Franklin hoped to tell the assembled Delanos about it in person over the Thanksgiving table at Fairhaven. At the beginning of November he fell ill, however, with what at first seemed simply a cold. After three days without improvement, an anxious Sara called in the family physician, Dr. George Draper, who examined the patient and confessed that he could not "quite see what was wrong." Sara was privately "sure it is liver," and it was eventually thought to be jaundice. He stayed home from class in any case, sitting listlessly by the fire. Eleanor was privately terrified but did her best to cheer him up during her frequent visits. Sara read aloud to him from the memoirs of Robert E. Lee. Rosy came to dine and play piquet.

Sara finally had to cancel plans to go to Fairhaven, but Franklin did write a letter announcing his news that was read aloud at the table, and the entire family wired back its congratulations. Franklin was largely recovered by the time the official announcement appeared in the newspapers but Eleanor was ill—with grippe, Sara said—"very weak and ill. Poor F. much upset and I am anxious." The next day she seemed better but "*very* weak and looks like a shadow."

Again, Eleanor not Franklin was the important Roosevelt in all the newspaper coverage of the coming wedding. She had "more claim to good looks than any of the Roosevelt cousins," according to *Town Topics*. "An attractive girl . . . unusually tall and very fair," another newspaper noted, "and has a charming grace of manner that has made her a favorite since her debut." Franklin was identified only as "a member of the New York Yacht Club," and as the former editor of the *Crimson* who "was defeated in a close struggle for election as a class day officer."

A blizzard of congratulatory letters descended upon the couple. Warren Delano IV, the oldest and most like their father of all Sara's brothers and sisters, vowed that Eleanor need never "doubt . . . being taken in by all her fiancé's family." Letters from the Hitches and Colliers and Delanos and from Aunt Dora all echoed his welcome. The Halls welcomed Franklin, too, Grandmother Hall attesting that he was "a fine man." Alice Roosevelt—who would be Eleanor's maid of honor—thought the news "simply too nice to be true." The Reverend Sherrard Billings of Groton wrote Franklin that it had been "a dream of mine for some years that you would be a man widely useful to your country, and a sympathetic wife will be a great help to you on the road to realizing my dream and I am thankful and glad."[9]

Here and there among the members of the family, public enthusiasm was secretly tempered by private fears for the future. Corinne Robinson Alsop remembered, for example, that her first thought on hearing news of the engagement had been that Eleanor had "lived through so much unhappiness, and then to [plan to marry] a man with a mother like Cousin Sally . . . A more determined and possessive woman than I have ever known." But to Eleanor she merely wrote "Hurrah, hurrah, hurrah," and boasted that she had been the first to predict it.

Franklin must have been especially pleased by a letter from the White House:

> Dear Franklin,
>
> We are greatly rejoiced over the good news. I am as fond of Eleanor as if she were my daughter; and I like you, and trust you, and believe in you. No other success in life—not the Presidency, or anything

9. In *This Is My Story,* Eleanor wrote that her engagement had already been announced before Thanksgiving in 1904, and that she and Franklin had spent that holiday with the Delanos at Fairhaven. Her mother-in-law's journal and family letters show that this was not the case, and the eloquent description of the impact upon her of the Delanos' closeness as a family that appears on pages 117–120 of that book must date from Thanksgiving of the following year, when the newlywed Roosevelts were indeed guests at the homestead.

The secret was well kept. The last members of the family to hear the news were Helen and Teddy Robinson, who were still traveling on their honeymoon in January of 1905 and were idly leafing through a heap of old newspapers in the lobby of their hotel in Colombo, Ceylon, when they came upon the announcement in a month-old copy of the *New York Herald.*

Source: Helen Roosevelt Robinson's diary, courtesy of Franklin D. Roosevelt, Jr.

else—begins to compare with the joy and happiness that come in and from the love of the true man and the true woman, the love which never sinks lover and sweetheart in man and wife. You and Eleanor are true and brave, and I believe you love each other unselfishly; and golden years open before you. May all good fortune attend you both, ever.

Give my love to your dear mother.

Your aff. cousin,
Theodore Roosevelt

Sara was surely proud of that letter, too, but not as proud as she must have been of the one the President's sister Bamie sent to Eleanor. "My own darling soft-eyed child," it said in part, "your letter has given me great joy. I love Franklin as you know on his own personal account because he is so attractive & also because I believe his character is like his Father's whom Uncle Will & I always feel was the most *absolutely* honorable upright gentleman (the last in its highest sense) that we ever knew."

Franklin asked Endicott Peabody to officiate at the wedding—"It would not be the same without you," he told the rector—and Peabody rearranged his schedule in order to be on hand. Meanwhile, Eleanor asked her Uncle Ted if he would be willing to stand in her father's place and give her away. He enthusiastically agreed, and the wedding was set for Friday afternoon, March 17, 1905—St. Patrick's Day, when the President was to be in the city to deliver two speeches.

The engaged couple would see a lot of him that month. He had been elected President in his own right in November by a landslide. ("I am no longer a political accident," he had told Edith.) Franklin had been pleased to cast his own first presidential vote for his cousin, still more pleased to be asked, along with Eleanor, to be Bamie's guest at the March 4 inaugural. He sat with his fiancée just behind the President's immediate family on the steps of the Capitol and heard TR pledge himself to a "square deal for every man." Eleanor was too excited to pay much attention to what her uncle was saying, she remembered; she was conscious only that she was witnessing history up close, and she "never expected to see another inauguration in the family." Franklin forgot nothing.

The two intervening weeks were filled with parties in honor of the bride and groom, their bridesmaids and ushers. Some 340 wedding gifts were received and gratefully acknowledged—leather-bound sets of Browning and Emerson, Stevenson and Brontë, because everyone knew Franklin was a collector; several gold cigarette cases, also for him; a drawing of Bamie for Eleanor; thirteen clocks for the new household, and as many silver trays.

The wedding was to be held in the drawing room of Mrs. Ludlow's house on East Seventy-sixth street; by opening the doors between her drawing room and Cousin Susy's next door, some 200 guests could comfortably be accommodated. Most of the wedding arrangements were left to Eleanor's Hall relations—the orchestra and refreshments, the palms and lilacs and roses that would fill the houses and form the bower beneath which the couple was to be married. And they made certain that the Hall side of Eleanor's heritage was not overlooked. Her satin wedding gown was covered with Brussels lace that had been worn by both her grandmother and her mother at their weddings; her long veil was held in place by a diamond crescent that had once belonged to her mother—whose birthday also happened to fall on her daughter's wedding day.

But otherwise the event was to be a Roosevelt celebration. Franklin saw to that. Rosy, suffering from one of the many mostly psychosomatic illnesses that now plagued him, was resting in Florida and unable at the last moment to act as the best man. Lathrop Brown stood in for him. All Franklin's ushers were cousins or classmates. Each wore a diamond stickpin incorporating the three feathers of the family crest of which Mr. James had been so fond; Franklin had designed them himself. And he made certain that Eleanor's bridesmaids—who included Alice Roosevelt and Corinne Robinson—also displayed the crest in a more startlingly realistic form: three authentic silver-tipped ostrich plumes worn in their hair. Eleanor wore the crest as well, as part of Franklin's wedding gift, a gold watch with her initials picked out in diamonds on the back, suspended from a diamond pin in the same triple-feather pattern.

Franklin spent the evening of March 16 quietly with his mother at 200 Madison Avenue—his "last night at home as a boy," she noted in her journal. And as the actual ceremony grew nearer the next afternoon, he was "calm and happy" she said; so calm and happy, in fact, that he lost track of the time, chatting about the old days at Groton with Lathrop and the rector in a small anteroom in the Ludlow house.

The guests began filing to their seats in the candle-lit Ludlow drawing room. Sara sat up front, not far from Grandmother Hall, and wearing a white dress covered with black lace that had belonged to her mother, Catherine Delano. Behind them sat the Oyster Bay Roosevelts and the Delanos—"Dora, Annie & Fred, Fred & Tilly, Kassie & ALL," Sara noted proudly.

While Eleanor and her bridesmaids were dressing upstairs a cable from England was handed to her. "*Bonheur,*" it said, and it was signed "Souvestre."[10]

The sounds of the St. Patrick's Day parade banging its way north along Fifth Avenue and of the crowds that lined the sidewalks to cheer it on drifted steadily into the drawing room, the shouting suddenly louder and more insistent at about three-thirty. The President's carriage had arrived. He was a little late as he waved his top hat to the crowd and hurried inside, a wilted shamrock drooping in his buttonhole. He took the Ludlow stairs two at a time.

The ceremony could begin. The orchestra swung into the wedding march, doing its best to overcome the relentless blare of "The Wearing of the Green." The bridesmaids appeared, gliding down the stairs and up the aisle beneath their gravely nodding plumes. Franklin, Lathrop, and the rector scrambled to their places at the altar beneath a bower of palms and pink roses.

Then Eleanor appeared on the staircase with the President. Franklin waited under the palms as she came slowly toward him, taller than the beaming uncle whose arm she held, and looking more lovely than she ever had before. Those among the guests who remembered her mother murmured to one another; for the first time she seemed to some of them to look like Anna Hall.

Peabody began the Episcopal service in his big confident voice, stumbling a little over the words in the dim, unsteady candlelight. When he asked "Who giveth this woman in marriage?" one guest recalled, TR answered in "loud emphatic tones," "*I* do!" instead of merely stepping forward to place his niece's hand in Franklin's. They joined hands anyway, and the rings and vows were at last exchanged.

"Well, Franklin," the President said as he reached up to kiss his niece. "There's nothing like keeping the name in the family." Then he led the way into the dining room, where a collation was being served. Most of the guests followed in his wake, eager to stay close to the expansive, voluble TR. The bride and groom trailed along behind. Even the cutting of the wedding cake failed to attract many onlookers until the President was persuaded to come and get his slice.

10. Mademoiselle Souvestre would die of cancer two days after her favorite pupil's wedding.

TR finally left at about five o'clock, running late for his speech to the Friendly Sons of St. Patrick at Delmonico's, and by the time the newlyweds had dressed to leave, only their closest friends and relatives remained to pelt them with rice.

They were to spend their first week alone together at Hyde Park.

Sara later told Franklin and Eleanor that "*Everyone* says it was the most perfect wedding, so simple & yet so 'elegant & refined,' etc etc. . . . I think it was all perfect & . . . I was very proud of both my dear children." She cannot have liked *Town Topics*' treatment of the event: Despite the presence of the President of the United States, it said, the wedding had frankly been a disappointment. The Parishes were chastised for their "pathetic economy"; the food "was supplied by an Italian caterer, not of the first class"; the flowers by "a Madison Avenue florist of no particular fame; and the narrow staircase in the Parish house [had] permitted only one person to ascend or descend at a time." It was noted that Mrs. Vanderbilt had stayed at the reception only ten minutes. But whatever Sara may have thought of the article as a whole, she must have been at least momentarily pleased by its conclusion: On the way out the front door, one guest had been overheard to say that "the bridegroom had been especially handsome," and another had agreed, adding, "Surprising for a Roosevelt."

The Roosevelt coachman met Franklin and his new bride at the Hyde Park depot that evening, and drove them home to Springwood. It was a clear starry night, but the wind off the river had turned cold, and Franklin and Eleanor sat close together in the carriage, a robe across their laps. They passed between the stone gates Mr. James had brought up the road from the ruins of Mount Hope nearly forty years before, and beneath the big trees that lined both sides of the drive, their bare branches just visible against the sky.

The windows of the big house glowed bright across the lawn, and when the carriage stopped and Franklin helped Eleanor down, Elespie, the old Scottish housekeeper, was waiting in the open door to greet them. Over the years she had seen to it that the wishes of both Rebecca Howland and Sara Delano Roosevelt were carried out, and she had once admitted to her mistress that if young Franklin had any faults she could not see them. Elespie had grown deaf in the Roosevelts' service and had to rely on a homemade ear trumpet to understand her orders now, but she was still alert, and Eleanor remembered that she "looked me over critically and appraisingly, wondering if I could come up to her expectations as the wife of 'her boy.' "

Franklin and Eleanor followed along behind the old lady as she slowly climbed the stairs, past the glass case containing Franklin's mounted birds and the portrait of him painted at fourteen, and showed them to their room.

Back in New York, Sara followed them as best she could in her imagination. "My precious Franklin & Eleanor," she wrote that evening. "It is a delight to write to you together & to think of you happy at dear Hyde Park, just where my great happiness began."

ACKNOWLEDGMENTS

When I began to work on this book I assumed the end result would be both slim and speculative. It is no longer slim, and it is all based on documentary evidence—more of it, and more of it previously unexplored, than I had imagined possible.

Not long after I started my research, I had dinner with David McCullough, the fearless biographer of those three great symbols of American optimism and energy—the Brooklyn Bridge, the Panama Canal, and Theodore Roosevelt. The task of burrowing my way through the massive FDR archives then seemed more daunting every day; so did the prospect of ever penetrating the private defenses of my subject; and I wondered, also, if too many years spent editing other people's manuscripts had spoiled my chances of producing one of my own. He heard me out, then gave me some cheering advice. "Remember," he said, "the great thing is that when you're finished it's *your* book. Nobody else's."

For better or worse, it is mine, and I accept full responsibility for its shortcomings. But for whatever virtues it has, I owe a great deal to the kindness and counsel of colleagues, friends, and members of my family. Most of those who helped me along the way are thanked in the Source Notes at the end of the book, but several need to be acknowledged here as well, and in greater detail.

I want first to express my appreciation to nine scholars who occupied the Roosevelt field long before I got there, but who never hesitated for a moment to offer help to a newcomer: Bernard Asbell, Kenneth Davis, Frank Freidel, Joseph P. Lash, David McCullough, Edmund and Sylvia Morris, Alfred B. Rollins, and Arthur Schlesinger, Jr. And I owe a unique debt to Professor R. J. C. Butow, whose discovery of the secret White House recordings got me started.

The President's sons, James and Franklin, Jr., and his grandson, John R. Boettiger, were enormously helpful, too, responding even to intrusive questions about their family with candor and care. And another member of the big Roosevelt clan, W. Sheffield Cowles, Jr.—FDR's distant cousin, the only child of Anna Roosevelt Cowles, Eleanor Roosevelt's beloved "Auntie Bye"—graciously told me a host of family tales which were not only full of fresh and intriguing information but which I found could be documented. Mr. Cowles is a biographer's dream—a superb storyteller who tells true stories.

I would also like to thank two individuals who were so close to Eleanor Roosevelt as to have seemed part of her family—Edna Gurewitsch and Maureen Corr. Although they knew her only in her last years, their insights into her mature personality and character were invaluable to me in trying to understand her youth.

I worked with original documents at Harvard University, at the New York Public Library and at the New-York Historical Society, and am grateful to the staffs of all three institutions. The employees of the National Park Service who look after Springwood and Val-Kill—especially Diane Boyce, Susan Brown, Donald McTernan, Margaret Partridge, and Emily Wright—were invariably helpful when confronted with my sometimes obsessively detailed questions about life at those two places long ago.

But most of my research time was inevitably spent in the reading room at the Franklin D. Roosevelt Library at Hyde Park, and I would like to thank individually those men and women on the library staff whose patience, knowledge, and good humor made my many weeks there so rewarding—and so much fun: Supervisory Archivists Frances Seeber and Raymond Teichman and librarian Joseph Marshall, as well as Susan Busanko, Elizabeth Denier, Shellynne Eickhoff, John Ferris, Marguerite Hubbard, Shirley Mahoney, Paul McLaughlin, Robert Parks, Irene Prentiss, Mark Renovitch, and William Stickel.

This book could not have been researched or written without the encouragement and informed advice of the library's director, Dr. William R. Emerson. He has been both my mentor and my friend.

A number of people believed in this project at moments when I was not entirely sure I did, among them Robbin Reynolds (now of Workman Press), Buz Wyeth and Terry Karten of Harper & Row, and especially Carl Brandt, my agent and friend.

Several other friends took the time to read and comment upon the entire manuscript: Richard and Carol Snow, who saved me from more embarrassments, large and small, than I care to admit; Professor Charles B. Strozier, who worked hard to keep honest my speculations about what went on in the minds of the reticent men and women about whom I chose to write; and Dr. Pauline G. Vorhaus, who has a lot to do with whatever coherence this book—and its author—may have.

Still closer to home, I want to apologize to Nathan, to Garrett, and to Kelly, whom I too often overlooked in favor of furthering my book; no writer could have a more loving and supportive family, and I only hope they like the result.

Finally, I want to thank my wife and close reader, Diane, without whom neither this book nor much else in my life could have been accomplished. She has heard a good deal about Delanos and Roosevelts over the past three years, and not the least miraculous thing about her is that she doesn't seem to mind that there is more to come.

SOURCE NOTES

A brief note on sources: This book is based very largely upon original documents, most of them found among the massive collections of the Franklin D. Roosevelt Library at Hyde Park. A list of the collections I consulted will be found in the Bibliography that follows these notes, along with the title, date, and place of publication for all the important books, articles, and other materials I found especially useful.

To save space, in the notes to the individual chapters, I have referred to the Roosevelt Library by the abbreviation FDRL, and have used initials to designate items from several frequently used collections:

OF: President's Official File, followed by file number;
PPF: President's Personal File, followed by file number;
PSF: President's Secretary's File, followed by file number.

PROLOGUE: THE RIVER ROAD

The story of FDR and the ghoulish bishop and the account of Roosevelt's visit to his mother's garden with Frances Perkins both come from her *The Roosevelt I Knew*, pages 145–146, supplemented by contemporary newspaper accounts of the cathedral service. Further amplification of Roosevelt's antagonism toward Bishop Freeman is given in an unpublished reminiscence by Will Alexander, Papers of the Franklin D. Roosevelt Memorial Foundation, FDRL.

Calvin Coolidge's chilly view of American prospects appears in William E. Leuchtenberg, *Franklin D. Roosevelt and the New Deal*, page 28. The roll call of Roosevelt legislation is here abridged from one offered by Arthur M. Schlesinger, Jr., in a speech delivered before a group of former New Deal officials and their allies, March 7, 1983, and kindly lent to me. Eleanor Roosevelt's summings-up of her husband's contributions on both the domestic and foreign fronts are from *This I Remember*, pages 347–348.

Merriman Smith and Harold Oliver remembered the sad singing at Charlotte and described it to Bernard Asbell in *When FDR Died*, page 158. Joseph Alsop discusses FDR's inclusiveness in his eloquent *FDR: A Centenary Remembrance.*

The President's original funeral instructions are on display at the FDRL. The details of the Hyde Park ceremony are drawn from many sources, including newsreels and radio reports; a series of recently discovered photographs of the second funeral train at the Hyde Park depot, FDRL; an anonymous letter from a member of the escort of honor; a brief unpublished memoir, "When FDR Came Home," written by the man responsible for planning and supervising the Hyde Park rites, Colonel A. J. McGehee, also recently deposited at the FDRL; and from Asbell, *When FDR Died*, pages 189–199; Jim Bishop, *FDR's Last Year*, pages 660–668; Kenneth S. Davis, *Invincible Summer*, page 166; and Henrietta Nesbitt, *White House Diary*, page 311.

Robert Sherwood's thoughts as he waited in the garden and his baffled assessment of Roosevelt's personality are from his *Roosevelt and Hopkins*, pages 9 and 882. Henry Morgenthau, Jr., is quoted on the difficulty of describing FDR in Sherwood, page 9; while his story of the left and right hands comes from his diary entry for May 21, 1936, and is quoted in John Morton Blum, *Roosevelt and Morgenthau*, page 127. Mrs. Roosevelt's admission that even she had not been her husband's confidante comes from a conversation she had with her son James and appears on page 315 of his *Affectionately, FDR*, written with Sidney Shalett. Mrs. Collier's wish to accompany FDR's body to Hyde Park is quoted in Bishop, page 660.

The number of times FDR visited Hyde Park during his presidency is my estimate, based on sampling the White House usher's diaries at the FDRL; I suspect that it is low.

1: MR. JAMES

James Roosevelt is an elusive figure. He was an upright and determinedly private man to begin with, persuaded that a gentleman's duty was to stay out of the newspapers. Then, too, all his papers written or received before 1866 were destroyed when Mount Hope was razed in that year. This account of his early years and first marriage, which I believe to be the fullest ever attempted, is largely drawn from his few surviving papers and from those of other members of his family in three collections at the FDRL—the Roosevelt Family Papers, the Roosevelt Family Papers Donated by the Children, and the "Rosedale Papers," available only on microfilm. The most important single source is the lively journal kept by Mr. James's fond first wife, Rebecca Howland Roosevelt, also among the Roosevelt Family Papers at the FDRL.

The story of the Roosevelts' purchase of the house that became Springwood is drawn from Rebecca's journal, plus Olin Dows, *Franklin Roosevelt at Hyde Park;* Clara and Hardy Steelholm, *The House at Hyde Park;* and George Y. Wilkins' unpublished Interior Department document, *A Report on the Birthplace and Home of Franklin Delano Roosevelt.* James Roosevelt's comparison of the house's profile to a train comes from FDR's own unpublished memorandum, *Notes on Hyde Park*, FDRL.

The genealogy of the Roosevelts has been explored in at least four books. The two best are Karl Shriftgiesser, *The Amazing Roosevelt Family: 1603–1942*, and Nathan Miller, *The Roosevelt Chronicles.* My brief account is based on them, as well as *FDR: The Beckoning of Destiny* by Kenneth S. Davis, the Roosevelt biographer who has devoted the most shrewd and thorough attention to his subject's antecedents. I am also grateful to the genealogist, Timothy Beard, who kindly shared with me some of his findings about the family.

The customs and attitudes of Knickerbocker society are admirably described in Douglas T. Miller, *Jacksonian Aristocracy: Class and Democracy in New York, 1830–1860,* and I have relied heavily upon it and to a lesser extent upon Dixon Wecter, *The Saga of American Society.* The small scale of New York society in 1830 is described by Joseph A. Scoville on page 9 of the first volume of his *Old Merchants of New York.* The devotions of family servants are recalled on page 13 of Abram C. Dayton's wry memoir, *Last Days of Knickerbocker Society in New York;* the description of Knickerbocker exclusivity is also from Dayton, page 196. Philip Hone's recollection of Isaac Roosevelt and his forbidding contemporaries is quoted in Miller, page 87. Francis Grund's encounters with aristocratic scorn for the lower classes and for politics are all from his elegant book *Aristocracy in America,* pages 170, 94, and 107.

Isaac Roosevelt's overly charitable brother-in-law is quoted in Steelholm, page 41. His own view of his son as "unruly" comes from his letter to James, May 14, 1843, Roosevelt Family Papers, FDRL. (Isaac is ostensibly writing here of John Aspinwall Roosevelt's behavior, not James's, but the allusion is inescapable.)

The story of the Reverend Alvan Hyde and his schoolmaster son Alexander comes from the reminiscences of townspeople, included in an unusually entertaining compilation, *The Centennial Celebration and Centennial History of the Town of Lee, Massachusetts,* put together by Alexander Hyde himself (with the Reverend C. M. Hyde) in 1877. Dr. Isaac's querulous letters to James and to Alexander Hyde are among the Roosevelt Family Papers at the FDRL.

Life at the Collegiate School at Poughkeepsie is described in Steelholm, pages 41–42. But that account has here been supplemented with fresh facts found in the *Poughkeepsie Eagle* anniversary edition, June 1911, and in the College Hill *Mercury,* the school's literary magazine published from June 30, 1850, to October 1852, and found at the NYHS.

Mr. James's difficulties at the University of New York (now NYU) come from its archives and were found for me through the kindness of the archivist, Bayrd Still.

My account of Union College and its president comes largely from Codman Hislop, *Eliphalet Nott.* The unpublished *My Personal Reminiscences* by Silas Burt at the NYHS and Frederick H. Seward's *Reminiscences of a Wartime Statesman and Diplomat* provided anecdotes about student pranks, Nott's charity toward miscreants, and his reputation for financial slipperiness. Details of campus life were also drawn from George F. Howe, *Chester A. Arthur: A Quarter-Century of Machine Politics,* and Thomas C. Reeves's excellent biography, *Gentleman Boss: The Life of Chester Alan Arthur.*

The shadowy story of James Roosevelt's Grand Tour has been pieced together from his father's and stepmother's letters and from his 1847 passport, all at the FDRL.

Franklin Roosevelt's account of his father's meeting with Sam Houston is given in a letter to Adolph Schwarz, March 18, 1935, in PPF 2324, FDRL.

Mr. James's decision to abandon the law for business comes from his own autobiographical "Summary of My Life," scrawled in pencil, Roosevelt Family Papers, FDRL. His business career is briefly sketched in most biographies of his son, but is most fully developed in Davis, *FDR: The Beckoning of Destiny* pages 28–29.

The honeymoon breakfast at Niagara Falls is recalled in a letter written to John at the time of his marriage in 1867, "Rosedale Papers," FDRL. My account of the Roosevelts' subsequent trip to London is based upon my interpretation of an FDR letter to the historian Roy F. Nichols, PPF 3012, FDRL. Buchanan's clothing crisis is recounted in James MacGregor Burns, *The Vineyard of Liberty*, and in George T. Curtis, *Life of Buchanan*, Volume I.

The details of Rosy's boyhood at Mount Hope are all drawn from James's letters to John Roosevelt, written in 1864, "Rosedale Papers," FDRL. The 1861 photograph of father and son is also at the FDRL.

The official family version of James Roosevelt's wartime career is given in a short biographical entry belatedly prepared for the *National Cyclopedia of American Biography* and reviewed by the President in 1935. James's letter offering counsel to John on enlistment was written on March 16, 1864, Roosevelt Family Papers Donated by the Children, FDRL. The chagrin Theodore Roosevelt, Sr., felt at having failed to fight is fully documented in David McCullough, *Mornings on Horseback*, pages 56–61.

The statistics on American tourism before the Civil War are from Foster Rhea Dulles, *Americans Abroad*, pages 44 and 83. The *Scotia* passenger list was published in the *New York Times*, May 18, 1865. My account of August Belmont is drawn largely from David Black, *The King of Fifth Avenue: The Fortunes of August Belmont*, and from the *Dictionary of American Biography*. The DAB also supplied the details for the brief portrait of Captain Charles Marshall and the fact that Andrew Carnegie delighted in small talk and Burns's poetry. Carnegie's mission in England is outlined in Harold C. Livesay, *Andrew Carnegie and the Rise of Big Business*, pages 80–81.

My account of the Roosevelts' long sojourn abroad has been compiled from three interrelated sources: Rebecca's journals, James Roosevelt's letters to John, and Rosy's schoolboy diary, all at the FDRL. My understanding of the Rebecca Roosevelt journals was greatly enhanced by the shoe-box index to its busy, shifting cast of characters, prepared by the late George Roach and supplied to me by the library staff; it is a great pity that Mr. Roach did not live to publish the annotated version of the journals he had planned.

James's theory about the Mount Hope fire is from FDR's memorandum "History of the President's Estate at Hyde Park With Anecdotes," FDRL.

General McClellan's musings are all drawn from his unpublished letters of the period, George Brinton McClellan Papers, Library of Congress.

Nathaniel Parker Willis's rapturous description of the Hudson at Hyde Park is from his book, *American Scenery*, and appears on page 266 of *The Hudson River in Literature: An Anthology*, edited by Arthur G. Adams. The ruminations about English aristocrats by William Hickling Prescott are included in *Transatlantic Crossing*, edited by Walter Allen, pages 69–71.

The population of Hyde Park is given in *Change in Hyde Park*, a senior thesis at Vassar College, written by Nancy Fogel, FDRL.

The idyllic details of life there are all from Rebecca's journal; so is the fact that Springwood was once Brierstone. The description of Leland Stanford's visit to Springwood was given by FDR in his "History of the President's Estate," FDRL. The story of Mr. James's early-morning arrival at Hyde Park comes from a letter he wrote to Anna Roosevelt, March 31, 1878, Theodore Roosevelt Papers, Harvard.

The story of Mr. James's one-sided romance with Anna Roosevelt was first told to me by her son, W. Sheffield Cowles, Jr. I found corroboration for it in a series of letters from Mr. James to Bamie in the Theodore Roosevelt Papers in the Houghton Library at Harvard. My description of Bamie's illness and character come from McCullough, pages 33–35. Mittie Roosevelt's remark about Mr. James's first impression of Sara Delano first appears without attribution in Rita Halle Kleeman's *Gracious Lady,* page 101; it must have come from Sara Delano Roosevelt herself.

2: ALGONAC

Sara Delano Roosevelt's early life is outlined in most biographies of her son. But she is also the subject of a lively biography of her own, *Gracious Lady: The Life of Sara Delano Roosevelt,* written during her lifetime by her friend Rita Halle Kleeman and published in 1935. It is a fond portrait, invariably tactful but filled with vivid and useful detail, most of it provided by Mrs. Roosevelt herself. The text was reviewed for indiscretions by the President's daughter, Anna, before it was published. Few were found. Its surprising conclusion—that Sara Delano Roosevelt "has no personal vanity at all"—was allowed to stand.

Mrs. Kleeman's notes for the book and for two completed but unpublished magazine articles on Mrs. Roosevelt's final years have been deposited with her papers at the FDRL. These include typed transcripts of interviews with Mrs. Roosevelt, her friends, and members of her family; notes on her visits to Algonac and Fairhaven; and a small stenographer's pad filled with scribbled verbatim remarks garnered on visits to Mrs. Roosevelt in her last days. In writing this and subsequent chapters I have drawn heavily on this collection for memories more frank and revealing than those Mrs. Kleeman finally chose to use.

The House at Hyde Park, written by Clara and Hardy Steelholm and published in 1950, is useful for details of life at Algonac as well as Springwood.

The Delanos themselves, however, were their own best historians. They thought themselves important and they seem to have kept everything. The Algonac diaries, which cover the years 1872–1894, are an indispensable guide to daily happenings within the family. In addition, there are hundreds, perhaps thousands, of Delano family letters and memorabilia scattered among several collections at the FDRL—the Roosevelt Family Papers, Roosevelt Family Papers Donated by the Children, Delano Family Papers, and the Papers of Frederic A. Delano.

Frederic A. Delano, Sara's youngest brother, was the Delanos' unofficial chronicler and his several nostalgic pamphlets written for members of the family provide both remarkably reliable history and a sensitive gauge of what the Delanos thought of themselves. Any writer on the Roosevelts and their background is in his debt.

Sara Delano's delight in her own good looks and those of her son are recorded in many places, including Nathan Miller, *The Roosevelt Chronicles.* Her ability still to dazzle at eighty-six is evident in newsreel #201-3105-4 at the FDRL. The story of her flower arranging during her first visit to Springwood was told by her daughter-in-law, Eleanor Roosevelt, and comes from a transcript of her recorded walking tour of Springwood, FDRL. Sara Roosevelt's pleasure at the memory of that visit is expressed in a letter to FDR, May 8, 1932, Roosevelt Family Papers, FDRL.

The story of Warren Delano's butter brick comes from Kleeman, page 31; his father established the custom and a newspaper clipping attesting to fat's effectiveness against TB pasted into one of the Algonac diaries implies that this was the rationale and that the practice was continued at Newburgh. Mr. Delano's firm views on religion, labor, and suitors and his surprise at Sara's engagement to Mr. James were all confided in letters to his son, Warren III, DFP, FDRL.

Elliott Roosevelt's irreverent view of Mr. James as a suitor is quoted in Joseph Lash, *Eleanor and Franklin*, page 114.

Mr. James's somewhat prickly exchange of letters with Bamie Roosevelt is in the Theodore Roosevelt Papers, Houghton Library, Harvard.

The early history of the Delano clan is set forth in Daniel W. Delano, Jr., *Franklin Roosevelt and the Delano Influence.* It is an odd book, more colorful than most genealogies but often unreliable and defensive, especially when dealing with unflattering events.

Warren Delano I described his own seafaring days to his son Edward in 1849, Delano Family Papers, FDRL.

The full story of Warren Delano's career in the China trade has not yet been written. My account is pieced together from a variety of sources. Some of his letters from China are among the DFP, FDRL; others having to do with his business dealings are with the papers of Russell and Company at the Baker Business Library at Harvard and among the papers of several members of the Forbes and Low families at the Massachusetts Historical Society in Boston.

Warren's younger brother Edward kept a diary during his years in Canton, and excerpts from it are published here for the first time; DFP, FDRL. Warren Delano's great-great-grandson, Frederic D. Grant, Jr., first suggested that I consult these. His Bates College history honors thesis, *Edward Delano and Warren Delano II: Case Studies in American China Trader Attitudes Toward the Chinese, 1834–1844* (1976) ably explores the minds of his ancestors, and I am grateful to him for sharing both his notes and his counsel with me.

Warren Delano is mentioned briefly in at least three firsthand accounts of the Canton trade: William C. Hunter's two gusty memoirs, *The Fan Kwae of Old Canton* and *Bits of Old China*, and Robert Bennet Forbes's *Personal Reminiscences.* He also appears in passing in Helen Augur, *Tall Ships to Cathay;* Maurice Collis, *Foreign Mud;* and Elma Loimes, *The China Trade Post-Bag of the Seth Low Family of Salem and New York.*

The part played by Americans in the opium business is perhaps most lucidly described in Jacques M. Downs, "American Merchants and the China Opium Trade, 1800–1840," *The Business History Review*, Volume XLII, Number 4 (Winter 1968). Professor Downs is soon to publish a full-scale study of the Americans at Canton which will include brief profiles of all the traders. He kindly allowed me to consult his sketch of Warren Delano's career in advance of publication.

My portrait of Canton, the China trade, and the Opium War as Warren Delano experienced them has been compiled from a number of books, including Foster Rhea Dulles, *The Old China Trade* and *China and America;* Arthur Cunnyngham, *The Opium War;* John King Fairbank, *Trade and Diplomacy on the China Coast;* and Osmond Tiffany, Jr., *The Canton Chinese.*

My account of Houqua's "chopstick dinner" comes from Augur, pages 38–39 and Edward Delano's diary. William Hunter's blissful memories of old Canton come from page 3 of *Bits of Old China.* Robert Forbes's justification of the opium business may be found on pages 144–145 of his autobiography; his woeful cooking is described on page 147.

Details for my profiles of Judge Joseph Lyman and his wife and Catherine Lyman Delano's first impressions of China come from *Memoir of the Life of Mrs. Anne Jean Lyman* by her daughter, Mrs. Susan Lesley. The newlywed Delanos' novel dinner eaten off the Cape of Good Hope is described in Forbes, page 167, and substantiated by Edward Delano's diary.

Details of Warren Delano's domestic business career are from Frederic Delano's unpublished 1928 sketch of his father's life and from his pamphlet *Algonac,* both among his papers at the FDRL. Additional facts come from an 1877 letter written to the *New Bedford Standard,* author unknown, DFP, FDRL.

Colonnade Row is described in Kleeman, pages 14–16, and attributed there to Seth Geer. The architectural historian Paul Goldberger has more recently credited the firm of Ithiel Town and Alexander Jackson Davis in his *The City Observed,* and I have followed his lead.

Warren Delano's longing for a country home of his own is described in Frederic Delano's *Algonac,* as are many details about the house and grounds. Kleeman, Steelholm, and the Algonac diaries provided more.

The use of the word "Algonac" as a Roosevelt code word for good news is described in *FDR: Personal Letters, 1905–1928,* pages 4–5.

My description of Andrew Jackson Downing is drawn from several sources, including his own *The Architecture of Country Houses,* Joseph Kastner's lively profile in *Notable American Architects,* Carl Carmer's *The Hudson,* and Steelholm.

Warren Delano's fondness for Oriental furnishings is described in Kleeman and Steelholm, amplified here by an examination of photographs at the FDRL.

Captain Warren Delano's pleasure at the simplicity of Sara's name is in Steelholm, page 8. Eight-year-old Dora is quoted in Kleeman, page 24. Kleeman's notes are the source of Sara's memories of her mother and father; her parents' aversion to American hotels and to her step-grandmother; details of clannishness at Fairhaven and her own speculations about its causes; her tribute to her father and to his "patriarchal spirit." Her sister Dora's views on Delano family loyalty come from Kleeman's notes of a separate interview with her.

Warren Delano's homily about the weather is from a 1938 compilation of Eleanor Roosevelt's *My Day* columns.

Edward Delano's scorn for his brother's plan to recoup his losses by returning to China in 1860 is from a letter he wrote to John Delano, DFP, FDRL. Frederic Delano described his mother's "firmness of purpose" in his *Algonac,* FDRL. Kleeman gives details of Algonac life without father. Sara's tribute to him is from her unpublished notes. Warren Delano's second stay in China is touched upon in Kwang-Ching Liu, *Anglo-American Steamship Rivalry in China: 1862–1874.*

My account of the family voyage to Hong Kong aboard the *Surprise* is drawn from Catherine Delano's meticulous log, discovered by her son Fred in 1928, Frederic A. Delano Papers, FDRL. Sara's reunion with her father was recounted to Kleeman and appears in her book, page 59.

Life at Rose Hill is described in Kleeman and Steelholm, supplemented here by an examination of photographs at the FDRL, especially those in the family albums of Dora Forbes and Annie Hitch. The opium record book, with its incongruous children's drawings still in place, is among the Delano Family Papers, FDRL; as are Sara's letters about her father's toilette; the Chinese scramble of 1877; and her joy at the Civil War's end.

The Delano sisters' sibling jousts are described in Kleeman, here supplemented by excerpts from the Algonac diaries, Kleeman's notes of an interview with a girlhood friend, and Sara's own letter to Warren on the birth of his son in 1877.

Warren Delano's admonitions to his son Warren III are among his letters, DFP, FDRL. That son's high collegiate spirits are amusingly described by his brother Fred in a privately printed tribute, *Warren Delano III,* delivered at his memorial service in 1920.

The story of Warren III's difficult courtship of Jennie Walters is outlined in Daniel Delano's family history, but has been amplified here with excerpts from the Algonac diaries and from Warren II's letters to his son, Delano Family Papers, FDRL.

My portrait of Stanford White as a boisterous young man is based upon Charles C. Baldwin, *Stanford White,* and several chatty letters written by his worshipful bride on their honeymoon in 1884, Stanford White Papers, New-York Historical Society. White's grandson Peter told me of his grandfather's early escapades with Boston women.

Details of the Roosevelt-Delano wedding come from the *New York World,* as reproduced in Kleeman, Steelholm, and Davis. Elizabeth Hissop, the wedding guest who remembered the tearful women at the wedding, was interviewed by Kleeman in the early 1930s.

The newlyweds' journey to Springwood is described in Kleeman, Steelholm, and Davis, here supplemented by details from the Algonac diary, FDRL. Ellen Roosevelt is quoted as to her Aunt Sally's beauty in Kleeman, page 111.

Warren Delano's indignation at the political disloyalty of his Irish servants and his report of Sara's sadness at leaving home are both from letters to his son, Warren, Delano Family Papers, FDRL.

Details of the Roosevelt honeymoon abroad were all found in Sara Delano Roosevelt's journal, FDRL.

My brief account of Philippe Delano, his death, and Sara's reaction to it are from the Kleeman notes, the Algonac diaries, Philippe's own amusing writings, and Sara's journal, all at the FDRL.

3: THE VERY NICE CHILD

Franklin Roosevelt's boyhood has received little attention from his biographers, in part because many family papers have only recently been opened but also, I believe, because its serene surface seems to yield so few telling incidents. I have returned to primary sources for the most part in developing my own account. But there are four very different works that have proved especially helpful, and I am indebted to the authors of all four.

Kenneth S. Davis in the early chapters of *FDR: The Beckoning of Destiny* gives the fullest previous portrait of the period, as well as a useful and provocative assessment of its meaning to Roosevelt's later development.

Dr. Nona S. Ferdon's unpublished Ph.D. thesis, *Franklin D. Roosevelt: A Psychological Interpretation of His Childhood and Youth,* seeks to apply the theoretical framework developed by Erik Erikson to FDR's formative years; this book would have been much harder to write without her pioneering research into early documents and her subsequent generous advice to the author.

Perhaps the most audacious investigator of Roosevelt's youth is Bernard A. Asbell, whose shrewd, intriguing book, *The FDR Memoirs,* deserves a far wider audience than it has received.

Finally, Robert Coles's *Privileged Ones* deals with rich children in our time, not Roosevelt's, but it is filled with sensitive insights into the obvious advantages and subtler disadvantages money and family confer upon the children of the wealthy; my interpretation of their impact on Franklin Roosevelt owes much to him.

This and the following chapter also draw heavily upon *My Boy Franklin* by Sara Delano Roosevelt, as told to Isabel Leighton and Gabrielle Forbush. The curious publishing history of this book will be given in my second volume; there is nothing remotely like it in presidential literature.

Franklin Roosevelt's memories of Hyde Park as "the center of the world" are from his untitled and unpublished reminiscences, dictated in the White House at an unknown date and never completed, FDRL.

My account of his difficult birth draws heavily upon Kenneth Davis, *FDR: The Beckoning of Destiny,* pages 51–52, and Sara Delano Roosevelt's diary, FDRL.

Mrs. Roosevelt's warm memories of her infant son are from *My Boy Franklin;* her approval of Helen McRorie is from her diary, FDRL. Winston Chruchill's tribute to his nurse is quoted in William Manchester, *The Last Lion,* page 116.

Warren Delano's delight in his grandson and his dashed hope that the baby might be named for him are from letters to his son Warren III and his brother Franklin, Delano Family Papers, FDRL. Sara's own disappointment at having to name her boy for someone else is noted in her diary, FDRL.

The story of FDR (and only FDR) being allowed to sleep in the ancestral Delano cradle is from the Kleeman notes, FDRL.

Dora Forbes's remark about "a beautiful frame" first appeared in Kleeman, page 170.

SDR's progress reports on the baby are all from Kleeman and from her own journals, FDRL, as are the stories of his poignant reactions to his parents' rare absences. Mittie Roosevelt's account of her quiet weekend at Springwood is from a letter to Elliott, among the Eleanor Roosevelt Papers, FDRL.

Roosevelt's own memories of his close call aboard the *Germania* are given in several places, but appeared first in Ernest K. Lindley, *Franklin D. Roosevelt: A Career in Progressive Democracy.* His mother's version, quoted here, is from Kleeman, pages 152–153. Additional details come from newspaper clippings describing the near disaster pinned into the Algonac diaries, FDRL.

FDR's fumbling with a cigarette and the memory it triggered are from the *Press Conferences of Franklin D. Roosevelt,* Volume I, December 14, 1933. James Roosevelt's theorizing about his father's "dread of fire" is from *My Parents: A Differing View,* page 81. Warren Delano's fondness for his daughter Laura and the story of her ghastly death come from the Algonac diaries, and from letters to Warren Delano III, written by his father and by SDR, Delano Family Papers, FDRL.

The photographs of FDR with his aunt, with his father, and at the wheel of the Roosevelt yacht are all at the FDRL.

SDR's version of the relationship between her son and her husband is from *My Boy Franklin,* pages 20–21. Mr. James's tobogganing mishap is noted in SDR's diary, FDRL. Roosevelt's own memories of the Blizzard of '88 are recorded in his unpublished and incomplete "History of the President's Estate at Hyde Park, N.Y., With Anecdotes," FDRL. The story of Mr. James and the old woman who believed herself Queen Victoria was told by FDR to the graduating class of nurses at the Hudson River State Hospital in 1937, and is quoted in Steelholm, page 99.

FDR's bout with typhoid fever is outlined in Sara's journal, FDRL.

SDR's cheerful account of life in Washington in the winter of 1887 is from her diary, FDRL. Her son's visit to the Cleveland White House is here drawn from the version in Kleeman, pages 145–146. His mother's lifelong goal for her son is given on page 4 of *My Boy Franklin.*

Mrs. Moschele's letter on the elder Roosevelt's fondness for one another was written to Elliott Roosevelt, FDRL.

Roosevelt's joy at being allowed to bathe himself is from his letter to his father, *FDR: His Personal Letters: Early Years* (Volume I), page 16. His mother's resolve to keep her son's mind on "nice things"; her discussion of an allowance and of his reading; the virtues of being an only child; the story of his scary defiance aboard the *Germania;* her efforts at discipline; and his one-day genteel rebellion, all come from *My Boy Franklin.* The Englishman who admired the young Roosevelt's manners was named Hulten; his daughter, the Honorable Mrs. Richard Bethels, wrote to remind FDR of it in 1939, PPF 6329, FDRL.

The life of James Roosevelt Roosevelt is largely uncharted territory. My account of his gaudy arrival at Hyde Park in the spring of 1884 is based upon one of the newspaper clippings he stored in the series of elaborately monogrammed scrapbooks he never quite got around to arranging, FDRL. Further details are drawn from an account of the trip from New York recorded in Reginald W. Rives, *The Coaching Club: Its History, Records and Activities.* (It is my assumption that FDR and his mother walked next door to see the coach drive up; they were at home at the time, Mr. James was aboard as a passenger, and it's hard to imagine that they would not have made the effort.)

Eleanor Roosevelt called Rosy "a terrible snob" in her interview with Louis Eisner, FDRL.

My account of the early Astors, of *the* Mrs. Astor, and of her courtier, Ward McAllister, is drawn from several sources, including Virginia Cowles, *The Astors;* Lucy Kavaler, *The Astors: An American Legend;* Dixon Wecter, *The Saga of American Society;* and Kate Simon, *Fifth Avenue: A Very Social History.* The photograph of Rosy in full Versailles splendor is at the FDRL; his mother's pleasure at how he looked may be found in the Rebecca Howland Roosevelt diary, FDRL.

W. Sheffield Cowles, Jr., recalled for me Rosy's great charm and somewhat casual attitude toward office work. The description of the finery worn at the Roosevelt-Astor wedding is from a clipping found among Rosy's papers, FDRL; the description of the work of the Downtown Relief Bureau comes from another.

My survey of Rosy's expensive and obsessive hobby is based upon a number of sources, including Reginald Rives's club history, cited above; Fairman Rogers, *Manual of Coaching;* "An Old Whip," *The Delights of Coaching;* Frank Kintrea, "When the Coachman Was a Millionaire," *American Heritage,* XVIII, Number 6, October 1967; Clarence Gohdes, "Driving a Drag in Old New York," *Bulletin of the New York Public Library,* June 1962. Rosy's own coaching activities are recorded in Rives, and in the many crumbling clippings in his personal albums.

My account of his first diplomatic experience is drawn from his scrapbooks and from his letter copybooks, FDRL.

The Thanksgiving tableau presented at Springwood by the three Roosevelt children is described in Kleeman, pages 178–79. Early signs of Taddy's troubles may be found in the copybooks kept by Rosy, FDRL. The tutor's remarks and Rosy's own worries are from copies of his letters to Endicott Peabody of Groton. Alice Roosevelt described the hair-pulling in a letter to FDR in 1898, FDRL.

My discussion of the River families draws heavily upon F. Kennon Moody's unpublished Ph.D. thesis, *FDR and His Neighbors,* FDRL. FDR spoke of the peripatetic gourmand Henry Madison while waiting for a press conference to begin on January 12, 1940. My account of his wanderings is supplemented by a newspaper clipping about him, found in a scrapbook kept by FDR's uncle, John A. Roosevelt, FDRL.

Anna Roosevelt's remark about FDR's childhood choice of playmates is from Asbell, *The FDR Memoirs.* Roosevelt's early letter to Archie Rogers is from *FDR: His Personal Letters: The Early Years* (Volume I), page 12. His mother's severe view of overnight visitors is from a 1917 letter to her son, FDRL. The story of the Whitney sisters was kindly sent to me by their cousin, Dawn Langley Simmons, of Hudson, New York. FDR's air of command while telling the servants' children what to do is described in *My Boy Franklin,* page 26.

Details of life for the children of Hyde Park and the stories of the boys who bobsledded and hunted snakes at Springwood were gleaned from listening to tape-recorded interviews with their descendants, made by Nancy Fogel and available at the FDRL. The story of the rabbits FDR took home to Springwood is found in PPF 5058, FDRL.

The Royal sleigh in which the Roosevelts rode may still be seen in the Springwood barn.

4: THE LOVING CONSPIRACY

My account of Mr. James's initial illness is drawn from Sara's journal, FDRL; the menu for a typical hunt breakfast at Springwood is from Steelholm, page 97.

Life at Nauheim and other German spas in the 1890s is described in Edward Gutman, *The Watering Places and Mineral Springs of Germany, Austria and Switzerland . . . A Popular Medical Guide* (New York, 1880); Karl Baedeker, *Northern Germany: A Handbook for Travelers* (Leipzig, 1904); Louise Chandler Moulton, *Lazy Tours in Spain and Elsewhere* (Boston, 1896); Photo-Club Bad Nauheim, *Das Schöne Bad Nauheim* (Bad Nauheim, 1956); E. S. Turner, *Taking the Cure* (London, 1967); Vivien and Charles Graves, *Enjoy Life Longer* (London, 1970).

The Roosevelts' experiences at Nauheim are given in Sara's journals and in Kleeman, pages 160–162. FDR's own terse memories of his first summer there and of his encounters with the little English invalid may be found in PPF 5612, FDRL. His

Spartan swimming lessons are mentioned in SDR's journal and more fully described in Roosevelt and Shalett, page 48. Herr Bommerscheim's nostalgic encomium to his American pupil is quoted in Davis, page 76; his contemporaneous progress report to Sara and Mr. James, FDRL, was kindly translated for me by the late Adolf Samet. Sara's scorn for the Germans is described in a letter to Franklin from Mr. James written June 9, 1897, Roosevelt Family Papers Donated by the Children, FDRL; he is describing a brief sojourn for an "after-cure" at Baden Baden, not Nauheim, but English visitors did dine by themselves at Nauheim, and the Roosevelts ate with their friends.

The comings and goings of Franklin's governesses and tutors are noted in Sara's journals, FDRL, and so are his "Sunday headaches" and crippling "bobos." The story of the intrusive Miss Gerver and of Franklin's reluctance to express his genuine feelings about her is told in *My Boy Franklin*, pages 23–24, augmented here by Sara's journal, FDRL. A journalist named Constance Drexel tracked down Mademoiselle Sandoz in Belgium in 1933, and a number of the incidents I have included about her are from Drexel's "Unpublished Letters of FDR," *Parents' Magazine*, XXVI, September 1951. (This article must be used with care, however, since several of the scenes described as having been witnessed by Mademoiselle Sandoz actually took place some years before she was employed by the family.) Mademoiselle Sandoz's first report to Franklin's parents is at the FDRL, along with a number of his exercise books and his essay on ancient Egypt. Sara's chagrin at her son's callousness toward his teacher's injuries are in her diary. The story of the unfortunate Miss Reinsberg is told in William Hassett, *Off the Record with FDR*, page 9.

Sara lectured her son on his obligations to those less fortunate than he in a letter written in 1917, FDRL. The Delanos' local largesse is acknowledged in a newspaper clipping pinned into the Algonac diaries, FDRL. Details of Annie Hitch's formidable career as a Newburgh benefactress are detailed in various clippings gathered by Sara at the time of her sister's death, FDRL. Sara's memory of Booker T. Washington's visit to Algonac is from the Kleeman notes, FDRL. Mr. James's address on "Work" is also at the FDRL.

FDR's boyhood discovery of Methodism is given in Dows, page 109; his favorite hymn is given on a list of "Personal Data Regarding President Roosevelt" kept by his White House secretaries, PPF 1A, FDRL. Eleanor Roosevelt recalled her religious discussion with FDR in *This Is My Story*, pages 149–150.

The story of the FDR Library is given in Bernard A. Weisberger's article on presidential libraries, "The Paper Trust," *American Heritage* magazine, April 1971. John T. Flynn's pharaonic comparison is from *The Roosevelt Myth*, page 278. FDR's own rueful description of himself as an insatiable collector is from an after-dinner speech he delivered before a Washington gathering of the Library's newly appointed trustees, February 4, 1939, FDRL.

Admiral McIntire's estimate of the number of hours FDR spent with his stamps is on pages 78–79 of his *White House Physician*. My account of the astonishing scope of Roosevelt's collections is gleaned from William J. Stewart and Charyll C. Pollard, "Franklin D. Roosevelt, Collector," *Prologue: The Journal of the National Archives*, Winter 1969, pages 13–28, and from a helpful talk with Marguerite Hubbard, current curator of the collections at Hyde Park.

The ship drawings from his first letter are reproduced in *FDR: His Personal Letters:*

Early Years. Sara's claim that she alone fostered her son's love of the sea is registered in *My Boy Franklin,* page 7; her account of reading aloud to him appears on page 34; the precious contents of his sea chest are given on page 30. FDR's own account of his grandfather's logbooks is from his introduction to *Whaleships of New Bedford* by Clifford W. Ashley (Boston, 1929). The small girl who remembered FDR's absorption in a robin's egg was Leonora Sill Ashton, daughter of the rector of St. James; my account is drawn from her article "Bird Lover of Hyde Park," that appeared in *Audubon* magazine in June, 1955.

FDR's childish essay "Guns and Squirrels" is at the FDRL; so is his bird-shooting tally. The tale of his assurance that his prey would wait for him to come and shoot it is told on pages 15–16 of *My Boy Franklin;* his independent journey to see the Foljambe birds is from the same source, page 17. "Spring Song," the overwritten essay which he appears to have plagiarized, is from the May 11, 1896, number of *The Foursome,* FDRL.

Mrs. Charles Hamlin's charming "Some Memories of Franklin Delano Roosevelt" is at the FDRL. Roosevelt's own memory of election night 1892 was given on election night 1944. Mr. James's pleasure at Grover Cleveland's victory and the music and musicians that heralded it all come from a letter to FDR, written by an eyewitness, an old Hyde Park Democrat named D. E. Howatt, in 1935, PPF 8, FDRL.

Rosy's own copybooks and scrapbooks provided most of the material for my account of his second diplomatic posting, the death of his wife, and his troubles with the education of Taddy. A copy of General Lawton's somewhat limited tribute to his abilities is among Rosy's papers. Sara's account of Helen's death and Mr. James's aggrieved reaction to the way Rosy treated him are found in her journal, FDRL. The story of Bamie's hope to wed Rosy and of her belated discovery of Betty Riley, Rosy's genteel mistress, was told to me by Bamie's son, W. Sheffield Cowles, Jr. Rosy's embarrassing failure to enlarge his children's Astor allowance was described in all the New York dailies of the time.

My brief profile of Endicott Peabody is drawn from *Peabody of Groton* by Frank D. Ashburn (New York, 1944) and from Frank Kintrea's " 'Old Peabo' and the School," *American Heritage,* October 1980. Rosy's letter to Peabody is among the Endicott Peabody Papers at Groton School—as are Mr. James's letters to him about a gentlemanly tutor for Franklin. The story of FDR's desire to go to Annapolis is recounted by Eleanor Roosevelt in *This Is My Story,* page 122, and was confided to Ernest K. Lindley as well: *Franklin D. Roosevelt: A Career in Progressive Democracy,* page 5.

Arthur Dumper's impression of Sara and his bafflement at FDR's idiosyncratic study habits were recalled for me by his son, Sargent Dumper.

Warren Delano's pleasure in the Chicago World's Fair is described in Frederic A. Delano's memoir of his mother and father, Delano Family Papers, FDRL. Catherine Delano's birthday note is there, too, and so are her sister Susan Lyman Lesley's memories of Mrs. Delano's last days.

My account of Franklin's final preschool European journey is taken from Lindley, pages 50–51; Kleeman, pages 164–165; *My Boy Franklin,* page 23. His trip to Bayreuth and his parting with his parents are from *My Boy Franklin,* page 36, SDR's letter to Dora Forbes, and from Sara's journal, both FDRL.

5: GETTING ON VERY WELL WITH THE FELLOWS

My picture of Groton is drawn from Frank D. Ashburn, *Peabody of Groton* and *Fifty Years On: Groton School, 1884–1934;* Francis Biddle, *A Casual Past;* George Biddle, *An American Artist's Story;* William Amory Gardner, *Groton Myths and Memories;* Frank Kintrea, " 'Old Peabo' and the School," *American Heritage,* October/November 1980; George W. Martin, "Preface to a Schoolmaster's Biography," *Harper's,* February 1944; Ellery Sedgwick, *The Happy Profession,* plus the school newspaper, the *Grotonian,* for the years FDR was in attendance.

All of Franklin's voluminous letters home are reproduced in Elliott Roosevelt, ed., *FDR: His Personal Letters: Early Years.* His parents' letters to him are at the FDRL, among the Roosevelt Family Papers Donated by the Children.

The description of the dark woodwork is from Ashburn's *Peabody,* page 92. Francis Biddle recalled the special misery of the boy who found the carpetless stairs so disheartening (page 186). Sherrard Billings was the master who described the relentless busyness of the Groton boy's day, quoted on page 95 of Ashburn's *Peabody.* Peabody's own stern views on "loafing" and how to combat it are quoted from Kintrea, page 98.

Francis Biddle is the source for the special terrors for new boys of the communal washroom (page 186). Sara Delano Roosevelt noted Mr. James's pleasure in Franklin's good academic standing in her journal. Peabody's recollections of Franklin's Groton career were written in 1932 to a graduate whose name is not given, and appear on page 341 of Ashburn's *Peabody.*

The story of the rector and the bookish newcomer is from Joseph Alsop, *FDR: A Centenary Remembrance,* page 35, as is FDR's confession that something went "sadly wrong" at Groton. Roosevelt is quoted as having felt "hopelessly out of things" in John Gunther's *Roosevelt in Retrospect* (page 178), bolstered by George Biddle (page 58). Eleanor Roosevelt's memory of having been told by FDR that he had always been an "outsider" is from *This I Remember,* page 43.

The former classmate who recalled Taddy as a "queer sort of boy" was James L. Goodwin, who entered the third form with Franklin in 1896. Another classmate, Dr. Edward Bell Krumbhaar, a Philadelphia physician and teacher, told Stefan Lorant of the hazing FDR endured; the story appears among the author's notes for his *FDR: A Pictorial Biography,* page 154.

George Biddle tells the pathetic story of his own aborted closeness to his brother, page 60. His brother Francis described pumping and his own participation in *A Casual Past,* pages 171–173.

Ashburn explains Peabody's fondness for football on page 101 of his *Peabody;* the rector's own tribute to the game as a training ground for life is from a 1909 letter to Walter Camp, reproduced on page 195 of the same book.

Franklin's misleading memory of his boxing prowess comes from an interview in the *New York Globe,* June 2, 1911, FDRL. His fabricated football injuries come from the Henry Morgenthau diary for July 26, 1939. (The latter story was kindly pointed out to me by Professor Frank Freidel.)

The former student who remembered Sherrard Billings' insistence on good form in all things is quoted on page 108 of Davis, *FDR: The Beckoning of Destiny.* The brilliant rambling of William Amory Gardner in the classroom and his desktop dance were recalled by a nameless graduate and appear on page 158 of Ashburn's *Peabody.* Gardner's idiosyncratic creed for good teaching is given on page 109 of Davis.

FDR's 1934 tribute to his old headmaster is from the *New York Times,* June 3, 1934, and is quoted here from Freidel, page 35. W. Averell Harriman's iconoclastic remark about the rector is quoted in Davis, page 107. George Biddle's icy assessment appears on page 67 of his autobiography. George Martin's article provided the rector's stern views of the stage, and Francis Biddle recalled his ferocity about impurity of every kind on page 179 of *A Casual Past.* Peabody's assurance about the reality of immortality is quoted in Kintrea, page 100. His equally strong self-confidence about his own decisions is from Davis, page 111.

The rector's hope that his boys would go forth to purify politics is from a letter written to an unnamed friend in 1894, and is quoted here from Ashburn's *Peabody,* pages 112–113. TR's own views of a Groton boy's special responsibilities are from his address to the seniors of 1904 in the same book, pages 176–177.

Mary Newbold Morgan's memories of Taddy were relayed to me by her son, Gerald Morgan, Jr., as was his grandmother's theory of the "Astor taint." Taddy's pathetic letter to Bamie Roosevelt is among the Theodore Roosevelt Papers at Harvard.

The comparison Franklin's nurse made between him and his Grandfather Delano appears in Kleeman, page 197.

Endicott Peabody's lukewarm recommendation of Taddy for Harvard is among the Peabody Papers at Harvard. George Biddle's memories of FDR at Groton are on page 58 of *An American Artist's Story;* his brother's are in his *In Brief Authority,* page 4. Eleanor Roosevelt's impressions of her husband's unhappiness at Groton were offered to Bess Furman and appear in her *Washington By-Line,* page 272.

The classmate who remembered FDR's sarcasm at Groton was James L. Goodwin, who entered Franklin's form two years late, just as he did, and appears on page 34 of *FDR: His Personal Letters: The Early Years.* Franklin's fury at the rector for his alleged favoritism appears here in full for the first time; the letter appears in truncated form on page 392 of the same volume.

President Roosevelt's fulsome recommendation of the rector for a Cambridge honorary degree appears in Davis, page 112. The Roosevelt aide who suggested FDR simply felt sorry for Peabody in his old age was speaking to John Gunther; the unattributed remark appears on page 174 of *Roosevelt in Retrospect.* FDR's own tribute to the rector is from Ashburn's *Peabody,* page 349. The story of Peabody's Union Club tribute to FDR and its silent reception comes from George Biddle, *An American Artist's Story,* page 67.

The rector's vote for Herbert Hoover in 1932 is recorded in his own words in Ashburn's *Peabody,* page 340. FDR, Jr., told me of Peabody's early-morning visit. Peabody's tribute to New Deal legislation as a shield against radical attacks is on page 345.

William Hassett's assessment of what FDR really thought of the rector is from his *Off the Record with FDR,* page 24.

Mrs. Peabody's exuberant welcome for the President is described in Ashburn's *Peabody,* page 296. Jeffrey Potter's account of President Roosevelt's visit to Groton on its fiftieth anniversary and of his father's dire threats and abject surrender are from his memoir "This Thing About Frank," *The New Yorker,* Volume 39, Number 25, August 10, 1963.

6: UNDER THE INFLUENCE OF HIS MOTHER

My account of FDR's Harvard years is drawn largely from his letters to his parents and his mother's letters to him; from her journals; and from his own terse "Line-A-Day" college diary; all at the FDRL. I have also relied on the Harvard chapters in several biographies, but especially Rexford G. Tugwell, *The Democratic Roosevelt;* Frank Freidel, *Franklin D. Roosevelt: The Apprenticeship;* and Kenneth S. Davis, *The Beckoning of Destiny.*

The story of Helen Roosevelt (Robinson) and her grandmother's jewels is from the transcript of an interview with her and Mary Newbold (Morgan) conducted by George Palmer, National Park Service, December 13, 1949.

The story of luckless Taddy, his embarrassing marriage, and the Roosevelts' reaction to it is told here from family letters, augmented with details from the *New York Times, Sun, World,* and *Herald,* plus the gossip sheet *Town Topics.* Deleted passages in Volume I of FDR's *Personal Letters* have here been restored.

Family letters and Sara's journals provided the sad details of Mr. James's last days and death. Rosy's stubborn Locomobile is described in Kleeman, pages 201–202. Condolence letters upon the death of James Roosevelt as well as calligraphed tributes to him may be found among his papers, FDRL. The size of Sara's two legacies and Franklin's share in them is given in Miller, *FDR: An Intimate History,* page 36.

Franklin's overenthusiastic essay on his ancestors' democratic tendencies is at the FDRL. The Byzantine process by which would-be members of Porcellian inched toward their goal is clearly set forth in Davis, *FDR: The Beckoning of Destiny,* pages 135–137, and was kindly supplemented for me by a present-day member of the club who prefers to remain anonymous. FDR spoke of his bitter disappointment at having been rejected to W. Sheffield Cowles, Jr., who reaffirmed the story to me. Eleanor Roosevelt's reference to her husband's alleged "inferiority complex" is quoted in Freidel, page 57. FDR's misadventure with the little Italian boy and his neighbors is recounted in his own words in Looker, pages 35–38. Lathrop Brown's assessment of the impact of the Porcellian's rebuff was given to Frank Freidel and appears (anonymously, at Brown's request) in *The Apprenticeship,* page 57. The memories of FDR's Harvard acquaintances Tom Beal and Walter E. Sachs were solicited in their old age by Richard Thayer Goldberg and appear in his *The Making of Franklin D. Roosevelt,* page 12; those of Arthur A. Ballantine and W. Russell Bowie appeared in an article on FDR's days on the *Crimson* published in that newspaper; so did FDR's own reasons for having opposed the shift of the *Crimson*'s headquarters to the basement of the Harvard Union. His ease with the printers is described in Lindley, *Franklin D. Roosevelt: A Career in Progressive Democracy,* page 64.

All of FDR's *Crimson* editorials may be found at the FDRL.

My account of Franklin's time at Harvard and, especially, of his tenure on the *Crimson* has benefited from a careful reading by one of his successors as editor of that journal, Spencer Klaw, currently the editor of the *Columbia Journalism Review.* I am grateful to him.

Mrs. Hartman Kuhn's letter offering her Boston home to Sara is among the James

Roosevelt Papers, FDRL. Corinne Alsop's memories of FDR as a suitor are offered in her son Joseph's *FDR: A Centenary Remembrance,* page 36. Alice Roosevelt's harsher views are quoted here from Joseph Lash, *Eleanor and Franklin,* page 103. The girl who grieved at the news of FDR's engagement was named Minerva Lyman Hannewell, and her story was told to him by her mother, Mrs. C. A. Lyman of Beverly Farms, Massachusetts, in a letter written in 1944, PSF 155, FDRL. Eleanor Roosevelt's memory of how FDR dealt with awkwardness and her friend Helen Wilmerding's assessment of Sara Roosevelt's relationship with her son are both from Lash, pages 113 and 116.

Dr. Nona Ferdon discovered four coded messages in FDR's college diary in 1971 and eventually had them deciphered. The process was described in *Prologue,* Spring 1972. The code appears to have been devised by Franklin himself, perhaps in order to thwart the curiosity of his intrusive mother. I discovered a fifth entry in 1983.

My discussion of Franklin's relationships with women and his secrecy and misdirection about them when writing to his mother owes much to Bernard Asbell's *The FDR Memoirs.*

The story of his early relationship with Alice Sohier is detailed here for the first time. It is based upon study of FDR's Harvard diary and SDR's journal, as well as conversations with three members of the Sohier family—Alice's son, Bramwell Shaw; her nephew, Dr. William D. Sohier; and especially her granddaughter, Emily Shaw, who also kindly provided me with the photograph of her grandmother that I have included among the illustrations. FDR's own brief memory of Alice's beauty is from a letter he wrote to her father in 1934, acknowledging receipt of a photograph of himself among the ushers at her 1904 coming-out dance, PPF 1355, FDRL. His curiously canted memory of his relationship with Alice is from a letter to Robert D. Washburn, August 18, 1928, FDRL.

7: E IS AN ANGEL

My account of the Fairhaven Thanksgiving at which Franklin so startled his mother with his plan to marry Eleanor is based upon SDR's journal and the Algonac diaries (which include Warren Delano's dinner-table toast to the family and mention of that autumn's plentiful crop of apples); both at the FDRL. Sara's memory of how she took the news is from *Gracious Lady.* The reassuring letters to her from Franklin and from Eleanor appear in the first volume of his *Personal Letters,* pages 517–518.

Eleanor Roosevelt was almost as open about her own past as her husband was reticent about his. Her writings include three volumes of autobiography—*This Is My Story, This I Remember,* and *On My Own*—as well as several other books and a blizzard of magazine articles and newspaper columns in which the events of her early years are examined and re-examined. And in Joseph P. Lash she found a biographer who was both sensitive and encyclopedic. His six volumes about her—*Eleanor Roosevelt: A Friend's Memoir; Eleanor and Franklin; Eleanor Roosevelt: The Years Alone; Eleanor Roosevelt and Her Friends* (Volumes I and II); and *Life Was Meant to Be Lived*—are indispensable to anyone trying to puzzle out the personality of the complex woman he knew so well.

Corinne Robinson Alsop's terse assessment of Eleanor's childhood comes from an unpublished interview with her and other members of the Oyster Bay family, conducted in 1954 by Herman and Mary Hagedorn of the Theodore Roosevelt Association.

Elliott Roosevelt remains an elusive figure. Even the nature of his illnesses remains a mystery. My portrait of his early years is based largely upon *The Rise of Theodore Roosevelt* by Edmund Morris, *Mornings on Horseback* by David McCullough, Corinne Robinson's delicate memoir *My Brother Theodore Roosevelt*, Frances (Smith) Parsons' *Perchance Some Day*, and upon his letters at the FDRL and at Harvard.

Anna Hall is less well known even than her husband. My account of her and her family draws heavily upon Lash, *Eleanor and Franklin* and *Love, Eleanor.* I have also worked with the Anna Hall Roosevelt Papers at the FDRL. Neither she nor Elliott always dated their letters, so any account based upon them—as mine largely is—has to proceed from internal evidence. The woman friend who described Anna's unique grace and need for praise was one of three who contributed memorial essays to a little privately printed volume, *In Loving Memory of Anna Hall Roosevelt*, at FDRL.

All of Eleanor's own memories of her childhood are here drawn from the first four chapters of *This Is My Story*, except where noted. Her account of her first visit to Franklin in his Springwood nursery is from the book of her father's letters she edited, *Hunting Big Game in the Eighties*, pages 36–37; his letter to her in which he urged her not to chew her fingernails is also from that book. The portrait of "Little Nell Scolding Elliott" is on display at the FDRL.

My account of the near sinking of the *Britannic* is based on newspaper stories that appeared at the time in the *New York World*, *Tribune*, *Sun*, and *Times*. Mrs. Gracie's letter about Eleanor's reaction to being left behind by her parents is quoted in Lash, *Eleanor and Franklin*, pages 29–30; Anna's concern for her from Europe is quoted from page 31 of the same volume.

Eleanor's views about the crippling impact of fear are from her last book, *You Learn by Living*, page 25.

Joseph Lash offers the most complete account of Elliott Roosevelt's slow disintegration in *Eleanor and Franklin* and in *Love, Eleanor;* and my account draws upon his but is supplemented by a fresh examination of his letters to Anna, to her mother, and to others at the FDRL and by a careful reading of Theodore Roosevelt's letters to Bamie at the Theodore Roosevelt Association.

Eleanor's letter about her brother Elliott's arrival is quoted on page 32 of *Eleanor and Franklin;* Tissie Mortimer's letter about Eleanor's anxiety at his absence is on page 33.

Elliott's anger over Eleanor's fearfulness was recalled in her draft of an article for *Look*, May 23, 1939, FDRL.

Eleanor's memory of her sad time at the French convent is drawn from *This Is My Story*, published in 1937; by the time she composed this account, however, she had forgotten—or repressed—the real motive for swallowing the coin: it was the only way she could think of to be sent back to the family that had left her there. That motive is included in her earlier account in *Hunting Big Game in the Eighties.*

The details of Elliott's life at Abingdon, Virginia, are drawn from two newspaper articles that appeared in a Washington County, Virginia, newspaper, March 4, 1933 (its masthead is missing from the clipping I consulted), and the *Richmond Times-Dispatch*, May 24, 1935, as well as from an unpublished manuscript entitled "Roosevelts in Virginia" by Goodridge Wilson; copies of all four may be found at the FDRL.

Edith Carow Roosevelt's suggestion that Eleanor be sent away to school to keep her out of her father's hands was made in an undated letter to Bamie, Theodore Roosevelt Collection, Harvard.

Eleanor's glowing tribute to her father as a giver of gifts appears in *Hunting Big Game in the Eighties.* The fragment of her composition about the little girl who lost her father may be found in the "Commonplace Book" her Aunt Pussie gave her, and appears here as quoted in Lash, *Eleanor and Franklin,* page 729. The story of Eleanor and her father's battered Bible appears in an unpublished interview with the Reverend William Turner Levy, conducted by Emily Wright of the National Park Service and is used here with the Reverend Levy's permission.

Corinne Robinson Alsop's memories of life with the Halls, of Grandmother Hall's weariness, and of the Roser and Dodsworth dancing classes both she and Eleanor attended all come from her unpublished memoir and an unpublished profile of her cousin, Alsop Family Papers, Harvard, and appear here by courtesy of her son, John Alsop.

The mysterious menace represented by Madeleine is recounted in *This Is My Story* and a somewhat shortened version of it appears in the condensed version of Mrs. Roosevelt's autobiography published in 1958. In the original version she merely "told" her grandmother of her terror; in the later one she "confessed it," and I have used that word in my account. The vigor with which her Uncle Ted greeted his favorite niece is described by his wife on page 72 of Lash, *Eleanor and Franklin.*

Alice Roosevelt Longworth's memory of Eleanor's swimming at Oyster Bay is from *Mrs. L.* by Michael Teague, page 42. Edith Carow's much-quoted judgment of Eleanor's dreary prospects is quoted here from Lash, *Eleanor and Franklin,* page 72.

The description of Mademoiselle Souvestre's physical appearance, of her erudition and dramatic power, and of her rapid-fire discussion of art are all from the novel *Olivia* by "Olivia," a pseudonymn for Dorothy Strachey-Bussy. Corinne Robinson's recollection of Eleanor's standing at the school and of the fondness of the other girls for her comes from her unpublished memoir and from Lash, *Eleanor and Franklin,* page 84; the memories of other girls who knew her are from his *Love, Eleanor,* page 27. Eleanor's own thoughts on the rarity of honesty among women are quoted here from Lash, *Eleanor and Franklin,* page 70.

The existence of the triple locks on Eleanor's bedroom door was revealed to me by Laura Chanler White, who stayed in the room as a young woman and had their purpose explained to her. Eleanor's sadness at having no real home is described in a letter from Corinne Robinson to her daughter, Corinne, and is quoted here from Lash, *Love, Eleanor,* page 36.

It was to her friend Lorena Hickock that Eleanor confessed in 1934 that she was "locked up," quoted on page 1 of Lash, *Love, Eleanor.*

Debutante terror at the prospect of the Assembly Ball is quoted from Lash, *Eleanor and Franklin,* page 92. Duncan Harris' gallant letter correcting Eleanor's self-depreciating portrait of her popularity as a debutante is among the Eleanor Roosevelt Papers, FDRL.

My account of the earliest days of Franklin's courting of Eleanor is based upon his Line-A-Day diary and his mother's journal. Corinne Robinson's admiring portrait of Franklin as a sailor is from her unpublished memoir, Alsop Family Papers, Houghton Library, Harvard.

FDR's unconventional congratulations for all brides as well as grooms comes from Grace Tully, *FDR, My Boss.* Eleanor's arboreal costume is briefly noted in SDR's journal, FDRL. Her remarks about the contrast between her own sense of insecurity and Franklin's is from her 1953 interview with Louis Eisner, FDRL. The friend who described Eleanor's precocious gravity was Isabella Selmes Greenway, and is quoted in Lash, *Eleanor and Franklin,* page 105.

Eleanor's 1903 visit to Campobello is skeletally described in SDR's journal, FDRL; Mrs. Hartman Kuhn later confided her early awareness of a budding romance to Eleanor in a letter quoted in Lash, *Eleanor and Franklin,* page 103. Eleanor's visit to Hyde Park and Franklin's first days back at Harvard in the autumn of 1903 are reconstructed here from his and SDR's journals and from his letters to his mother and Eleanor's responses to letters from him, FDRL.

SDR's anxious solicitude for the failing Miss Clay is noted in her diary, FDRL.

Eleanor's discussion of courtship customs is from *This Is My Story,* pages 109–110.

The fateful weekend at Cambridge and Groton is reconstructed here from FDR's diary, FDRL. Late in her life, Eleanor recalled what she could of Franklin's proposal and her own response to it to her close friend Dr. David Gurewitsch, who, in turn, recounted it to Joseph Lash. It appears here as given in *Eleanor and Franklin,* page 107.

8: KEEPING THE NAME IN THE FAMILY

The sources for this chapter are largely the same as for the last—Sara's letters and journal; Franklin's letters and Line-A-Day diary; and Eleanor's letters, all at the FDRL.

Eleanor's discussion of Franklin's resentment of the rebuff by Porcellian is from her interview with Louis Eisner, FDRL. The scorn of his Oyster Bay contemporaries is from Corinne Robinson Alsop's unpublished articles on Franklin and Eleanor Roosevelt, Alsop Papers, Harvard.

Eleanor's explanation for her haste in marrying is from *This Is My Story,* page 111. Mademoiselle Souvestre's counsel of caution is quoted in Lash, *Eleanor and Franklin,* page 90. Eleanor's memories of her first winter in society, her philanthropic duties, her Uncle Vallie's mixed motives for his own charity work, and her delight and satisfaction in work at the Rivington Street Settlement are all from *This Is My Story,* pages 100–123.

The letter to the newspaper about Anna Hall's kindness was found pinned into the memorial scrapbook someone prepared for Eleanor after her mother's death, Eleanor Roosevelt Papers, FDRL.

Eleanor's memories of Cousin Susie Parish and her somewhat restricted hospitality are from *This Is My Story,* pages 106–107.

The drawing at Sara's request showing how she might be buried with her husband is among the James Roosevelt Papers, FDRL.

Joseph P. Lash was the first to spot the aptness of Eleanor's interest in Candida; see *Eleanor and Franklin,* pages 124–125.

The story of Sara's visit to Joseph Choate with Franklin in tow first appeared in Rita Halle Kleeman, *Gracious Lady.* Someone other than Mrs. Roosevelt evidently told Kleeman of the incident and when she was asked about it, Sara said she had "forgotten" the event until reminded of it.

FDR's sadness at not having his father present to see him graduate from Harvard was recalled to me many years later in a conversation with his son, James.

Corinne Alsop's account of FDR's unheralded visit to Dark Harbor and his later stop at Orange are from her unpublished journals, Alsop Papers, Harvard.

Mrs. Kuhn's letter to Eleanor is quoted in Lash, *Eleanor and Franklin,* page 105.

Franklin's careful attention to the selection of a ring at Tiffany's is recorded in his Line-A-Day diary, FDRL.

My account of the Roosevelt wedding is drawn largely from the detailed description of it in Lash, *Eleanor and Franklin,* supplemented here by newspaper accounts. Eleanor's account of her arrival at Springwood and Elespie's careful scrutiny of her is from Alfred Steinberg, *Mrs. R,* page 54.

BIBLIOGRAPHY

To list the subject of every personal interview and oral history transcript, the title of every thesis and book and magazine article I read or consulted in the course of writing this book would serve only to make a fat volume fatter. Items read merely for background have therefore been omitted; everything that follows had a direct bearing on the final result.

I. UNPUBLISHED MATERIAL

A. Manuscript Collections Consulted at the Franklin D. Roosevelt Library

Bye, George
Clemens, Cyril
Delano Family Papers
Delano, Frederic A.
Dows, Olin
Early, Stephen T.
Forbush, Gabrielle
Franklin D. Roosevelt Library, Inc.
Franklin D. Roosevelt Memorial Foundation
Freidel, Frank
Hackett, Henry T. and John
Hall Family
Halsted, Anna Roosevelt
Harper and Brothers
Hassett, William D.
Hickock, Lorena

Howe, Louis M.
Joseph, Nannine
Kleeman, Rita Halle
Lape, Esther
Livingston Family
McIntyre, Ross T.
Marvin, Langdon P.
Mellett, Lowell
Morgenthau, Henry, Jr.
O'Connor, Basil
Perkins, Frances
Rollins, Alfred B.
"Rosedale Papers" (microfilm)
Roosevelt, Anna Eleanor
Roosevelt, Anna Eleanor and Franklin D. (reminiscences by contemporaries)
Roosevelt, Franklin D.: Papers Pertaining to Family, Business, and Personal Affairs
Roosevelt, Franklin D.: Papers as New York State Senator, 1910–1913
Roosevelt, Franklin D.: Papers as Assistant Secretary of the Navy, 1913–1920
Roosevelt, Franklin D.: Papers as Vice-Presidential Candidate, 1920
Roosevelt, Franklin D.: Papers, 1920–1928
Roosevelt, Franklin D.: Papers as President, Alphabetical File
Roosevelt, Franklin D.: Papers as President, Official File
Roosevelt, Franklin D.: Papers as President, President's Personal File
Roosevelt, Franklin D.: Papers as President, President's Secretary's File
Roosevelt, James (son of the President)
Roosevelt Family
Roosevelt Family: Papers Donated by the Children of Franklin D. and Eleanor Roosevelt
Rosenman, Samuel I.
Schary, Dore
Secret Service

Note: The audiovisual section of the FDRL houses scores of photograph albums, hundreds of thousands of individual photographs, and mile upon mile of film, both newsreels and home movies. I have drawn heavily upon its collections, not only for illustrations, but as a source for the sort of intimate detail about the world in which Franklin Roosevelt grew up unavailable anywhere else.

B. Other Manuscript Collections Consulted

Alsop Family Papers, Houghton Library, Harvard University
Silas Burt Papers, New-York Historical Society
George Brinton McClellan Papers, Manuscript Division, Library of Congress
Endicott Peabody Papers, Groton School
Theodore Roosevelt Collection, Houghton Library, Harvard University
Theodore Roosevelt Collection, Theodore Roosevelt Birthplace, New York City
Stanford White Papers, New-York Historical Society

C. Author's Interviews

John R. Boettiger
Marquis Childs
Maureen Corr
W. Sheffield Cowles, Jr.
Hamilton Fish
Edna Gurewitsch
Edward Hermann
Mary D. Keyserling
Gerald Morgan
Thomas Morgan
Franklin D. Roosevelt, Jr.
James Roosevelt
Laura Chanler White
Peter White

D. Oral History Transcripts

Oral Histories, FDRL
Dickerman, Marion
Forbush, Gabrielle
Palmer, George: interviews relating to FDR at Hyde Park
Roosevelt, Anna Eleanor
Rosenman, Samuel I.

Eleanor Roosevelt Oral History Transcripts, FDRL

Bell, Minnewa
Berge, Otto
Boettiger, John R.
Calhoun, Gilbert
Connell, Catherine, and O'Neill, Gabrielle
Corr, Maureen
Curnan, Archie H. ("Tubby")
Daniels, Jonathan
Dows, Olin
Drewry, Elizabeth B.
Entrup, Marguerite
Farley, Harold
Gellhorn, Martha
Gurewitsch, Edna P.
Gurievitch, Grania
Halsted, Diana Hopkins
Halsted, James A.
Harriman, W. Averell
Hoffman, Anna Rosenberg
Kidd, Gordon

Lash, Trude W.
McVitty, Honoria Livingston
Nixon, Edgar; Deyo, Jerome; and Stickle, William
Redmond, Roland
Roosevelt, Elliott
Roosevelt, James
Seagraves, Eleanor
Tugwell, Rexford G.

National Park Service Val-Kill Transcripts, FDRL

Berge, Otto
Boettiger, John R.
Corr, Maureen
Curnan, Archie
Entrup, Marguerite
Gellhorn, Martha
Levy, William Turner
Redmond, Roland
Roosevelt, Elliott
Wotkyns, Eleanor

I also consulted a collection of 31 transcripts of interviews with friends, relatives, employees and servants of the Roosevelts, conducted in the late 1940s by George Palmer and Fred Rath of the National Park Service, as well as others in the collections of the Columbia University Oral History Research Library, on microfilm at the FDRL.

E. Theses and Reports

Note: This short list does not include the considerable number of unpublished manuscripts and drafts by FDR, Eleanor Roosevelt, members of their family, and their friends upon which I drew, almost all of which are to be found scattered among the various manuscript collections at the FDRL. The titles of these are given in the notes for the individual chapters.

Ferdon, Nona S. *Franklin D. Roosevelt: A Psychological Interpretation of His Childhood and Youth.* Ph.D. dissertation, University of Hawaii, 1971.

Fogel, Nancy. *Change in Hyde Park: Interviews with 24 People.* Senior thesis, Vassar College, 1979. (Copies of the tape-recorded interviews upon which this thesis was based are on deposit at the FDRL; several of the anecdotes I used in the book were gleaned by listening to these.)

Grant, Frederic D., Jr. *Edward Delano and Warren Delano II: Case Studies in American China Trader Attitudes Toward the Chinese, 1834–1844.* History honors thesis, Bates College, 1976.

Moody, F. Kennon. *FDR and His Neighbors: A Study of the Relationship Between Franklin D. Roosevelt and the Residents of Dutchess County.* Ph.D. dissertation, SUNY, Albany, 1981.

Snell, Charles W. *Historic Site and Grounds Report Bellefield Mansion and Estate, Home of Franklin D. Roosevelt National Historic Site, Hyde Park, New York.* National Park Service, Denver Service Center, 1977.

Wilkins, George Y. *A Report on the Birthplace and Home of Franklin D. Roosevelt.* Prepared for the National Park Service, 1950.

II. PUBLISHED MATERIALS

A. Books Bearing Directly Upon the Roosevelts and Delanos

Alsop, Joseph. *FDR: A Centenary Remembrance.* New York, 1982.

Asbell, Bernard. *When FDR Died.* New York, 1961.

———. *The FDR Memoirs.* New York, 1973.

———, ed. *Mother and Daughter: The Letters of Eleanor and Anna Roosevelt.* New York, 1982.

Ashley, Clifford W. *Whaleships of New Bedford,* with introduction by Franklin D. Roosevelt. Boston, 1929.

Beschloss, Michael P. *Kennedy and Roosevelt: The Uneasy Alliance.* New York, 1980.

Biddle, Francis. *A Casual Past.* Garden City, 1961.

———. *In Brief Authority.* Garden City, 1962.

Biddle, George. *An American Artist's Story.* New York, 1939.

Bishop, Jim. *FDR's Last Year.* New York, 1974.

Blum, John Morton. *From the Morgenthau Diaries: Years of Crisis.* Boston, 1959; *Years of Urgency,* Boston, 1965; *Years of War,* Boston, 1967.

———. *Roosevelt and Morgenthau.* Boston, 1970.

Boettiger, John R. *A Love in Shadow.* New York, 1978.

Burns, James MacGregor. *Roosevelt: The Lion and the Fox.* New York, 1956.

———. *Roosevelt: The Soldier of Freedom.* New York, 1970.

Burt, Nathaniel. *First Families.* Boston, 1970.

Busch, Noel. *What Manner of Man.* New York, 1944.

Carmer, Carl. *The Hudson.* New York, 1939.

Churchill, Allen. *The Roosevelts: American Aristocrats.* New York, 1965.

Cooper, John Milton, Jr. *The Warrior and the Priest: Woodrow Wilson and Theodore Roosevelt.* Cambridge, 1983.

Daniels, Jonathan. *White House Witness.* Garden City, 1975.

Davis, Kenneth S. *FDR: The Beckoning of Destiny, 1882–1928.* New York, 1971.

———. *Invincible Summer: An Intimate Portrait of the Roosevelts.* New York, 1974.

Delano, Daniel W., Jr. *Franklin Roosevelt and the Delano Influence.* Pittsburgh, 1946.

Dow, Dorothy. *Eleanor Roosevelt: An Eager Spirit.* New York, 1984.

Dows, Olin. *Franklin Roosevelt at Hyde Park.* New York, 1949.

Faber, Doris. *The Mothers of American Presidents.* New York, 1968.

———. *The Life of Lorena Hickock: E. R.'s Friend.* New York, 1980.

Flynn, John T. *Country Squire in the White House.* New York, 1940.

———. *The Roosevelt Myth.* Garden City, 1948.

Franklin D. Roosevelt Library. *The Press Conferences of Franklin D. Roosevelt* (22 volumes).

Freedman, Max, ed. *Roosevelt and Frankfurter: Their Correspondence, 1928–1948.* Boston, 1967.

Freidel, Frank. *Franklin D. Roosevelt: The Apprenticeship.* Boston, 1952.

Geddes, Donald Potter, ed. *Franklin Delano Roosevelt: A Memorial.* New York, 1945.

Goldberg, Richard Thayer. *The Making of Franklin D. Roosevelt: Triumph Over Disability.* Cambridge, 1981.

Graff, Robert D.; Ginna, Robert Emmett; and Butterfield, Roger. *FDR.* New York, 1962.

Gunther, John. *Roosevelt in Retrospect.* New York, 1950.

Gurewitsch, A. David. *Eleanor Roosevelt: Her Day.* New York, 1973.

Hareven, Tamara. *Eleanor Roosevelt: An American Conscience.* Chicago, 1968.

Harrity, Richard, and Martin, Ralph G. *Eleanor Roosevelt: Her Life in Pictures.* New York, 1958.

———. *The Human Side of FDR.* New York, 1960.

Hassett, William D. *Off the Record with FDR.* New Brunswick, 1958.

Hess, Stephen. *America's Political Dynasties.* Garden City, 1966.

Hickock, Lorena. *The Road to the White House: FDR: The Pre-Presidential Years.* New York, 1962.

Hoff-Wilson, Joan, and Lightman, Marjorie, eds. *Without Precedent: The Life and Times of Eleanor Roosevelt.* Bloomington, 1984.

Johnson, Alvin Page. *Franklin Roosevelt's Colonial Ancestors.* Boston, 1946.

Johnson, Gerald W. *Roosevelt: An American Study.* New York, 1942.

Kavaler, Lucy. *The Astors: An American Legend.* New York, 1972.

Kearney, James R. *Anna Eleanor Roosevelt: The Evolution of a Reformer.* Boston, 1968.

Kinnaird, Clark, ed. *The Real FDR.* New York, 1945.

Kleeman, Rita Halle. *Gracious Lady: The Life of Sara Delano Roosevelt.* New York, 1935.

Lash, Joseph P. *Eleanor Roosevelt: A Friend's Memoir.* Garden City, 1964.

———. *Eleanor and Franklin.* New York, 1971.

———. *Eleanor: The Years Alone.* New York, 1972.

———. *Love, Eleanor: Eleanor Roosevelt and Her Friends,* Volume I. Garden City, 1982.

———. *A World of Love: Eleanor Roosevelt and Her Friends,* Volume II. Garden City, 1984.

———. *Life Was Meant to Be Lived: A Centenary Tribute.* New York, 1984.

Lesley, Susan. *Memoir of the Life of Mrs. Anne Jean Lyman.* Cambridge, 1875.

Leuchtenberg, William E. *Franklin D. Roosevelt and the New Deal, 1932–1940.* New York, 1963.

———. *In the Shadow of FDR: From Harry Truman to Ronald Reagan.* Ithaca, 1983.

Lindley, Ernest K. *Franklin D. Roosevelt: A Career in Progressive Democracy.* New York, 1932.

———. *Halfway with Roosevelt.* New York, 1936.

Looker, Earle. *This Man Roosevelt.* New York, 1932.

Lorant, Stefan. *FDR: A Pictorial Biography.* New York, 1950.

Ludwig, Emil. *Roosevelt: A Study in Fortune and Power.* New York, 1938.

McCullough, David. *Mornings on Horseback.* New York, 1981.

McIntire, Ross T. *White House Physician.* New York, 1946.

Mackenzie, Compton. *Mr. Roosevelt.* New York, 1944.

MacLeish, Archibald. *The Eleanor Roosevelt Story.* Boston, 1965.
Miller, Nathan. *The Roosevelt Chronicles.* Garden City, 1979.
———. *FDR: An Intimate History.* Garden City, 1983.
Morris, Edmund. *The Rise of Theodore Roosevelt.* New York, 1979.
Morris, Sylvia Jukes. *Edith Kermit Roosevelt.* New York, 1980.
Nesbitt, Henrietta. *White House Diary.*
Parsons, Mrs. James Russell (Smith). *Perchance Some Day.* Privately printed, 1951.
Partridge, Bellamy. *The Roosevelt Family in America.* New York, 1936.
Perkins, Frances. *The Roosevelt I Knew.* New York, 1946.
Rollins, Alfred B., Jr. *Roosevelt and Howe.* New York, 1962.
———, ed. *Franklin D. Roosevelt and the Age of Action.* New York, 1962.
Roosevelt, Eleanor. *This Is My Story.* New York, 1937.
———. *This I Remember.* New York, 1949.
———. *On My Own.* New York, 1958.
———. *The Autobiography of Eleanor Roosevelt.* New York, 1961.
———. *You Learn by Living.* New York, 1960.
———, ed. *Hunting Big Game in the Eighties.* New York, 1933.
———. *My Day.* New York, 1938.
———. *Franklin D. Roosevelt and Hyde Park* (pamphlet).
Roosevelt, Elliott, ed. *FDR: His Personal Letters: Early Years* (Volume I). New York, 1947.
———. *FDR: His Personal Letters, 1905–1928* (Volume II). New York, 1948.
———, and James Brough. *An Untold Story: The Roosevelts of Hyde Park.* New York, 1973.
———. *A Rendezvous with Destiny: The Roosevelts of the White House.* New York, 1975.
———. *Mother R.* London, 1978.
Roosevelt, Hall, ed. *Odyssey of an American Family.* New York, 1939.
Roosevelt, James, with Sidney Shalett. *Affectionately, FDR: A Son's Story of a Lonely Man.* New York, 1956.
———, with Bill Libby. *My Parents: A Differing View.* Chicago, 1976.
Roosevelt, Sara Delano (as told to Isabel Leighton and Gabrielle Forbush). *My Boy Franklin.* New York, 1933.
Rosenman, Samuel I. *Working with Roosevelt.* New York, 1952.
———, ed. *The Public Papers and Addresses of Franklin D. Roosevelt* (13 volumes). New York, 1938–50.
Schlesinger, Arthur M., Jr. *The Age of Roosevelt: The Crisis of the Old Order* (Volume I). Boston, 1957.
Schriftgiesser, Karl. *The Amazing Roosevelt Family, 1603–1942.* New York, 1942.
Sherwood, Robert E. *Roosevelt and Hopkins.* New York, 1948.
Steelholm, Clara and Hardy. *The House at Hyde Park.* New York, 1950.
Steinberg, Alfred. *Mrs. R: The Life of Eleanor Roosevelt.* New York, 1958.
Teague, Michael. *Mrs. L: Conversations with Alice Roosevelt Longworth.* Garden City, 1981.
Teichman, Howard. *Alice: The Life and Times of Alice Roosevelt Longworth.* Englewood Cliffs, 1979.
Trohan, Walter. *Political Animals.* Garden City, 1975.
Tugwell, Rexford G. *The Democratic Roosevelt.* New York, 1957.
———. *In Search of Roosevelt.* Cambridge, 1972.

Tully, Grace. *FDR, My Boss.* New York, 1949.
"Unofficial Observer" (pseudonym for John Carter Vincent). *The New Dealers.* New York, 1934.
Wharton, Don, ed. *The Roosevelt Omnibus.* New York, 1934.
White, William S. *Majesty and Mischief: A Mixed Tribute to FDR.* New York, 1961.
Young, James C. *Roosevelt Revealed.* New York, 1936.
Youngs, J. William T. *Eleanor Roosevelt: A Personal and Public Life.* Boston, 1985.

B. Books on Aspects of the Roosevelts' World

"An Old Whip." *The Delights of Coaching.* New York, 1883.
Ashburn, Frank D. *Fifty Years On: Groton School, 1884–1934.* Privately printed, New York, 1934.
———. *Peabody of Groton.* New York, 1944.
Auchincloss, Louis. *The Rector of Justin.* Boston, 1964.
———. *Life, Law and Letters: Essays and Sketches.* Boston, 1979.
Augur, Helen. *Tall Ships to Cathay.* Garden City, 1951.
Baedeker, Karl. *Northern Germany: A Handbook for Travelers.* Leipzig, 1904.
Beachley, Charles E. *History of the Consolidated Coal Company, 1864–1934.* New York, 1934.
Benepe, Barry, and Downs, Arthur Channing, Jr. *Newburgh Revealed.* Newburgh, 1975.
Black, David. *The King of Fifth Avenue: The Fortunes of August Belmont.* New York, 1981.
Burns, James MacGregor. *The American Experiment: The Vineyard of Liberty.* New York, 1982.
Cable, Mary. *Top Drawer.* New York, 1984.
Clemens, Clara. *My Father, Mark Twain.* New York, 1931.
Coles, Robert. *Privileged Ones: The Well-Off and the Rich in America.* Boston, 1977.
Collis, Maurice. *Foreign Mud.* New York, 1952.
Cowles, Virginia. *The Astors.* New York, 1979.
Cunnyngham, Arthur. *The Opium War.* Philadelphia, 1845.
Curtis, George T. *James Buchanan.* New York, 1883.
Dayton, Abram C. *Last Days of Knickerbocker Society in New York.* New York, 1882.
Downing, Andrew Jackson. *The Architecture of Country Houses.* New York, 1850.
Dulles, Foster Rhea. *The Old China Trade.* Boston, 1930.
———. *China and America.* Ann Arbor, 1946.
———. *Americans Abroad.* Ann Arbor, 1964.
Fairbank, John King. *Trade and Diplomacy on the China Coast.* Cambridge, 1953.
Forbes, Robert Bennet. *Personal Reminiscences.* Boston, 1878.
Furman, Bess. *Washington By-Line.* New York, 1949.
Gardner, William Amory. *Groton Myths and Memories.* Groton, 1928.
Goldberger, Paul. *The City Observed.* New York, 1975.
Graves, Vivien and Charles. *Enjoy Life Longer.* London, 1970.
Griffin, Eldon. *Clippers and Consuls.* Ann Arbor, 1938.
Grund, Francis. *Aristocracy in America* (reprint). New York, 1959.
Gutman, Edward. *The Watering Places and Mineral Springs of Germany, Austria and Switzerland . . . A Popular Medical Guide.* New York, 1880.

Haswell, Charles H. *Reminiscences of an Octogenarian.* New York, 1897.
Hislop, Codman. *Eliphalet Nott.* Middletown, 1971.
Hone, Philip. *The Diary of Philip Hone, 1828–1851,* edited by Bayard Tuckerman. New York, 1889.
Howe, George F. *Chester A. Arthur: A Quarter-Century of Machine Politics.* New York, 1935.
Hunter, William C. *The Fan Kwae of Old Canton Before Treaty Days.* London, 1882.
———. *Bits of Old China.* London, 1885.
Hyde, Alexander, with the Reverend C. M. Hyde. *The Centennial Celebration and Centennial History of the Town of Lee, Massachusetts.* Springfield, 1878.
Jackson, Stanley. *Caruso.* New York, 1972.
James, Henry. *Richard Olney and His Public Services.* New York, 1923.
Liu, Kwang-Ching. *Anglo-American Steamship Rivalry in China: 1862–74.* Cambridge, 1962.
Livesay, Harold C. *Andrew Carnegie and the Rise of Big Business.* Boston, 1975.
Loimes, Emma. *The China Trade Post-Bag of the Seth Low Family of Salem and New York.* Manchester, 1953.
MacCracken, Henry Noble. *Blithe Dutchess.* New York, 1950.
———. *Old Dutchess, Forever!* New York, 1958.
Manchester, William. *The Last Lion.* New York, 1983.
Miller, Douglas T. *Jacksonian Aristocracy: Class and Democracy in New York, 1830–1860.* New York, 1967.
Moulton, Louise Chandler. *Lazy Tours in Spain and Elsewhere.* Boston, 1896.
Nevins, Allan. *The Life of Henry White.* New York, 1930.
Photoclub Bad Nauheim. *Das Schöne Bad-Nauheim.* Bad Nauheim, 1956.
Reeves, Thomas C. *Gentleman Boss: The Life of Chester Alan Arthur.* New York, 1975.
Rives, Reginald W. *The Coaching Club: Its History, Records and Activities.* Privately printed, New York, 1935.
Robbins, Christine Chapman. *David Hosack, Citizen of New York.* Philadelphia, 1964.
Rogers, Fairman. *A Manual of Coaching.* Philadelphia, 1900.
Scoville, Joseph A. *Old Merchants of New York.* New York, 1863.
Sedgwick, Ellery. *The Happy Profession.* Boston, 1946.
Seward, Frederick H. *Reminiscences of a Wartime Statesman and Diplomat.* New York, 1916.
Simon, Kate. *Fifth Avenue: A Very Social History.* New York, 1978.
Tansill, Charles C. *The Foreign Policy of Thomas F. Bayard, 1885–1897.* New York, 1940.
Turner, E. S. *Taking the Cure.* London, 1967.
Union College. *Union College in the Civil War, 1861–65.* Schenectady, 1915.
Waley, Arthur. *The Opium War Through Chinese Eyes.* London, 1958.
Wexter, Dixon. *The Saga of American Society: A Record of Social Aspiration, 1607–1937.* New York, 1970.

C. Journals and Newspapers

The *New York Times* has been my primary journalistic source, but often supplemented by other New York newspapers, including the *Graphic, Herald, Journal, Sun,* and *Tribune.*

In addition, I examined issues of the *Poughkeepsie Eagle* and *Courier*, as well as the *College Hill Mercury* (1850–1852), New-York Historical Society; the *Grotonian* (1895–1904); the Harvard *Crimson* (1900–1905); the *Hyde Park Historian;* and *Town Topics.*

D. Articles

Basso, Hamilton. "The Roosevelt Legend." *Life,* November 3, 1947.
Cowperthwaite, L. LeRoy. "FDR at Harvard." *Quarterly Journal of Speech,* February 1952.
Crowell, Laura. "Roosevelt the Grotonian." *Quarterly Journal of Speech,* February 1952.
Davis, Kenneth S. "FDR As a Biographer's Problem." *The American Scholar,* Winter 1983/84.
Downs, Jacques M. "American Merchants and the China Opium Trade, 1800–1840." *The Business History Review,* Winter 1968.
Drexel, Constance. "Unpublished Letters of FDR to His French Governess." *Parents' Magazine,* September 1951.
Erickson, Joan. "Nothing to Fear." *Daedalus,* Spring 1964.
Fabricant, Noah D. "FDR's Nose and Throat Ailments." *Eye, Ear, Nose and Throat Monthly,* February 1957.
———. "FDR's Tonsillectomy and Poliomyelitis." *Eye, Ear, Nose and Throat Monthly,* June 1957.
———. "FDR, the Common Cold and American History." *Eye, Ear, Nose and Throat Monthly,* March 1958.
Freidel, Frank. "Roosevelt's Father." *The FDR Collector,* November 1952.
Gohdes, Clarence. "Driving a Drag in Old New York." *Bulletin of the New York Public Library,* June 1962.
Kastner, Joseph. "Andrew Jackson Downing." *Notable American Architects,* New York, 1981.
Kintrea, Frank. "When the Coachman was a Millionaire." *American Heritage,* October 1967.
———. " 'Old Peabo' and the School." *American Heritage,* October 1980.
Martin, George W. "Preface to a Schoolmaster's Biography." *Harper's,* February 1944.
Pollard, Charyll C. "FDR—Collector." *Prologue,* Winter 1969.
Potter, David M. "Sketches for the Roosevelt Portrait." *Yale Review,* Autumn 1949.
Potter, Jeffrey. "This Thing About Frank." *The New Yorker,* August 10, 1963.
Sill, Leonora. "Bird Lover of Hyde Park." *Audubon,* June 1955.
Straight, Michael. "A Dutchess County Boy." *New Republic,* April 15, 1946.
Tugwell, Rexford G. "The Two Great Roosevelts." *The Western Political Quarterly,* March 1952.
Weisberger, Bernard A. "The Paper Trust." *American Heritage,* April 1971.
Whitehead, James L. "A President Goes Birding." *Conservationist,* May-June 1977.
Wilson, Theodore A., and McKinzie, Richard D. "The Masks of Power: FDR and the Conduct of American Diplomacy," in *Makers of American Diplomacy,* edited by Frank J. Merli and Theodore A. Wilson. New York, 1974.

INDEX

Europe he might easily have followed

- "Taddy," his tragic half-nephew and boyhood rival, whose scandalous private life helped kill Franklin's father
- Cousin Theodore—the great TR—whom Franklin began openly to emulate while still a schoolboy

And it tells for the first time anywhere the story of Franklin's romance with Alice Sohier, the beautiful, sharp-tongued Boston girl, who spurned his offer of marriage and helped drive him into the arms of his sympathetic cousin Eleanor—whose own girlhood, courtship, and motives for marrying are examined in the light of fresh evidence.

Before the Trumpet is a richly detailed, immensely readable family epic, played out on two continents and full of surprises. It is a tale that would grip the reader even if its central character had not grown up to become the most important president of this century.

Jacket design © Paul Perlow
Author's photograph © Gary Green

Harper & Row, Publishers
10 East 53rd Street
New York, N.Y. 10022